Microsoft

Microsoft® Word 2010

Step by Step

Joyce Cox
Joan Lambert

PUBLISHED BY
Microsoft Press
A Division of Microsoft Corporation
One Microsoft Way
Redmond, Washington 98052-6399

Library of Congress Control Number: 2010928516

Printed and bound in the United States of America.

3 4 5 6 7 8 9 10 11 QGT 6 5 4 3 2 1 0

A CIP catalogue record for this book is available from the British Library.

Microsoft Press books are available through booksellers and distributors worldwide. For further information about international editions, contact your local Microsoft Corporation office or contact Microsoft Press International directly at fax (425) 936-7329. Visit our Web site at www.microsoft.com/mspress. Send comments to mspinput@ microsoft.com.

Microsoft, Microsoft Press, Access, ActiveX, Excel, Internet Explorer, Outlook, PowerPoint, SharePoint, SkyDrive, SmartArt, SQL Server, Windows, Windows Live, and Windows Vista are either registered trademarks or trademarks of the Microsoft group of companies. Other product and company names mentioned herein may be the trademarks of their respective owners.

The example companies, organizations, products, domain names, e-mail addresses, logos, people, places, and events depicted herein are fictitious. No association with any real company, organization, product, domain name, e-mail address, logo, person, place, or event is intended or should be inferred.

This book expresses the author's views and opinions. The information contained in this book is provided without any express, statutory, or implied warranties. Neither the authors, Microsoft Corporation, nor its resellers, or distributors will be held liable for any damages caused or alleged to be caused either directly or indirectly by this book.

Acquisitions Editor: Juliana Aldous
Developmental Editor: Devon Musgrave
Project Editor: Joel Panchot
Editorial Production: Online Training Solutions, Inc.
Cover: Girvin

Body Part No. X16-95387

[2011-10-14]

Contents

What do you think of this book? We want to hear from you!

Microsoft is interested in hearing your feedback so we can continually improve our books and learning resources for you. To participate in a brief online survey, please visit:

microsoft.com/learning/booksurvey

What do you think of this book? We want to hear from you!

Microsoft is interested in hearing your feedback so we can continually improve our books and learning resources for you. To participate in a brief online survey, please visit:

> microsoft.com/learning/booksurvey

Introducing Microsoft Word 2010

Microsoft Word 2010 is a sophisticated word processing program that helps you quickly and efficiently author and format all the business and personal documents you are ever likely to need. You can use Word to:

- Create professional-looking documents that incorporate impressive graphics such as charts and diagrams.

- Give documents a consistent look by applying styles and themes that control the font, size, color, and effects of text and the page background.

- Store and reuse ready-made content and formatted elements such as cover pages and sidebars.

- Create personalized e-mail messages and mailings to multiple recipients without repetitive typing.

- Make information in long documents accessible by compiling tables of contents, indexes, and bibliographies.

- Safeguard your documents by controlling who can make changes and the types of changes that may be made, as well as by removing personal and confidential information.

Word 2010 builds on previous versions to provide powerful tools for all your word processing needs. This introduction provides an overview of new features that we explore throughout the book.

New Features

If you're upgrading to Word 2010 from a previous version, you're probably most interested in the differences between the old and new versions and how they will affect you, as well as how to find out about them in the quickest possible way. The following sections list new features you will want to be aware of, depending on the version of Word you are upgrading from.

If You Are Upgrading from Word 2007

If you have been using Word 2007, you might be wondering how Microsoft could have improved on what seemed like a pretty comprehensive set of features and tools. The list of new features includes the following:

- **The Backstage view** Finally, all the tools you need to work with your files, as opposed to their content, really are accessible from one location. You display the Backstage view by clicking the File tab, which replaces the Microsoft Office Button at the left end of the ribbon.

- **Customizable ribbon** The logical next step in the evolution of the command center introduced with Word 2007: Create your own tabs and groups to suit the way you work.

- **Navigation task pane** The replacement for the Document Map not only provides a means of navigating to any heading but also to any page or to any search term you enter.

- **Unsaved file recovery** How many times have you responded No without thinking to the "save changes" message when closing files, only to find that you have discarded work you wanted to keep? Word now preserves your unsaved files for a period of time, allowing you to recover them if you need them.

- **Paste preview** No more trial and error when moving items to new locations. Preview what an item will look like in each of the available formats, and then pick the one you want.

- **Coauthoring** A team of authors can now work simultaneously on a document stored on a Microsoft SharePoint 2010 server or in Windows Live SkyDrive.

- **Language support** These days, more business is conducted internationally across language lines than ever before. Not only can you easily tailor the language of your working environment, but you can also use new translation tools to collaborate with team members in other countries.

- **Graphics editing** Found the perfect picture, but its colors or style aren't quite right for your document? Now after inserting a picture, you can edit it in new ways. In addition to changing color, brightness, and contrast, you can remove the background and, most exciting of all, apply artistic effects that make it appear like a watercolor, pencil drawing, or pastel sketch.

- **Text effects** WordArt has had a makeover. Not only can WordArt be used to create distinctive headlines but its effects can be used on any text.

- **Screenshots** You no longer need to go outside of Word when you want to insert a screenshot into a document. This capability is now built into Word.

- **Improved SmartArt Graphics tool** A whole new category has been added to SmartArt so that you can include pictures as well as text in your diagrams.

If You Are Upgrading from Word 2003

In addition to the features listed in the previous section, if you're upgrading from Word 2003, you'll want to take note of the new features that were introduced in Word 2007. The 2007 upgrade provided a more efficient working environment and included a long list of new and improved features, including the following:

- **The Microsoft Office Fluent Ribbon** No more hunting through menus, submenus, and dialog boxes. This new interface organizes all the commands most people use in a new way, making them quickly accessible from tabs at the top of the program window.

- **Live Preview** See the effect of a formatting option before you apply it.

- **Building blocks** Think AutoText on steroids! Predefined building blocks include sets of matching cover pages, quote boxes, sidebars, and headers and footers.

- **Style sets and document themes** Quickly change the look of a document by applying a different style set or theme, previewing its effect before making a selection.

- **SmartArt Graphics tool** Use this awesome new diagramming tool to create sophisticated diagrams with three-dimensional shapes, transparency, drop shadows, and other effects.

- **Improved charting** Enter data in a linked Microsoft Excel worksheet and watch as your data is instantly plotted in the chart type of your choosing.

- **Document cleanup** Have Word check for and remove comments, hidden text, and personal information stored as properties before you declare a document final.

- **New file format** The new Microsoft Office Open XML Formats reduce file size and help avoid loss of data.

Let's Get Started!

We've been working with Word since its debut, and each version has offered something that made daily document creation a little easier. Microsoft Word 2010 is no exception, and we look forward to showing you around.

Modifying the Display of the Ribbon

The goal of the Microsoft Office working environment is to make working with Office documents, including Microsoft Word documents, Excel workbooks, PowerPoint presentations, Outlook e-mail messages, and Access database tables, as intuitive as possible. You work with an Office document and its contents by giving commands to the program in which the document is open. All Office 2010 programs organize commands on a horizontal bar called the *ribbon*, which appears across the top of each program window whether or not there is an active document.

A typical program window ribbon.

Commands are organized on task-specific tabs of the ribbon, and in feature-specific groups on each tab. Commands generally take the form of buttons and lists. Some appear in galleries. Some groups have related dialog boxes or task panes that contain additional commands.

Throughout this book, we discuss the commands and ribbon elements associated with the program feature being discussed. In this topic, we discuss the general appearance of the ribbon, things that affect its appearance, and ways of locating commands that aren't visible on compact views of the ribbon.

See Also For detailed information about the ribbon in Microsoft Word, see "Working in the User Interface" in Chapter 1, "Explore Word 2010."

Tip Some older commands no longer appear on the ribbon, but are still available in the program. You can make these commands available by adding them to the Quick Access Toolbar. For more information, see "Customizing the Quick Access Toolbar" in Chapter 16, "Work in Word More Efficiently."

Dynamic Ribbon Elements

The ribbon is dynamic, meaning that the appearance of commands on the ribbon changes as the width of the ribbon changes. A command might be displayed on the ribbon in the form of a large button, a small button, a small labeled button, or a list entry. As the width of the ribbon decreases, the size, shape, and presence of buttons on the ribbon adapt to the available space.

For example, when sufficient horizontal space is available, the buttons on the Review tab of the Word program window are spread out and you're able to see more of the commands available in each group.

The Review tab of the Word program window at 1024 pixels wide.

If you decrease the width of the ribbon, small button labels disappear and entire groups of buttons hide under one button that represents the group. Click the group button to display a list of the commands available in that group.

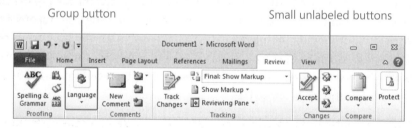

The Review tab of the Word program window at 675 pixels wide.

When the window becomes too narrow to display all the groups, a scroll arrow appears at its right end. Click the scroll arrow to display hidden groups.

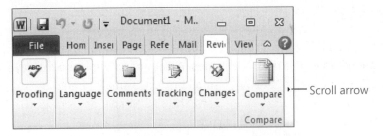

Scroll arrow

The Review tab of the Word program window at 340 pixels wide.

Changing the Width of the Ribbon

The width of the ribbon is dependent on the horizontal space available to it, which depends on these three factors:

- **The width of the program window** Maximizing the program window provides the most space for ribbon elements. You can resize the program window by clicking the button in its upper-right corner or by dragging the border of a non-maximized window.

  Tip On a computer running Windows 7, you can maximize the program window by dragging its title bar to the top of the screen.

- **Your screen resolution** Screen resolution is the size of your screen display expressed as pixels wide × pixels high. The greater the screen resolution, the greater the amount of information that will fit on one screen. Your screen resolution options are dependent on your monitor. At the time of writing, possible screen resolutions range from 800 × 600 to 2048 × 1152. In the case of the ribbon, the greater the number of pixels wide (the first number), the greater the number of buttons that can be shown on the ribbon, and the larger those buttons can be.

  On a computer running Windows 7, you can change your screen resolution from the Screen Resolution window of Control Panel.

You set the resolution by dragging the pointer on the slider.

● **The density of your screen display** You might not be aware that you can change the magnification of everything that appears on your screen by changing the screen magnification setting in Windows. Setting your screen magnification to 125% makes text and user interface elements larger on screen. This increases the legibility of information, but means that less fits onto each screen.

On a computer running Windows 7, you can change the screen magnification from the Display window of Control Panel.

You can choose one of the standard display magnification options, or create another by setting a custom text size.

The screen magnification is directly related to the density of the text elements on screen, which is expressed in dots per inch (dpi) or points per inch (ppi). (The terms are interchangeable, and in fact are both used in the Windows dialog box in which you change the setting.) The greater the dpi, the larger the text and user interface elements appear on screen. By default, Windows displays text and screen elements at 96 dpi. Choosing the Medium - 125% display setting changes the dpi of text and screen elements to 120 dpi. You can choose a custom setting of up to 500% magnification, or 480 dpi, in the Custom DPI Setting dialog box.

You can choose a magnification of up to 200% from the lists, or choose a greater magnification by dragging across the ruler from left to right.

See Also For more information about display settings, refer to *Windows 7 Step by Step* (Microsoft Press, 2009), *Windows Vista Step by Step* (Microsoft Press, 2006), or *Windows XP Step by Step* (Microsoft Press, 2002) by Joan Lambert Preppernau and Joyce Cox.

Adapting Exercise Steps

The screen images shown in the exercises in this book were captured at a screen resolution of 1024 × 768, at 100% magnification, and the default text size (96 dpi). If any of your settings are different, the ribbon on your screen might not look the same as the one shown in the book. For example, you might see more or fewer buttons in each of the groups, the buttons you see might be represented by larger or smaller icons than those shown, or the group might be represented by a button that you click to display the group's commands.

When we instruct you to give a command from the ribbon in an exercise, we do it in this format:

● On the **Insert** tab, in the **Illustrations** group, click the **Chart** button.

If the command is in a list, we give the instruction in this format:

● On the **Page Layout** tab, in the **Page Setup** group, click the **Breaks** button and then, in the list, click **Page**.

The first time we instruct you to click a specific button in each exercise, we display an image of the button in the page margin to the left of the exercise step.

If differences between your display settings and ours cause a button on your screen to look different from the one shown in the book, you can easily adapt the steps to locate the command. First, click the specified tab. Then locate the specified group. If a group has been collapsed into a group list or group button, click the list or button to display the group's commands. Finally, look for a button that features the same icon in a larger or smaller size than that shown in the book. If necessary, point to buttons in the group to display their names in ScreenTips.

If you prefer not to have to adapt the steps, set up your screen to match ours while you read and work through the exercises in the book.

Features and Conventions of This Book

This book has been designed to lead you step by step through all the tasks you're most likely to want to perform in Microsoft Word 2010. If you start at the beginning and work your way through all the exercises, you will gain enough proficiency to be able to create and work with all the common types of Word documents. However, each topic is self contained. If you have worked with a previous version of Word, or if you completed all the exercises and later need help remembering how to perform a procedure, the following features of this book will help you locate specific information:

- **Detailed table of contents** Search the listing of the topics and sidebars within each chapter.

- **Chapter thumb tabs** Easily locate the beginning of the chapter you want.

- **Topic-specific running heads** Within a chapter, quickly locate the topic you want by looking at the running heads at the top of odd-numbered pages.

- **Glossary** Look up the meaning of a word or the definition of a concept.

- **Keyboard Shortcuts** If you prefer to work from the keyboard rather than with a mouse, find all the shortcuts in one place.

- **Detailed index** Look up specific tasks and features in the index, which has been carefully crafted with the reader in mind.

You can save time when reading this book by understanding how the *Step by Step* series shows exercise instructions, keys to press, buttons to click, and other information. These conventions are listed in the table on the next page.

Convention	Meaning
SET UP	This paragraph preceding a step-by-step exercise indicates the practice files that you will use when working through the exercise. It also indicates any requirements you should attend to or actions you should take before beginning the exercise.
CLEAN UP	This paragraph following a step-by-step exercise provides instructions for saving and closing open files or programs before moving on to another topic. It also suggests ways to reverse any changes you made to your computer while working through the exercise.
1 2	Blue numbered steps guide you through hands-on exercises in each topic.
1 2	Black numbered steps guide you through procedures in sidebars and expository text.
See Also	This paragraph directs you to more information about a topic in this book or elsewhere.
Troubleshooting	This paragraph alerts you to a common problem and provides guidance for fixing it.
Tip	This paragraph provides a helpful hint or shortcut that makes working through a task easier.
Important	This paragraph points out information that you need to know to complete a procedure.
Keyboard Shortcut	This paragraph provides information about an available keyboard shortcut for the preceding task.
Ctrl+B	A plus sign (+) between two keys means that you must press those keys at the same time. For example, "Press Ctrl+B" means that you should hold down the Ctrl key while you press the B key.
	Pictures of buttons appear in the margin the first time the button is used in a chapter.
Black bold	In exercises that begin with SET UP information, the names of program elements, such as buttons, commands, windows, and dialog boxes, as well as files, folders, or text that you interact with in the steps, are shown in black, bold type.
Blue bold	In exercises that begin with SET UP information, text that you should type is shown in blue bold type.

Using the Practice Files

Before you can complete the exercises in this book, you need to copy the book's practice files to your computer. These practice files, and other information, can be downloaded from the book's support page, located at:

http://go.microsoft.com/fwlink/?Linkid=192147

Display the support page in your Web browser and follow the instructions for downloading the files.

Important The Microsoft Word 2010 program is not available from this Web site. You should purchase and install that program before using this book.

The following table lists the practice files for this book.

Chapter	File
Chapter 1: Explore Word 2010	Prices_start.docx Procedures_start.docx Rules_start.docx
Chapter 2: Edit and Proofread	Bamboo_start.docx Brochure_start.docx Letter_start.docx Orientation_start.docx RulesRegulations_start.docx
Chapter 3: Change the Look of Text	AgendaA_start.docx AgendaB_start.docx Information_start.docx OrientationDraft_start.docx RulesDraft_start.docx
Chapter 4: Organize Information in Columns and Tables	ConsultationA_start.docx ConsultationB_start.docx RepairCosts_start.docx RoomPlanner_start.docx

(continued)

Chapter	File
Chapter 5: Add Simple Graphic Elements	Announcement_start.docx
	Authors_start.docx
	Flyer_start.docx
	Joan.jpg
	Joyce.jpg
	MarbleFloor.jpg
	OTSI-Logo.png
Chapter 6: Preview, Print, and Distribute Documents	InfoSheetA_start.docx
	InfoSheetB_start.docx
	InfosheetC_start.docx
	OfficeInfo_start.docx
Chapter 7: Insert and Modify Diagrams	Garden.jpg
	Park.jpg
	Pond.jpg
	ServiceA_start.docx
	ServiceB_start.docx
	Woods.jpg
Chapter 8: Insert and Modify Charts	CottageA_start.docx
	CottageB_start.docx
	CottageC_start.docx
	Temperature.xlsx
Chapter 9: Use Other Visual Elements	AgendaDraft_start.docx
	AuthorsDraft_start.docx
	OTSI-Logo.jpg
	Welcome_start.docx
Chapter 10: Organize and Arrange Content	BambooInfo_start.docx
	DeliveryTruckPurchase.docx
	Loan.xlsx
	LoanComparisons_start.docx
	OfficeProcedures_start.docx

Chapter	File
Chapter 11: Create Documents for Use Outside of Word	BlogPost.docx ParkingRules_start.docx RoomPlannerWeb_start.docx
Chapter 12: Explore More Text Techniques	Conductors.docx ProceduresFields_start.docx RulesBookmarks_start.docx VisitorGuide_start.docx
Chapter 13: Use Reference Tools for Longer Documents	AllAboutBamboo_start.docx BambooBibliography_start.docx ProceduresContents_start.docx RulesIndex_start.docx
Chapter 14: Work with Mail Merge	AnniversaryLetter_start.docx CustomerList_start.xlsx ThankYouEmail_start.docx
Chapter 15: Collaborate on Documents	CompetitiveAnalysisA_start.docx CompetitiveAnalysisB_start.docx InfoSheetReviewA_start.docx InfoSheetReviewB_start.docx InfoSheetReviewC_start.docx LoansProtected_start.docx ProceduresRestricted_start.docx ServiceCP_start.docx ServiceSH_start.docx ServiceTA_start.docx
Chapter 16: Work in Word More Efficiently	AgendaSH_start.docx AuthorsTemplate_start.docx ProceduresEdited_start.docx

Your Companion eBook

The eBook edition of this book allows you to:

- **Search the full text**
- **Print**
- **Copy and paste**

To download your eBook, please see the instruction page at the back of this book.

Getting Help

Every effort has been made to ensure the accuracy of this book. If you do run into problems, please contact the sources listed in the following sections.

Getting Help with This Book

If your question or issue concerns the content of this book or its practice files, please first consult the book's errata page, which can be accessed at:

http://go.microsoft.com/fwlink/?Linkid=192147

This page provides information about known errors and corrections to the book. If you do not find your answer on the errata page, send your question or comment to Microsoft Press Technical Support at:

mspinput@microsoft.com

Getting Help with Word 2010

If your question is about Microsoft Word 2010, and not about the content of this book, your first recourse is the Word Help system. This system is a combination of tools and files stored on your computer when you installed Word and, if your computer is connected to the Internet, information available from Office.com. You can find general or specific Help information in the following ways:

- To find out about an item on the screen, you can display a ScreenTip. For example, to display a ScreenTip for a button, point to the button without clicking it. The ScreenTip gives the button's name, the associated keyboard shortcut if there is one, and unless you specify otherwise, a description of what the button does when you click it.

- In the Word program window, you can click the Microsoft Word Help button (a question mark in a blue circle) at the right end of the ribbon to display the Word Help window.

- After opening a dialog box, you can click the Help button (also a question mark) at the right end of the dialog box title bar to display the Word Help window. Sometimes, topics related to the functions of that dialog box are already identified in the window.

To practice getting help, you can work through the following exercise.

SET UP You don't need any practice files to complete this exercise. Start Word, and then follow the steps.

1. At the right end of the ribbon, click the **Microsoft Word Help** button.

   The Word Help window opens.

You can maximize the window or adjust its size by dragging the handle in the lower-right corner. You can change the size of the font by clicking the Change Font Size button on the toolbar.

If you are connected to the Internet, clicking any of the buttons below the Microsoft Office banner (Products, Support, Images, and Templates) takes you to a corresponding page of the Office Web site.

2. Below the bulleted list under **Browse Word 2010 support**, click **see all**.

   The window changes to display a list of help topics.

3. In the list of topics, click **Activating Word**.

Word Help displays a list of topics related to activating Microsoft Office programs. You can click any topic to display the corresponding information.

4. On the toolbar, click the **Show Table of Contents** button.

   The window expands to accommodate two panes. The Table Of Contents pane appears on the left. Like the table of contents in a book, it is organized in sections. If you're connected to the Internet, Word displays sections, topics, and training available from the Office Online Web site as well as those stored on your computer.

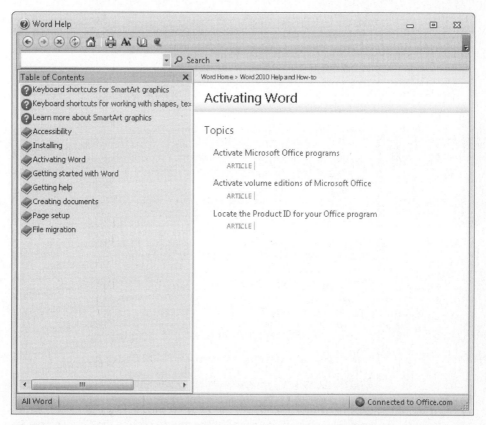

Clicking any section (represented by a book icon) displays that section's topics (represented by help icons).

5. In the **Table of Contents** pane, click a few sections and topics. Then click the **Back** and **Forward** buttons to move among the topics you have already viewed.

6. At the right end of the **Table of Contents** title bar, click the **Close** button.

7. At the top of the **Word Help** window, click the **Type words to search for** box, type **saving**, and then press the Enter key.

   The Word Help window displays topics related to the word you typed.

Next and Back buttons appear to make it easier to search for the topic you want.

8. In the results list, click the **Recover earlier versions of a file in Office 2010** topic.

    The selected topic appears in the Word Help window.

9. Below the title at the top of the topic, click **Show All**.

    Word displays any hidden auxiliary information available in the topic and changes the Show All button to Hide All. You can jump to related information by clicking hyperlinks identified by blue text.

    Tip You can click the Print button on the toolbar to print a topic. Only the displayed information is printed.

✖ CLEAN UP Click the Close button at the right end of the Word Help window.

More Information

If your question is about Microsoft Word 2010 or another Microsoft software product and you cannot find the answer in the product's Help system, please search the appropriate product solution center or the Microsoft Knowledge Base at:

support.microsoft.com

In the United States, Microsoft software product support issues not covered by the Microsoft Knowledge Base are addressed by Microsoft Product Support Services. Location-specific software support options are available from:

support.microsoft.com/gp/selfoverview/

Part 1
Basic Word Documents

Chapter at a Glance

Work in the user interface, **page 4**

The office hours are from 8:00 A.M. to 9:00 P.M., Monday through Saturday. Customers who rent mailboxes have access to them 24 hours a day.

Warehouse

The rear of the building contains the warehouse, which occupies the major portion of the building space. The warehouse is divided into four separate areas: Receiving, Shipping, Packaging, and Inventory storage:

- The Receiving area consists of two loading docks (also used for Shipping), and a 12 x 12 ft. area with racks for holding incoming packages. The racks are divided by shipping company.
- The Shipping area just opposite the Receiving area shares the loading dock space and also has a 12 x 12 ft. area with racks for holding packages waiting to be shipped. The racks are divided by shipping company.
- The Packaging area has two tables, and two racks that contain various size boxes, bubble wrap, tape, Styrofoam peanuts, and labeling materials.
- The Inventory area has three racks for overflow supplies.

Phone System

The phone system i[
connection to enabl
employees. Please f
phone to connect be

To use the intercom

1. Pick up the earpiece, and press 1 on the number pad.
2. Press 2 to contact the kitchen from the office.
3. When you hear a click, press the Speaker button.

To connect without the intercom:

4. Press 1.
5. Wait for an answer.

Ordering Supplies

Business Stationery, Letterheads, Invoices, Packing Slips, Receipts

Supplies

Business Stationery, Letterheads, Invoices, Packing Slips, Receipts

   Vendor: Lucerne Publishing
   Web Address: www.lucernepublishing.com

Account access info:

   E-mail address: andrew@consolidatedmessenger.com

View documents in different ways, **page 29**

Create, enter text in, and save documents, **page 16**

Navigation

Search Document

1. Definitions
2. General Rules
3. Birds, Wild Animals, a...
4. Storage
5. Garbage
6. Parking and Vehicles
7. Landscaping
8. Architectural and Stru...
9. Common Area Mainte...
10. Building Maintenance
11. Homeowners Dues
12. Renting and Leasing
13. Complaints and Rul...

Open, move around in, and close documents, **page 23**

1 Explore Word 2010

In this chapter, you will learn how to

✔ Work in the user interface.

✔ Create, enter text in, and save documents.

✔ Open, move around in, and close documents.

✔ View documents in different ways.

When you use a computer program to create, edit, and produce text documents, you are performing a task known as *word processing*. Microsoft Word 2010 is one of the most sophisticated word-processing programs available. With Word 2010, it is easy to efficiently create a wide range of business and personal documents, from the simplest letter to the most complex report. Word includes many desktop publishing features that you can use to enhance the appearance of documents so that they are visually appealing and easy to read. Even novice users will be able to work productively in Word after only a brief introduction to the program.

For many people, Word is the first—or possibly the only—Microsoft Office program they will use. All the Office 2010 programs share a common working environment, called the *user interface*, so you can apply basic techniques that you learn in Word, such as those for creating and working with files, to other Office programs.

In this chapter, you'll first familiarize yourself with the Word working environment. Next you'll create and save a document and then save an existing document in a different location. Then you'll open an existing Word document, learn ways of moving around in it, and close it. Finally, you'll explore various ways of viewing documents so that you know which view to use for different tasks and how to tailor the program window to meet your needs.

Practice Files Before you can complete the exercises in this chapter, you need to copy the book's practice files to your computer. The practice files you'll use to complete the exercises in this chapter are in the Chapter01 practice file folder. A complete list of practice files is provided in "Using the Practice Files" at the beginning of this book.

Working in the User Interface

As with all programs in Office 2010, the most common way to start Word is from the Start menu displayed when you click the Start button at the left end of the Windows Taskbar.

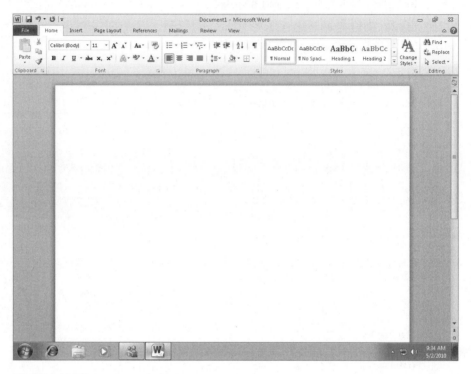

The Word 2010 program window.

When you start Word without opening a specific document, the program window appears, displaying a new blank document. The program window contains the following elements:

- The title bar displays the name of the active document. At the left end of the title bar is the Word icon, which you click to display commands to move, size, and close the program window. At the right end of the title bar are three buttons that control the window. You can temporarily hide the program window by clicking the Minimize button, adjust the size of the window by clicking the Restore Down/Maximize button, and close the active document or exit Word by clicking the Close button.

These three buttons serve the same function in all Windows programs.

Tip Windows 7 introduced many fun and efficient new window-management techniques. For information about ways to work with the Word program window on a Windows 7 computer, refer to *Windows 7 Step by Step* by Joan Lambert Preppernau and Joyce Cox (Microsoft Press, 2009).

● By default, the Quick Access Toolbar appears to the right of the Word icon at the left end of the title bar, and displays the Save, Undo, and Redo buttons. You can change the location of the Quick Access Toolbar and customize it to include any command that you use frequently.

The default buttons on the Quick Access Toolbar.

Tip If you create and work with complicated documents, you might achieve greater efficiency if you add all the commands you use frequently to the Quick Access Toolbar and display it below the ribbon, directly above the workspace. For information, see "Customizing the Quick Access Toolbar" in Chapter 16, "Work in Word More Efficiently."

● Below the title bar is the ribbon. All the commands for working with your Word document content are available from this central location so that you can work efficiently with the program.

The ribbon.

Troubleshooting The appearance of buttons and groups on the ribbon changes depending on the width of the program window. For information about changing the appearance of the ribbon to match our images, see "Modifying the Display of the Ribbon" at the beginning of this book.

● Across the top of the ribbon is a set of tabs. Clicking a tab displays an associated set of commands.

● Commands related to managing Word and Word documents (rather than document content) are gathered together in the Backstage view, which you display by clicking the colored File tab located at the left end of the ribbon. You access commands in the Backstage view from the left pane. Simple file-management commands that interact with the Windows operating system—Save, Save As, Open, and Close—are available at the top of the pane. Two program management commands—Options and Exit—are available at the bottom of the pane. Commands related to managing Word documents are organized on pages, which you display by clicking the tabs in the pane.

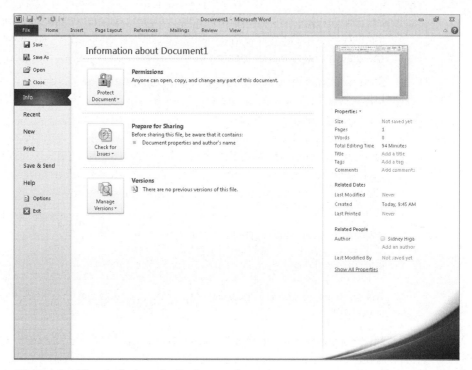

Clicking the File tab displays the Backstage view, where you can manage files and customize the program.

● Commands related to working with document content are represented as buttons on the remaining tabs. The Home tab is active by default.

Tip Don't be alarmed if your ribbon has tabs not shown in our screens. You might have installed programs that add their own tabs to the Word ribbon.

● On each tab, buttons are organized into named groups.

Tip You might find that obscure commands you used in the past are not available from the ribbon. However, these legacy commands are still available. You can make legacy commands accessible by adding them to the Quick Access Toolbar. For more information, see "Customizing the Quick Access Toolbar" in Chapter 16, "Work in Word More Efficiently."

● If a button label isn't visible, you can display the command, a description of its function, and its keyboard shortcut (if it has one) in a ScreenTip by pointing to the button.

Tip You can control the display of ScreenTips and of feature descriptions in ScreenTips. Simply display the Backstage view, click Options to open the Word Options dialog box, and change settings in the User Interface Options area of the General page. You can also change the language of ScreenTip content on the Language page and control the display of keyboard shortcuts in ScreenTips in the Display area of the Advanced page. For more information, see "Changing Default Program Options" in Chapter 16, "Work in Word More Efficiently."

- Related but less common commands are not represented as buttons in a group. Instead they are available in a dialog box or task pane, which you display by clicking the dialog box launcher located in the lower-right corner of the group.

- Some buttons include an integrated or separate arrow. To determine whether a button and arrow are integrated, point to the button or arrow to display its border. If a button and its arrow are integrated within one border, clicking the button will display options for refining the action of the button. If the button and arrow have separate borders, clicking the button will carry out the default action indicated by the button's current icon. You can change the default action of the button by clicking the arrow and then clicking the action you want.

The arrow of the Change Styles button is integrated, and the arrow of the Paste button is separate.

- To the right of the ribbon tab names, below the Minimize/Maximize/Close buttons, is the Minimize The Ribbon button. Clicking this button hides the commands but leaves the tab names visible. You can then click any tab name to temporarily display its commands. Clicking anywhere other than the ribbon hides the commands again. When the full ribbon is temporarily visible, you can click the button at its right end, shaped like a pushpin, to make the display permanent. When the full ribbon is hidden, you can click the Expand The Ribbon button to redisplay it.

  Keyboard Shortcut Press Ctrl+F1 to minimize or expand the ribbon.

  See Also To see a complete list of keyboard shortcuts, see "Keyboard Shortcuts" at the end of this book.

- Clicking the Word Help button at the right end of the ribbon displays the Word Help window in which you can use standard techniques to find information.

  Keyboard Shortcut Press F1 to display the Word Help window.

  See Also For information about the Word Help system, see "Getting Help" at the beginning of this book.

- Across the bottom of the program window, the status bar displays information about the current document and provides access to certain program functions. You can control the contents of the status bar by right-clicking it to display the Customize Status Bar menu, on which you can click any item to display or hide it.

Customize Status Bar	
Formatted Page Number	1
Section	1
✓ Page Number	1 of 1
Vertical Page Position	1"
Line Number	1
Column	1
✓ Word Count	0
✓ Number of Authors Editing	
✓ Spelling and Grammar Check	No Errors
✓ Language	
✓ Signatures	Off
✓ Information Management Policy	Off
✓ Permissions	Off
Track Changes	Off
Caps Lock	Off
Overtype	Insert
Selection Mode	
✓ Macro Recording	Not Recording
✓ Upload Status	
✓ Document Updates Available	No
✓ View Shortcuts	
✓ Zoom	100%
✓ Zoom Slider	

You can specify which items you want to display on the status bar.

● At the right end of the status bar are the View Shortcuts toolbar, the Zoom Level button, and the Zoom Slider. These tools provide you with convenient methods for adjusting the display of document content.

You can change the document view by clicking buttons on the View Shortcuts toolbar and change the magnification by clicking the Zoom Level button or adjusting the Zoom slider.

See Also For information about changing the document view, see "Viewing Documents in Different Ways" later in this chapter.

The goal of all these features of the Word environment is to make working on a document as intuitive as possible. Commands for tasks you perform often are readily available, and even those you might use infrequently are easy to find.

For example, when a formatting option has several choices available, they are often displayed in a gallery of thumbnails. These galleries give you an at-a-glance picture of each choice. If you point to a thumbnail in a gallery, the Live Preview feature shows you what that choice will look like if you apply it to your document.

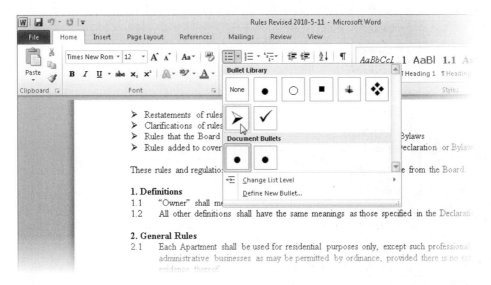

Live Preview shows the effect on the document of clicking the thumbnail you are pointing to.

In this exercise, you'll start Word and explore the tabs and groups on the ribbon. Along the way, you'll get a glimpse of galleries and Live Preview.

SET UP You don't need any practice files to complete this exercise; just follow the steps.

1. On the **Start** menu, click **All Programs**, click **Microsoft Office**, and then click **Microsoft Word 2010**.

    Tip If this is the first time you have started an Office 2010 program, Office prompts you to enter your full name and initials. The programs in the Office 2010 use this information when tracking changes, responding to messages, and so on. Next, Office prompts you to select the type of information you want to share over the Internet, and offers the option of signing up for automatic program updates from the Microsoft Update service. None of these options places you at risk, and all can be quite useful.

    The Word program window opens in Print Layout view, displaying a blank document. On the ribbon, the Home tab is active. Buttons related to working with document content are organized on this tab in five groups: Clipboard, Font, Paragraph, Styles, and Editing.

2. Point to each button on the **Home** tab.

Word displays information about the button in a ScreenTip.

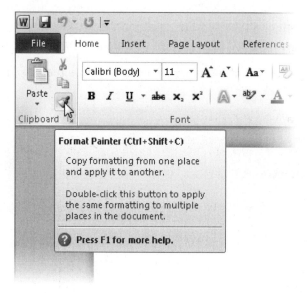

The ScreenTip for the Format Painter button displays the button's name, its keyboard shortcut, and its function.

Tip A button representing a command that cannot be performed on the selected document element is inactive (gray), but pointing to it still displays its ScreenTip.

3. Click the **Insert** tab, and then explore its buttons.

Buttons related to all the items you can insert into a document are organized on this tab in seven groups: Pages, Tables, Illustrations, Links, Header & Footer, Text, and Symbols.

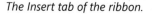

The Insert tab of the ribbon.

4. Click the **Page Layout** tab, and then explore its buttons.

Buttons related to the appearance of your document are organized on this tab in five groups: Themes, Page Setup, Page Background, Paragraph, and Arrange.

The Page Layout tab of the ribbon.

5. In the **Page Setup** group, display the ScreenTip for the **Margins** button.

   The ScreenTip tells you how you can adjust the margins of the document.

6. In the lower-right corner of the **Page Setup** group, click the **Page Setup** dialog box launcher.

   The Page Setup dialog box opens.

In this dialog box, you can specify several page layout options in one location.

Across the top of this dialog box are three tabs: Margins, Paper, and Layout. Clicking a tab displays a page of related options.

See Also For information about the Page Setup dialog box, see "Previewing and Adjusting Page Layout" in Chapter 6, "Preview, Print, and Distribute Documents."

7. Click **Cancel** to close the dialog box.

8. In the **Themes** group, click the **Themes** button.

   A gallery of the available themes appears.

   The theme controls the color scheme, fonts, and special effects applied to the text of a document.

9. Press the Esc key to close the gallery without making a selection.

10. In the **Page Background** group, click the **Page Color** button, and when a color palette appears, point to each box in the top row under **Theme Colors**.

    The blank document page shows a live preview of what it will look like if you click the color you are pointing to. You can see the effect of the selection without actually applying it.

11. Press Esc to close the palette without making a selection.

12. Click the **References** tab, and then explore its buttons.

Buttons related to items you can add to documents are organized on this tab in six groups: Table Of Contents, Footnotes, Citations & Bibliography, Captions, Index, and Table Of Authorities. You will usually add these items to longer documents, such as reports.

The References tab of the ribbon.

13. Click the **Mailings** tab, and then explore its buttons.

Buttons related to creating mass mailings are organized on this tab in five groups: Create, Start Mail Merge, Write & Insert Fields, Preview Results, and Finish.

The Mailings tab of the ribbon.

14. Click the **Review** tab, and then explore its buttons.

Buttons related to proofreading documents, working in other languages, adding comments, tracking and resolving document changes, and protecting documents are organized on this tab in seven groups: Proofing, Language, Comments, Tracking, Changes, Compare, and Protect.

The Review tab of the ribbon.

15. Click the **View** tab, and then explore its buttons.

Buttons related to changing the view and other aspects of the display are organized on this tab in five groups: Document Views, Show, Zoom, Window, and Macros.

The View tab of the ribbon.

16. On the ribbon, click the **File** tab, which is color-coded to match the color assigned by Microsoft to the Word program.

    The Backstage view of Word 2010 is displayed. Commands related to managing documents (rather than document content) are available in this view.

17. If the **Info** page is not already displayed in the Backstage view, click **Info** in the left pane.

    On the Info page of the Backstage view, the middle pane provides commands for controlling who can work on the document, removing properties (associated information), and accessing versions of the document automatically saved by Word. The right pane displays the associated properties, as well as dates of modification, creation, and printing, and who created and edited the document.

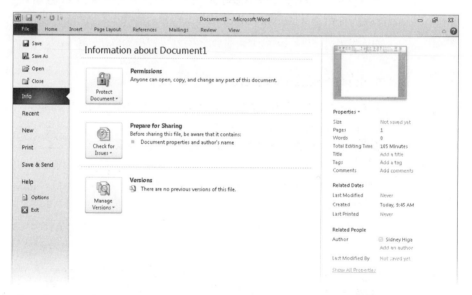

The Info page of the Backstage view provides commands for changing the information attached to a document.

> **See Also** For information about working with properties, see "Preparing Documents for Electronic Distribution" in Chapter 6, "Preview, Print, and Distribute Documents."

18. In the left pane, click **Recent**.

    The Recent page displays the names of the documents you recently worked on. By default a maximum of 20 names is displayed. You can change this number on the Advanced page of the Word Options dialog box.

> **See Also** For information about the Word Options dialog box, see "Changing Default Program Options" in Chapter 16, "Work in Word More Efficiently."

19. In the left pane, click **New**.

    The New page displays all the templates on which you can base a new document.

    See Also For information about creating documents, see the next topic, "Creating, Entering Text in, and Saving Documents."

20. In the left pane, click **Print**.

    The Print page gathers together all print-related commands and provides a pane for previewing the current document as it will appear when printed.

    See Also For information about printing, see Chapter 6, "Preview, Print, and Distribute Documents."

21. In the left pane, click **Save & Send**.

    The Save & Send page displays all the commands related to making the current document available to other people.

    See Also For information about working with other people on documents, see Chapter 15, "Collaborate on Documents."

22. In the left pane, click **Help**.

    The Help page displays all the ways you can get help and support for Word.

The right pane of the Help page displays your Office edition, its version number, and your product ID, which you will need if you contact Microsoft Product Support.

23. On the **Help** page, under **Tools for Working With Office**, click **Options**.

    The Word Options dialog box opens. In this dialog box are program settings that control the way the program looks and behaves.

You can also display this dialog box by clicking Options in the left pane of the Backstage view.

See Also For information about the Word Options dialog box, see "Changing Default Program Options" in Chapter 16, "Work in Word More Efficiently."

24. At the bottom of the **Word Options** dialog box, click **Cancel**.

    You return to the current document with the Home tab active on the ribbon.

Creating, Entering Text in, and Saving Documents

When you start Word without opening a specific document, a blank document is displayed, and you can simply type your content. The blinking cursor shows where the next character you type will appear. When the cursor reaches the right margin, the word you are typing moves to the next line. You press the Enter key only to start a new paragraph, not a new line.

If you want to create a document during a Word session, you display the Backstage view by clicking the File tab on the ribbon, and then click New.

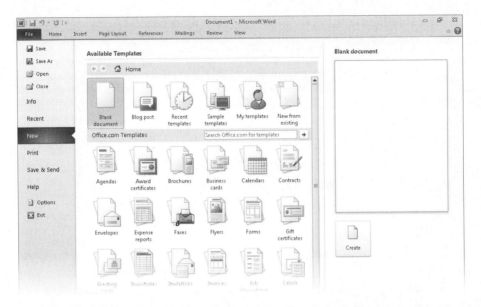

The New page displays icons for the different types of documents you can create.

Troubleshooting Because more types of documents are constantly being added to the list of those available, your New page might be different from ours.

The documents listed on the New page are based on templates, which are sets of formats that have been saved in such a way that you can use them as a pattern for new documents. The icons in the top row are:

● **Blank document** This type of document is selected by default.

● **Blog post** Clicking this icon opens a document suitable for posting to a blog.

● **Recent templates** Clicking this icon displays a page with icons for the last few templates you have used.

> **Tip** Clicking the Back button or the Home button takes you back to the New page.

● **Sample templates** Clicking this icon displays a page with the icons of sample documents that come with Word.

● **My templates** Clicking this icon displays a dialog box in which you can select a template you have created as the basis for a new document.

● **New from existing** Clicking this icon displays a dialog box in which you can select an existing document as the basis for a new document.

The icons in the Office.com Templates section represent categories of common types of documents. Clicking one of these icons displays the templates available from the Office.com Web site. You can also search for specific documents by entering the type you want in the Search Office.com For Templates box and clicking the Start Searching button.

See Also For information about templates, see "Working with Styles and Templates" in Chapter 16, "Work in Word More Efficiently."

When you find a template you might want to use as the basis for your new document, clicking its icon displays a preview of that type of document in the right pane. You can then click the Create button in the right pane to create the document.

Tip Double-clicking an icon creates that type of document without first displaying it in the preview pane.

Each document you create is temporary unless you save it as a file with a unique name or location. To save a document for the first time, you click the Save button on the Quick Access Toolbar or click Save in the Backstage view. Either action displays the Save As dialog box, where you can assign the name and storage location.

The Save As dialog box.

Troubleshooting This graphic shows the Save As dialog box as it appears when Word is running on Windows 7. If you are using a different version of the Windows operating system, your dialog box will look different but the functionality will be similar.

Troubleshooting If you don't see the Navigation pane and toolbar, click Organize on the toolbar, click Layout, and then click Navigation Pane.

If you want to save the document in a folder other than the one shown in the Address bar at the top of the dialog box, you can click the arrow or chevrons in the Address bar or click locations in the Navigation pane on the left to display the folder you want. If you want to create a folder in which to store the document, you can click the New Folder button on the toolbar.

After you save a document the first time, you can save changes simply by clicking the Save button. The new version of the document then overwrites the previous version.

Keyboard Shortcut Press Ctrl+S to save the current document.

If you want to keep both the new version and the previous version, click Save As in the Backstage view, and then save the new version with a different name in the same location or with the same name in a different location. (You cannot store two files of the same type with the same name in the same folder.)

Tip By default, Word periodically saves the document you are working on in case the program stops responding or you lose electrical power. To adjust the time interval between automatic saves, display the Backstage view, click Options, click Save in the left pane of the Word Options dialog box, and specify the period of time in the box to the right of the Save AutoRecover Information Every check box. Then click OK.

In this exercise, you'll create a blank document, enter text, and save the document in a folder that you create.

 SET UP You don't need any practice files to complete this exercise; just follow the steps.

1. On the ribbon, click the **File** tab. Then in the left pane of the Backstage view, click **New**.

2. On the **New** page, double-click **Blank document**.

    Word creates a blank document temporarily called *Document2* and displays it in its own program window in Print Layout view. Document1 is still open, but its window is hidden by the Document2 window.

    See Also For information about switching between open windows, see "Viewing Documents in Different Ways" later in this chapter.

3. With the cursor at the beginning of the new document, type **Parks Appreciation Day**, and then press the Enter key.

    The text appears in the new document.

4. Type **Help beautify our city by participating in the annual cleanup of Log Park, Swamp Creek Park, and Linkwood Park. This is a lot of fun! Volunteers receive a free T-shirt and barbeque lunch. Bring your own gardening tools and gloves.** (Include the period.)

   Notice that you did not need to press Enter when the cursor reached the right margin because the text wrapped to the next line.

   > Parks Appreciation Day
   >
   > Help beautify our city by participating in the annual cleanup of Log Park, Swamp Creek Park, and Linkwood Park. This is a lot of fun! Volunteers receive a free T-shirt and barbecue lunch. Bring your own gardening tools and gloves.

   You press Enter at the end of each paragraph; the Word Wrap feature takes care of wrapping each line.

   Tip If a red wavy line appears under a word or phrase, Word is flagging a possible error. For now, ignore any errors.

5. Press Enter, and then type **The Service Committee is coordinating groups to participate in this event. If you are interested in spending time outdoors with your family and friends while improving the quality of our parks, contact Paul Shen at paul@treyresearch.net.**

6. On the Quick Access Toolbar, click the **Save** button.

   The Save As dialog box opens, displaying the contents of the Documents library. In the File Name box, Word suggests the first words of the document as a possible name.

7. Using standard Windows techniques, navigate to the location where you have stored the practice files for this book. Then double-click your **Chapter01** practice file folder.

8. On the dialog box's toolbar, click the **New folder** button, type **My New Documents** as the name of the new folder, and press Enter. Then double-click the **My New Documents** folder.

9. In the **File name** box, click anywhere in **Parks Appreciation Day** to select it, and then replace this name by typing **My Announcement**.

   Important Programs that run on the Windows operating systems use file name extensions to identify different types of files. For example, the extension .docx identifies Word 2010 documents. Windows 7 does not display these extensions by default, and you shouldn't type them in the Save As dialog box. When you save a file, Word automatically adds whatever extension is associated with the type of file selected in the Save As Type box.

10. Click **Save**.

    The Save As dialog box closes, Word saves the My Announcement document in the My New Documents folder, and the name of the document, My Announcement, appears on the program window's title bar.

11. Display the Backstage view, and then click **Save As**.

    The Save As dialog box opens.

The dialog box displays the contents of the My New Documents folder, because that is the last folder you worked with.

12. In the **Address** bar of the **Save As** dialog box, to the left of **My New Documents**, click **Chapter01**.

    The dialog box now displays the contents of the Chapter01 folder, which is the folder that contains the My New Documents folder.

    See Also For information about saving a document in a different file format, see "Saving Files in Different Formats" in Chapter 11, "Create Documents for Use Outside of Word." For information about working with the file properties that appear at the bottom of the Save As dialog box, see "Preparing Documents for Electronic Distribution" in Chapter 6, "Preview, Print, and Distribute Documents."

13. Click **Save**.

Word saves the My Announcement document in the Chapter01 folder. You now have two versions of the document saved with the same name but in different folders.

CLEAN UP At the right end of the title bar, click the Close button (the X) to close the My Announcement document, leaving Document1 open for the next topic.

Document Compatibility with Earlier Versions of Word

The Microsoft Office 2010 programs use file formats based on XML, called the *Microsoft Office Open XML Formats*, that were introduced with Microsoft Office 2007. By default, Word 2010 files are saved in the .docx format, which is the Word variation of this file format. The .docx format provides the following benefits:

- File size is smaller because files are compressed when saved, decreasing the amount of disk space needed to store the file, and the amount of bandwidth needed to send files in e-mail, over a network, or across the Internet.

- Recovering at least some of the content of damaged files is possible because XML files can be opened in a text program such as Notepad.

- Security is greater because .docx files cannot contain macros, and personal data can be detected and removed from the file. (Word 2010 and Word 2007 provide a different file format—.docm—for documents that contain macros.)

You can open a .doc document created with earlier Word versions in Word 2010, but the new features of Word 2010 will not be available. The document name appears in the title bar with *[Compatibility Mode]* to its right. You can work in Compatibility mode, or you can convert the document to the .docx format by displaying the Backstage view, clicking Info, and clicking the Convert button in the Compatibility Mode section. You can also click Save As in the Backstage view to save the document as a different file in the .docx format.

If you work with people who are using a version of Word earlier than 2007, you can save your documents in a format that they will be able to open and use. If your colleagues regularly receive .docx files, they might want to download the Microsoft Office Compatibility Pack For Word, Excel, And PowerPoint 2007 File Formats from the office.microsoft.com Web site so that they can open .docx files in their version of Word.

See Also For information about saving files in other formats, see "Saving Files in Different Formats" in Chapter 11 "Create Documents for Use Outside of Word."

Opening, Moving Around in, and Closing Documents

If Word isn't already running, you can start the program and simultaneously open an existing Word document from Windows Explorer by double-clicking the document's file name. While Word is running, you can open an existing document from the Backstage view. If you have recently worked on the document you want to open, you can display the Recent page and simply click the document you want in the list. If the document is not available on the Recent page, clicking Open in the left pane displays the Open dialog box.

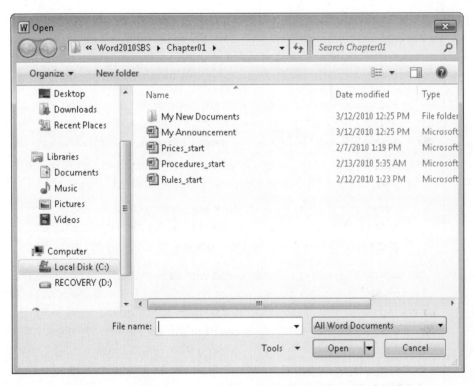

The Open dialog box, displaying the contents of the Chapter01 practice file folder.

The first time you use this command, the dialog box displays your Documents library. If you display the dialog box again in the same Word session, it displays the contents of whatever folder you last used. To see the contents of a different folder, you use standard Windows navigation techniques. After you locate the document you want to work with, you can click its file name and then click Open in the lower-right corner of the dialog box, or you can simply double-click the file name.

Tip Clicking a file name and then clicking the Open arrow displays a list of alternative ways in which you can open the document. To look through the document without making any inadvertent changes, you can open it as read-only, or you can open an independent copy of the document. After a computer crash or similar incident, you can tell Word to open the document and attempt to repair any damage. And you can display the file in other versions and formats, discussion of which is beyond the scope of this book.

If you open a document that is too long to fit entirely on the screen, you can bring off-screen content into view without changing the location of the cursor by using the vertical scroll bar.

- Click the scroll arrows to move up or down by one line.
- Click above or below the scroll box to move up or down one windowful.
- Drag the scroll box on the scroll bar to display the part of the document corresponding to the location of the scroll box. For example, dragging the scroll box to the middle of the scroll bar displays the middle of the document.

If the document is too wide to fit on the screen, Word displays a horizontal scroll bar that you can use in similar ways to move from side to side.

You can also move around in a document by moving the cursor. To place the cursor in a specific location, you simply click there. To move the cursor one page backward or forward, you click the Previous Page and Next Page buttons below the vertical scroll bar.

You can also press a keyboard shortcut on the keyboard to move the cursor. For example, pressing the Home key moves the cursor to the left end of a line, and pressing Ctrl+Home moves it to the beginning of the document.

Tip The location of the cursor is displayed on the status bar. By default, the status bar tells you which page the cursor is on, but you can also display its location by section, line, and column, and in inches from the top of the page. Simply right-click the status bar and click the option you want to display.

The following table lists ways to use your keyboard to move the cursor.

Cursor movement	Key or keyboard shortcut
Left one character	Left Arrow
Right one character	Right Arrow
Down one line	Down Arrow
Up one line	Up Arrow
Left one word	Ctrl+Left Arrow
Right one word	Ctrl+Right Arrow
To the beginning of the current line	Home
To the end of the current line	End
To the beginning of the document	Ctrl+Home
To the end of the document	Ctrl+End
Up one screen	Page Up
Down one screen	Page Down
To the beginning of the previous page	Ctrl+Page Up
To the beginning of the next page	Ctrl+Page Down

In a long document, you might want to move quickly among elements of a certain type; for example, from graphic to graphic. Clicking the Select Browse Object button at the bottom of the vertical scroll bar displays a gallery of browsing options, such as Browse By Page and Browse By Graphic. (These options are also available on the Go To page of the Find And Replace dialog box, which you display by clicking the Find arrow in the Editing group of the Home tab and then clicking Go To.) You can also display the Navigation task pane and move from heading to heading or page to page.

Keyboard Shortcut Press Ctrl+G to display the Go To page of the Find And Replace dialog box.

See Also For information about using the Navigation task pane to search for specific content in a document, see "Finding and Replacing Text" in Chapter 2, "Edit and Proofread Text."

If more than one document is open, you can close the active document without exiting Word by clicking the Close button at the right end of the title bar. If only one document is open, clicking the Close button closes the document and also exits Word. If you want to close that document but leave Word running, you must click Close in the Backstage view.

In this exercise, you'll open an existing document and explore various ways of moving around in it. Then you'll close the document.

→ **SET UP** You need the Rules_start document located in your Chapter01 practice file folder to complete this exercise.

1. With Document1 open, display the Backstage view, and then click **Open**.

   The Open dialog box opens, showing the contents of the folder you used for your last open or save action.

2. If your **Chapter01** practice file folder is not displayed, navigate to that folder.

3. Click the **Rules_start** document, and then click **Open**.

   The Rules_start document opens in the Word program window.

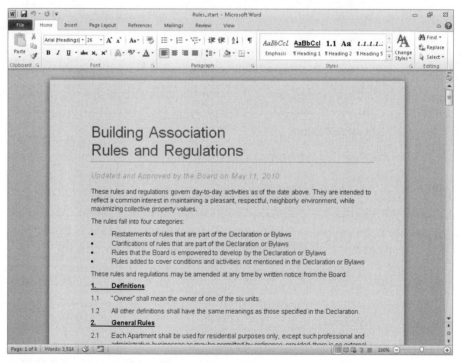

An existing document displayed in Print Layout view.

4. Display the Backstage view, and in the left pane, click **Save As**.

5. In the **Save As** dialog box, change the file name to **Rules**, and then click **Save**.

   Now you can experiment with the document without fear of overwriting the original.

6. In the second line of the document title, click at the right end of the paragraph to position the cursor.

7. Press the Home key to move the cursor to the beginning of the line.

8. Press the Right Arrow key six times to move the cursor to the beginning of the word **and** in the heading.

9. Press the End key to move the cursor to the end of the line.

10. Press Ctrl+End to move the cursor to the end of the document.

11. Press Ctrl+Home to move the cursor to the beginning of the document.

12. At the bottom of the vertical scroll bar, click the **Next Page** button.

13. Click above the scroll box on the scroll bar to change the view of the document by one windowful.

14. Drag the scroll box to the top of the scroll bar.

   The beginning of the document comes into view. Note that the location of the cursor has not changed—just the view of the document.

15. Click to the left of the first line of the title to place the cursor at the top of the document, and then near the bottom of the vertical scroll bar, click the **Select Browse Object** button.

   A gallery of browsing choices appears.

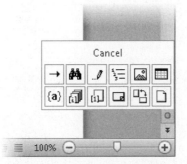

The Select Browse Object gallery.

16. Move the pointer over the buttons representing the objects you can browse among.

   As you point to each button, the name of the browsing option appears at the top of the gallery.

17. Click the **Browse by Page** button.

    The cursor moves from the beginning of page 1 to the beginning of page 2.

18. Click the **View** tab, and then in the **Show** group, select the **Navigation Pane** check box.

    The Navigation task pane opens on the left side of the screen, displaying an outline of the headings in the document. The heading of the section containing the cursor is highlighted.

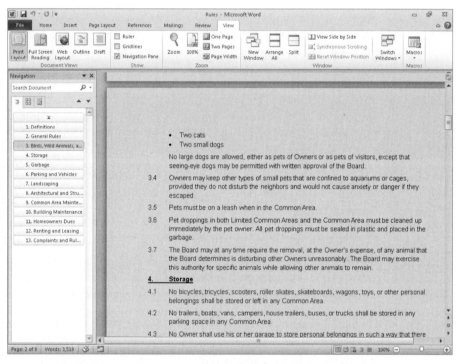

Using the Navigation task pane, you can move from heading to heading or from page to page.

19. In the **Navigation** task pane, click the **Landscaping** heading.

    Word scrolls the document and moves the cursor to the selected heading.

20. In the **Navigation** task pane, click the **Browse the pages in your document** tab (the one with the icon of four small pages). Then scroll the thumbnails in the task pane, and click page **5**.

21. At the right end of the **Navigation** task pane title bar, click the **Close** button.

22. At the right end of the program window title bar, click the **Close** button.

    The Rules document closes, and Document1 becomes the active document.

23. Display the Backstage view, and then click **Close**. If Word asks whether you want to save changes to this document, click **Don't Save.**

   Document1 closes, leaving Word running.

   Troubleshooting In step 23, if you click the Close button at the right end of the title bar instead of clicking Close in the Backstage view, you'll close the open Word document and exit the Word program. To continue working, start Word again.

Viewing Documents in Different Ways

In Word, you can display a document in a variety of views, each suited to a specific purpose. You switch the view by clicking the buttons in the Document Views group on the View tab, or those on the View Shortcuts toolbar in the lower-right corner of the program window.

- **Print Layout view** This view displays a document on the screen the way it will look when printed. You can see elements such as margins, page breaks, headers and footers, and watermarks.

- **Full Screen Reading view** This view displays as much of the content of the document as will fit on the screen at a size that is comfortable for reading. In this view, the ribbon is replaced by one toolbar at the top of the screen with buttons for saving and printing the document, accessing reference and other tools, highlighting text, and making comments. You can move from page to page and adjust the view by selecting options from the View Options menu. You can edit the document only if you turn on the Allow Typing option on this menu, and you can switch views only by clicking the Close button to return to the previous view.

- **Web Layout view** This view displays the document the way it will look when viewed in a Web browser. You can see backgrounds and other effects. You can also see how text wraps to fit the window and how graphics are positioned.

   See Also For information about Web documents, see "Creating and Modifying Web Documents" in Chapter 11, "Create Documents for Use Outside of Word."

- **Outline view** This view displays the structure of a document as nested levels of headings and body text, and provides tools for viewing and changing its hierarchy.

   See Also For information about outlining, see "Reorganizing Document Outlines" in Chapter 10, "Organize and Arrange Content."

- **Draft view** This view displays the content of a document with a simplified layout so that you can type and edit quickly. You cannot see layout elements such as headers and footers.

When you want to focus on the layout of a document, you can display rulers and gridlines to help you position and align elements. Simply click the corresponding check boxes in the Show group on the View tab. You can also adjust the magnification of the document by using the tools available in the Zoom group on the View tab or the Zoom Level button or Zoom Slider at the right end of the status bar. Clicking either the Zoom button or Zoom Level button displays a dialog box where you can select or type a percentage; or you can drag the Zoom Slider to the left or right or click the Zoom Out or Zoom In button on either side of the slider to change the percentage incrementally.

You are not limited to working with one document at a time. You can easily switch between open documents, and you can display more than one program window simultaneously. If you want to work with different parts of the same document, you can open the active document in a second window and display both, or you can split a single window into two panes and scroll each pane independently.

Tip At the right end of the View tab is the Macros group, which includes commands for viewing, recording, and pausing macros. A discussion of macros is beyond the scope of this book. If you are interested in finding out about them, enter *macros* in Word Help.

Not represented on the View tab is a feature that can be invaluable when you are fine-tuning the layout of a document. Clicking the Show/Hide ¶ button in the Paragraph group on the Home tab turns the display of formatting marks and hidden characters on and off. Formatting marks, such as tabs and paragraph marks, control the layout of your document, and hidden characters provide the structure for behind-the-scenes processes, such as indexing. When you are developing a document, you might want to turn these marks and characters on, and when you want to see what the finished piece will look like to other people, you will want to turn them off.

Tip You can hide any text by selecting it, clicking the Font dialog box launcher in the lower-right corner of the Font group on the Home tab, selecting the Hidden check box, and clicking OK. When the Show/Hide ¶ button is turned on, hidden text is visible and is identified in the document by a dotted underline.

In this exercise, you'll first explore various ways that you can customize Print Layout view to make the work of developing documents more efficient. You'll turn white space on and off, zoom in and out, display the rulers and Navigation task pane, and view formatting marks and hidden characters. Then you'll switch to other views, noticing the differences so that you have an idea of which one is most appropriate for which task. Finally, you'll switch between open documents and view documents in more than one window at the same time.

SET UP You need the Procedures_start and Prices_start documents located in your Chapter01 practice file folder to complete this exercise. Open the Procedures_start document, and save it as *Procedures*. Then follow the steps.

1. With the document displayed in Print Layout view (the default), scroll through the document.

   As you can see, on all pages but the first, the printed document will have the title in the header at the top of the page, the page number in the right margin, and the date in the footer at the bottom of each page.

   See Also For information about headers and footers, see "Inserting Building Blocks" in Chapter 5, "Add Simple Graphic Elements."

2. Point to the gap between any two pages, and when the pointer changes to two opposing arrows, double-click the mouse button. Then scroll through the document again.

   The white space at the top and bottom of each page and the gray space between pages is now hidden.

   Facilities

   Office

   Warehouse

   Phone System

   Page 2

   Office

   The Consolidated Messenger front office and lobby is located at the front of the building and serves as the main entrance for our office employees and our customers.

   Hiding white space makes it quicker to scroll through a long document and easier to compare the content on two pages.

3. Restore the white space by pointing to the line that separates one page from the next and double-clicking the mouse button.

4. Press Ctrl+Home to move to the top of the document, and then on the **View Shortcuts** toolbar near the right end of the status bar, click the **Zoom Level** button, which currently indicates that the document is displayed at 100%.

   The Zoom dialog box opens.

100%

You can click a built-in zoom percentage or specify your own.

5. Click **Many pages**. Then click the monitor button, click the second page thumbnail in the top row, and click **OK**.

   The magnification changes so that you can see two pages side by side.

You can now scroll through the document two pages at a time.

6. At the bottom of the vertical scroll bar, click the **Next Page** button to display the third and fourth pages of the document.

7. On the **View** tab, click the **Zoom** button. Then in the **Zoom** dialog box, click **75%**, and click **OK**.

   Notice that the Zoom Level percentage and slider position are adjusted to reflect the new setting.

8. At the left end of the **Zoom Slider**, click the **Zoom Out** button two times.

   As you click the button, the Zoom Level percentage decreases and the slider moves to the left.

9. At the right end of the **Zoom Slider**, click the **Zoom In** button until the **Zoom Level** percentage is 100 percent.

10. On the **View** tab, in the **Show** group, select the **Ruler** check box.

    Horizontal and vertical rulers appear above and to the left of the page. On the rulers, the content area of the page is white and the margins are gray.

11. On the **Home** tab, in the **Paragraph** group, click the **Show/Hide ¶** button.

    Formatting marks such as spaces, tabs, and paragraph marks are now visible.

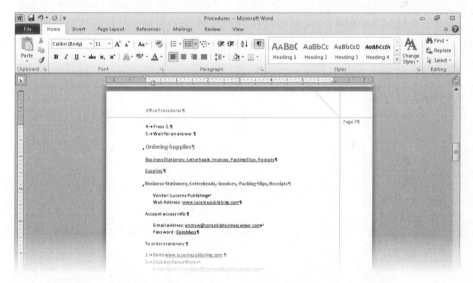

You can display the formatting marks that control the layout of the content.

12. On the **View Shortcuts** toolbar, click the **Full Screen Reading** button.

    Word displays the document in a format that is easy to read.

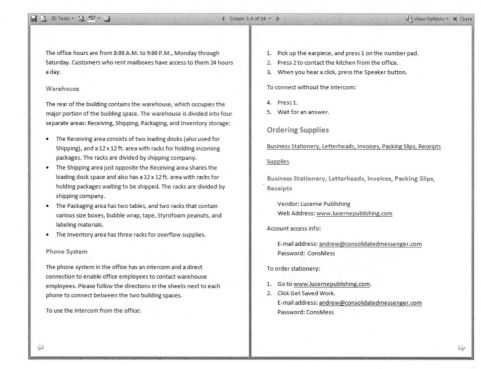

You cannot edit content in Full Screen Reading view unless you select Allow Typing on the View Options menu.

13. In the lower-right corner of the window, click the **Forward** button.

    You can now read the next two screens of information.

14. To the right of the screen indicator at the top of the window, click the **Previous Screen** button.

15. Point to each button on the toolbar at the top of the window to display its ScreenTip. Then in the upper-right corner, click the **Close** button to return to Print Layout view.

16. Press Ctrl+Home. Then on the **View Shortcuts** toolbar, click the **Web Layout** button, and scroll through the document.

    In a Web browser, the text column will fill the window, and there will be no page breaks.

17. Press Ctrl+Home, and then on the **View Shortcuts** toolbar, click the **Outline** button.

    Word displays the document's hierarchical structure, and the Outlining tab appears on the ribbon.

18. On the **Outlining** tab, in the **Outline Tools** group, click the **Show Level** arrow, and in the list, click **Level 2**.

    The document collapses to display only the Level 1 and Level 2 headings.

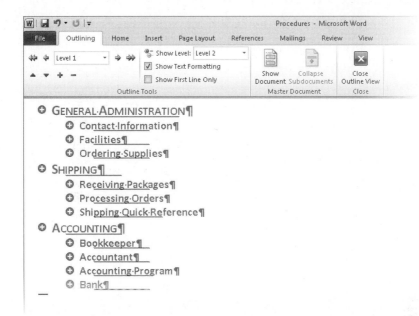

You can control the level of detail shown in the document's outline.

19. On the **View Shortcuts** toolbar, click the **Draft** button, and then scroll through the document.

    You can see the basic content of the document without any extraneous elements, such as margins and headers and footers. The active area on the ruler indicates the width of the text column, dotted lines indicate page breaks, and scrolling is quick and easy.

20. Display the Backstage view, click **Open**, and then in the **Open** dialog box, double-click **Prices_start**.

    The Prices_start document opens in Print Layout view in its own window. Notice that the telephone number in the body of the memo has a dotted underline, which indicates that it is formatted as hidden.

21. Save the **Prices_start** document as **Prices** so that you can work with it without overwriting the original.

22. On the **Home** tab, in the **Paragraph** group, click the **Show/Hide ¶** button to turn it off.

    The telephone number is no longer visible.

23. On the **View** tab, in the **Window** group, click the **Switch Windows** button, and then in the list of open documents, click **Procedures**.

    The Procedures document is displayed in Draft view with formatting marks and hidden text turned on. You can control the view and formatting marks for each window.

24. On the **View** tab, in the **Window** group, click the **Arrange All** button.

    The open windows are sized and stacked one above the other. Each window has a ribbon, so you can work with each document independently.

You can display more than one window at the same time.

> **Tip** The ribbons in each window take up a lot of screen space. To see more of each document, you can click the Minimize The Ribbon button to hide all but the tab names.

25. At the right end of the **Procedures** title bar, click the **Close** button.

26. At the right end of the **Prices** title bar, click the **Maximize** button.

    The window expands to fill the screen.

27. On the **View** tab, in the **Show** group, clear the **Ruler** check box to turn off the rulers.

✖ **CLEAN UP** Close the Prices document.

Key Points

- You can open more than one Word document, and you can view more than one document at a time, but only one document can be active at a time.

- You create Word documents by selecting a template and typing text at the cursor. It's easy to move the cursor by clicking in the text or by pressing keys and keyboard shortcuts.

- When you save a Word document, you specify its name, location, and file format in the Save As dialog box.

- You can view a document in a variety of ways, depending on your needs as you create the document and on the purpose for which you are creating it.

Chapter at a Glance

Find and replace text, **page 49**

Make text changes, **page 40**

Fine-tune text, **page 55**

Correct spelling and grammatical errors, **page 63**

Insert saved text, **page 69**

Navigation

parking

8 matches

campers, house trailers, buses, or trucks shall be stored in any **parking** space in any Common Area.

4.4 No Owner shall use his or her **parking** spaces in the common garage to store personal belongings

be stored in the front end of the assigned **parking** stall or in the Owner's unused assigned stall

6. **Parking** and Vehicles

6.3 Five **parking** spaces are reserved for guest parking for the entire complex. Commercial vehicles

File   Home   Insert   Page Layout

Constantia (Boc   11

B *I* U abc x₂ x²

Paste Options:

Font

Paste Special...

Set Default Paste...

Visit our showroom and purchase a Room Planner look around and see what really appeals to you. Son designed around just one or two special pieces, so something already what to cho our des is available walking professiona

Bilingual Dictionary

wardrobe
for clothes armoire *féminin, (clothes)* garde-robe *féminin*

As an exam bedro new bed, a wardrobe, or perhaps a chair to sit in wh The Room Planner can be used countless times for

current economic and environmental conditions, as well as of political issues that our ability to maintain a viable business. When we select our product sources, we only to improve the local economy but to ensure the preservation of fragile ecolo complex balancing act, but we are committed to maximizing our positive impacts whi no corresponding negative impacts.

An exciting to discuss any may contact S sidney@wide available May

In the meantim suppliers, a tra which outlines

Sincerely,

Spelling and Grammar: English (U.S.)

Repeated Word:

When we select our product sources, we strive to not only to improve the local economy but to to ensure the preservation of fragile ecologies.

Suggestions:

Ignore Once
Ignore All
Add to Dictionary

Delete
Delete All
AutoCorrect

☑ Check grammar

Undo   Cancel

Quick Parts

General

Contact Block

Wide World Importers
Furniture and accessories for your world
(925) 555-0167
www.wideworldimporters.com

AutoText

Document Property

Field...

Building Blocks Organizer...

Save Selection to Quick Part Gallery...

2 Edit and Proofread Text

In this chapter, you will learn how to

- ✔ Make text changes.
- ✔ Find and replace text.
- ✔ Fine-tune text.
- ✔ Correct spelling and grammatical errors.
- ✔ Insert saved text.

As you learned in Chapter 1, "Explore Word 2010," entering text is a simple matter of typing. However, even the most accurate typists occasionally make mistakes, also known as *typos* (for *typographical errors*). Unless the documents you create are intended for no one's eyes but your own, you need to ensure that they are not only correct but also persuasive. Whether you are a novice or experienced writer, Microsoft Word 2010 has several tools that make creating professional documents easy and efficient.

- **Editing tools** These tools provide quick-selection techniques and drag-and-drop editing to make it easy to move and copy text anywhere you want it.

- **Search tools** These tools can be used to locate and replace words, phrases, and special characters, either one at a time or throughout a document.

  See Also For information about using the search tools to find and replace formatting, see the sidebar "Finding and Replacing Formatting" in Chapter 3, "Change the Look of Text."

- **Research tools** These tools make it easy to find synonyms, look up information, and translate words and phrases.

- **AutoCorrect and Spelling And Grammar** These features make it easy to correct typographical and grammatical errors before you share a document with others.

- **Quick Parts** These building blocks can be used to save and recall specialized terms or standard paragraphs.

  Tip Word also includes formatted building blocks for document elements such as cover pages, headers, and footers. For information, see "Inserting Building Blocks" in Chapter 5, "Add Simple Graphic Elements."

In this chapter, you'll edit the text in a document by inserting and deleting text, copying and pasting a phrase, and moving a paragraph. Then you'll replace one phrase with another throughout the entire document. Next, you'll replace a word with a synonym and translate another word. You'll also add misspelled words to the AutoCorrect list and check the spelling and grammar of a document. Finally, you'll save a couple of building blocks for insertion later in a document.

> **Practice Files** Before you can complete the exercises in this chapter, you need to copy the book's practice files to your computer. The practice files you'll use to complete the exercises in this chapter are in the Chapter02 practice file folder. A complete list of practice files is provided in "Using the Practice Files" at the beginning of this book.

Making Text Changes

You'll rarely write a perfect document that doesn't require any editing. You'll almost always want to add or remove a word or two, change a phrase, or move text from one place to another. You can edit a document as you create it, or you can write it first and then revise it. Or you might want to edit a document that you created for one purpose so that you can use it for a different purpose. For example, a letter might make an ideal starting point for a flyer, or a report might contain all the information you need for a Web document.

Inserting text is easy; you click to position the cursor and simply begin typing. Any existing text to the right of the cursor moves to make room for the new text.

Deleting text is equally easy. If you want to delete only one or a few characters, you can simply position the cursor and then press the Backspace or Delete key until the characters are all gone. Pressing Backspace deletes the character to the left of the cursor; pressing Delete deletes the character to the right of the cursor.

To delete more than a few characters efficiently, you need to know how to select the text. Selected text appears highlighted on the screen. You can drag through a section of text to select it, or you can select specific items as follows:

● **Word** Double-click anywhere in the word. The word and the space immediately following it are selected, but not any punctuation following the word.

● **Sentence** Click anywhere in the sentence while holding down the Ctrl key. Word selects all the characters in the sentence, from the first character through the space following the ending punctuation mark.

● **Paragraph** Triple-click anywhere in the paragraph. Word selects the text of the paragraph and the paragraph mark.

● **Adjacent words, lines, or paragraphs** Position the cursor at the beginning of the text you want to select, hold down the Shift key, and then press the Arrow keys to select one character or line at a time; hold down the Shift and Ctrl keys and press the Arrow keys to select one word at a time; or click at the end of the text that you want to select.

● **Non-adjacent words, lines, or paragraphs** Make the first selection, and then hold down the Ctrl key while selecting the next text block.

Tip When you select text, Word displays a box called the *Mini Toolbar* so that you can quickly format the selection. You can ignore this toolbar for now. For more information, see "Manually Changing the Look of Characters" in Chapter 3, "Change the Look of Text."

As an alternative way of selecting, you can use an invisible area in the document's left margin, called the *selection area*, to select items.

● **Line** Click in the selection area to the left of the line.

● **Paragraph** Double-click in the selection area to the left of the paragraph.

● **Entire document** Triple-click in the selection area.

Keyboard Shortcut Press Ctrl+A to select all the content in the body of the document.

See Also To see a complete list of keyboard shortcuts, see "Keyboard Shortcuts" at the end of this book.

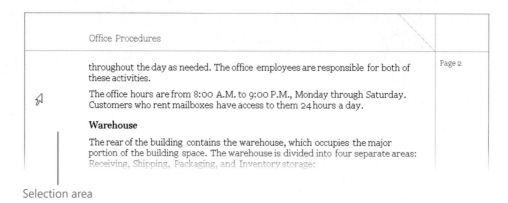

Selection area

In the selection area, the pointer becomes a right-pointing arrow.

After selecting the text you want to delete, press either Backspace or Delete.

Tip To release a selection, click anywhere in the window other than the selection area.

If you want to move or copy the selected text, you have three options:

- **Drag-and-drop editing** Use this feature, which is frequently referred to simply as *dragging*, when you need to move or copy text only a short distance—for example, within a paragraph. Start by using any of the methods described previously to select the text. Then point to the selection, hold down the mouse button, drag the text to its new location, and release the mouse button. To copy the selection, hold down the Ctrl key while you drag.

- **Cut, Copy, and Paste buttons** Use this method when you need to move or copy text between two locations that you cannot see at the same time—for example, between pages or between documents. Select the text, and click the Cut or Copy button in the Clipboard group on the Home tab. (The cut or copied item is stored in an area of your computer's memory called the *Microsoft Office Clipboard*, hence the name of the group.) Then reposition the cursor, and click the Paste button to insert the selection in its new location. If you click the Paste arrow instead of the button, Word displays a list of different ways to paste the selection.

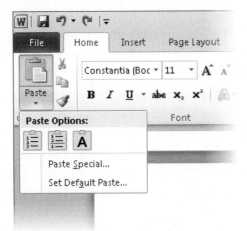

Under Paste Options, buttons represent the ways in which you can paste the item.

Pointing to a button under Paste Options displays a preview of how the cut or copied item will look when pasted into the text in that format, so you can experiment with different ways of pasting until you find the one you want.

See Also For more information about the Clipboard, see the sidebar "About the Clipboard" later in this chapter.

● **Keyboard shortcuts** It can be more efficient to press key combinations to cut, copy, and paste selections than to click buttons on the ribbon. The main keyboard shortcuts for editing tasks are shown in the following table.

Task	Keyboard shortcut
Cut	Ctrl+X
Copy	Ctrl+C
Paste	Ctrl+V
Undo	Ctrl+Z
Repeat/Redo	Ctrl+Y

Using a keyboard shortcut to cut or copy a selection stores the item on the Clipboard, just as if you had clicked the corresponding button.

Tip No matter which method you use, when you cut text, Word removes it from its original location. When you copy text, Word leaves the text in the original location and repeats it in the new location.

If you make a change to a document and then realize that you made a mistake, you can easily reverse the change. You can undo your last editing action by clicking the Undo button on the Quick Access Toolbar. To undo an earlier action, click the Undo arrow and then click that action in the list.

Tip Selecting an action from the Undo list undoes that action and all the editing actions you performed after that one. You cannot undo only one action other than the last one you performed.

If you make a change to a document and want to repeat that change elsewhere, you can click the Repeat button on the Quick Access Toolbar. If the last task you performed was to undo an action, the Repeat button is replaced by the Redo button. So if you change your mind about whatever you undid, you can click the Redo button to return the text to its previous state. You can't redo multiple actions by clicking them in a list as you can with the Undo button, but you can click the Redo button repeatedly until the text is restored to what you want.

In this exercise, you'll edit the text in a document. You'll insert and delete text, undo the deletion, copy and paste a phrase, and move a paragraph.

SET UP You need the Orientation_start document located in your Chapter02 practice file folder to complete this exercise. Open the Orientation_start document, and save it as *Orientation*. Then follow the steps.

1. If formatting marks such as spaces and paragraph marks are not visible in the document, on the **Home** tab, in the **Paragraph** group, click the **Show/Hide ¶** button.

   Keyboard Shortcut Press Ctrl+* to turn formatting marks on or off. (You need to hold down the Shift key to activate the * key. So in effect, you are pressing Ctrl+Shift+8.)

2. In the second bullet point under **Project Goals**, double-click the word **natural** to select it, and then press Backspace.

3. In the third bullet point, click to the left of the **a** in the word **and**, hold down the Shift key, and then click to the right of the **e** in the word **motivate**.

   Word selects the text between the two clicks.

   Troubleshooting If Word selects the word *Engage* as well, you clicked before the space instead of after it. Click anywhere in the document to release the selection, and then repeat step 3, being sure to click after the space but before the word *and*.

Community·Service·Committee¶
Employee·Orientation¶

Proposal↵
Last·updated:·January·25,·2010¶

Project·Goals¶
- → Familiarize·employees·with·the·concept·of·service.¶
- → Make·service·a·part·of·their·lives.¶
- → Engage·and·motivate·them.¶
- → Forge·a·sense·of·teamwork·among·all·employees·across·departments.¶
- → Provide·appropriate·skills·development·through·brainstorming,·planning,·and·leadership· opportunities.¶

You can use the Shift+click method to select as much text as you want.

4. Press Delete to delete the selection.

   Word also deletes the space after the selection.

5. In the fourth bullet point, double-click the word **Forge**, and then replace it by typing **Build**.

   Notice that you don't have to type a space after _Build_. Word inserts the space for you.

   Tip Word inserts and deletes spaces because the Use Smart Cut And Paste check box is selected on the Advanced page of the Word Options dialog box. If you want to be able to control the spacing yourself, click the Options button in the Backstage view, click Advanced, clear this check box (located in the Cut, Copy, And Paste area), and then click OK.

6. Scroll the page, and position the mouse pointer at the edge of the page to the left of the first bullet point under **Questions for Team Leaders**. Then with the pointer in the selection area, click to select the entire paragraph.

   Tip Clicking once selects this paragraph because it is only one line long. If the paragraph contained more than one line, you would need to double-click.

7. On the **Home** tab, in the **Clipboard** group, click the **Copy** button.

   The selection is copied to the Clipboard.

8. If you can't see the bulleted list under **Questions for Department Reps**, click the **Next Page** button below the vertical scroll bar to move to the beginning of the next page. Then click to the left of **What** in the first bullet point under **Questions for Department Reps**, and in the **Clipboard** group, click the **Paste** arrow.

   The Paste Options menu opens.

```
Paste Options:

 [≣] [≣] [A]

    Paste Special...
    Set Default Paste...
```

   The Paste Options menu includes buttons representing pasting options.

9. Point to the **Merge List** button, notice how the text will look with this paste option implemented, and then click the button.

   The Paste Options button appears below and to the right of the inserted bullet point. You can click this button to display a list of paste options if you want to change the way the text has been pasted or the default way Word pastes. In this case, you can just ignore it.

10. In the **Set Up Team** section, triple-click anywhere in the paragraph that begins **The Committee will pursue** to select the entire paragraph.

11. In the **Clipboard** group, click the **Cut** button.

12. Press the Up Arrow key to move to the beginning of the preceding paragraph, and then in the **Clipboard** group, click the **Paste** button.

    The two paragraphs switch places.

13. On the Quick Access Toolbar, click the **Undo** arrow, and then in the **Undo** list, click the third action (**Paste Merge List**).

Word undoes the previous cut-and-paste operation and the pasting of the copied text.

14. Press Ctrl+Home to move to the top of the document. Then position the pointer in the selection area adjacent to the third bullet point under **Project Goals**, and click to select the paragraph.

15. Point to the selection, hold down the mouse button, and then drag the paragraph up to the left of the word **Make** at the beginning of the preceding bullet point.

    When you release the mouse, the bullet point moves to its new location.

16. With the text still selected, press the End key.

    Word releases the selection and moves the cursor to the end of the paragraph.

17. Press the Spacebar, and then press Delete.

    Word deletes the paragraph mark and merges the two bullet points.

Community·Service·Committee¶
Employee·Orientation¶

Proposal↵
Last·updated:··January· 25,·2010¶

·Project·Goals¶
- → Familiarize·employees·with·the·concept·of·service.¶
- → Engage·them.··Make·service·a·part·of·their·lives.¶
- → Build·a·sense·of·teamwork·among·all·employees·across·departments.¶
- → Provide·appropriate·skills·development·through·brainstorming,·planning,·and·leadership· opportunities.¶
- → Meet·genuine·community·needs.¶

In the second bullet point, two bullets have now been combined into one.

✖ **CLEAN UP** If you prefer not to see formatting marks, turn them off. Then save and close the Orientation document.

About the Clipboard

You can view the items that have been cut or copied to the Clipboard in the Clipboard task pane, which you display by clicking the Clipboard dialog box launcher on the Home tab.

The Clipboard stores items that have been cut or copied from any Office program.

To paste an individual item at the cursor, you simply click the item in the Clipboard task pane. To paste all the items, click the Paste All button. You can point to an item, click the arrow that appears, and then click Delete to remove it from the Clipboard and the task pane, or you can remove all the items by clicking the Clear All button.

You can control the behavior of the Clipboard task pane by clicking Options at the bottom of the pane, and choosing the circumstances under which you want the task pane to appear.

To close the Clipboard task pane, click the Close button at the right end of its title bar.

Finding and Replacing Text

One way to ensure that the text in your documents is consistent and accurate is to use the Find feature to search for every occurrence of a particular word or phrase. For example, if you are responsible for advertising a trademarked product, you might want to search your marketing materials to check that every occurrence of the product's name is correctly identified as a trademark.

Clicking the Find button (not the arrow) in the Editing group on the Home tab displays the Navigation task pane with the Search tab active. As you type characters in the Search Document box at the top of the task pane, Word highlights all occurrences of those characters in the document and displays them in the search results list in the Navigation task pane.

Keyboard Shortcut Press Ctrl+F to display the Search tab of the Navigation task pane.

The Navigation task pane shows enough of the text surrounding the search term to identify its context.

When you point to a particular search result in the Navigation task pane, a ScreenTip displays the number of the page on which that result appears. You can click a search result to scroll the document to display the result's location.

Tip The beauty of the Navigation task pane is that you can continue editing your document as you normally would, without closing the pane.

If you want to be more specific about the text you are looking for—for example, if you want to look for occurrences that match the exact capitalization of your search term—click the arrow at the right end of the Search Document box in the Navigation task pane and then click Advanced Find to display the Find page of the Find And Replace dialog box. Clicking More in the lower-left corner expands the dialog box to make additional search options available.

You can make a search more specific by using the criteria in the Search Options area of the Find And Replace dialog box.

In the expanded dialog box, you can do the following:

● Guide the direction of the search by selecting Down, Up, or All from the Search list.

● Locate only text that matches the capitalization of the Find What text by selecting the Match Case check box.

● Exclude occurrences of the Find What text that appear within other words by selecting the Find Whole Words Only check box.

● Find two similar words, such as *effect* and *affect* by selecting the Use Wildcards check box and then entering a wildcard character in the Find What box. The two most common wildcard characters are:

  ○ ?, which represents any single character in this location in the Find What text.

  ○ *, which represents any number of characters in this location in the Find What text.

  Tip To see a list of the available wildcards, use Help to search for the term *wildcards*.

● Find occurrences of the search text that sound the same but are spelled differently, such as *there* and *their*, by selecting the Sounds Like check box.

● Find occurrences of a particular word in any form, such as *try*, *tries*, and *tried*, by selecting the Find All Word Forms check box. You can match a prefix or a suffix, and you can ignore punctuation and white space.

● Locate formatting, such as bold, or special characters, such as tabs, by selecting them from the Format or Special list.

  See Also For information about finding and replacing formatting, see the sidebar "Finding and Replacing Formatting" in Chapter 3, "Change the Look of Text."

If you want to substitute a specific word or phrase for another, you can use the Replace feature. Clicking the Replace button in the Editing group of the Home tab displays the Replace page of the Find And Replace dialog box.

Find and Replace			? ✕

Find | **Replace** | Go To

Find what: Susie

Replace with: Suzy

More >>   Replace   Replace All   Find Next   Cancel

Correcting errors and inconsistencies is easy with the Replace feature.

Keyboard Shortcut Press Ctrl+H to display the Replace page of the Find And Replace dialog box.

Tip If the Navigation task pane is open, you can click the arrow at the right end of the Search Document box and then click Replace. The Find And Replace dialog box opens with the search term from the Navigation task pane already in the Find What box.

On the Replace page, you can click the following:

- **Find Next** Finds the first occurrence or leaves the selected occurrence as it is and locates the next one

- **Replace** Replaces the selected occurrence with the text in the Replace With box and moves to the next occurrence

- **Replace All** Replaces all occurrences with the text in the Replace With box

    Tip Before clicking Replace All, ensure that the replacement is clearly defined. For example, if you want to change *trip* to *journey*, be sure to tell Word to find only the whole word *trip*; otherwise, *triple* could become *journeyle*.

As on the Find page, clicking More displays the options you can use to carry out more complicated replacements.

In this exercise, you'll find a phrase and make a correction to the text. Then you'll replace one phrase with another throughout the entire document.

SET UP You need the RulesRegulations_start document located in your Chapter02 practice file folder to complete this exercise. Open the RulesRegulations_start document, and save it as *RulesRegulations*. Then follow the steps.

1. With the cursor at the beginning of the document, on the **Home** tab, in the **Editing** group, click the **Find** button (not its arrow).

    The Navigation task pane opens, displaying the Search tab.

2. With the cursor in the **Search Document** box, type **Board**. (Don't type the period.)

The Navigation task pane displays 62 matches with the word *Board* and highlights every occurrence in the document.

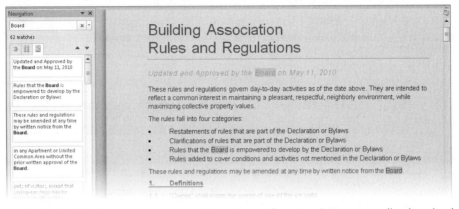

In the Navigation task pane, you can click each match to view its corresponding location in the document.

3. In the **Navigation** task pane, click the fifth match in the search results to jump to page **2**.

    Notice that under the heading *4. Storage*, Word has highlighted the *board* portion of *skateboards*. You need to restrict the search to the whole word *Board*.

4. In the **Navigation** task pane, click the arrow at the right end of the **Search Document** box.

    A menu of options for refining the search appears.

You can click options that allow you to find specific types of objects as well as text.

5. In the top part of the list, click **Advanced Find**.

    The Find And Replace dialog box opens with the Find page displayed. The Find What box already contains the search term from the Navigation task pane.

6. In the lower-left corner of the dialog box, click **More**.

   The dialog box expands to display options for refining the search.

7. In the **Search Options** area of the dialog box, select the **Match case** and **Find whole words only** check boxes. Then click **Reading Highlight**, click **Highlight All**, and click **Close**.

   Under the *4. Storage* heading, the word *skateboards* is no longer highlighted.

8. Press Ctrl+Home to move the cursor to the beginning of the document.

9. In the **Navigation** task pane, display the search options list again, and then click **Replace**.

   The Find And Replace dialog box opens with the Replace page active. The Find What box retains the entry from the previous search, and the Match Case and Find Whole Words Only check boxes are still selected.

10. Click **Less** to reduce the size of the box, and then drag the box by its title bar toward the top of the document.

11. Click the **Replace with** box, type **Association Board**, and then click **Find Next**.

    Word highlights the first occurrence of *Board*.

12. In the dialog box, click **Replace**.

    Word replaces the first occurrence of *Board* with *Association Board* and then finds the next occurrence.

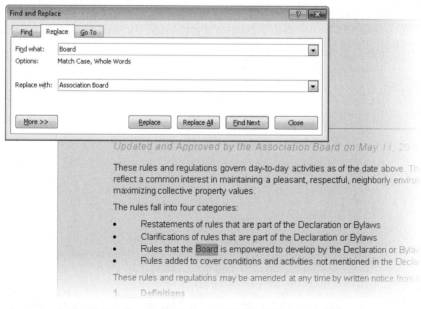

If you don't want to replace an occurrence, click Find Next to skip it.

13. Having tested the replacement, click **Replace All**.

14. When Word tells you how many replacements it made, click **OK** to close the message box. Then in the **Find and Replace** dialog box, click **Close**.

15. Press Ctrl+Home to move to the beginning of the document.

    In the *Updated and Approved* line of text, the word *Association* is now duplicated.

16. Use your new find and replace skills to replace any instances of **Association Association** in the document with **Association**.

✖ CLEAN UP Close the Navigation task pane. Then save and close the RulesRegulations document.

Fine-Tuning Text

Language is often contextual—you use different words and phrases in a marketing brochure than you would in a letter requesting immediate payment of an invoice or in an informal memo about a social gathering after work. To help you ensure that you're using the words that best convey your meaning in any given context, Word provides a thesaurus where you can look up alternative words, called *synonyms*, for a selected word. The Thesaurus is one of a set of research services provided by Word.

To look up alternatives for a word, you can right-click the word, and then click Synonyms to display a list from which you can choose the one you want. Alternatively, you can select the word and then click the Thesaurus button in the Proofing group on the Review tab. The Research task pane opens, displaying the selected word in the Search For box and synonyms for that word in the Thesaurus list.

Keyboard Shortcuts Press Shift+F7 to open the Research task pane and display Thesaurus entries for the active word, which is also displayed in the Search For box.

```
Research                          ▼ ✕
Search for:
┌──────────────────────────┐ ┌──┐
│ chips                    │ │→ │
└──────────────────────────┘ └──┘
┌────────────────────────────┐ ┌─┐
│ Thesaurus: English (U.S.)  │ │▼│
└────────────────────────────┘ └─┘
┌──────────────┐ ┌──────────┐
│ ⊕ Back  │ ▼ │ │ ⊕  │ ▼    │
└──────────────┘ └──────────┘
◢ Thesaurus: English (U.S.)   ▲
   ◢ fries (n.)
     fries
     French-fried potatoes …
     French fries (Dictionar…   ▤
     deep fried potatoes (Di…
     pommes frites (Diction…
   ◢ marks (n.)
     marks
     damages
     imperfections
     flaws
     blemishes
   ◢ pieces (n.)
     pieces
     bits
     crumbs
     flakes
     chunks
     morsels
   ◢ tokens (n.)            ▼
🌐 Get services on Office
   Marketplace
🔍 Research options…
```

You can click a synonym to display its synonyms and click again to repeat that process until you find exactly the word you want.

To replace the selected word with a synonym, point to your chosen synonym, click the arrow that appears, and then click Insert.

In addition to the Thesaurus, the Research task pane provides access to a variety of informational resources. You first open the Research task pane by clicking the Research button in the Proofing group and then enter a topic in the Search For box, specifying in the box below which resource Word should use to look for information about that topic.

Keyboard Shortcut Press the Alt key and click anywhere in the document to display the Research task pane.

You can choose a specific resource from the list or click All Reference Books or All Research Sites to widen the search.

Clicking Research Options at the bottom of the Research task pane displays the Research Options dialog box. In this dialog box, you can specify which of a predefined set of reference materials and other Internet resources will be available from the list.

Research Options

To activate a service for searching, select the check box associated with that service.

Services:

Reference Books
- [ ] Diccionario de la Real Academia Española
- [x] Encarta Dictionary: English (North America)
- [ ] Encarta Dictionary: English (U.K.)
- [ ] Encarta Dictionary: French
- [ ] Foreign Word Spelling Look Up (Korean)
- [ ] Hangul Word Romanization (Korean)
- [ ] Local Address Search (Korean)
- [ ] Thesaurus: English (U.K.)
- [x] Thesaurus: English (U.S.)
- [x] Thesaurus: French (France)
- [x] Thesaurus: Spanish (International Sort)
- [x] Translation

Research Sites
- [x] Bing [Current Favorite]

Properties...
Favorite...

Add Services...   Update/Remove...   Parental Control...

OK   Cancel

You can click Add Services to include your favorite reference resources in the list.

Word also comes with three translation tools with which you can quickly translate words and phrases, or even entire documents.

● **Mini Translator** You turn the Mini Translator on or off by clicking the Translate button in the Language group of the Review tab and then clicking Mini Translator. When the Mini Translator is turned on, you can point to a word or selected phrase to display a translation in the specified language. When the box containing the translation is displayed, you can click the Expand button to display the Research task pane, where you can change the translation language. You can also copy the translated word or phrase, or hear the word or phrase spoken for you.

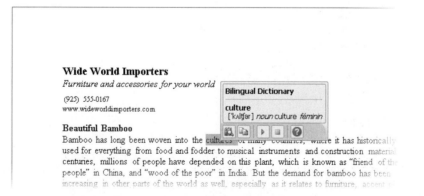

Using the Mini Translator is the quickest way to obtain the translation of a selection.

- **Online bilingual dictionary** To obtain the translation of a word that does not appear in the text of a document, you can click Translate Selected Text in the Translate menu to display the Research task pane, type the word in the Search For box, specify the language you want, and then click Start Searching. Word consults the online bilingual dictionary for the language you chose and displays the result. You can then click Insert to enter a translated word in the document at the cursor.

You can use the bilingual dictionary to translate a selected word or the word you type in the Search For box.

● **Online machine translator** To translate an entire document, you can click Translate Document on the Translate menu. When Word displays a message that the document will be sent for translation by the Microsoft Translator service (which is free), click Send. The document and its translation then appear side by side in your Web browser. You can set the translation from and translation to languages in the boxes at the top of the Web page and click buttons to change the view.

The Microsoft Translator service translates complete documents into the language you select.

To change the default language used by the Mini Translator or the machine translator, you click Choose Translation Language on the Translate menu. Then in the Translation Language Options dialog box, you can select different language pairs for each type of translator.

You can translate from and to many languages, including Arabic, Chinese, Greek, Hebrew, Italian, Japanese, Korean, Polish, Portuguese, Russian, Spanish, and Swedish.

In this exercise, you'll use the Thesaurus to replace one word with another. Then you'll experiment with the Mini Translator.

SET UP You need the Brochure_start document located in your Chapter02 practice file folder to complete this exercise. Open the Brochure_start document, and save it as *Brochure*. Then follow the steps.

1. Double-click the word **acclaimed** in the second line of the first paragraph.

2. On the **Review** tab, in the **Proofing** group, click the **Thesaurus** button.

   The Research task pane opens, listing synonyms for the word *acclaimed*.

3. In the task pane, under **much-admired**, click **commended**.

   The word *commended* replaces *acclaimed* in the Search For box at the top of the task pane.

Synonyms for commended *are now listed in the task pane.*

4. Point to the word **celebrated**, click the arrow that appears to its right, and then click **Insert**.

   The word *celebrated* replaces *acclaimed* in the document.

5. Close the **Research** task pane.

   Tip You can open the Research task pane at any time by clicking the Research button in the Proofing group on the Review tab.

6. In the **Language** group, click the **Translate** button, and then click **Choose Translation Language**.

   The Translation Language Options dialog box opens.

7. Under **Choose Mini Translator language**, click the **Translate to** arrow, click **French (France)** in the list, and then click **OK**.

8. In the **Language** group, click the **Translate** button, and then click **Mini Translator [French (France)]**.

   The Mini Translator is now turned on.

9. In the last paragraph of the document, point to the word **wardrobe**, and then move the pointer over the shadow box that appears above the word.

   The Mini Translator appears, showing two French translations for the word *wardrobe*: *armoire* and *garde-robe*.

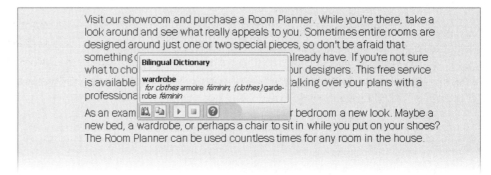

You can click the Play button to hear the translated word.

10. In the **Mini Translator** box, click the **Expand** button.

    The Research task pane opens, displaying the settings for translating from English into French.

11. Under **Bilingual Dictionary** in the **Research** task pane, double-click **armoire** to select it.

12. Right-click the selection, and click **Copy**.

13. In the document, double-click the word **wardrobe**.

14. Right-click the selection, and under **Paste Options** in the list, point to (don't click) the **Keep Text Only** button.

    Word displays a live preview of what the text will look like if you replace *wardrobe* with *armoire*.

15. Press the Esc key to close the shortcut menu and leave the word *wardrobe* in the text.

✖ CLEAN UP Close the Research task pane, and turn off the Mini Translator by clicking the Translate button in the Language group and clicking Mini Translator. Then save and close the Brochure document.

Correcting Spelling and Grammatical Errors

In the days of handwritten and typewritten documents, people might have tolerated a typographical or grammatical error or two because correcting such errors without creating a mess was difficult. Word-processing programs such as Word have built-in spelling and grammar checkers, so now documents that contain these types of errors are likely to reflect badly on their creators.

Tip Although Word can help you eliminate misspellings and grammatical errors, its tools are not infallible. You should always read through your document to catch any problems that the Word tools can't detect—for example, homonyms such as *their*, *there*, and *they're*.

Word provides these three tools to help you with the chore of eliminating spelling and grammar errors:

- **AutoCorrect** This feature corrects commonly misspelled words, such as *adn* to *and*, so that you don't have to correct them yourself. AutoCorrect comes with a long list of frequently misspelled words and their correct spellings. If you frequently misspell a word that AutoCorrect doesn't change, you can add it to the list in the AutoCorrect dialog box. If you deliberately mistype a word and don't want to accept the AutoCorrect change, you can reverse the correction by clicking the Undo button before you type anything else.

- **Error indicators** Word underlines potential spelling errors with red wavy underlines and grammatical errors with green wavy underlines. You can right-click an underlined word or phrase to display suggested corrections in a shortcut menu.

- **Spelling and Grammar dialog box** If you want to check the spelling or grammar of the entire document, you can click the Spelling & Grammar button in the Proofing group on the Review tab. Word then works its way through the document and displays the Spelling And Grammar dialog box if it encounters a potential error.

The buttons in the Spelling And Grammar dialog box are dynamic and reflect the type of error found.

Keyboard Shortcut Press F7 to start checking the spelling and grammar from your current location in the document.

If the error is a misspelling, the Spelling And Grammar dialog box suggests corrections; if the error is a breach of grammar rules, the Spelling And Grammar dialog box tells you which rule you have broken and suggests corrections. You can implement a suggestion by double-clicking it in the Suggestions box.

In this exercise, you'll change an AutoCorrect setting and add a word to the AutoCorrect list. You'll check the spelling in the document and add terms to the custom dictionary, and then you'll find, review, and correct a grammatical error.

SET UP You need the Letter_start document located in your Chapter02 practice file folder to complete this exercise. Open the Letter_start document, and save it as *Letter*. Then follow the steps.

1. Click immediately to the left of **negative** in the last line of the first paragraph, and then type **coresponding**, followed by a space.

   As soon as you press the Spacebar, AutoCorrect changes *coresponding* to *corresponding*.

2. Click the **File** tab to display the Backstage view, and then click **Options**.

3. In the left pane of the **Word Options** dialog box, click **Proofing**, and then on the **Proofing** page, click **AutoCorrect Options**.

   The AutoCorrect dialog box opens, displaying the AutoCorrect page.

A selected check box indicates an error that AutoCorrect will automatically correct.

> **Tip** You can clear the check box of any item you don't want corrected. For example, if you don't want AutoCorrect to capitalize the first letter that follows a period, clear the Capitalize First Letter Of Sentences check box.

4. In the **Replace** box, type **avalable**.

   Word scrolls the list below to show the entry that is closest to what you typed.

5. Press the Tab key to move the cursor to the **With** box, and then type **available**.

6. Click **Add** to add the entry to the correction list, and then click **OK**.

7. Click **OK** to close the **Word Options** dialog box.

8. Position the cursor at the end of the second paragraph, press the Spacebar, and then type **Sidney will not be avalable May 10-14** followed by a period.

   The word *avalable* changes to *available*.

9. In the first paragraph, right-click **sorces**, the first word with a red wavy underline.

   Word lists possible correct spellings for this word.

sources

sores

scores

source's

forces

Ignore

Ignore All

Add to Dictionary

AutoCorrect ▶

Language ▶

Spelling...

Loo**k** Up | ▶

Cut

Copy

Paste Options:

A

The shortcut menu also lists actions you might want to carry out, such as adding the word to the AutoCorrect list.

10. In the list, click **sources**.

    Word removes the red wavy underline and inserts the correction.

Tip Word's grammar checker helps identify phrases and clauses that don't follow traditional grammatical rules, but it's not always accurate. It's easy to get in the habit of ignoring green wavy underlines. However, it's wise to scrutinize them all to be sure that your documents don't contain any embarrassing mistakes.

11. Press Ctrl+Home to move to the beginning of the document, and then on the **Review** tab, in the **Proofing** group, click the **Spelling & Grammar** button.

    The Spelling And Grammar dialog box opens, with the duplicate word *to* in red in the Repeated Word box.

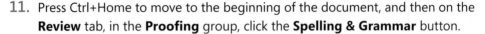

Behind the dialog box, Word has highlighted the duplicate to *in the document.*

Troubleshooting If the errors we mention don't appear to be in the practice file, click Options at the bottom of the Spelling And Grammar dialog box. Then in the Word Options dialog box, under When Correcting Spelling And Grammar In Word, click Recheck Document. Click Yes to reset the spelling and grammar checkers, and then click OK.

12. Click **Delete**.

    Word deletes the second *to* and then displays the first word it does not recognize, *commited*, in red in the Not In Dictionary box.

13. With **committed** selected in the **Suggestions** box, click **AutoCorrect**.

    Word adds the misspelling and the selected correction to the AutoCorrect list, so that the next time you type *commited* by mistake, the spelling will be corrected for you as you type. The program then identifies a possible grammatical error.

Spelling and Grammar: English (U.S.)

Comma Use:

> An exciting and challenging **venture**, and we would like to invite you to visit our corporate office to discuss any information you might need with Sidney Higa, one of our purchasing

Ignore Once

Ignore Rule

Ne**x**t Sentence

Suggestio**n**s:

> venture

Change

Explain...

☑ Check grammar

Options... **U**ndo

Close

This grammatical error is identified as an incorrect use of a comma.

You need to read the sentence and then decide whether and how to correct the error. In this case, the error is not related to the comma after *venture* but to the fact that there is no verb in the first half of the sentence.

14. In the **Comma Use** box, double-click the word **An** at the beginning of the sentence with the error, and type **The import business is an**. Then click **Change**.

Word flags *Contoso* as a word it doesn't recognize.

Troubleshooting If Word does not proceed to the next potential error after you click Change, click Resume to tell Word to continue with the spelling and grammar check.

Contoso is a proper noun and is spelled correctly. You could click Ignore All to cause Word to skip over any other instances of this word in this document. However, if this name appears frequently in your documents, you can prevent Word from continuing to flag it by adding the word to the custom dictionary.

15. Click **Add to Dictionary**.

Word displays a message indicating that it has finished checking the spelling and grammar of the document.

16. Click **OK** to close the message box.

Tip The grammar checker doesn't always catch awkward phrasing. For example, note the error in the second sentence of the first paragraph of the Letter document. It's a good example of why you should always proofread your documents, to catch the things that Word doesn't.

 CLEAN UP Save the Letter document, and then close it.

Viewing Document Statistics

As you type, Word keeps track of the number of pages and words in your document and displays this information at the left end of the status bar. To see the number of words in only part of the document, such as a few paragraphs, simply select that part. The status bar then displays the number of words in the selection, expressed as a fraction of the total, such as 250/800.

You can see more statistics in the Word Count dialog box, which you open by clicking the Word Count button in the Proofing group on the Review tab.

Word Count	?	x
Statistics:		
Pages	1	
Words	184	
Characters (no spaces)	979	
Characters (with spaces)	1,157	
Paragraphs	6	
Lines	22	

☑ Include textboxes, footnotes and endnotes

Close

In addition to counting pages and words, Word counts characters, paragraphs, and lines.

Word also gives you the option of including or excluding words in text boxes, footnotes, and endnotes.

Inserting Saved Text

Another way to ensure consistency in your documents while also saving time is to use building blocks. These are saved items that are available for use in any document. Word 2010 comes with many built-in building blocks for formatted items such as cover pages, headers and footers, tables, and text boxes. You can also save your own building blocks by using the Quick Parts feature.

See Also For information about the building blocks that come with Word, see "Inserting Building Blocks" in Chapter 5, "Add Simple Graphic Elements."

A custom building block can be a simple phrase or sentence that you type often, or it can include multiple paragraphs, formatting, graphics, and so on. The trick is to first ensure that the text is exactly the way you want it. Then you can save the building block and use it confidently wherever you need it.

To create a building block, you select the item you want to save, click Quick Parts in the Text group on the Insert tab, and save the selection in the Quick Parts gallery with an assigned name. You can then insert the building block at the cursor by clicking Quick Parts to display the gallery and clicking the thumbnail of the building block you want. Or you can insert it elsewhere by right-clicking the thumbnail in the gallery and then clicking one of the specified locations.

Quick Parts ▾	

General

(925) 555-0167

(925) 555-0167	
	Insert at Current Document Position
	Insert at Page Header
	Insert at Page Footer
	Insert at Beginning of Section
	Insert at End of Section
	Insert at Beginning of Document
	Insert at End of Document
	Edit Properties...
	Organize and Delete...
	Add Gallery to Quick Access Toolbar

You can insert a custom building block by selecting a location from a list.

Tip In a document, you can type the name of any building block and then press the F3 key to insert it at the cursor.

When you create a custom building block, Word saves it in a special file called the *Building Blocks template*. When you exit Word, you'll be asked whether you want to save this template. If you want to discard the building blocks you have created in this Word session, click Don't Save. If you want them to be available for future documents, click Save.

In this exercise, you'll save a company contact-information block and the Latin name of a plant as building blocks so that you can insert them elsewhere in a document.

SET UP You need the Bamboo_start document located in your Chapter02 practice file folder to complete this exercise. Open the Bamboo_start document, and save it as *Bamboo*. Then follow the steps.

1. At the top of the document, select the first four lines by using any of the selection techniques described earlier in this chapter.

2. On the **Insert** tab, in the **Text** group, click the **Quick Parts** button, and then click **Save Selection to Quick Part Gallery**.

   The Create New Building Block dialog box opens.

Word suggests the first few words of the selection as the name of the building block.

3. In the **Name** box, type **Contact Block**, and then click **OK**.

   Word saves the selection in the Quick Parts gallery.

4. In the third paragraph of the document, select **otatea acuminata aztectorum** (don't select the period). Then in the **Text** group, click the **Quick Parts** button.

   Notice that the company contact information now appears as a building block in the Quick Parts gallery.

The Quick Parts gallery displays only the building blocks you create. The built-in building blocks are available from other galleries, such as the Cover Page gallery.

5. Click **Save Selection to Quick Part Gallery**, type **oaa** in the **Name** box, and then click **OK**.

6. Press Ctrl+End to move the cursor to the end of the document, and then press the Spacebar.

7. Type **In particular, we recommend oaa** (don't type a period).

8. Press F3, and then type a period.

   Word replaces *oaa* with its building block, *obatea acuminata aztectorum*.

   Troubleshooting Pressing F3 substitutes the corresponding building block only if there is a space to the left of the building block name and the cursor is immediately to its right. If you want to enter a building block in existing text (rather than at the end of it), you need to ensure that there is a space after the cursor. Type two spaces, position the cursor between them, type the building block name, and then press F3.

9. Press Enter. Then in the **Text** group, click the **Quick Parts** button, and in the gallery, click the **Contact Block** entry.

   The company contact information appears at the cursor.

   very adaptable, with some species deciduous and others evergreen. Although there isn't yet a complete knowledge about this plant, there are believed to be between 1100 and 1500 different species of bamboo. The color range is from light green leaves and culms (stems) to dark, rich shades of green or some combination thereof.

   Because they are so easy to grow in such a variety of climates, there is a plant available for just about anyone who wishes to grow one in the backyard. Some dwarf species include chimonobambusa marmorea, indocalamus tessellatus, and pleioblastus chino vaginatus. Also suitable for the personal garden are those categorized as mid size. Examples of these types of plants are bambusa glaucophylla and otatea acuminata aztectorum. Plant starts and seeds are easier to find than ever, being available at nurseries and through mail order.

   Choosing bamboo as part of home or garden design makes sense on many levels. Not only does it have an appealing look, but it supports the environment as well as the countries that produce it. In particular, we recommend otatea acuminata aztectorum.

   Wide World Importers
   Furniture and accessories for your world

   (925) 555-0167
   www.wideworldimporters.com

The two custom building blocks are inserted with just a few clicks.

CLEAN UP Save the Bamboo document, and then close it. When you exit Word, remember to click Don't Save when you are asked whether you want to save changes to the Building Blocks template.

Inserting One Document into Another

Sometimes you'll want to insert one saved document into another document. For example, you might want to compile four quarterly reports so that you can edit them to create an annual report. In this situation, it would be tedious to have to select and copy the text of each report and then paste it into the annual document. Instead, you can have Word insert the existing documents for you. Here's how:

1. Position the cursor where you want to insert the existing document, and then on the Insert tab, in the Text group, click the Object arrow.

2. In the list, click Text From File.

   The Insert File dialog box opens.

3. Locate the file you want, and double-click it to insert it at the cursor.

Key Points

- You can cut or copy text and paste it elsewhere in the same document or in a different document. Cut and copied text is stored on the Clipboard.

- Undo one action or the last several actions you performed by clicking the Undo button (or its arrow) on the Quick Access Toolbar. Click the Redo button if you change your mind again.

- You can find each occurrence of a word or phrase and replace it with another.

- Rely on AutoCorrect to correct common misspellings. Correct other spelling and grammatical errors individually as you type or by checking the entire document in one pass.

- You don't have to type and proof the same text over and over again. Instead, save the text as a building block and insert it with a few mouse clicks.

Chapter at a Glance

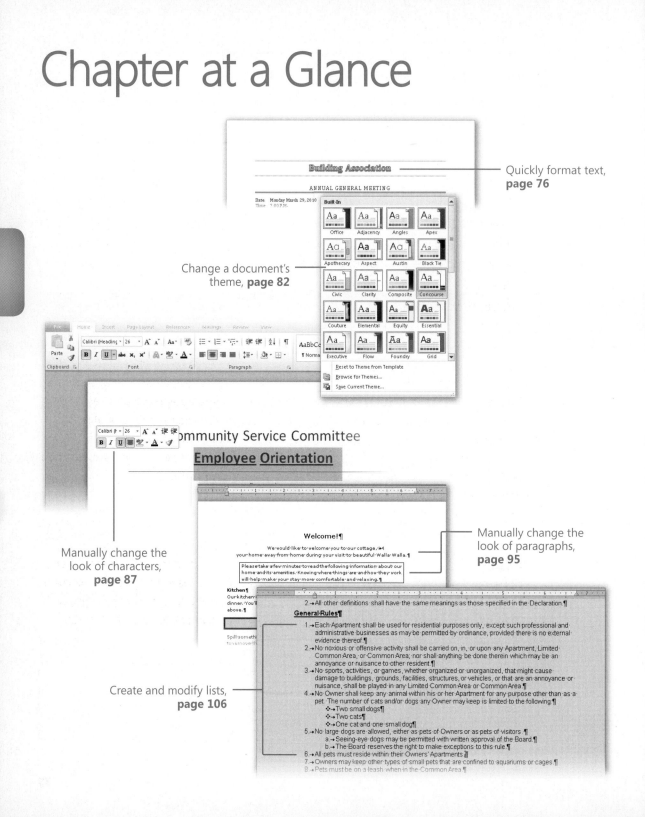

Quickly format text, **page 76**

Change a document's theme, **page 82**

Manually change the look of characters, **page 87**

Manually change the look of paragraphs, **page 95**

Create and modify lists, **page 106**

3 Change the Look of Text

In this chapter, you will learn how to

✔ Quickly format text.

✔ Change a document's theme.

✔ Manually change the look of characters.

✔ Manually change the look of paragraphs.

✔ Create and modify lists.

The appearance of your documents helps to convey their message. Microsoft Word 2010 can help you develop professional-looking documents whose appearance is appropriate to their contents. You can easily format the characters and paragraphs so that key points stand out and your arguments are easy to grasp. You can also change the look of major elements within a document by applying predefined sets of formatting called *Quick Styles*, and you can change the look of selected text by applying predefined combinations called *text effects*. In addition, you can change the fonts, colors, and effects throughout a document with one click by applying one of the built-in themes.

Tip A font consists of alphabetic characters, numbers, and symbols that share a common design.

In this chapter, you'll first experiment with built-in Quick Styles and text effects, and then you'll change the theme applied to a document. You'll change the look of individual words, and then you'll change the indentation, alignment, and spacing of individual paragraphs. You'll also add borders and shading to make paragraphs stand out. Finally, you'll create and format both bulleted and numbered lists.

> **Practice Files** Before you can complete the exercises in this chapter, you need to copy the book's practice files to your computer. The practice files you'll use to complete the exercises in this chapter are in the Chapter03 practice file folder. A complete list of practice files is provided in "Using the Practice Files" at the beginning of this book.

Quickly Formatting Text

You don't have to know much about character and paragraph formatting to be able to format your documents in ways that will make them easier to read and more professional looking. With a couple of mouse clicks, you can easily change the look of words, phrases, and paragraphs by using Quick Styles.

Word has several types of predefined Quick Styles, but the simplest are those you can apply to text.

- **Paragraph styles** You apply these to entire paragraphs, such as headings.
- **Character styles** You apply these to words.
- **Linked styles** You apply these to either paragraphs or words.

By default, Word makes just a few of the predefined Quick Styles available in the Quick Styles gallery in the Styles group on the Home tab. Quick Styles apply a combination of character formatting (such as font, size, and color) and paragraph formatting (such as line spacing).

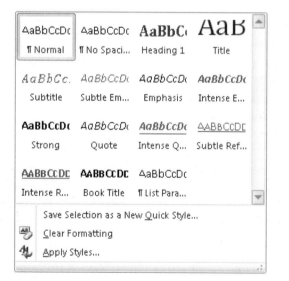

The Quick Styles gallery.

The styles displayed as thumbnails in the Quick Styles gallery have been designed to go well together, so applying styles from the gallery produces a harmonious effect. After you apply styles from the current set of styles, you can easily change the look of the entire document by switching to a different style set. The Quick Style names are the same; only their defined formatting changes. So if you have applied the Heading 1 style to a paragraph, you can change its formatting simply by changing the style set.

You display the list of available style sets by clicking the Change Styles button and then clicking Style Set.

Clicking one of these style sets displays thumbnails of its styles in the Quick Styles gallery.

You can point to any style set in the list to see a live preview of how the applied styles in a set will look, and you can click a style set to apply its definitions to the document.

See Also For information about creating custom styles, see "Working with Styles and Templates" in Chapter 16, "Work in Word More Efficiently."

In addition to applying Quick Styles to quickly change the look of paragraphs and characters, you can apply predefined text effects to a selection to add more zing. Clicking the Text Effects button in the Font group on the Home tab displays a gallery of effects to choose from.

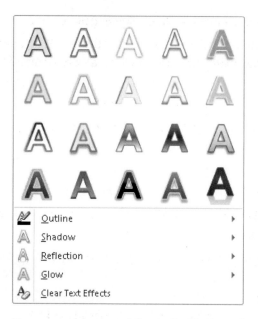

You can apply any predefined effect in the gallery to selected text, or you can click options at the bottom of the gallery and define a custom effect.

These effects are dramatic, so you'll probably want to restrict their use to document titles and similar elements to which you want to draw particular attention.

In this exercise, you'll experiment with Quick Styles and text effects.

SET UP You need the AgendaA_start document located in your Chapter03 practice file folder to complete this exercise. Open the AgendaA_start document, and save it as *AgendaA*. Then follow the steps.

1. In the lower-right corner of the program window, at the left end of the **Zoom Slider**, click the **Zoom Out** button until you can see all of the text.

   For example, if your current view is 100% and your resolution is 1024x768, you can click the Zoom Out button three times to set the zoom percentage to 70%.

2. Ensure that the cursor is located at the top of the document, at the beginning of the **Building Association** paragraph. Then on the **Home** tab, in the **Styles** group, point to each thumbnail in the displayed row of the **Quick Styles** gallery.

   The formatting of the first line changes to show you a live preview of how its text will look if you click the style you are pointing to. You don't have to actually apply the formatting to see its effect.

3. Without making a selection, click the **Down** arrow to the right of the gallery.

   The next row of the Quick Styles gallery appears.

4. Point to each thumbnail in this row of the **Quick Styles** gallery.

   Only the styles that are paragraph or linked styles affect the text. You cannot see a live preview of character styles unless the cursor is within a word or multiple words are selected.

5. To the right of the **Quick Styles** gallery, click the **More** button.

   Word displays the entire Quick Styles gallery. The style applied to the paragraph containing the cursor is surrounded by a border.

6. In the gallery, click the **Title** thumbnail.

   Word applies that style to the paragraph containing the cursor.

7. Click anywhere in the **ANNUAL GENERAL MEETING** line, and then in the gallery, click the **Heading 1** thumbnail.

8. Click anywhere in the **Agenda** line, and then in the gallery, click the **Heading 1** thumbnail.

   Notice that although you applied the same Heading 1 style to *ANNUAL GENERAL MEETING* and *Agenda*, the first heading looks bigger because of the use of all capital letters.

Building Association
_____

ANNUAL GENERAL MEETING
Date: Monday March 29, 2010
Time: 7:00 P.M.

Agenda
Preliminaries

Call to order

Proof of notice of meeting

The styles make it easy to distinguish information.

Tip We have hidden formatting marks for this exercise.

9. Point in the selection area to the left of the **Preliminaries** line, and click to select the line. Then hold down the Ctrl key while clicking adjacent to the following lines:

   Approval of Minutes
   Board Reports
   Election of Board Members
   New Business
   Adjournment

10. Apply the **Heading 1** style to the selected lines. Then without moving the selection, click the **More** button and, in the gallery, click **Emphasis**.

    Applying the Emphasis character style on top of the Heading 1 paragraph style makes these headings italic, which looks lighter.

11. Select the **Date** and **Time** lines, and then in the **Quick Styles** gallery, click the **No Spacing** thumbnail.

12. Apply the **No Spacing** style to the three lines under **Preliminaries**, the two lines under **Board Reports**, and the two lines under **Election of Board Members**.

13. Press Ctrl+Home to release the selection and move the cursor to the top of the document.

    As you can see, the results look very professional.

Building Association

ANNUAL GENERAL MEETING
Date: Monday March 29, 2010
Time: 7:00 P.M.

Agenda

Preliminaries
Call to order
Proof of notice of meeting
Roll call to establish quorum

Approval of Minutes

Board Reports
Financial report
New rules and regulations

You have clearly defined the hierarchy of the agenda with just a few clicks.

14. In the **Styles** group, click the **Change Styles** button, point to **Style Set**, and then point to each style set in turn, watching the effect on the document.

15. When you finish exploring, click **Formal**.

    The formatting of the document changes and the headings and text take on the look assigned to this style set.

The Title, Heading 1, and Emphasis style definitions in the Formal style set produce a different look from those in the default set.

16. Select the document title. Then in the **Font** group, click the **Text Effects** button.

Word displays the Text Effects gallery.

17. Point to each thumbnail in the gallery, observing the effect on the title behind the gallery.

18. Click the right-most thumbnail in the third row (**Fill - Red, Accent 2, Double Outline - Accent 2**). Then click away from the title to release the selection.

The effect applied to the title makes it really stand out.

By using text effects, you can apply complex sets of formatting with a few clicks.

CLEAN UP Save the AgendaA document, and then close it.

Changing a Document's Theme

To enhance the look of a Word document whose components have been styled, you can apply a predefined theme. A theme is a combination of colors, fonts, and effects that project a certain feeling or tone. For example, the Flow theme uses a palette of blues and greens, the Calibri and Constantia fonts, and understated effects. You apply a theme to the entire document by clicking the Themes button in the Themes group on the Page Layout tab, and then making a selection from the Themes gallery.

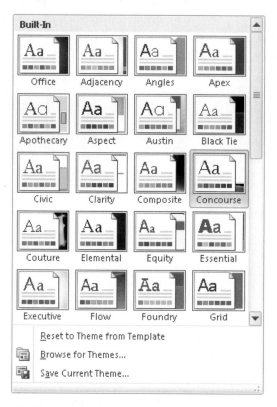

The Themes gallery.

If you like the colors of one theme and the fonts of another, you can mix and match theme elements. First apply the theme that most closely resembles the look you want, and then in the Themes group, change the colors by clicking the Theme Colors button or the fonts by clicking the Theme Fonts button.

If you create a combination of colors and fonts that you would like to be able to use with other documents, you can save the combination as a new theme. By saving the theme in the default Document Themes folder, you make the theme available in the Themes gallery. However, you don't have to store custom themes in the Document Themes folder; you can store them anywhere on your hard disk, on removable media, or in a network location. To use a theme that is stored in a different location, you click the Themes button, and then click Browse For Themes at the bottom of the gallery. Locate the theme you want in the Choose Theme Or Themed Document dialog box, and then click Open to apply that theme to the current document.

Tip The bottom section of the Themes gallery displays themes downloaded from the Microsoft Office Online Web site. You can visit this Web site at office.microsoft.com to find additional themes and templates created by Microsoft and by other people.

In this exercise, you'll apply a theme to an existing document and change the colors and fonts. Then you'll save the new combination as a custom theme.

SET UP You need the AgendaB_start document located in your Chapter03 practice file folder to complete this exercise. Open the AgendaB_start document, and save it as *AgendaB*. Then follow the steps.

1. On the **Page Layout** tab, in the **Themes** group, click the **Themes** button.

   The Themes gallery appears.

2. Point to each thumbnail in turn to display a live preview of the theme. (Scroll through the gallery so that you can explore all the themes.)

3. In the **Themes** gallery, click **Trek**.

   The colors and fonts change to those defined for the selected theme.

4. In the **Themes** group, click the **Theme Colors** button.

   The Theme Colors gallery appears. (The currently selected color set, which is not shown in the graphic on the next page, is indicated by a border.)

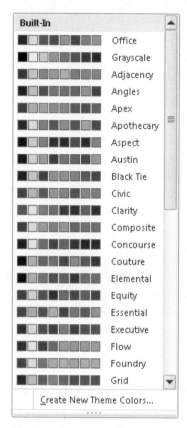

The Theme Colors gallery.

5. Preview any color set that interests you, and then in the gallery, click **Newsprint**.

   The Newsprint colors replace the Trek colors, but nothing else in the document changes.

6. In the **Themes** group, click the **Theme Fonts** button.

   The Theme Fonts gallery appears. The currently selected font set is highlighted. Each built-in option includes a set of two fonts—the first is used for headings and the second for body text.

Slipstream
Trebuchet MS
Trebuchet MS

Solstice
Gill Sans MT
Gill Sans MT

Technic
Franklin Gothic Bo...
Arial

Thatch
Tw Cen MT
Tw Cen MT

Trek
Franklin Gothic M...
Franklin Gothic Book

Create New Theme Fonts...

The Theme Fonts gallery.

7. Preview any set of fonts that interests you, and then in the gallery, click **Apex**.

   The Apex fonts replace the Trek fonts, but the colors remain the same.

8. In the **Themes** group, click the **Themes** button, and then below the gallery, click **Save Current Theme**.

   The Save Current Theme dialog box opens and displays the contents of the Document Themes folder. (This dialog box resembles the Save As dialog box.) The Document Themes folder is the default location for saving any new themes you create.

9. In the **File name** box, replace the suggested name with **My Theme**, and then click **Save**.

10. In the **Themes** group, click the **Themes** button to display the gallery.

    Your new theme appears in the Custom section at the top of the gallery.

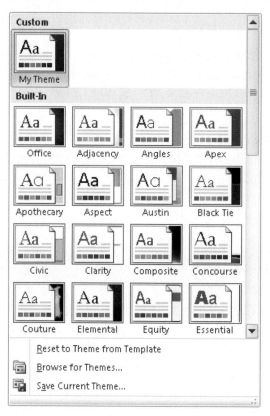

You can apply the custom theme to any document.

11. Click away from the gallery to close it without making a selection.

CLEAN UP Save the AgendaB document, and then close it.

Tip If you want to delete the theme you created in this topic, open Windows Explorer and navigate to the C:\Users\<user name>\AppData\Roaming\Microsoft\Templates\Document Themes folder. (In Windows 7, you can click the Start button, type *Document Themes* in the Search box at the bottom of the Start menu, and then click the folder in the search results.) Then select My Theme, and press Delete.

Manually Changing the Look of Characters

As you have seen, Word 2010 makes changing the look of content in a styled document almost effortless. But styles can't do everything. To be able to precisely control the look of your text, you need to know how to manually change individual elements.

When you type text in a document, it is displayed in a particular font. By default the font used for text in a new Word document is Calibri, but you can change the font of any element at any time. The available fonts vary from one computer to another, depending on the programs installed. Common fonts include Arial, Verdana, and Times New Roman.

You can vary the look of a font by changing the following attributes:

- **Size** Almost every font comes in a range of sizes, which are measured in points from the top of letters that have parts that stick up (ascenders), such as *h*, to the bottom of letters that have parts that drop down (descenders), such as *p*. A point is approximately 1/72 of an inch (about 0.04 centimeters).

- **Style** Almost every font comes in a range of styles. The most common are regular (or plain), italic, bold, and bold italic.

- **Effect** Fonts can be enhanced by applying effects, such as underlining, small capital letters (small caps), or shadows.

- **Color** A palette of coordinated colors is available, and you can also specify custom colors.

- **Character spacing** You can alter the spacing between characters by pushing them apart or squeezing them together.

Although some attributes might cancel each other out, they are usually cumulative. For example, you might use a bold font in various sizes and various shades of green to make words stand out in a newsletter. Collectively, the font and its attributes are called *character formatting*.

You apply character formatting from one of three locations:

- **Mini Toolbar** Several common formatting buttons are available on the Mini Toolbar that appears when you point to selected text.

The Mini Toolbar is transparent until you point to it.

- **Font group on the Home tab** This group includes buttons for changing the font and most of the font attributes you are likely to use.

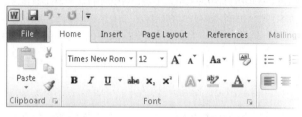

The Font group.

- **Font dialog box** If you are looking for an attribute, such as small caps, and don't see it in the Font group, click the Font dialog box launcher. All the attributes are gathered together on the Font page of the dialog box, except character spacing, which is on the Advanced page.

The Font page of the Font dialog box.

In this exercise, you'll format the text in a document by changing its font, style, size, color, and character spacing. You'll also highlight a few words. Then you'll return selected text to its original condition by clearing some formatting you no longer want.

SET UP You need the OrientationDraft_start document located in your Chapter03 practice file folder to complete this exercise. Open the OrientationDraft_start document, and save it as *OrientationDraft*. Then follow the steps.

1. In the **Employee Orientation** heading, click anywhere in the word **Orientation**.

2. On the **Home** tab, in the **Font** group, click the **Underline** button.

   Keyboard Shortcut Press Ctrl+U to underline the active word or selection.

   See Also To see a complete list of keyboard shortcuts, see "Keyboard Shortcuts" at the end of this book.

   The word containing the cursor is now underlined. Notice that you did not have to select the entire word.

   Tip If you click the Underline arrow, you can choose an underline style and color from the Underline gallery.

3. In the same heading, click anywhere in the word **Employee**, and then on the Quick Access Toolbar, click the **Repeat** button.

   Keyboard Shortcut Press Ctrl+Y to repeat an action.

   Word repeats the previous formatting command. Again, although you did not select the entire word, it is now underlined.

4. In the selection area, click adjacent to **Employee Orientation** to select the entire heading.

   Word displays a transparent version of the Mini Toolbar. You can use the common commands on the Mini Toolbar to quickly change the look of the selection.

5. Point to the Mini Toolbar to make it fully visible. Then on the Mini Toolbar, click the **Bold** button.

   Keyboard Shortcut Press Ctrl+B to make the active word or selection bold.

The heading is now bold. The active buttons on the Mini Toolbar and in the Font group on the Home tab indicate the attributes you applied to the selection.

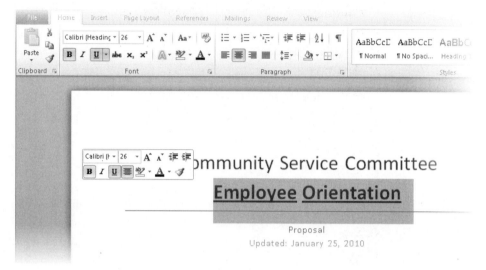

The ribbon reflects the settings in the Mini Toolbar.

Troubleshooting The appearance of buttons and groups on the ribbon changes depending on the width of the program window. For information about changing the appearance of the ribbon to match our screen images, see "Modifying the Display of the Ribbon" at the beginning of this book.

6. On the Mini Toolbar, click the **Format Painter** button. Then move the pointer into the selection area to the left of the **Proposal** heading, and click the mouse button.

   Tip The Format Painter button is also available in the Clipboard group on the Home tab.

   Word applies the formatting of *Employee Orientation* to *Proposal*.

7. Select **Employee Orientation**, and then on the **Home** tab, in the **Font** group, click the **Font** arrow.

   The Font gallery appears.

Theme Fonts	
Calibri	(Headings)
Constantia	(Body)

All Fonts

O Agency FB

O **Aharoni**   אבגד הוז

O ALGERIAN

O Andalus   أبجد هوز

O Angsana New   ส วัสดี

O AngsanaUPC   ส วัสดี

O Aparajita   देवनागरी

O Arabic Typesetting   أبجد هوز

O Arial

O **Arial Black**

O Arial Narrow

O **Arial Rounded MT Bold**

O Arial Unicode MS

O Baskerville Old Face

O Batang

O BatangChe

O **Bauhaus 93**

Word comes with many fonts.

8. Scroll through the gallery of available fonts, and then click **Impact**.

   Troubleshooting If Impact is not available, select any heavy font that catches your attention.

   The *Employee Orientation* heading now appears in the new font.

9. In the **Font** group, click the **Font Size** arrow, and then in the list, click **20**.

   The size of the heading text decreases to 20 points.

   Tip You can increase or decrease the font size in set increments by clicking the Grow Font and Shrink Font buttons in the Font group, or by clicking the same buttons on the Mini Toolbar that appears when you select text. You can also press Ctrl+> or Ctrl+<.

10. Click the **Font** dialog box launcher.

    Keyboard Shortcut Press Ctrl+Shift+F to display the Font dialog box.

    The Font dialog box opens.

11. Click the **Underline style** arrow, and then in the list, click **(none)**.

12. In the **Effects** area, select the **Small caps** check box.

13. Click the **Advanced** tab.

    Notice that the Spacing option is currently set to Expanded.

Font	? ✕

Font / **Advanced**

Character Spacing

Scale: 100%

Spacing: Expanded   By: 0.25 pt

Position: Normal   By:

☑ Kerning for fonts: 14   Points and above

OpenType Features

Ligatures: None

Number spacing: Default

Number forms: Default

Stylistic sets: Default

☐ Use Contextual Alternates

Preview

EMPLOYEE ORIENTATION

This font style is imitated for display. The closest matching style will be printed.

Set As Default   Text Effects...   OK   Cancel

The Advanced page of the Font dialog box.

14. To the right of the **Spacing** option, in the **By** box, select **0.25 pt**, type **10 pt** (the *pt* stands for *points*), and click **OK**. Then press Home to release the selection.

    The manually formatted text appears in small capital letters with the spacing between the characters expanded by 10 points.

You can expand and contract the spacing between letters to create different effects.

15. Select **Employee Orientation** again. In the **Font** group, click the **Font Color** arrow, and then under **Theme Colors** in the palette, click the box at the right end of the top row (**Lime, Accent 6**).

    The selected words are now lime green.

    Tip To apply the Font Color button's current color, you can simply click the button (not its arrow). If you want to apply a color that is not shown under Theme Colors or Standard Colors, click More Colors at the bottom of the palette, and in the Colors dialog box, click the color you want in the color wheel.

16. In the first bullet point, select the phrase **concept of service**. Then in the **Font** group, click the **Text Highlight Color** arrow, and click the **Turquoise** box in the top row.

    The selected phrase is now highlighted in turquoise, and the Text Highlight Color button shows turquoise as its active color.

    Tip If you click the Text Color Highlight button without first making a selection, the shape of the mouse pointer changes to a highlighter that you can drag across text. Click the button again, or press Esc, to turn off the highlighter.

17. In the fifth bullet point, double-click the word **brainstorming**. Then hold down the Ctrl key while double-clicking **planning** and **leadership**.

18. In the **Font** group, click the **Change Case** button, and click **UPPERCASE**. Then click away from the bullet point to release the selection.

    The selected words now appear in all capital letters.

    Community Service Committee
    E M P L O Y E E   O R I E N T A T I O N

    # Proposal

    Updated: January 25, 2010

    Project Goals
    - Familiarize employees with the concept of service.
    - Make service a natural part of their lives.
    - Engage and motivate them.
    - Forge a sense of teamwork among all employees across departments.
    - Provide appropriate skills development through BRAINSTORMING, PLANNING, and LEADERSHIP opportunities.
    - Meet genuine community needs.

    Instead of retyping, you can have Word change the case of words.

19. Select the **Proposal** line. Then on the **Home** tab, in the **Font** group, click the **Clear Formatting** button.

    Keyboard Shortcut Press Ctrl+Spacebar to clear manually applied formatting.

    The formatting of the selected text is removed.

    Tip You cannot click the Clear Formatting button to remove highlighting. If the highlight is the same color as that shown on the Text Highlight Color button, you can select the text and click the button to remove the highlighting. If the button shows a different color, select the text, click the Text Highlight Color arrow, and then click No Color.

 CLEAN UP Save the OrientationDraft document, and then close it.

Character Formatting and Case Considerations

The way you use case and character formatting in a document can influence its visual impact on your readers. Used judiciously, case and character formatting can make a plain document look attractive and professional, but excessive use can make it look amateurish and detract from the message. For example, using too many fonts in the same document is the mark of inexperience, so don't use more than two or three.

Bear in mind that lowercase letters tend to recede, so using all uppercase (capital) letters can be useful for titles and headings or for certain kinds of emphasis. However, large blocks of uppercase letters are tiring to the eye.

Tip Where do the terms *uppercase* and *lowercase* come from? Until the advent of computers, individual characters made of lead were assembled to form the words that would appear on a printed page. The characters were stored alphabetically in cases, with the capital letters in the upper case and the small letters in the lower case.

Manually Changing the Look of Paragraphs

As you know, you create a paragraph by typing text and then pressing the Enter key. The paragraph can consist of one word, one sentence, or multiple sentences. You can change the look of a paragraph by changing its indentation, alignment, and line spacing, as well as the space before and after it. You can also put borders around it and shade its background. Collectively, the settings you use to vary the look of a paragraph are called *paragraph formatting*.

In Word, you don't define the width of paragraphs and the length of pages by defining the area occupied by the text; instead you define the size of the white space—the left, right, top, and bottom margins—around the text. You click the Margins button in the Page Setup group on the Page Layout tab to define these margins, either for the whole document or for sections of the document.

See Also For information about setting margins, see "Previewing and Adjusting Page Layout" in Chapter 6, "Preview, Print, and Distribute Documents." For information about sections, see "Controlling What Appears on Each Page" in the same chapter.

Although the left and right margins are set for a whole document or section, you can vary the position of the paragraphs between the margins. The quickest way to indent a paragraph from the left is to click the Increase Indent button; clicking the Decrease Indent button has the opposite effect. You cannot increase or decrease the indent beyond the margins.

Another way to control the indentation of lines is by dragging markers on the horizontal ruler to indicate where each line of text starts and ends.

- **First Line Indent** Begins a paragraph's first line of text at this marker

- **Hanging Indent** Begins a paragraph's second and subsequent lines of text at this marker at the left end of the ruler

- **Left Indent** Indents the text to this marker

- **Right Indent** Wraps the text when it reaches this marker at the right end of the ruler

You display the ruler by clicking the Ruler check box in the Show group on the View tab, or by clicking the View Ruler button located at the top of the vertical scroll bar.

Bamboo has long been woven into the cultures of many countries, where it has historically been used for everything from food and fodder to musical instruments and construction material.

Here at Wide World Importers, we are proud to offer a wide range of bamboo furniture and accessories from around the globe, as well as plants for that special spot on a deck or patio.

For centuries, millions of people have depended on this plant, which is known as "friend of the people" in China, and "wood of the poor" in India. But the demand for bamboo has been increasing in other parts of the world as well, especially as it relates to furniture, accent pieces, and flooring. More and more, people are seeing the value and beauty of using bamboo in their homes to achieve modern-day fashion with an ethnic flavor.

There are many different sizes and varieties of bamboo. It is both tropical and subtropical, growing in climates as diverse as jungles and mountainsides. Actually giant, woody grasses, it is

You can manually change a paragraph's indentation by moving markers on the horizontal ruler.

Setting a right indent indicates where the lines in a paragraph should end, but sometimes you might want to specify where only one line should end. For example, you might want to break a title after a particular word to make it look balanced on the page. You can end an individual line by inserting a text wrapping break (more commonly known as a *line break*). After positioning the cursor where you want the break to occur, you click the Breaks button in the Page Setup group on the Page Layout tab, and then click Text Wrapping. Word indicates the line break with a bent arrow. Inserting a line break does not start a new paragraph, so when you apply paragraph formatting to a line of text that ends with a line break, the formatting is applied to the entire paragraph, not just that line.

Keyboard Shortcut Press Shift+Enter to insert a line break.

You can also determine the positioning of a paragraph between the left and right margins by changing its alignment. You can click buttons in the Paragraph group on the Home tab to align paragraphs.

- **Align Left** Aligns each line of the paragraph at the left margin, with a ragged right edge

  Keyboard Shortcut Press Ctrl+L to left-align a paragraph.

- **Center** Aligns the center of each line in the paragraph between the left and right margins, with ragged left and right edges

  Keyboard Shortcut Press Ctrl+E to center-align a paragraph.

- **Align Right** Aligns each line of the paragraph at the right margin, with a ragged left edge

  Keyboard Shortcut Press Ctrl+R to right-align a paragraph.

- **Justify** Aligns each line between the margins, creating even left and right edges

  Keyboard Shortcut Press Ctrl+J to justify a paragraph.

Tip If you know that you want to create a centered paragraph, you don't have to type the text and then align the paragraph. You can use the Click And Type feature to create appropriately aligned text. Move the pointer to the center of a blank area of the page, and when the pointer's shape changes to an I-beam with centered text attached, double-click to insert the cursor in a centered paragraph. Similarly, you can double-click at the left edge of the page to enter left-aligned text and at the right edge to enter right-aligned text.

You can align lines of text in different locations across the page by using tab stops. The easiest way to set tab stops is to use the horizontal ruler. By default, Word sets left-aligned tab stops every half inch (1.27 centimeters), as indicated by gray marks below the ruler. To set a custom tab stop, you start by clicking the Tab button located at the left end of the ruler until the type of tab stop you want appears. You have the following options:

- **Left Tab** Aligns the left end of the text with the tab stop

- **Center Tab** Aligns the center of the text with the tab stop

- **Right Tab** Aligns the right end of the text with the tab stop

- **Decimal Tab** Aligns the decimal point in the text (usually a numeric value) with the tab stop

- **Bar Tab** Draws a vertical line at the position of the tab stop

After selecting the type of tab stop you want to set, you simply click the ruler where you want the tab stop to be. Word then removes any default tab stops to the left of the one you set.

This ruler has a custom left-aligned tab stop at the 1.5 inch mark and default tab stops every half inch to the right of the custom tab stop.

To change the position of an existing custom tab stop, you drag it to the left or right on the ruler. To delete a custom tab stop, you drag it away from the ruler.

To align the text to the right of the cursor with the next tab stop, you press the Tab key. The text is then aligned on the tab stop according to its type. For example, if you set a center tab stop, pressing Tab moves the text so that its center is aligned with the tab stop.

Tip To fine-tune the position of tab stops, click the Paragraph dialog box launcher on either the Home or Page Layout tab. In the Paragraph dialog box, click Tabs to display the Tabs dialog box. You might also open this dialog box if you want to use tab leaders—visible marks such as dots or dashes connecting the text before the tab with the text after it. For example, tab leaders are useful in a table of contents to carry the eye from the text to the page number.

To make it obvious where one paragraph ends and another begins, you can add space between them by adjusting the Spacing After and Spacing Before settings in the Paragraph group on the Page Layout tab. You can adjust the spacing between the lines in a paragraph by clicking the Line And Paragraph Spacing button in the Paragraph group on the Home tab.

The Line Spacing options.

When you want to make several adjustments to the alignment, indentation, and spacing of selected paragraphs, it is sometimes quicker to use the Paragraph dialog box than to click buttons and drag markers. Clicking the Paragraph dialog box launcher on either the Home tab or the Page Layout tab opens the Paragraph dialog box.

The Indents And Spacing page of the Paragraph dialog box.

You can do a lot with the options in the Paragraph dialog box, but to make a paragraph really stand out, you might want to put a border around it or shade its background. (For real drama, you can do both.) Clicking the Border arrow in the Paragraph group on the Home tab displays a gallery of border options.

The Borders gallery.

Clicking Borders And Shading at the bottom of the list displays the Borders And Shading dialog box, where you can select the style, color, width, and location of the border.

![Borders and Shading dialog box]

The Border page of the Borders And Shading dialog box.

In this exercise, you'll change text alignment and indentation, insert and modify tab stops, modify paragraph and line spacing, and add borders and shading to paragraphs.

SET UP You need the Information_start document located in your Chapter03 practice file folder to complete this exercise. Open the Information_start document, and save it as *Information*. Then click the Show/Hide ¶ button to turn on the display of formatting marks, and follow the steps.

1. Set the zoom percentage so that you can see almost all of the paragraphs in the document. Then on the **View** tab, in the **Show** group, select the **Ruler** check box.

   Tip In the following steps, we give measurements in inches. You can substitute approximate measurements in your own measuring system. If you want to change the measuring system Word uses, display the Backstage view, click Options, and in the Word Options dialog box, display the Advanced page. Then under Display, click the system you want in the Show Measurements In Units Of list, and click OK.

2. Select the first two paragraphs (**Welcome!** and the next paragraph). Then on the **Home** tab, in the **Paragraph** group, click the **Center** button.

   The lines are now centered between the margins.

   Tip When applying paragraph formatting, you don't have to select the entire paragraph.

3. After the comma in the second paragraph, click to the left of **your**. Then on the **Page Layout** tab, in the **Page Setup** group, click the **Breaks** button, and click **Text Wrapping**.

   Word inserts a line break character and moves the part of the paragraph that follows that character to the next line.

The bent arrow after cottage indicates that you have inserted a line break.

   See Also For information about page and section breaks, see "Controlling What Appears on Each Page" in Chapter 6, "Preview, Print, and Distribute Documents."

4. Click anywhere in the next paragraph, and then on the **Home** tab, in the **Paragraph** group, click the **Justify** button.

   Word inserts space between the words in the lines of the paragraph so that the edges of the paragraph are flush against both the left and right margins.

5. Without moving the cursor, on the horizontal ruler, drag the **Left Indent** marker to the **0.5** inch mark.

   The First Line Indent and Hanging Indent markers move with the Left Indent marker.

6. At the right end of the ruler, drag the **Right Indent** marker to the **6** inch mark.

   The paragraph is now indented a half inch in from each of the side margins.

Left and right indents are often used to make paragraphs such as quotations stand out.

7. Click in the **Be careful** paragraph, and then in the **Paragraph** group, click the **Increase Indent** button.

8. Select the **Pillows**, **Blankets**, **Towels**, and **Dish towels** paragraphs, and with the **Left Tab** stop active at the left end of the ruler, click the ruler at the **2** mark.

   Word removes the default tab stops (indicated by gray lines below the ruler) up to the 2-inch mark and inserts a custom left-aligned tab at that location on the ruler.

9. Click to the left of **There** in the **Pillows** paragraph, and press the Tab key. Then insert tabs to the left of **You**, **These**, and **There** in the next three paragraphs.

   The part of each paragraph that follows the colon is now aligned at the 2-inch mark, producing more space than you need.

10. Select the four paragraphs containing tabs, and on the ruler, drag the **Left Tab** stop to the **1.25** mark.

11. Without changing the selection, on the ruler, drag the **Hanging Indent** marker to the **1.25** mark. Then press Home to release the selection.

   The Left Indent marker has moved as well, causing the second line of the second selected paragraph to start in the same location as the tab stop.

Hanging indents are often used to create table-like effects.

12. At the bottom of the document, select the three paragraphs containing dollar amounts. Where the horizontal and vertical rulers meet, click the **Tab** button until the **Decimal Tab** button is displayed and then click the ruler at the **3** mark.

13. Insert a tab to the left of each dollar amount.

    Word aligns the three paragraphs on the decimals.

14. Select the first paragraph containing tabs (**Pillows**), hold down the Ctrl key, and then select the paragraphs that begin with the following:

    Blankets
    Towels
    Limousine winery tour
    In-home massage

15. On the **Home** tab, in the **Paragraph** group, click the **Line Spacing** button, and click **Remove Space After Paragraph**. Then press the Home key.

    Now only the last paragraphs of the two lists have extra space after them.

Removing internal space from lists makes them easier to read.

16. Scroll up until the top of the document is in view, and click anywhere in the **Please take a few minutes** paragraph. On the **Home** tab, in the **Paragraph** group, click the **Border** arrow, and then click **Outside Borders**.

17. Click anywhere in the **Be careful** paragraph, click the **Border** arrow, and then at the bottom of the list, click **Borders and Shading**.

    The Borders And Shading dialog box opens, with the Borders page displayed.

18. Under **Setting**, click the **3-D** icon to select that border style. Scroll through the **Style** list and click the fourth style from the bottom. Then click the **Color** arrow, and under **Theme Colors** in the palette, click the **Red, Accent 2** box.

    Tip If you want only one, two, or three sides of the selected paragraphs to have a border, click the buttons surrounding the image in the Preview area.

19. Click the **Shading** tab.

    You can use the options on this page to format the background of the selected paragraph.

The Shading page of the Borders And Shading dialog box.

20. Click the **Fill** arrow, and under **Theme Colors**, click the lightest color in the red column (**Red, Accent 2, Lighter 80%**). Then click **OK** to close the **Borders and Shading** dialog box.

A border surrounds the paragraph, and a light red color fills its background. The border stretches all the way to the right margin.

21. To achieve a more balanced look, in the **Paragraph** group, click the **Decrease Indent** button. Then click the **Center** button.

The paragraph is now centered between the page margins and within its surrounding box.

A combination of a border and shading really makes text stand out. Don't overdo it!

CLEAN UP Leave the rulers and formatting marks displayed for the next exercise, but change the zoom percentage back to 100%. Save the Information document, and then close it.

Finding and Replacing Formatting

In addition to searching for words and phrases in the Find And Replace dialog box, you can use the dialog box to search for a specific format and replace it with a different one.

See Also For information about finding and replacing text, see "Finding and Replacing Text" in Chapter 2, "Edit and Proofread Text."

To search for a specific format and replace it with a different format:

1. On the Home tab, in the Editing group, click the Replace button.

   Keyboard Shortcut Press Ctrl+H to display the Replace tab of the Find And Replace dialog box.

   The Find And Replace dialog box opens, displaying the Replace tab.

2. Click More to expand the dialog box. Then click Format, and on the Format menu, click either Font or Paragraph.

   Tip You can click Style to search for paragraph styles or character styles.

   The Find Font or Find Paragraph dialog box opens.

3. In the dialog box, click the format you want to find, and then click OK.

4. Click the Replace With text box, click Format, click Font or Paragraph, click the format you want to substitute for the Find What format, and then click OK.

5. Click Find Next to search for the first occurrence of the format, and then click Replace to replace that one occurrence or Replace All to replace every occurrence.

Creating and Modifying Lists

Lists are paragraphs that are usually formatted with a hanging indent so that the first line of each paragraph is longer than subsequent lines. Fortunately, Word takes care of the formatting of lists for you. You simply indicate the type of list you want to create. When the order of items is not important—for example, for a list of supplies needed to carry out a task—a bulleted list is the best choice. And when the order is important—for example, for the steps in a procedure—you will probably want to create a numbered list.

You can indicate the start of a list as follows:

- **Bulleted list** Type * (an asterisk) at the beginning of a paragraph, and then press the Spacebar or the Tab key before entering the list item text. Or click the Bullets button in the Paragraph group on the Home tab.

- **Numbered list** Type *1.* (the number 1 followed by a period) at the beginning of a paragraph, and then press the Spacebar or the Tab key before entering the list item text. Or click the Numbering button in the Paragraph group on the Home tab.

When you start a list in this fashion, Word automatically formats it as a bulleted or numbered list. When you press Enter to start a new item, Word continues the formatting to the new paragraph. Typing items and pressing Enter adds subsequent bulleted or numbered items. To end the list, press Enter twice; or click the Bullets arrow or Numbering arrow in the Paragraph group on the Home tab, and then in the library, click None.

Tip If you want to start a paragraph with an asterisk or number but don't want to format the paragraph as a bulleted or numbered list, click the AutoCorrect Options button that appears after Word changes the formatting, and then in the list, click the appropriate Undo option. You can also click the Undo button on the Quick Access Toolbar.

If you want to create a list that has multiple levels, you start off by creating the list in the usual way. Then when you want the next paragraph to be a level lower (indented more), you press the Tab key after pressing Enter and before you type the text of the item. If you want the next paragraph to be a level higher (indented less), you press Shift+Tab after pressing Enter. In the case of a bulleted list, Word changes the bullet character for each item level. In the case of a numbered list, Word changes the type of numbering used, based on a predefined numbering scheme.

Tip To create a multilevel numbered list with a scheme that is different from the default, you can click the Multilevel List button in the Paragraph group of the Home tab and then select a scheme from the List gallery. You can also define your own scheme.

If you type a set of paragraphs containing a series of items and then decide you want to turn the set into a list, you can select the paragraphs and then click the Bullets or Numbering button.

After you create a list, you can modify, format, and customize the list as follows:

- You can move items around in a list, insert new items, or delete unwanted items. If the list is numbered, Word automatically updates the numbers.

- You can sort items in a bulleted list into ascending or descending order by clicking the Sort button in the Paragraph group on the Home tab.

- For a bulleted list, you can change the bullet symbol by clicking the Bullets arrow in the Paragraph group and making a selection from the Bullets gallery. You can also define a custom bullet (even a picture bullet) by clicking Define New Bullet.

- For a numbered list, you can change the number style by clicking the Numbering arrow in the Paragraph group and making a selection from the Numbering gallery. You can also define a custom style by clicking Define New Number Format.

- You can modify the indentation of the list by dragging the indent markers on the horizontal ruler. You can change both the overall indentation of the list and the relationship of the first line to the other lines.

   See Also For information about paragraph indentation, see "Manually Changing the Look of Paragraphs" earlier in this chapter.

In this exercise, you'll create a bulleted list and a numbered list and then modify lists in various ways.

SET UP You need the RulesDraft_start document located in your Chapter03 practice file folder to complete this exercise. Open the RulesDraft_start document, and save it as *RulesDraft*. Then follow the steps.

1. With formatting marks and the rulers displayed, select the first four paragraphs under **The rules fall into four categories**, and then on the **Home** tab, in the **Paragraph** group, click the **Bullets** button.

   The selected paragraphs are reformatted as a bulleted list. Word indents the list and precedes each item with a bullet and a tab. The program also removes the space after all paragraphs except the last one.

2. With the paragraphs still selected, in the **Paragraph** group, click the **Bullets** arrow.

   The Bullets gallery appears.

The Bullets gallery offers several predefined bullet choices.

3. Under **Bullet Library**, point to each bullet character to display a live preview of its effect on the selected list items, and then click the bullet composed of four diamonds.

   The bullet character that begins each item in the selected list changes.

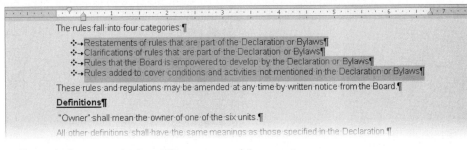

Different bullets are suited to different types of documents.

4. Select the two paragraphs below the **Definitions** heading, and then in the **Paragraph** group, click the **Numbering** button.

   Word numbers the two selected paragraphs sequentially.

5. Select the first four paragraphs below the **General Rules** heading, and then click the **Numbering** button.

   Word restarts the second numbered list from 1.

6. Select the next three paragraphs, and then in the **Paragraph** group, click the **Bullets** button.

   Word formats the paragraphs as a bulleted list, using the symbol you specified earlier. These three bullets are a second-level list of the preceding numbered item and should be indented.

7. With the three bulleted items still selected, in the **Paragraph** group, click the **Increase Indent** button.

   The bulleted paragraphs move to the right.

   Tip You can also adjust the indent level of a bulleted list by selecting its paragraphs, and on the horizontal ruler, dragging the Left Indent marker to the left or right. You can move just the Hanging Indent marker to adjust the space between the bullets and their text.

8. Select the remaining three paragraphs, and click the **Numbering** button.

   Word restarts this numbered list from 1, but you want it to continue the sequence of the previous numbered list.

9. Click anywhere in the **No large dogs** item, and then click the **Numbering** arrow.

   The Numbering gallery appears.

The Numbering gallery offers several predefined number formats.

10. At the bottom of the gallery, click **Set Numbering Value**.

The Set Numbering Value dialog box opens.

In this dialog box, you specify how this numbered list relates to the previous one.

11. Change the **Set value to** setting to **5**, and then click **OK**.

    Word renumbers the list after the bullet items so that it continues from the previous list.

12. In the **No large dogs** numbered item, click to the left of **Seeing**, press Enter, and then press Tab.

    Word first creates a new number 6 item and renumbers all subsequent items. However, when you press Tab to make the item second level, Word changes the 6 to a, indents the item, and restores the original numbers to the subsequent items.

13. Press the End key, and then press Enter. Then type **The Board reserves the right to make exceptions to this rule.** (type the period), and press Enter.

14. Click the **Numbering** arrow, click **Change List Level** at the bottom of the gallery, and click the first **1.** option. Then in the new first-level item, type **All pets must reside within their Owners' Apartments.**

    The lists are now organized hierarchically.

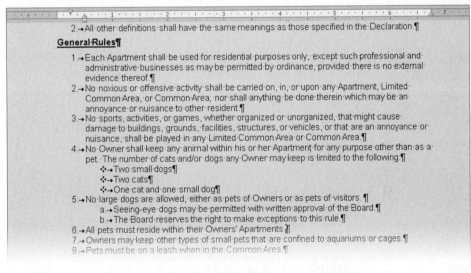

Word takes the work out of creating hierarchical lists.

15. Select the three bulleted paragraphs, and then in the **Paragraph** group, click the **Sort** button.

Formatting Text as You Type

The Word list capabilities are just one example of the program's ability to intuit how you want to format an element based on what you type. You can learn more about these and other AutoFormatting options by exploring the AutoCorrect dialog box. Display the Backstage view, click Options, click Proofing in the left pane of the Word Options dialog box, and then on the Proofing page, click AutoCorrect Options.

On the AutoFormat As You Type page, you can see the options Word implements by default, including bulleted and numbered lists. You can select and clear options to control AutoFormatting behavior.

The AutoFormat As You Type page of the AutoCorrect dialog box.

One interesting option is Border Lines. When this check box is selected, typing three consecutive hyphens (-) or three consecutive underscores (_) and pressing Enter draws a single line across the page. Three consecutive equal signs (=) draw a double line, and three consecutive tildes (~) draw a zigzag line.

The Sort Text dialog box opens.

You can sort text in lists in ascending or descending order.

16. With the **Ascending** option selected, click **OK**.

   The order of the bulleted items changes to ascending alphabetical order.

CLEAN UP If you want, turn off the rulers and formatting marks. Then save and close the RulesDraft document.

Key Points

- Quick Styles and style sets make it simple to apply combinations of character and paragraph formatting to give your documents a professional look.

- The same document can look very different depending on the theme applied to it. Colors, fonts, and effects can be combined to create just the look you want.

- You can format characters with an almost limitless number of combinations of font, size, style, and effect. For best results, resist the temptation to use more than a handful of combinations.

- You can change the look of paragraphs by varying their indentation, spacing, and alignment and by setting tab stops and applying borders and shading. Use these formatting options judiciously to create a balanced, uncluttered look.

- Bulleted and numbered lists are a great way to present information in an easy-to-read, easy-to-understand format. If the built-in bulleted and numbered formats don't provide what you need, you can define your own formats.

Chapter at a Glance

Present information in columns, **page 116**

Create tabbed lists, **page 123**

Present information in tables, **page 125**

Format tables, **page 136**

4 Organize Information in Columns and Tables

In this chapter, you will learn how to

✔ Present information in columns.

✔ Create tabbed lists.

✔ Present information in tables.

✔ Format tables.

Information in documents is most commonly presented as paragraphs of text. To make a text-heavy document more legible, you can flow the text in two or more columns, or you can display information in a table. For example, flowing text in multiple columns is a common practice in newsletters, flyers, and brochures; and presenting information in tables is common in reports.

When you need to present data in a document, using a table is often more efficient than describing the data in a paragraph, particularly when the data consists of numeric values. Tables make the data easier to read and understand. A small amount of data can be displayed in simple columns separated by tabs, which creates a tabbed list. A larger amount of data, or more complex data, is better presented in a table, which is a structure of rows and columns, frequently with row and column headings.

In this chapter, you'll first create and modify columns of text. Then you'll create a simple tabbed list. Finally, you'll create tables from scratch and from existing text, and format a table in various ways.

> **Practice Files** Before you can complete the exercises in this chapter, you need to copy the book's practice files to your computer. The practice files you'll use to complete the exercises in this chapter are in the Chapter04 practice file folder. A complete list of practice files is provided in "Using the Practice Files" at the beginning of this book.

Presenting Information in Columns

By default, Microsoft Word 2010 displays text in one column that spans the width of the page between the left and right margins. You can specify that text be displayed in two, three, or more columns to create layouts like those used in newspapers and magazines. When you format text to flow in columns, the text fills the first column on each page and then moves to the top of the next column. You can manually indicate where you want the text within each column to end.

The Columns gallery in the Page Setup group on the Page Layout tab displays several standard options for dividing text into columns. You can choose one, two, or three columns of equal width or two columns of unequal width. If the standard options don't suit your needs, you can specify the number and width of columns. The number of columns is limited by the width and margins of the page, and each column must be at least a half inch wide.

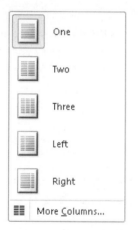

The Columns gallery displays the predefined column options.

No matter how you set up the columns initially, you can change the layout or column widths at any time.

You can format an entire document or a section of a document in columns. When you select a section of text and format it as columns, Word inserts section breaks at the beginning and end of the selected text to delineate the area in which the columnar formatting is applied. Within the columnar text, you can insert column breaks to specify where you want to end one column and start another. Section and column breaks are visible when you display formatting marks in the document.

Tip You can apply many types of formatting, including page orientation, to content within a specific section of a document without affecting the surrounding text. For information about sections, see "Controlling What Appears on Each Page" in Chapter 6, "Preview, Print, and Distribute Documents."

See Also For information about formatting marks, see "Viewing Documents in Different Ways" in Chapter 1, "Explore Word 2010."

You can apply character and paragraph formatting to columnar text in the same way you would any text. Here are some formatting tips for columnar text:

- When presenting text in narrow columns, you can justify the paragraphs (align the text with the left and right edges) to achieve a neat and clean appearance. To justify the paragraphs, Word adjusts the spacing between words, essentially moving the empty space that would normally appear at the end of the line into the gaps between words.

- To more completely fill columns, you can have Word hyphenate the text to break words into syllables to fill up the gaps.

In this exercise, you'll flow the text in one section of a document into three columns. You'll justify the text in the columns, change the column spacing, and hyphenate the text. You'll then break a column at a specific location instead of allowing the text to flow naturally from one column to the next.

SET UP You need the RoomPlanner_start document located in your Chapter04 practice file folder to complete this exercise. Open the RoomPlanner_start document, and save it as *RoomPlanner*. Then display formatting marks and the rulers, and follow the steps.

1. Click at the beginning of the paragraph that begins **Take a look** (do not click in the selection area). Then scroll down until you can see the end of the document, hold down the Shift key, and click to the right of the paragraph mark after **credit cards**.

   Word selects the text from the *Take a look* paragraph through the end of the last paragraph (but not the empty paragraph).

   Tip If you want to format an entire document with the same number of columns, you can simply click anywhere in the document—you don't have to select the text.

2. On the **Page Layout** tab, in the **Page Setup** group, click the **Columns** button, and then in the **Columns** gallery, click **Three**.

   Word inserts a section break above the selected text and flows the text within the section into three columns.

3. Press Ctrl+Home to move to the top of the document.

The section break is visible above the columns.

Simple·Room·Design¶

With·the·Room·Planner,·you'll·never·make·a·design·mistake·again.··Created·by·acclaimed·interior· designers·to·simplify·the·redecorating·process,·this·planning·tool·incorporates·elements·of·color,· dimension,·and·style·to·guide·your·project.·It·includes·a·furniture·location·guide;·room·grid;·drawing· tools;·and·miniature·furniture,·rugs,·accessories,·and·color·swatches·that·match·our·large·in-store· selection.·Here's·how·to·use·the·planner·to·create·the·room·of·your·dreams!¶

¶ ·················Section Break (Continuous)·················

Take·a·look·at·how·your· home·is·decorated·and·note· the·things·you·like·and· dislike.·Pay·special·attention· to·the·color·scheme·and·to· how·each·room·"feels"·to· you.·Is·it·inviting?·Does·it· feel·comfortable?·Does·it· relax·you·or·does·it· invigorate·you?¶

Focus·on·the·room(s)·you·

love,·and·the·rest·will·fall· into·place.¶

Take·your·Room·Planner· home·and·get·to·work!· Adjust·the·planner·so·that·it· models·the·room· dimensions.·Don't·forget·to· place·the·windows·and· doors.·Arrange·the·furniture· placeholders·to·mirror·how· your·room·is·currently·set·

design·for·a·day·or·two.· Then·review·it·again.·Does·it· still·look·perfect,·or·is· something·not·quite·right?· You·might·need·to·"live"· with·the·new·plan·for·a·few· days,·especially·if·you've· made·big·changes.·When· everything·feels·just·right·to· you,·you're·ready·for·the· next·big·step!¶

A continuous section break changes the formatting of the subsequent text but keeps it on the same page.

4. On the **Home** tab, in the **Editing** group, click the **Select** button, and then click **Select All**.

Keyboard Shortcut Press Ctrl+A to select all the text in the document.

See Also To see a complete list of keyboard shortcuts, see "Keyboard Shortcuts" at the end of this book.

5. In the **Paragraph** group, click the **Justify** button.

Keyboard Shortcut Press Ctrl+J to justify paragraphs.

The spacing between the words changes to align all the paragraphs in the document with both the left and right margins. Because you applied the formatting to the entire document, the title is no longer centered. However, it is often quicker to apply formatting globally and then deal with the exceptions.

6. Press Ctrl+Home to move to the paragraph containing the document title. Then in the **Paragraph** group, click the **Center** button.

   Keyboard Shortcut Press Ctrl+E to center text.

   Word centers the document title between the left and right margins.

7. Adjust the zoom percentage until you can see about two-thirds of the first page of the document.

   See Also For information about adjusting the zoom percentage, see "Viewing Documents in Different Ways" in Chapter 1, "Explore Word 2010."

8. Click anywhere in the first column.

   On the horizontal ruler, Word indicates the margins of the columns.

On the ruler, the indent markers show the indentation of the active column.

Tip If your rulers aren't turned on, select the Ruler check box in the Show group of the View tab.

9. On the **Page Layout** tab, display the **Columns** gallery, and click **More Columns**.

   The Columns dialog box opens. The spacing between columns is set by default to a half inch.

Because the Equal Column Width check box is selected, you can adjust the width and spacing of only the first column.

Tip To separate the columns with vertical lines, select the Line Between check box.

10. In the **Width and spacing** area, in the **Spacing** box for column 1, type or select **0.2"**.

    Word changes the measurement in the Spacing box for column 2, and widens all the columns in the Preview area to reflect the new setting.

11. Click **OK**.

    Word reflows the columns to fit their new margins.

Simple·Room·Design¶

With·the·Room·Planner,·you'll·never·make·a·design·mistake·again.·Created·by·acclaimed·interior·designers·to·simplify·the·redecorating·process,·this·planning·tool·incorporates·elements·of·color,·dimension,·and·style·to·guide·your·project.·It·includes·a·furniture·location·guide;·room·grid;·drawing·tools;·and·miniature·furniture,·rugs,·accessories,·and·color·swatches·that·match·our·large·in-store·selection.·Here's·how·to·use·the·planner·to·create·the·room·of·your·dreams!¶

¶———————————————————Section·Break·(Continuous)———————————————————

Take·a·look·at·how·your·home·is·decorated·and·note·the·things·you·like·and·dislike.·Pay·special·attention·to·the·color·scheme·and·to·how·each·room·"feels"·to·you.·Is·it·inviting?·Does·it·feel·comfortable?·Does·it·relax·you·or·does·it·invigorate·you?¶

Focus·on·the·room(s)·you·would·most·like·to·change.·Brainstorm·all·the·things·you·would·change·in·that·room·if·you·could.·Don't·give·a·thought·to·any·financial·considerations·

Take·your·Room·Planner·home·and·get·to·work!·Adjust·the·planner·so·that·it·models·the·room·dimensions.·Don't·forget·to·place·the·windows·and·doors.·Arrange·the·furniture·placeholders·to·mirror·how·your·room·is·currently·set·up.·Add·the·current·colors,·too.¶

This·is·where·the·fun·begins!·Start·changing·things·around·a·bit.·Move·the·furniture,·add·different·colors,·and·watch·the·room·come·together!·Here's·where·you·can·tell·if·that·rich·

changes.·When·everything·feels·just·right·to·you,·you're·ready·for·the·next·big·step!¶

Come·back·to·the·store.·Look·again·at·the·pieces·you·liked·during·your·last·visit·and·see·if·you·still·love·them.·If·you're·not·quite·sure,·go·back·to·your·planner·for·a·little·more·tweaking.·If·you·are·sure,·take·a·look·around·the·store·one·more·time·to·see·if·anything·else·catches·your·eye.·Then·make·your·purchases.·You're·almost·there!¶

Wider columns generally look neater on the page.

12. Click at the beginning of the **Take a look** paragraph. Then in the **Page Setup** group, click the **Hyphenation** button, and click **Automatic**.

   Word hyphenates the text of the document, which fills in some of the large gaps between words.

13. Click anywhere in the **NOTE** paragraph in the third column.

14. On the horizontal ruler, at the left end of the third column, drag the **Hanging Indent** marker 0.25 inch (two marks) to the right.

   All the lines in the *NOTE* paragraph except the first are now indented, offsetting the note from the paragraphs above and below it.

Take a look at how your home is decorated and note the things you like and dislike. Pay special attention to the color scheme and to how each room "feels" to you. Is it inviting? Does it feel comfortable? Does it relax you or does it invigorate you?¶

Focus on the room(s) you would most like to change. Brainstorm all the things you would change in that room if you could. Don't give a thought to any financial considerations; just let your imagination go wild! It might be helpful to write down all the negatives and positives. You don't need to come up with solutions all at once. Just be clear on what you like and what you hate about that room.¶

Visit our showroom and purchase a Room Planner. While planner so that it models the room dimensions. Don't forget to place the windows and doors. Arrange the furniture placeholders to mirror how your room is currently set up. Add the current colors, too.¶

This is where the fun begins! Start changing things around a bit. Move the furniture, add different colors, and watch the room come together! Here's where you can tell if that rich red rug you saw in the showroom enhances or overwhelms your room. What about that overstuffed chair that caught your eye? Place a furniture or accessory shape, and then color it. Does it look great or is it too jarring? Change the color... does that help? Don't forget about the walls. Try different colors to see the effect on the room overall.¶

just right to you, you're ready for the next big step!¶

Come back to the store. Look again at the pieces you liked during your last visit and see if you still love them. If you're not quite sure, go back to your planner for a little more tweaking. If you are sure, take a look around the store one more time to see if anything else catches your eye. Then make your purchases. You're almost there!¶

NOTE: If you decided to paint your room, do that before your new pieces are delivered. You'll want to start enjoying your new room as soon as your purchases arrive.¶

After a few weeks, ask yourself whether the room is as great as you thought it would be. Does it achieve the look and feel you

You can change the indentation of individual paragraphs within a column.

15. Display the bottom of page **1**. In the first column on page **1**, click at the beginning of the **Take your Room Planner home** paragraph. Then in the **Page Setup** group, click the **Breaks** button, and click **Column**.

Word inserts a column break. The text that follows the column break moves to the top of the second column.

16. At the bottom of the third column on page **1**, click at the beginning of the **If you're not sure** paragraph, and then on the Quick Access Toolbar, click the **Repeat Insertion** button to insert another column break.

Keyboard Shortcut Press Ctrl+Y to repeat the previous action.

Word inserts a column break. The text that follows the column break moves to the top of the first column on page 2.

✖ **CLEAN UP** Return the Zoom Level setting to 100%, and then save and close the RoomPlanner document.

Creating Tabbed Lists

If you have a relatively small amount of data to present, you might choose to display it in a tabbed list, which arranges text in simple columns separated by tabs. You can align the text within the columns by using left, right, centered, or decimal tab stops.

See Also For more information about setting tab stops, see "Manually Changing the Look of Paragraphs" in Chapter 3, "Change the Look of Text."

When entering text in a tabbed list, inexperienced Word users have a tendency to press the Tab key multiple times to align the columns of the list with the default tab stops. If you do this, you have no control over the column widths. To be able to fine-tune the columns, you need to set custom tab stops rather than relying on the default ones.

When setting up a tabbed list, you should press Tab only once between the items that you want to appear in separate columns. Next you apply any necessary formatting. And finally, you set the custom tab stops. Set left, right, centered, and decimal tabs to control the alignment of the column content, or set a bar tab to add a vertical line to visually separate list columns. By setting the tabs in order from left to right, you can check the alignment of the text within each column as you go.

In this exercise, you'll first enter text separated by tabs and format the text. Then you'll set custom tab stops to create a tabbed list.

 SET UP You need the ConsultationA_start document located in your Chapter04 practice file folder to complete this exercise. Open the ConsultationA_start document, and save it as *ConsultationA*. Then display formatting marks and the rulers, and follow the steps.

1. Set the zoom percentage to a level that is comfortable for you, and then press Ctrl+End to move the cursor to the blank line at the end of the document.

2. Type **Location**, press Tab, type **Discount Applies**, press Tab, type **Hourly Rate**, and then press Enter.

3. Add three more lines to the list by typing the following text, pressing the Tab and Enter keys where indicated.

In home Tab No Tab $50.00 Enter
Phone Tab Yes Tab $35.00 Enter
In store Tab Yes Tab $40.00 Enter

The tab characters push the items to the next default tab stop, but because some items are longer than others, they do not line up.

```
Available·Consultants·(check·your·consultant's·name)¶
Susan·Burk¶
Andy·Ruth¶
Carlos·Carvallo¶

Consultation·Fee·Schedule¶
Location  →  Discount·Applies  →  Hourly·Rate¶
In·home  →  No  →  $50.00¶
Phone·Yes  →  $35.00¶
In·store  →  Yes  →  $40.00¶
¶
```

In a tabbed list, it's important to press the Tab key only once between items.

4. Select the first line of the tabbed list, and then on the Mini Toolbar that appears, click the **Bold** button.

Troubleshooting If the Mini Toolbar doesn't appear, click the Bold button in the Font group on the Home tab.

Keyboard Shortcut Press Ctrl+B to apply bold.

5. Select all four lines of the tabbed list, and then on the Mini Toolbar, click the **Increase Indent** button.

Tip It's more efficient to make all character and paragraph formatting changes to the text before setting tab stops. Otherwise, you might have to adjust the tab stops after applying the formatting.

6. With the tabbed list still selected, on the **Page Layout** tab, in the **Paragraph** group, under **Spacing**, change the **After** setting to **0 pt**.

7. Click the tab setting button at the junction of the horizontal and vertical rulers until the **Center Tab** button is active. (You will probably have to click only once.) Then click the **2.5** inch mark on the horizontal ruler.

On the ruler, Word sets a center-aligned tab stop that looks like the Center Tab icon. The items in the second column of the tabbed list center themselves at that position.

8. Click the tab setting button once.

   The Right Tab button is now active.

9. With the **Right Tab** button active, click the horizontal ruler at the **4.5** inch mark.

   On the ruler, Word sets a right-aligned tab stop that looks like the Right Tab icon. The items in the third column of the tabbed list right-align themselves at that position.

10. On the **Home** tab, in the **Paragraph** group, click the **Show/Hide ¶** button to hide the tabs, paragraph marks, and other formatting marks. Then click away from the tabbed list to see the results.

    The tabbed list resembles a simple table.

Available Consultants (check your consultant's name)
Susan Burk
Andy Ruth
Carlos Carvallo

Consultation Fee Schedule

Location	Discount Applies	Hourly Rate
In home	No	$50.00
Phone	Yes	$35.00
In store	Yes	$40.00

You have created a simple table-like layout with just a few clicks.

✖ **CLEAN UP** Save the ConsultationA document, and then close it.

Presenting Information in Tables

A table is a structure of vertical columns and horizontal rows. Each column and each row can be named with a heading, although some tables have only column headings or only row headings. At the junction of each column and row is a box called a *cell* in which data (text or numeric information) is stored.

You can create empty or predefined tables in a Word document in the following ways:

● The Insert Table gallery, which is available from the Tables group on the Insert tab, displays a simple grid.

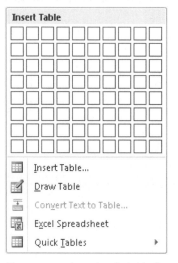

You can create a simple table from the grid in the Insert Table gallery.

Clicking a cell in the grid inserts an empty table the width of the text column. The table has the number of rows and columns you indicated in the grid, with all the rows one line high and all the columns of an equal width.

● To insert a more customized empty table, you can click Insert Table on the menu at the bottom of the Insert Table gallery to open the Insert Table dialog box, in which you can specify the number of rows and columns and customize the column width.

You can create a custom-width table from the Insert Table dialog box.

● To insert a less clearly defined empty table, you can click Draw Table below the grid in the Insert Table gallery. This command displays a pencil with which you can draw cells directly in the Word document to create a table. The cells you draw connect by snapping to a grid, but you have some control over the size and spacing of the rows and columns.

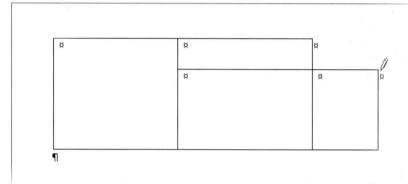

You can draw a table directly on the page.

See Also For information about drawing tables, see "Using Tables to Control Page Layout" in Chapter 10, "Organize and Arrange Content."

● In addition to empty tables, you can insert any of the available Quick Tables, which are predefined tables of formatted data that you can replace with your own information. Built-in Quick Tables include a variety of calendars, simple tables, tables with subheadings, and tabbed lists. You can also save your own custom tables to the Quick Tables gallery so that you can easily insert a frequently used table structure and data into any document.

Enrollment in local colleges, 2010

College	New students	Graduating students	Change
Undergraduate			
Cedar University	110	103	+7
Elm College	223	214	+9
Maple Academy	197	120	+77
Pine College	134	121	+13
Oak Institute	202	210	-8
Graduate			
Cedar University	24	20	+4
Elm College	43	53	-10
Maple Academy	3	11	-8
Pine College	9	4	+5
Oak Institute	53	52	+1
Total	998	908	90

Source: Fictitious data, for illustration purposes only

The Quick Tables gallery includes a selection of predefined tables such as this one.

A new table appears in the document as a set of cells, usually bordered by gridlines. (In some Quick Tables, the gridlines are turned off.) Each cell contains an end-of-cell marker, and each row ends with an end-of-row marker. (The end-of-cell markers and end-of-row markers are identical in appearance, and are visible only when you display formatting marks in the document.) When you point to a table, a move handle appears in its upper-left corner and a size handle in its lower-right corner. When the cursor is in a table, two Table Tools contextual tabs—Design and Layout—appear on the ribbon.

A table has its own controls and its own contextual ribbon tabs.

Tip The move handle and size handle appear only in Print Layout view and Web Layout view.

After you create a table, you can enter data (such as text, numbers, or graphics) into the table cells and press the Tab key to move the cursor from cell to cell. Pressing Tab when the cursor is in the last cell of a row moves the cursor to the first cell of the next row. Pressing Tab when the cursor is in the last cell of the last row adds a new row to the table and moves the cursor to the first cell of that row.

Tip You can move and position the cursor by pressing the Tab key or the Arrow keys, or by clicking in a table cell.

If the data you want to present in a table already exists in the document, either as regular text or as a tabbed list, you can convert the text to a table by selecting it and then clicking Convert Text To Table in the Insert Table gallery. Conversely, you can convert an active table to regular text by clicking the Convert To Text button in the Data group on the Layout tab.

You can modify a table's structure by changing the size of the table, changing the size of one or more columns or rows, or adding or removing rows, columns, or individual cells.

Tip To change a table's structure, you often need to select the entire table or a specific column or row. The simplest way to do this is to position the cursor in the table, column, or row, click the Select button in the Table group on the Layout tab, and then click the table element you want. Alternatively, you can point to the top edge of a column or left edge of a row and, when the pointer changes to an arrow, click to select the column or row.

The basic methods for manipulating a table or its contents are as follows:

● **Insert a row or column** Click anywhere in a row or column adjacent to where you want to make the insertion. Then on the Layout tab, in the Rows & Columns group, click the Insert Above, Insert Below, Insert Left, or Insert Right button.

The Rows & Columns group of the Layout tab.

Selecting more than one row or column before you click an Insert button inserts that number of rows or columns in the table.

Tip You can insert cells by clicking the Rows & Columns dialog box launcher and specifying in the Insert Cells dialog box how adjacent cells should be moved to accommodate the new cells.

● **Delete a row or column** Click anywhere in the row or column, and in the Rows & Columns group, click the Delete button. Then click Delete Cells, Delete Columns, Delete Rows, or Delete Table.

● **Resize an entire table** Drag the size handle.

● **Resize a single column or row** Without selecting the column, drag its right border to the left or right. Without selecting the row, drag its bottom border up or down. (If you select a column or row and then drag its border, only the selected column or row changes.)

● **Move a table** Point to the table, and then drag the move handle that appears in its upper-left corner to a new location. Or use the Cut and Paste commands in the Clipboard group on the Home tab to move the table.

● **Merge cells** Create cells that span multiple columns or rows by selecting the cells you want to merge and clicking the Merge Cells button in the Merge group on the Layout tab. For example, to center a title in the first row of a table, you can merge all the cells in the row to create one merged cell that spans the table's width.

● **Split cells** Divide one cell into multiple cells by clicking the Split Cells button in the Merge group on the Layout tab and then specifying the number of columns and rows you want.

● **Sort information** Click the Sort button in the Data group on the Layout tab to sort the rows in ascending or descending order by the data in any column. For example, in a table that has the column headings Name, Address, ZIP Code, and Phone Number, you can sort on any one of those columns to arrange the information in alphabetical or numerical order.

In this exercise, you'll work with two tables. First you'll create an empty table, enter and align text in the table cells, add rows to the table, and merge cells. Then you'll create a second table by converting an existing tabbed list, change the width of a column, and change the width of the entire table.

SET UP You need the ConsultationB_start document located in your Chapter04 practice file folder to complete this exercise. Open the ConsultationB_start document, and save it as *ConsultationB*. Then display formatting marks and the rulers, and follow the steps.

1. Click to the left of the second blank paragraph below **Please complete this form**.

2. On the **Insert** tab, in the **Tables** group, click the **Table** button. Then in the **Insert Table** gallery, point to (don't click) the cell that is five columns to the right and five rows down from the upper-left corner of the grid.

   Word highlights the cells that will be in the table, indicates the table dimensions in the gallery header, and creates a temporary table in the document.

You can preview the table with the number of columns and rows you have specified.

3. Click the cell.

    Word creates a blank table consisting of five columns and five rows. The cursor is located in the first cell. Because the table is active, Word displays the Design and Layout contextual tabs.

4. In the selection area to the left of the table, point to the first row of the table, and then click once to select it.

Merge Cells

5. On the **Layout** contextual tab, in the **Merge** group, click the **Merge Cells** button.

    Word combines the five cells in the first row into one cell.

6. With the merged cell selected, in the **Alignment** group, click the **Align Center** button.

    The end-of-cell marker moves to the exact center of the merged cell to indicate that anything you type there will be centered both horizontally and vertically.

7. Type **Consultation Estimate**.

    The table now has content that looks like a table title.

Consultation· Estimate¤				
¤	¤	¤	¤	¤
¤	¤	¤	¤	¤
¤	¤	¤	¤	¤
¤	¤	¤	¤	¤

Merged cells are often used for table titles and column headings.

8. Click the first cell in the second row, type **Type**, and then press Tab.

9. Type **Location**, **Consultant**, **Hourly Rate**, and **Total**, pressing Tab after each entry.

    Pressing Tab after the *Total* heading moves the cursor to the first cell of the third row. The table now has a row of column headings.

10. Select the column heading row, and then on the Mini Toolbar, click the **Bold** button.

11. In the third row, type **Window treatments**, **In home**, **Andy Ruth**, **$50.00**, and **$50.00**, pressing Tab after each entry.

    You have entered a complete row of data.

12. Select the last two rows, and then on the **Layout** tab, in the **Rows & Columns** group, click the **Insert Below** button.

Insert Below

    Word adds two new rows and selects them.

13. In the last row, click the first cell, hold down the Shift key, and then press the Right Arrow key four times to select the first four cells in the row.

14. In the **Merge** group, click the **Merge Cells** button.

    Word combines the selected cells into one cell.

15. In the **Alignment** group, click the **Align Center Right** button.

16. Type **Subtotal**, and then press Tab twice.

    Word adds a new row with the same structure to the bottom of the table.

Consultation· Estimate¤				
Type¤	**Location**¤	**Consultant**¤	**Hourly· Rate**¤	**Total**¤
Window· treatments¤	In·home¤	Andy· Ruth¤	$50.00¤	$50.00¤
¤	¤	¤	¤	¤
¤	¤	¤	¤	¤
¤	¤	¤	¤	¤
			Subtotal¤	¤
			¤	¤

When you add a new row, it has the same format as the one it is based on.

17. Type **Add trip fee**, press Tab twice to add a new row, and then type **Total**.

    Now you'll create a different table by converting existing text.

18. Scroll down to the bottom of the document, and select the rows of the tabbed list beginning with **Distance** and ending with **$20.00**.

19. On the **Insert** tab, in the **Tables** group, click the **Table** button, and then click **Convert Text to Table**.

    The Convert Text To Table dialog box opens.

You can separate text into columns based on the symbol you specify.

20. Verify that the **Number of columns** box displays **2**, and then click **OK**.

    The selected text appears in a table with two columns and six rows.

21. Click anywhere in the table to release the selection, and then point to the right border of the table. When the pointer changes to two opposing arrows, double-click the border.

    Word adjusts the width of the right column to accommodate its longest cell entry.

    Tip You can also adjust the column width by changing the Table Column Width setting in the Cell Size group on the Layout tab.

22. Point to the **In-Home Trip Charge** table.

    Word displays the move handle in the upper-left corner and the size handle in the lower-right corner.

23. Drag the size handle to the right, releasing the mouse button when the right edge of the table aligns approximately with the **4** inch mark on the horizontal ruler.

    The width of the table expands.

The table is now approximately as wide as the tabbed list above, creating a nice balance.

✖ **CLEAN UP** Save the ConsultationB document, and then close it.

Performing Calculations in Tables

When you want to perform calculations with the numbers in a Word table, you can create a formula that uses a built-in mathematical function. You construct a formula by using the tools in the Formula dialog box, which you display by clicking the Formula button in the Data group on the Layout contextual tab.

The Formula dialog box.

A formula consists of an equal sign (=), followed by a function name (such as SUM), followed by parentheses containing the location of the cells you want to use for the calculation. For example, the formula =SUM(Left) totals the cells to the left of the cell containing the formula.

To use a function other than SUM in the Formula dialog box, you click the function you want in the Paste Function list. You can use built-in functions to perform a number of calculations, including averaging (AVERAGE) a set of values, counting (COUNT) the number of values in a column or row, or finding the maximum (MAX) or minimum (MIN) value in a series of cells.

Although formulas commonly refer to the cells above or to the left of the active cell, you can also use the contents of specified cells or constant values in formulas. To use the contents of a cell, you type the cell address in the parentheses following the function name. The cell address is a combination of the column letter and the row number—for example, A1 is the cell at the intersection of the first column and the first row. A series of cells in a row can be addressed as a range consisting of the first cell and the last cell separated by a colon, such as A1:D1. For example, the formula =SUM(A1:D1) totals the values in row 1 of columns A through D. A series of cells in a column can be addressed in the same way. For example, the formula =SUM(A1:A4) totals the values in column A of rows 1 through 4.

Other Layout Options

You can control many aspects of a table in the Table Properties dialog box, which you display by clicking the Properties button in the Table group on the Layout tab. You can set the following options:

- On the Table page, you can specify the width of the entire table, as well as the way it interacts with the surrounding text.

- On the Row page, you can specify the height of each row, whether a row is allowed to break across pages, and whether a row of column headings should be repeated at the top of each page.

  Tip The Repeat As Header Row option is available only if the cursor is in the top row of the table.

- On the Column page, you can set the width of each column.

- On the Cell page, you can set the width of cells and the vertical alignment of text within them.

  Tip You can also control the widths of selected cells by changing the settings in the Cell Size group on the Layout tab.

- On either the Table page or Cell page, you can control the margins of cells (how close text comes to the cell border) by clicking Options and specifying top, bottom, left, and right settings.

  Tip You can also control the margins by clicking the Cell Margins button in the Alignment group on the Layout tab.

- On the Alt Text page, you can enter text that describes what the table is about.

Formatting Tables

Formatting a table to best convey its data can be a process of trial and error. With Word 2010, you can quickly get started by applying one of the table styles available in the Table Styles gallery on the Design contextual tab.

The table styles include a variety of borders, colors, and other attributes to give the table a professional look.

If you want to control the appearance of a table more precisely, you can use the commands on the Design and Layout tabs. You can also format the table content. As you saw in the previous exercise, you can apply character formatting to the text in tables just as you would to regular text, by clicking buttons on the Mini Toolbar. You can also click the buttons in the Font group on the Home tab. You can apply paragraph formatting, such as alignment and spacing, by clicking buttons in the Paragraph group on the Home tab. And you can apply both character and paragraph styles from the Quick Styles gallery.

In this exercise, you'll first apply a table style to a table. Then you'll format a table row and column. You'll also apply character and paragraph formatting to various cells so that the table's appearance helps the reader understand its data.

SET UP You need the RepairCosts_start document located in your Chapter04 practice file folder to complete this exercise. Open the RepairCosts_start document, and save it as *RepairCosts*. If formatting marks are displayed, hide them, and then follow the steps.

1. Click anywhere in the table, and then on the **Design** tab, point to each thumbnail in the first row of the **Table Styles** gallery to see its live preview.

2. In the **Table Style Options** group, clear the **Banded Rows** check box, and select the **Total Row** check box.

   The table style thumbnails no longer have banded rows, reflecting your changes.

3. In the **Table Styles** group, click the **More** button.

   The Table Styles gallery appears.

4. Preview all the styles in the gallery. When you finish exploring, click the second thumbnail in the fifth row (**Medium Shading 2 – Accent 1**).

   The style needs to be modified to suit the data, but it's a good starting point.

Building Association Estimated Repair Costs

Item	Repair Type	Quantity	Cost, $
Elastomeric Decks	Resurface	400 sq. ft.	1,600
Wood Decks	Replace	1,200 sq. ft.	6,500
Building Exterior	Repaint	9,000 sq. ft.	9,000
Roof	Reseal	5,000 sq. ft.	2,700
Entry Doors	Repaint	4	600
Carpet	Replace	150 sq. yds.	4,500
Intercom	Replace	1	2,500
Garage Door Opener	Replace	1	2,000
Steel Doors	Repaint	10	750
Exterior Trim	Repaint	800 ft.	4,500
Elevator Hydraulics	Replace	1	55,000
Fire Alarm System	Replace	1	3,000
TOTAL			**110,550**

This table style applies formatting to the header and total rows, the first column, and the text of the table.

Borders

5. Select all the cells in the last row by clicking in the selection area to its left. Then in the **Table Styles** group, click the **Borders** arrow, and click **Borders and Shading**.

   The Borders And Shading dialog box opens, displaying the borders applied to the selected cells.

6. On the **Borders** page of the dialog box, scroll to the top of the **Style** list, and click the thick black border.

7. In the **Preview** area, click the top border button once to remove the current border, and click again to apply the thick black border.

8. Click the **Shading** tab, and click the **Fill** arrow. Under **Theme Colors** in the palette, click the fifth box in the top row (**Blue, Accent 1**). Then click **OK**.

9. Without moving the selection, on the **Home** tab, in the **Font** group, click the **Font Color** arrow, and under **Theme Colors** in the palette, click the white box. Then press Home to release the selection.

   The table now has the same border at the top and bottom.

Building Association Estimated Repair Costs

Item	Repair Type	Quantity	Cost, $
Elastomeric Decks	Resurface	400 sq. ft.	1,600
Wood Decks	Replace	1,200 sq. ft.	6,500
Building Exterior	Repaint	9,000 sq. ft.	9,000
Roof	Reseal	5,000 sq. ft.	2,700
Entry Doors	Repaint	4	600
Carpet	Replace	150 sq. yds.	4,500
Intercom	Replace	1	2,500
Garage Door Opener	Replace	1	2,000
Steel Doors	Repaint	10	750
Exterior Trim	Repaint	800 ft.	4,500
Elevator Hydraulics	Replace	1	55,000
Fire Alarm System	Replace	1	3,000
TOTAL			110,550

You can customize a table style to meet your needs.

10. Point to the left side of the **Elastomeric Decks** cell, and when the pointer changes to a black right-pointing arrow, drag downward to select all the cells in the **Item** column *except* the **TOTAL** cell.

Shading

11. On the **Design** tab, in the **Table Styles** group, click the **Shading** arrow, and under **Theme Colors**, click the third box in the blue column (**Blue, Accent 1, Lighter 40%**).

12. Select all the cells containing amounts in the **Cost, $** column, including the cell with the total. Then on the **Layout** tab, in the **Alignment** group, click the **Align Center Right** button.

   Tip If the first row of your table has several long headings that make it difficult to fit the table on one page, you can turn the headings sideways. Simply select the heading row and click the Text Direction button in the Alignment group on the Layout tab.

   Now you can judge how well the table displays its data.

Building Association Estimated Repair Costs

Item	Repair Type	Quantity	Cost, $
Elastomeric Decks	Resurface	400 sq. ft.	1,600
Wood Decks	Replace	1,200 sq. ft.	6,500
Building Exterior	Repaint	9,000 sq. ft.	9,000
Roof	Reseal	5,000 sq. ft.	2,700
Entry Doors	Repaint	4	600
Carpet	Replace	150 sq. yds.	4,500
Intercom	Replace	1	2,500
Garage Door Opener	Replace	1	2,000
Steel Doors	Repaint	10	750
Exterior Trim	Repaint	800 ft.	4,500
Elevator Hydraulics	Replace	1	55,000
Fire Alarm System	Replace	1	3,000
TOTAL			110,550

The total now stands out better, and the amounts are easier to read.

   Tip If you will need to use this formatted table with different data in the future, you can save it as a Quick Table. For information about saving customized tables for future use, see the sidebar "Quick Tables" on the next page.

✖ **CLEAN UP** Save the RepairCosts document, and then close it.

Quick Tables

With Word 2010, you can create Quick Tables—preformatted tables with sample data that you can customize. To create a Quick Table:

1. On the Insert tab, in the Tables group, click the Table button, and then point to Quick Tables.

   The Quick Tables gallery appears.

The predefined Quick Tables meet several common needs.

2. Scroll through the gallery, noticing the types of tables that are available, and then click the one you want.

   For example, this is the Matrix Quick Table.

City·or·Town¤	Point·A¤	Point·B¤	Point·C¤	Point·D¤	Point·E¤	¤
Point·A¤	—¤	¤	¤	¤	¤	¤
Point·B¤	87¤	—¤	¤	¤	¤	¤
Point·C¤	64¤	56¤	—¤	¤	¤	¤
Point·D¤	37¤	32¤	91¤	—¤	¤	¤
Point·E¤	93¤	35¤	54¤	43¤	—¤	¤
¶						

The Matrix Quick Table includes row and column headings, placeholder data, and no summary data, such as totals.

3. On the Design tab, apply formatting to tailor the Quick Table to your needs.

   For example, here's the Matrix Quick Table after we formatted it.

City or Town	Point A	Point B	Point C	Point D	Point E
Point A	—				
Point B	87	—			
Point C	64	56	—		
Point D	37	32	91	—	
Point E	93	35	54	43	—

It is easy to customize a Quick Table for your own needs.

If you will use the table again, you can save it in the Quick Tables gallery. Select the table, display the Quick Tables gallery, and click Save Selection To Quick Tables Gallery. Then in the Create New Building Block dialog box, assign a name to the table, and click OK. Provided you save the Building Blocks template when Word prompts you to, the table will be available in the Quick Tables gallery for future use.

See Also For information about building blocks, see "Inserting Building Blocks" in Chapter 5, "Add Simple Graphic Elements."

Key Points

- To vary the layout of a document, you can divide text into columns. You can control the number of columns, the width of the columns, and the space between the columns.

- To clearly present a simple set of data, you can use tabs to create a tabbed list, with custom tab stops controlling the width and alignment of columns.

- You can create a table from scratch, or convert existing text to a table. You can control the size of the table and its individual structural elements.

- By using the built-in table styles, you can quickly apply professional-looking cell and character formatting to a table and its contents.

- You can enhance a table and its contents by applying text attributes, borders, and shading.

Chapter at a Glance

Insert and modify pictures, **page 144**

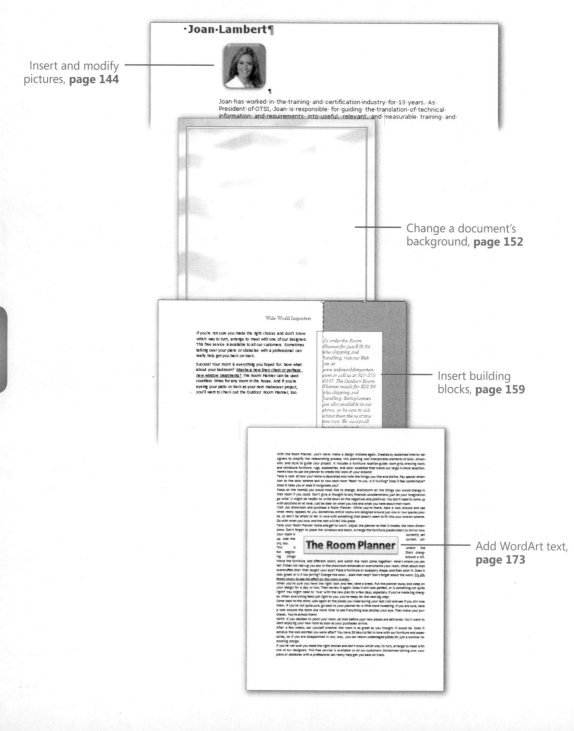

Change a document's background, **page 152**

Insert building blocks, **page 159**

Add WordArt text, **page 173**

5 Add Simple Graphic Elements

In this chapter, you will learn how to

✔ Insert and modify pictures.

✔ Change a document's background.

✔ Insert building blocks.

✔ Add WordArt text.

Some documents that you create in Microsoft Word 2010 are straightforward and require nothing more than words. Others might benefit from the addition of graphic elements to reinforce their concepts, to grab the reader's attention, or to make them more visually appealing. These graphic elements can include a wide variety of objects and effects, including:

● **Pictures** These objects are created outside of Word—photographs from digital cameras, clip art images, or files created on a computer with a graphics program. No matter what the origin of the picture, you can change its size and its position in relation to other content after you insert it in the Word document. For some types of pictures, you can make additional changes from within Word, such as cropping the picture or embellishing it by applying artistic effects.

● **Drawing objects** These objects are created within Word—text boxes, WordArt text, diagrams, charts, shapes, and other such objects. As with pictures, you can size, move, and format drawing objects from within Word.

See Also For information about diagrams, see Chapter 7, "Insert and Modify Diagrams." For information about charts, see Chapter 8, "Insert and Modify Charts." For information about shapes, see "Drawing and Modifying Shapes" in Chapter 9, "Use Other Visual Elements."

- **Building blocks** You can draw attention to specific information and add graphic appeal by incorporating ready-made graphic building blocks (also called *Quick Parts*) into a document. These building blocks are combinations of drawing objects (and sometimes pictures) in a variety of formatting styles that you can select to insert elements such as cover pages, quotations pulled from the text (called *pull quotes*), and sidebars. You can also create your own building blocks, which then become available in the Quick Parts gallery.

- **Backgrounds** You can apply a variety of backgrounds to the pages of your document, including plain colors, gradients, textures, patterns, and pictures.

In this chapter, you'll first insert and modify pictures in a document. You'll experiment with page backgrounds, and then add three types of building blocks to a document. Finally, you'll have a bit of fun with WordArt.

> **Practice Files** Before you can complete the exercises in this chapter, you need to copy the book's practice files to your computer. The practice files you'll use to complete the exercises in this chapter are in the Chapter05 practice file folder. A complete list of practice files is provided in "Using the Practice Files" at the beginning of this book.

Inserting and Modifying Pictures

You can insert digital photographs or pictures created in almost any program into a Word document. You specify the source of the picture you want to insert by clicking one of these two buttons, which are located in the Illustrations group on the Insert tab:

- **Picture** Click this button to insert a picture that is saved as a file on your computer, or on a device (such as an external hard drive or a digital camera) that is connected to your computer.

- **Clip Art** Click this button to insert one of hundreds of clip art images, such as photos and drawings of people, places, and things.

  > **See Also** For information about clip art, see the sidebar "About Clip Art" later in this chapter.

After you insert a picture in a document, you can modify the image by using commands on the Format contextual tab, which is displayed only when a picture or drawing object is selected. For example, you can click buttons in the Adjust group to change the picture's brightness and contrast, recolor it, apply artistic effects to it, and compress it to reduce the size of the document containing it. The Picture Styles group offers a wide range of picture styles that you can apply to a picture to change its shape and orientation, as well as add borders and picture effects. And finally, you can use the commands in the Size group for cropping and resizing pictures.

The ribbon image showing Picture Tools Format contextual tab.

The Format contextual tab for pictures.

Troubleshooting The appearance of buttons and groups on the ribbon changes depending on the width of the program window. For information about changing the appearance of the ribbon to match our screen images, see "Modifying the Display of the Ribbon" at the beginning of this book.

See Also For information about using the commands in the Arrange group, see "Arranging Objects on the Page" in Chapter 10, "Organize and Arrange Content."

In this exercise, you'll insert a couple of photographs and size and crop them. You'll modify one of them and then copy the modifications to the other one. Then you'll insert an illustration and apply an artistic effects to it.

SET UP You need the Authors_start document, the Joan and Joyce photographs, and the OTSI-Logo illustration located in your Chapter05 practice file folder to complete this exercise. Open the Authors_start document, and save it as *Authors*. Display the rulers and formatting marks, and then follow the steps.

1. Click to the left of the **Joyce has 30 years' experience** paragraph, press the Enter key, and press the Up Arrow key. Then on the **Insert** tab, in the **Illustrations** group, click the **Picture** button.

   The Insert Picture dialog box opens, displaying the contents of your Pictures library.

2. Navigate to the **Chapter05** practice file folder, and double-click the **Joyce** picture.

   Word inserts the picture at the cursor and displays the Format contextual tab on the ribbon.

   Troubleshooting If Word inserts a frame the size of the picture but displays only a sliver of the picture itself, Word cannot increase the line spacing to accommodate the picture because it is set to a specific amount. To correct this problem, click the Paragraph dialog box launcher, and in the Paragraph dialog box, change the Line Spacing setting to Single.

   Tip In this exercise, you insert pictures in blank paragraphs. By default, Word inserts the picture in-line with the text, meaning that Word increases the line spacing as necessary to accommodate the picture. If you were to type text adjacent to the picture, the bottom of the picture would align with the bottom of the text on the same line. After you insert a picture, you can change its position and the way text wraps around it.

   See Also For more information about positioning objects and wrapping text around them, see "Adding WordArt Text" later in this chapter and "Arranging Objects on the Page" in Chapter 10, "Organize and Arrange Content."

3. In the lower-right corner of the picture, point to the handle (the circle). When the pointer changes to a double arrow, drag up and to the left until the right side of the picture's shadow frame is in line with the **1.75** inch mark on the horizontal ruler.

   When you release the mouse button, the picture assumes its new size.

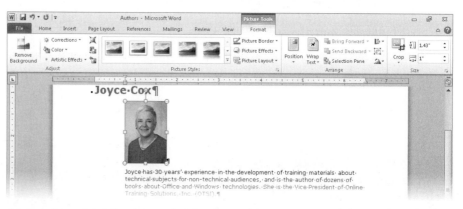

Because the ratio of the picture's height to its width (called the aspect ratio*) is locked, the height and width change proportionally.*

Tip You can fine-tune the size of a graphic by adjusting the Shape Height and Shape Width settings in the Size group on the Format tab.

4. On the **Format** contextual tab, in the **Size** group, click the **Crop** button.

   Word surrounds the picture with crop handles.

5. Point to the bottom-middle handle, and when the pointer changes to a black T, drag upward until the picture is about 1 inch high.

   Word grays out the part of the picture you have cropped away.

Word will not actually crop the picture until you turn off the crop button.

6. Click the **Crop** button to turn it off.

   Word removes the crop handles and discards the gray part of the picture.

Tip In addition to cropping a picture manually, you can click the Crop arrow and select from various options, including having Word crop a picture to fit a shape you select, cropping to a precise width:height ratio, filling an area with a picture, or fitting a picture to an area.

7. Click to the left of the **Joan has worked** paragraph, press Enter, and then press the Up Arrow key. Then repeat steps 1 through 6 to insert, size, and crop the **Joan** picture below the **Joan Lambert** heading.

8. With the **Joan** picture still selected, on the **Format** contextual tab, in the **Adjust** group, click the **Color** button.

Color ▾

The Color gallery appears.

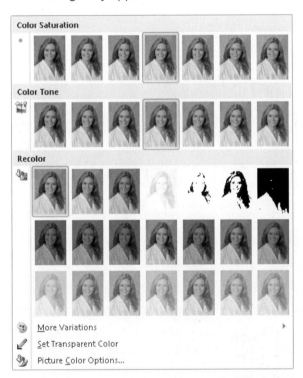

You can change the saturation and tone, as well as recolor the picture.

9. Under **Recolor** in the **Color** gallery, preview each option, and then click the second thumbnail in the first row (**Grayscale**).

The picture is grayscaled—that is, each color is converted into a shade of gray.

10. In the **Adjust** group, click the **Corrections** button. Then in the **Corrections** gallery, under **Brightness and Contrast**, preview each option, and then click the fourth thumbnail in the top row (**Brightness: +20% Contrast: -40%**).

Corrections ▾

11. In the **Picture Styles** group, click the **More** button.

The Picture Styles gallery appears.

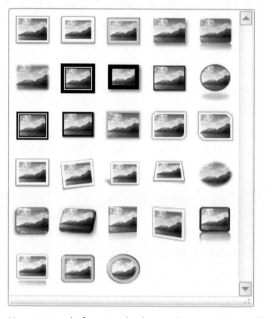

You can apply frames, shadows, glows, and 3-D effects from the Picture Styles gallery.

Troubleshooting The number of thumbnails per row in your galleries might be different than ours, depending on the screen resolution and the width of the program window. In the steps, look for the thumbnail with the name specified.

12. In the gallery, preview each thumbnail, and then click the first thumbnail in the fifth row (**Bevel Rectangle**). Click away from the picture to see the effect.

The photograph now has a three-dimensional appearance.

This picture style gives the effect of a padded square button.

13. Click the **Joan** picture to select it, and then on the **Home** tab, in the **Clipboard** group, click the **Format Painter** button.

14. If necessary, scroll up in the document, and click the **Joyce** picture.

    Word copies the grayscale format, color corrections, and picture style from one picture to the other.

15. Scroll down until the **Online Training Solutions, Inc. (OTSI)** heading is visible, click to the left of the **OTSI specializes** paragraph, press Enter, and then press Up Arrow.

16. On the **Insert** tab, in the **Illustration** group, click the **Picture** button. Then in the **Chapter05** folder displayed in the **Insert Picture** dialog box, double-click the **OTSI-Logo** graphic.

17. With the logo selected, on the **Format** contextual tab, in the **Adjust** group, click the **Artistic Effects** button.

18. In the **Artistic Effects** gallery, preview each thumbnail, and then click the last thumbnail in the fifth row (**Glow Edges**). Click away from the picture to see the effect.

    The logo now has a black-and-white stylized effect.

You can use artistic effects to make pictures look like paintings, pencil sketches, cutouts and more.

Tip To move a picture, simply drag it to the desired location. Tocopy a graphic, hold down the Ctrl key while you drag, releasing first the mouse button and then the Ctrl key. (If you release Ctrl first, Word will move the image instead of copying it.)

CLEAN UP Save the Authors document, and then close it.

About Clip Art

If you want to dress up a document with a graphic but you don't have a suitable picture, you might want to search for a clip art image. Clip art comes in many different styles and formats, including illustrations, photographs, videos, and audio clips. The only thing the clips have in common is that they are free and available without any copyright restrictions.

Clicking the Clip Art button displays the Clip Art task pane, where you can enter a search term to look for an image on your computer or on the Office.com Web site. When clip art images matching your search term are displayed in the task pane, you can click an image to insert it in your document. If you don't want to insert an image at the cursor but want it to be available for use somewhere else, you can point to the image in the Clip Art task pane, click the arrow that appears, and then click Copy to store a copy of the image on the Microsoft Office Clipboard. If you find an image on Office.com and want to be able to insert it in documents when you are not online, you can point to the arrow, click Make Available Offline, and then store it in a clip art collection. You can also edit the keywords associated with an image and view its properties.

To find and insert a clip art image:

1. Position the cursor where you want the image to appear. Then on the Insert tab, in the Illustrations group, click the Clip Art button.

2. In the Clip Art task pane, select the current entry in the Search For box (or click in the box if there is no entry), and enter a keyword for the type of clip art you are looking for, such as *cats*. Then select the Include Office.com Content check box, and click Go.

   Tip You can restrict the search results to a particular type of clip art by selecting the type in the Results Should Be list.

   The task pane displays any clip art images that have your keyword associated with them.

Cat-related clip art images from your computer and Office.com.

3. In the task pane, click the image you want to insert into the document.

   You can then manipulate the clip art image the same way you would a picture.

Changing a Document's Background

Whether you're creating a document that will be printed, viewed on a computer, or published on the Internet and viewed in a Web browser, you can make your document stand out by adding a background color, texture, or picture to every page in a document. You can also add borders to every page.

See Also For information about creating documents for the Web, see "Creating and Modifying Web Documents" in Chapter 11, "Create Documents for Use Outside of Word."

When it comes to backgrounds, the trick is to not overdo it. Your effects need to be subtle enough that they do not interfere with the text or other elements on the page.

In this exercise, you'll first apply a solid background color to every page. Then you'll create a two-color gradient across the pages. You'll fill the pages with one of the textures that come with Word and then fill them with a picture. Finally, you'll put a border around every page.

SET UP You need the MarbleFloor picture located in your Chapter05 practice file folder to complete this exercise. Open a blank document, turn off the rulers and formatting marks, and then follow the steps.

1. In the lower-right corner of the program window, click the **Zoom Level** button, and set the zoom percentage to display the whole page.

2. On the **Page Layout** tab, in the **Page Background** group, click the **Page Color** button, and then under **Theme Colors**, in the column of green boxes, click the second box from the top (**Olive Green, Accent 3, Lighter 60%**).

   The background of the document changes to the selected color.

3. In the **Page Background** group, click the **Page Color** button, and then click **Fill Effects**.

   The Fill Effects dialog box opens.

The Gradient page of the Fill Effects dialog box.

4. In the **Colors** area, click **Two colors**, and then leaving **Color 1** set to light green, click the **Color 2** arrow, and in the fifth column of boxes, select the top box (**Blue, Accent 1, Lighter 80%**).

    The Variants and Sample areas change to show graded combinations of the two colors.

5. In the **Shading styles** area, click each option in turn and observe the effects in the **Variants** and **Sample** areas. Then click **Diagonal Up**.

6. In the **Variants** area, click the option in the upper-left corner, and then click **OK**.

    The background of the document is now shaded from light green to light blue.

7. Display the **Fill Effects** dialog box again, and click the **Texture** tab.

   On this page, you can select from a number of texture files that come with Word.

The Texture page of the Fill Effects dialog box.

8. Click the effect in the second column of the third row (**White Marble**), and then click **OK**.

   The background changes to display the effect rather than the color.

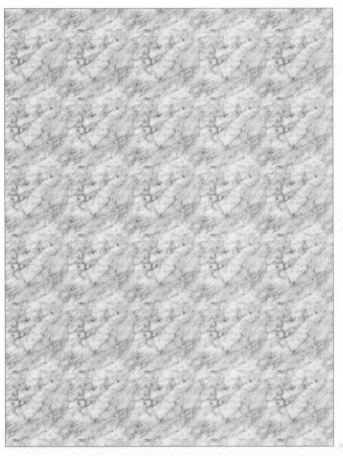

The page with the White Marble texture applied to the background.

9. Display the **Fill Effects** dialog box again, and click the **Picture** tab. Then click **Select Picture**, and with the contents of your **Chapter05** practice file folder displayed in the **Select Picture** dialog box, double-click **MarbleFloor**. In the **Fill Effects** dialog box, click **OK**.

The background changes to display a blurred picture of a marble floor in the Doge's Palace in Venice.

The page with the MarbleFloor picture applied to the background.

Tip Word fills the page with as much of the picture as will fit. If one copy of the picture does not completely fill the page, Word inserts another copy, effectively "tiling" the image.

Page Borders   10. In the **Page Background** group, click the **Page Borders** button.

The Borders And Shading dialog box opens with the Page Border page active.

The Page Border page is almost the same as the Borders page, except that an Art option is available at the bottom of the center pane.

11. In the **Setting** area of the **Borders and Shading** dialog box, click **Box**. Then in the **Color** list, click the third box in the blue column (**Blue, Accent 1, Lighter 40%**).

12. In the **Art** list, scroll down, clicking any art option you like to see it applied to the page in the **Preview** pane. When you find a style you like, click **OK**.

We chose a classic double border near the bottom of the Art list.

The page with a double border applied on top of the picture background.

13. Press Ctrl+Enter to insert a page break, and then scroll to the second page.

    When you apply a background, it is reflected in all the pages of the document.

CLEAN UP If you want, save the document as *PageBackground*, and then close it.

Inserting Building Blocks

To simplify the creation of professional-looking text elements, Word 2010 comes with ready-made visual representations of text, known as *building blocks*, which are available from various groups on the Insert tab. You can insert the following types of building blocks:

- **Cover page** You can quickly add a formatted cover page to a longer document such as a report by selecting a style from the Cover Page gallery. The cover page includes text placeholders for elements such as a title so that you can customize the page to reflect the content of the document.

  Tip You can also insert a blank page anywhere in a document—even in the middle of a paragraph—by positioning the cursor and then clicking the Blank Page button in the Pages group on the Insert tab.

- **Header and footer** You can display information on every page of a document in regions at the top and bottom of a page by selecting a style from the Header or Footer gallery. Word indicates the header and footer areas by displaying dotted borders and displays a Design contextual tab on the ribbon. You can enter information in the header and footer areas the same way you enter ordinary text. You can have a different header and footer on the first page of a document and different headers and footers on odd and even pages.

  Tip If your document contains section breaks, each successive section inherits the headers and footers of the preceding section unless you break the link between the two sections. You can then create a different header and footer for the current section. For information about sections, see "Controlling What Appears on Each Page" in Chapter 6, "Preview, Print, and Distribute Documents."

- **Page number** You can quickly add headers and footers that include only page numbers and require no customization by selecting the style you want from one of the Page Number galleries.

- **Text box** To reinforce key concepts and also alleviate the monotony of page after page of plain text, you can insert text boxes such as sidebars and quote boxes by selecting a style from the Text Box gallery. The formatted text box includes placeholder text that you replace with your own.

If you frequently use a specific element in your documents, such as a formatted title-subtitle-author arrangement at the beginning of reports, you can define it as a custom building block. It is then available from the Quick Parts gallery.

See Also For information about saving frequently used text as a custom building block, see "Inserting Saved Text" in Chapter 2, "Edit and Proofread Text."

You can see a list of all the available building blocks by clicking the Quick Parts button in the Text group on the Insert tab and then clicking Building Blocks Organizer.

The Building Blocks Organizer dialog box.

Initially the building blocks are organized by type, as reflected in the Gallery column. If you want to insert building blocks of the same design in a document, you might want to sort the list alphabetically by design name, by clicking the Name column heading. For example, a cover page, footer, header, quote box, and sidebar are all available with the Pinstripes design. Some elements, such as bibliographies, equations, tables of contents, tables, and watermarks, are not part of a design family and have their own unique names.

Tip You can see more information about each building block by dragging the horizontal scroll box to display the right side of the Building Blocks list.

At the bottom of the Building Blocks Organizer dialog box, you can click Edit Properties to display a dialog box where you can see the information about a selected building block in a more readable format. If you are viewing the properties associated with a custom building block, you can change them in this dialog box, but we don't recommend changing the properties assigned to a building block that came with Word.

Modify Building Block	? ✕
Name:	Pinstripes Sidebar
Gallery:	Text Boxes
Category:	Built-In
Description:	Right-aligned sidebar with accent shadow
Save in:	Building Blocks
Options:	Insert content only
	OK Cancel

The Modify Building Block dialog box.

You can delete a selected custom building block from the list by clicking Delete at the bottom of the Building Blocks Organizer dialog box, and you can insert a selected building block into the document by clicking Insert.

In this exercise, you'll insert a cover page and add a header and footer to a document. You'll also insert two kinds of text boxes with the same design. Finally, you'll save a customized sidebar as a building block.

SET UP You need the Flyer_start document located in your Chapter05 practice file folder to complete this exercise. Open the Flyer_start document, and save it as *Flyer*. Then follow the steps.

1. Click the **Zoom Level** button in the lower-right corner of the program window. In the **Zoom** dialog box, click **Whole page**, and then click **OK**.

2. With the cursor at the top of the document, on the **Insert** tab, in the **Pages** group, click the **Cover Page** button.

The Cover Page gallery appears.

The thumbnails show the designs of the available cover pages.

3. Scroll through the **Cover Page** gallery to see the available options, and then click **Pinstripes**.

   Word inserts the cover page at the beginning of the document and adds placeholders for the title, subtitle, date, company name, and author name.

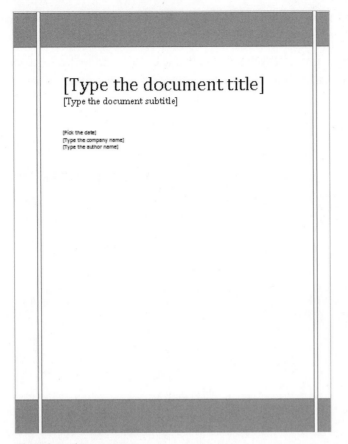

The selected cover page.

Tip If any of the required information is attached to the document as properties, Word inserts the information instead of the placeholder.

4. Click anywhere in the title placeholder, and type **Simple Room Design**. Then click the **Pick the date** placeholder, click the arrow that appears, and in the calendar, click today's date (indicated by a red box). Delete the remaining placeholder paragraphs.

5. On the **Insert** tab, in the **Header & Footer** group, click the **Header** button. Scroll through the **Header** gallery, and then click **Pinstripes**.

   Word displays the Design contextual tab, dims the text of the document, and indicates the header and footer areas with dotted lines.

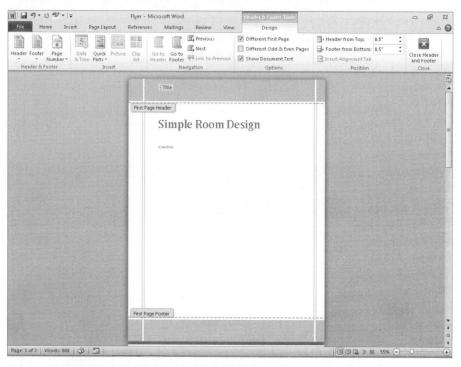

   Because the Different First Page check box in the Options group on the Design tab is selected, the header area is labeled First Page Header.

6. In the **Navigation** group, click the **Next** button.

   Word moves to the next section of the document, which is the page after the cover page.

7. Type **Wide World Importers**. Then on the **Home** tab, in the **Paragraph** group, click the **Center** button.

8. On the **Design** tab, in the **Navigation** group, click the **Go to Footer** button.

   The cursor moves to the footer area at the bottom of the page.

9. In the **Header & Footer** group, click the **Page Number** button, point to **Current Position** in the list, and then in the gallery, click **Large Color**.

   Except for the first page of the document, the pages now have a header and footer.

Headers and footers can include any information you want repeated on each page in a section, including graphics.

Tip To use a numbering scheme other than Arabic numerals, to number pages by chapter, or to control the starting number, click the Page Number button in the Header & Footer group, and then click Format Page Numbers. In the Page Number Format dialog box, click the Number Format arrow, and then in the list, click the format you want.

10. In the **Close** group, click the **Close Header and Footer** button.

11. At the top of the second page, delete **Simple Room Design**. Then on the **Insert** tab, in the **Text** group, click the **Quick Parts** button, and click **Building Blocks Organizer**.

    The Building Blocks Organizer shown at the beginning of this topic opens. The left pane displays a complete list of all the building blocks available on your computer. Clicking a building block in the left pane displays a preview in the right pane.

    Tip The Building Blocks list you see on your computer includes AutoText entries for your user name and initials. To change either of these entries, display the Backstage view, click Options, and then on the General page of the Word Options dialog box, update your information and click OK.

12. Scroll through the **Building blocks** list, previewing a few of the building blocks. Then click the **Name** column heading, and scroll through the list again.

    Notice that page elements of the same theme are coordinated.

The Building Blocks Organizer dialog box, after the Name column has been sorted.

13. In the **Building blocks** list, click **Pinstripes Quote** (the first of the **Pinstripes** text boxes), and then below the list, click **Insert**.

    Word inserts the quote box halfway down the right side of the page.

Placeholder text in the quote box tells you how to insert your own text and format the block.

14. Click the **Zoom Out** button on the **Zoom Slider** until you can read the text of the document. Then select and copy the last sentence of the fourth paragraph (**Go with what you love...**).

15. Click the quote box to select the placeholder text. Then on the **Home** tab, in the **Clipboard** group, click the **Paste** arrow, and under **Paste Options**, click the **Keep Text Only** button.

The copied text replaces the placeholder, and because it was pasted as unformatted text, it retains the formatting of the placeholder text. The quote box automatically resizes to fit its new contents.

See Also   For information about text boxes, see the sidebar "Drawing Text Boxes" later in this chapter.

16. Display the whole page again. Then scroll to the last page of the document, and click anywhere on the page.

17. On the **Insert** tab, in the **Text** group, click the **Text Box** button, scroll through the gallery, and click **Pinstripes Sidebar**.

Word inserts the sidebar down the right side of the page.

This sidebar consists of two overlapping, coordinated boxes.

18. If necessary, zoom out so that you can see the text well enough to edit it. Then at the beginning of the last paragraph of the document, delete **NOTE:** (including the colon and following space).

19. Select the last paragraph, and on the **Home** tab, in the **Clipboard** group, click the **Cut** button.

> **Keyboard Shortcut** Press Ctrl+X to cut the selected content to the Clipboard.
>
> **See Also** For more information about keyboard shortcuts, see "Keyboard Shortcuts" at the end of this book.

20. Click the sidebar to select the placeholder text. Then in the **Clipboard** group, click the **Paste** arrow, and under **Paste Options**, click the **Keep Text Only** button.

The sidebar now contains the cut text.

Wide World Importers

If you're not sure you made the right choices and don't know which way to turn, arrange to meet with one of our designers. This free service is available to all our customers. Sometimes talking over your plans or obstacles with a professional can really help get you back on track.

Success! Your room is everything you hoped for. Now what about your bedroom? Maybe a new linen chest or perhaps new window treatments? The Room Planner can be used countless times for any room in the house. And if you're eyeing your patio or deck as your next makeover project, you'll want to check out the Outdoor Room Planner, too.

To order the Room Planner for just $39.99 plus shipping and handling, visit our Web site at www.wideworldimporters.com or call us at 925-555-0167. The Outdoor Room Planner retails for $29.99 plus shipping and handling. Both planners are also available in our stores, so be sure to ask about them the next time you visit. We accept all major credit cards.

The pasted text takes on the formatting assigned to the text box.

21. To widen the sidebar so that the Web site address fits on one line, click the sidebar text, and drag the blue handle on the dotted line at the left side of the white box to the left, until it sits slightly to the left of the frame of the white box.

If the Web site address still doesn't fit, adjust the width of the sidebar again.

22. Click at the top of the sidebar's blue box. Then on the **Insert** tab, in the **Text** group, click the **Quick Parts** button, and click **Save Selection to Quick Part Gallery**.

    Troubleshooting If you click the text in the sidebar or elsewhere in the document after resizing the sidebar, the sidebar will no longer be selected and the Save Selection To Quick Part Gallery command will not be available.

    The Create New Building Block dialog box opens.

23. Replace the text in the **Name** box with **Order Sidebar**, and then click **OK**.

    You can now insert this custom sidebar from the Quick Parts gallery into other documents.

24. In the **Text** group, click the **Quick Parts** button.

    The Quick Parts gallery appears.

The Order Sidebar custom building block appears at the top of the gallery.

25. Click **Building Blocks Organizer**, and then in the **Building Blocks Organizer** dialog box, click the **Category** column heading to sort the **Building blocks** list by that column.

26. In the **Building blocks** list, scroll to the **General** category, and click **Order Sidebar** once.

The building block you just created appears in the preview pane.

The General category includes your custom building block and the user name and initials AutoText entries.

CLEAN UP If you want, delete the building block you just created before you close the Building Blocks Organizer dialog box. Then save the Flyer document, and close it.

Important When you exit Word after saving a custom building block, you'll be asked whether you want to save changes to the template in which you stored the building block. If you want the building block to be available for future documents, click Save; otherwise, click Don't Save.

Drawing Text Boxes

If none of the predefined text-box building blocks meets your needs, you can draw your own text box. At the bottom of the Text Box gallery, click Draw Text Box, and then drag a box the size you want anywhere on the page. You can immediately start typing at the blinking cursor, and you can format the text the way you would any other text.

When a text box is surrounded by a dashed border, it's selected for text editing. To manipulate the text box itself, you need to click its frame.

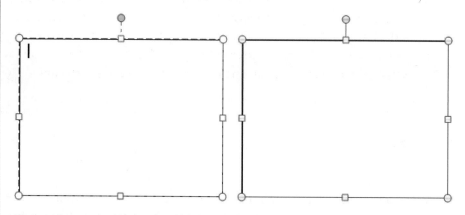

The text box on the left is selected for editing, and the one on the right is selected for manipulation.

When a text box has a solid border, you can reposition it by dragging it to another location, and you can change its size by dragging the size handles around its frame. You can change the outline and fill colors by using the commands in the Shape Styles group on the Format contextual tab.

You can link text boxes so that text flows from one to the next. To do so:

1. Click the first text box.

2. In the Text group on the Format contextual tab, click Create Link.

   The mouse pointer changes to a small pitcher.

3. Point to the second text box, and then when the mouse pointer changes to a pouring pitcher, click once.

   Note that the second text box must be empty.

Adding WordArt Text

If you're familiar with WordArt in earlier versions of Word, you're in for a surprise. WordArt has matured from the fun little tool you might have used in the past to create headings in molded shapes and gaudy colors. Its capabilities are now oriented toward creating more sophisticated display-text objects that you can position anywhere on the page. Although the WordArt object is attached to the paragraph that contained the cursor when you created it, you can move it independently from the text, even positioning it over the text if you want.

To insert a WordArt object, you click the WordArt button in the Text group on the Insert tab, and click a text style in the WordArt gallery. (The WordArt styles are the same as the text effects available in the Text Effects gallery in the Font group of the Home tab.) Then you enter your text in the text box that appears. You can edit the text, adjust the character formatting in the usual ways, and change the text style at any time.

Tip You can also select existing text before clicking the WordArt button to convert that text into a WordArt object.

See Also For information about character formatting, see "Manually Changing the Look of Characters" in Chapter 3, "Change the Look of Text." For information about text effects, see "Quickly Formatting Text" in the same chapter.

When a WordArt object is selected, the Format contextual tab appears on the ribbon. You can use the commands on this tab to format the WordArt object to meet your needs. For example, from the Format tab, you can add effects such as shadows and 3-D effects, change the fill and outline colors, and change the text direction and alignment. You can also position the WordArt object in any of several predefined locations on the page, as well as specify how the text should wrap around the object.

Tip Don't go too wild with WordArt formatting. Many WordArt Styles and Shape Styles take up space and can involve trial and error to produce a neat effect.

In this exercise, you'll insert a new WordArt object, modify it, and then position it on the page. Then you'll change the way it relates to the text on the page.

SET UP You need the Announcement_start document located in your Chapter05 practice file folder to complete this exercise. Open the Announcement_start document and save it as *Announcement*. Then with the rulers and formatting marks turned off, follow the steps.

1. On the **Insert** tab, in the **Text** group, click the **WordArt** button.

   The WordArt gallery appears, displaying the same formatted letters you see when you click the Text Effects button.

2. Click the third thumbnail in the fifth row (**Fill – Red, Accent 2, Warm Matte Bevel**).

   Word inserts a WordArt object with that text effect at the cursor. Because a graphic object is selected, the Format contextual tab appears on the ribbon.

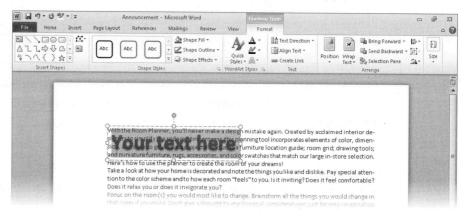

The WordArt object contains placeholder text in the style you chose.

Tip If formatting marks are displayed, you see an anchor icon adjacent to the first paragraph. You can ignore it for now.

See Also For information about anchoring objects, see "Arranging Objects on the Page" in Chapter 10, "Organize and Arrange Content."

3. With **Your Text Here** selected, type **The Room Planner**. (Don't type the period.)

   Tip WordArt objects can accommodate multiple lines. Simply press Enter if you want to start a new line.

4. Without moving the cursor, on the **Home** tab, in the **Paragraph** group, click the **Center** button.

5. Click the border of the text box to select the box, and then change the zoom percentage so that you can see the whole page.

6. On the **Format** contextual tab, in the **Arrange** group, click the **Position** button.

   The Position gallery appears.

You can position the WordArt object in one of 10 predefined positions.

7. Point to each thumbnail in turn to preview where each option will place the object. Then under **With Text Wrapping**, click the second thumbnail in the second row (**Position in Middle Center with Square Text Wrapping**).

   The object moves to the middle of the page.

   Don't worry if the word *Planner* is now truncated. Because of the interaction of the object with its surrounding text, sometimes not all the WordArt text fits in its box after you position it. You'll fix that in a minute.

8. In the **Arrange** group, click the **Wrap Text** button.

   The Wrap Text gallery appears.

You can change the text wrapping without changing the position.

9. Point to each thumbnail in turn to preview their effects, and then click **Tight**.

10. In the **Arrange** group, click the **Wrap Text** button, and then click **More Layout Options**.

The Layout dialog box opens with the Text Wrapping page active.

If you know what kind of text wrapping you want, you can select it on this page of the dialog box, but you can't preview it.

11. In the **Distance from text** area, change the **Left** and **Right** settings to **0.3"**, and then click **OK**.

The text outside the box is no longer encroaching on the box.

If the word *Planner* was truncated in your box, the entire word should now be displayed. If it isn't, try increasing the Distance From Text settings to 0.4".

12. In the **WordArt Styles** group, display the **WordArt Quick Styles** gallery, and then click the fourth thumbnail in the third row (**Gradient Fill – Blue, Accent 1**).

Troubleshooting Depending on your screen resolution and program window size, you might have to click the Quick Styles button to display the gallery.

13. In the **Shape Styles** group, display the **Shape Styles** gallery, and then click the fourth thumbnail in the fourth row (**Subtle Effect – Olive Green, Accent 3**).

14. Press Ctrl+Home.

    Now you can see the effect of the WordArt text.

This simple text banner is a stylish alternative to a traditional title.

15. If you want, experiment with combinations of the styles and formatting available on the **Format** tab.

    For example, you might want to try some of the Text Effects options, such as the molding effects available in the Transform gallery.

✖ CLEAN UP Save the Announcement document, and then close it.

Formatting the First Letter of a Paragraph

Many books, magazines, and reports begin the first paragraph of a section or chapter by using an enlarged, decorative capital letter. Called a *dropped capital*, or simply a *drop cap*, this effect can be an easy way to give a document a finished, professional look.

The Drop Cap gallery provides two basic drop-cap styles:

- **Dropped** Sits in the text column and displaces paragraph text
- **In margin** Hangs in the margin adjacent to the paragraph text

In either case, the drop cap is as tall as three lines of text and uses the same font as the rest of the paragraph.

To insert a drop cap:

1. Click anywhere in a paragraph of text, and then on the Insert tab, in the Text group, click the Drop Cap button.

2. Point to each thumbnail to display its live preview, and then click the one you want.

   Word inserts the first letter of the paragraph in a box. If you selected Dropped, Word rewraps the text to the right of the graphic.

For more options, click Drop Cap Options at the bottom of the Drop Cap gallery to open the Drop Cap dialog box. You can choose a font that is different from the paragraph and adjust the drop cap's height and distance from the text.

If you want to make the first word of the paragraph stand out, you can click to the right of the drop cap and type the rest of the word. If you do this, don't forget to delete the word from the beginning of the paragraph!

Key Points

- You can insert illustrations created with most graphics programs, as well as digital photos, into a Word document.
- A background color, texture, pattern, or picture can really give a document pizzazz, but be careful that it doesn't overwhelm the text.
- Word comes with predefined building blocks that quickly add graphic elements to a document.
- Using WordArt, you can easily add fancy text to a document and then format and position it for the best effect.

Chapter at a Glance

Preview and adjust
page layout, **page 182**

Print documents,
page 193

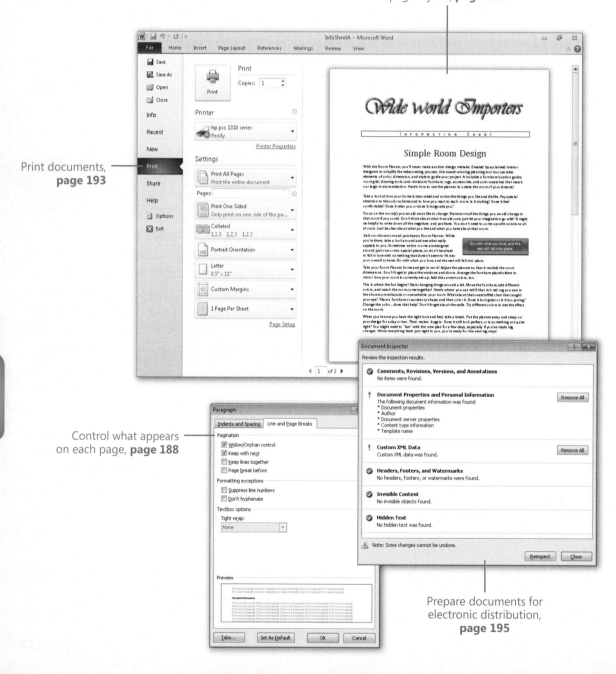

Control what appears
on each page, **page 188**

Prepare documents for
electronic distribution,
page 195

6 Preview, Print, and Distribute Documents

In this chapter, you will learn how to

✔ Preview and adjust page layout.

✔ Control what appears on each page.

✔ Print documents.

✔ Prepare documents for electronic distribution.

When you finish developing a document, you'll often want to distribute either a printed version or an electronic version. Before committing the document to paper, you should check that the pages are efficiently laid out and that there are no glaring problems, such as headings that print on separate pages from their text. Microsoft Word 2010 provides several tools you can use to manipulate how much text appears on each page and to control page layout. It also provides tools for finalizing an electronic document and ensuring that the end product of all your hard work contains no traces of personal or confidential information. When you are ready to print, you can control precisely how many copies and what parts of your document appear on paper.

In this chapter, you'll first preview a document and make some adjustments to improve its presentation. Then you'll look at the options available for controlling page breaks. You'll print a document, and finally, you'll inspect and finalize it for electronic distribution.

> **Practice Files** Before you can complete the exercises in this chapter, you need to copy the book's practice files to your computer. The practice files you'll use to complete the exercises in this chapter are in the Chapter06 practice file folder. A complete list of practice files is provided in "Using the Practice Files" at the beginning of this book.

Previewing and Adjusting Page Layout

Usually while you're creating a document, you'll make decisions about the size of the margins and the direction of the page (called the *orientation*) to best suit your content. You can use the Margins and Orientation commands in the Page Setup group of the Page Layout tab to make any necessary adjustments to the document, and you can use the Size command to change the paper size.

You can also display the Page Setup dialog box, where you can make these basic layout changes all in one place.

You can adjust all the page layout settings in one place.

Working on your document in Print Layout view helps to ensure that the document looks tidy on the page. However, before you print the document, you'll almost always want to check how it will look on paper by previewing it. Previewing is essential for multipage documents but is helpful even for one-page documents. To preview a document, you display the Print page of the Backstage view and then page through the document displayed in the right pane. This view shows exactly how each page of the document will look when printed on the specified printer.

The Print page of the Backstage view.

If you don't like what you see in the preview pane of the Print page, you don't have to leave the Backstage view to make adjustments. The middle pane of the Print page provides tools for making the following changes:

- **Orientation** You can switch the direction in which a page is laid out on the paper. The default orientation is Portrait, in which the page is taller than it is wide. You can set the orientation to Landscape, in which the page is wider than it is tall.

- **Paper size** You can switch to one of the sizes available for the selected printer by making a selection from a list.

- **Margins** Changing the margins of a document changes where information can appear on each page. You can select one of Word's predefined sets of top, bottom, left, and right margins, or set custom margins.

  Tip All the pages of a document have the same orientation and margins unless you divide the document into sections. Then each section can have independent orientation and margin settings. For more information about sections, see "Controlling What Appears on Each Page" later in this chapter.

If your printer is capable of scaling the pages of your document, you'll also see an option to set the number of pages to print per sheet of paper, up to 16. You might use this option to print a booklet with two pages per sheet that will be folded in the middle. You might also be tempted to use this option to save paper, but bear in mind that the smaller the pages, the harder it is to read them.

You can also open the Page Setup dialog box from the Print page to make multiple adjustments in one place.

In this exercise, you'll preview a document, change the orientation, and adjust the margins.

SET UP You need the InfoSheetA_start document located in the Chapter06 practice file folder, and an active printer connection, to complete this exercise. Open the InfoSheetA_start document, and save it as *InfoSheetA*. Then follow the steps.

1. Display the Backstage view, and in the left pane, click **Print**.

   Keyboard Shortcut Press Ctrl+P to display the Print page of the Backstage view.

   See Also For more information about keyboard shortcuts, see "Keyboard Shortcuts" at the end of this book.

The Print page is displayed, with a preview of the document on the right. The shaded background of the document is not displayed because it will not be printed.

`61%`

2. In the lower-right corner of the preview pane, click the **Zoom** button, and then in the **Zoom** dialog box, click **Many pages**, click the monitor button, and click the second page icon in the top row of the grid (**1x2 Pages**). Then click **OK**.

Word displays the two pages of the document side by side.

You can preview multiple pages.

Tip If you want to preview a multipage document as it will look when printed on both sides of the page and bound, add a blank page to the beginning of the document before previewing it.

3. Under **Settings** in the middle pane, click **Custom Margins**.

The gallery of margin options appears.

Normal
Top: 1"   Bottom: 1"
Left: 1"   Right: 1"

Narrow
Top: 0.5"   Bottom: 0.5"
Left: 0.5"   Right: 0.5"

Moderate
Top: 1"   Bottom: 1"
Left: 0.75"   Right: 0.75"

Wide
Top: 1"   Bottom: 1"
Left: 2"   Right: 2"

Mirrored
Top: 1"   Bottom: 1"
Inside: 1.25"   Outside:1"

Office 2003 Default
Top: 1"   Bottom: 1"
Left: 1.25"   Right: 1.25"

Custom Margins

Custom Margins...

You can select predefined margins or set your own.

4. In the list, click **Wide**.

   The text rewraps within the new margins.

5. In the page range in the lower-left corner of the preview pane, click the **Next Page** button.

   The page range updates to show that the document now has three pages and that page 2 is the active page.

6. Click the **Next Page** button again to see the last page of the document.

7. At the bottom of the middle pane, click **Page Setup**.

   The Page Setup dialog box opens, displaying the Margins page. Notice that selecting Wide margins on the Print page set the left and right margins to 2 inches.

8. In the **Pages** area, display the **Multiple pages** list, and click **Mirror Margins**.

   The Preview area now displays two pages side by side, and in the Margins area, Left and Right have changed to Inside and Outside.

9. In the **Margins** area, change the value in the **Outside** box to **1"**.

    Tip You can either type a new value or click the down arrow at the right end of the box.

    In the pages in the Preview area, the width of the outside margins decreases.

You might use the Mirror Margins setting if you were planning on printing on both sides of the paper and then stapling the pages.

10. Return the **Multiple pages** setting to **Normal**, and in the **Margins** area, change the value in the **Left** box to **1"**.

11. If you want, in the **Page Setup** dialog box, click the **Paper** tab and then the **Layout** tab, and notice the available options on those pages. Then click **OK**.

    On the Print page, the margins setting is now Normal Margins, and the page range indicator shows that the number of pages in the document has decreased to two.

✖ CLEAN UP Save the InfoSheetA document, and then close it.

Controlling What Appears on Each Page

When a document includes more content than will fit between its top and bottom margins, Word creates a new page by inserting a soft page break. If you want to break a page before Word would normally break it, you can insert a manual page break in one of three ways:

- Click Page Break in the Pages group on the Insert tab.
- Click Breaks in the Page Setup group on the Page Layout tab, and then click Page.
- Press Ctrl+Enter.

Tip As you edit the text in a document, Word changes the location of the soft page breaks, but the program cannot change the location of any manual page breaks you might have inserted.

If a paragraph breaks so that most of it appears on one page but its last line appears at the top of the next page, the line is called a *widow*. If a paragraph breaks so that its first line appears at the bottom of one page and the rest of the paragraph appears on the next page, the line is called an *orphan*. These single lines of text can make a document hard to read, so by default, Word specifies that a minimum of two lines should appear at the top and bottom of each page. However, on the Line And Page Breaks page of the Paragraph dialog box, you can change whether page breaks are allowed to create widows and orphans. You can also change the following options:

- **Keep with next** This option controls whether Word will break a page between the paragraph containing the cursor and the following paragraph.
- **Keep lines together** This option controls whether Word will break a page within a paragraph.
- **Page break before** This option controls whether Word will break a page before the paragraph containing the cursor.

The Line And Page Breaks page of the Paragraph dialog box.

Tip You can apply these options to individual paragraphs, or you can incorporate them into the styles you define for document elements such as headings. For information about styles, see "Working with Styles and Templates" in Chapter 16, "Work in Word More Efficiently."

In addition to page breaks, you can insert section breaks in your documents. A section break identifies a part of the document that has page settings, such as orientation or margins, that are different from those of the rest of the document. For example, you might want to put a large table in its own section so that you can turn it sideways by changing its orientation to Landscape.

You insert a section break by clicking Breaks in the Page Setup group on the Page Layout tab and then selecting from the following section types:

- **Next Page**   Starts the following section on the next page
- **Continuous**   Starts a new section without affecting page breaks
- **Even Page**   Starts the following section on the next even-numbered page
- **Odd Page**   Starts the following section on the next odd-numbered page

If formatting marks are displayed, a section break appears in Print Layout view as a double-dotted line from the preceding paragraph mark to the margin, with the words *Section Break* and the type of section break in the middle of the line.

Tip   To remove a page or section break, click at the left end of the break and then press the Delete key.

In this exercise, you'll insert page and section breaks, and ensure that the pages break in logical places.

SET UP   You need the OfficeInfo_start document located in the Chapter06 practice file folder to complete this exercise. Open the OfficeInfo_start document, and save it as *OfficeInfo*. Display formatting marks, and then follow the steps.

1. Scroll through the document, noticing any awkward page breaks, such as a topic or list that starts close to the bottom of a page.

2. On the **Home** tab, in the **Editing** group, click the **Select** button, and then click **Select All**.

3. Click the **Paragraph** dialog box launcher, and then in the **Paragraph** dialog box, click the **Line and Page Breaks** tab.

   Because different settings have been applied to different paragraphs in the document, all the check boxes have a solid filling.

Paragraph   [?] [x]

| Indents and Spacing | Line and Page Breaks |

Pagination
- ▣ Widow/Orphan control
- ▣ Keep with next
- ▣ Keep lines together
- ▣ Page break before

Formatting exceptions
- ▣ Suppress line numbers
- ▣ Don't hyphenate

Textbox options
Tight wrap:
[▾]

When multiple paragraphs are selected, solid check boxes indicate that the paragraphs have different settings.

4. Double-click all the check boxes to clear them.

5. Select the **Keep lines together** check box (click more than once if necessary), and then click **OK**.

   This setting ensures that none of the paragraphs will be broken across two pages. Word alerts you to the presence of this formatting by displaying a square symbol to the left of each paragraph.

6. Press Ctrl+Home to release the selection, and then scroll through the document, again looking for untidy page breaks.

7. Click to the left of the **Facilities** heading.

8. On the **Insert** tab, in the **Pages** group, click the **Page Break** button.

   Keyboard Shortcut Press Ctrl+Enter to insert a page break.

   Word breaks the page and moves the *Facilities* heading and the following text to the next page.

9. Scroll down to the bottom of page **3**, select the **Supplies** heading and the three lines that follow it (the third line is at the top of page **4**), and then display the **Line and Page Breaks** page of the **Paragraph** dialog box.

10. In the **Pagination** area, leave the **Keep lines together** check box selected, select the **Keep with next** check box, and then click **OK**.

    Word moves the selection to the next page.

11. Scroll down to page **9**, and click to the left of the **Shipping Quick Reference** heading.

    Tip If you drag the scroll box in the scroll bar, Word displays a ScreenTip with the number of the page that will be displayed if you release the mouse button.

12. On the **Page Layout** tab, in the **Page Setup** group, click the **Breaks** button, and then under **Section Breaks**, click **Next Page**.

    Word pushes the heading to the next page.

13. Scroll up until the text on page **9** is displayed.

    A double dotted line with the words *Section Break (Next Page)* appears at the right end of the paragraph preceding the section break.

The section break indicator.

14. Scroll down to page **10**, and with the cursor in the **Shipping Quick Reference** heading, on the **Page Layout** tab, in the **Page Setup** group, click the **Margins** button. Then in the **Margins** gallery, click **Wide**.

    The table in the new section shrinks in width to fit between the wider margins.

15. On the **Insert** tab, in the **Header & Footer** group, click the **Header** button, and then click **Edit Header**.

    In the Navigation group of the Design contextual tab, the Link To Previous button is selected, meaning that the header of the new section has inherited the settings of the preceding section. Because the preceding section has no header on its first page, this one doesn't have one either.

16. On the **Design** contextual tab, in the **Options** group, clear the **Different First Page** check box. Then click the **Close Header and Footer** button.

Now the header from pages 2 through 9 of the preceding section is repeated on page 10 in this section.

Office-Procedures¶

Page-10¶

. Shipping·Quick·Reference¶

	Package·for·shipment¤	¤
.Customer·information,·existing·account?¤		¤
.PO·for·payment·with·existing·account?¤		¤
.Shipping·company/method·of·shipment?¤		¤
.Delivery·when?¤		¤
.Invoice·and·tracking·slip¤		¤
.Process·order¤		¤
.Paperwork·to·customer¤		¤

You might have to adjust the header settings after creating a new section.

✖ **CLEAN UP** Save the OfficeInfo document, and then close it.

Printing Documents

When you are ready to print a document, you display the Print page of the Backstage view, and then, to print one copy on the current printer with the settings shown, you simply click the Print button.

If you need to use settings other than the defaults, you can change the following:

● **Number of copies** Click the arrows or type the number you need.

● **Printer** Switch to a different printer, or click Printer Properties to change the printer options.

● **Print range** Print the entire document, the selected text, the current page, or a custom range of pages. (Point to the information icon to the right of the Pages box to see the format in which to enter a custom range.)

● **Sides of the paper** Print on one side or both sides, either manually or, if your printer has duplex capability, automatically.

● **Collation** For multiple copies of a multipage document, print all the pages in the document as a set or print all the copies of each page as a set.

If your printer has multiple paper trays or a manual paper feeder, you can select the paper source you want to use, on the Paper page of the Page Setup dialog box.

In this exercise, you'll see how to select a different printer before sending two copies of the current page of a document to be printed.

 SET UP You need the InfoSheetB_start document located in the Chapter06 practice file folder, and multiple active printer connections, to complete this exercise. Open the InfoSheetB_start document, and save it as *InfoSheetB*. Then follow the steps.

1. Display the Backstage view, and in the left pane, click **Print**.

   If you don't need to change any settings, you can simply click the Print button at the top of the middle pane of the Print page.

2. If you have more than one printer available and you want to switch printers, under **Printer** in the middle pane, click the option displaying the name of the default printer, and in the list, click the printer you want.

3. Point to the information icon to the right of the **Printer** area heading.

   Tip You can also point to the selected printer.

   Information about your printer's status is displayed.

   Printer Status

   Status: Ready
   Type: hp psc 1310 series
   Where: USB001
   Comment:

   You can check your printer's status without leaving the Print page.

4. In the **Copies** box next to the **Print** button, change the number of copies to **2**.

5. Under **Settings**, click the arrow to the right of the first box to expand the list of print options, and then in the list, click **Print Current Page**.

6. Leaving the other settings as they are, click the **Print** button at the top of the middle pane.

   Word prints two copies of the document's first page on the designated printer, and returns you to the document.

 CLEAN UP Close the InfoSheetB document.

Preparing Documents for Electronic Distribution

When a document is complete, you can distribute it in two basic ways: on paper or electronically. If you distribute it electronically, you need to ensure that no private or inappropriate information is attached to the file and that it can be viewed by the people to whom you are sending it.

Many documents go through several revisions, and some are scrutinized by multiple reviewers. During this development process, documents can accumulate information that you might not want in the final version, such as the names of people who worked on the document, comments that reviewers have added to the file, or hidden text about status and assumptions. This extraneous information is not a concern if the final version is to be delivered as a printout. However, these days, more and more files are delivered electronically, making this information available to anyone who wants to read it.

To examine some of the attached information, you can display the document's proper-ties on the Info page of the Backstage view. You can change or remove the information in either the Document Panel or the Properties dialog box. However, Word provides a tool called the *Document Inspector* to automate the process of finding and removing all extraneous and potentially confidential information. After you run the Document Inspector, you see a summary of its search results, and you have the option of removing all the items found in each category.

Word also includes two other finalizing tools:

- **Check Accessibility** Checks for document elements and formatting that might be difficult for people with certain kinds of disabilities to read.

- **Check Compatibility** Checks for the use of features not supported in earlier versions of Word.

After you have handled extraneous information and accessibility and compatibility issues, you can mark a document as final and make it a read-only file, so that other people know that they should not make changes to this released document.

In this exercise, you'll inspect a document for inappropriate information and mark it as final.

➡ **SET UP** You need the InfoSheetC_start document located in the Chapter06 practice file folder to complete this exercise. Open the InfoSheetC_start document, and save it as *InfoSheetC*. Then follow the steps.

1. Display the Backstage view, and in the left pane, click **Info**.

   In the right pane you see the properties that have been saved with the file. Some of the information, including the name of the author, was attached to the file by Word. Other information, such as the title, was added by a user.

Properties ▾

Size	466KB
Pages	2
Words	814
Total Editing Time	29 Minutes
Title	INFORMATION SHEET
Tags	infosheets;handouts
Comments	background color under ...

Related Dates

Last Modified	Yesterday, 2:07 PM
Created	Yesterday, 2:07 PM
Last Printed	Today, 10:23 AM

Related People

Author	☐ Marlene Lambert
	Add an author
Last Modified By	☐ Sidney Higa

Related Documents

📁 Open File Location

The properties attached to this document.

Properties ▾

2. In the right pane, click the **Properties** button, and then in the list, click **Advanced Properties**.

   The Properties dialog box for this document opens. On the General page of the dialog box are properties maintained by Word.

3. Click the **Summary** tab.

   Notice that additional identifying information is displayed on this page.

InfoSheetC Properties ? ✕

| General | Summary | Statistics | Contents | Custom |

Title: INFORMATION SHEET

Subject: Room Makeover

Author: Marlene Lambert

Manager:

Company: Online Training Solutions, Inc

Category:

Keywords: infosheets;handouts

Comments: background color under discussion

Hyperlink base:

Template: Normal

☐ Save Thumbnails for All Word Documents

OK   Cancel

These properties were entered by the people who worked on the document.

Tip To make a document easier to find in Windows Explorer, you can add tags in the Properties area of the Info page or keywords in the Properties dialog box.

4. Click **Cancel** to close the **Properties** dialog box.

5. In the **Prepare for Sharing** area of the **Info** page, click **Check for Issues**, and then click **Inspect Document**.

   Troubleshooting If Word asks whether you want to save changes to the file, click Yes.

   The Document Inspector dialog box opens, listing the items that will be checked.

6. Without changing the default selections in the **Document Inspector** dialog box, click **Inspect**.

The Document Inspector reports the presence of the properties you viewed earlier, as well as some custom XML data.

The results of the inspection.

7. To the right of **Document Properties and Personal Information**, click **Remove All**.

8. To the right of **Custom XML Data**, click **Remove All**.

9. Click **Reinspect**, and then click **Inspect**.

Word has removed the properties and XML data.

10. In the **Document Inspector** dialog box, click **Close**.

The right pane of the Info page now shows that there are no custom properties attached to the document.

11. In the **Permissions** area of the **Info** page, click **Protect Document**, and then click **Mark As Final**.

    A message tells you that the document will be marked as final and then saved.

12. Click **OK**.

    A message tells you that the document has been marked as final and that typing, editing commands, and proofing marks are turned off.

13. Click **OK**.

    The Permissions area now indicates that the file is final.

    Permissions
    This document has been marked as final to discourage editing.

    Protect
    Document

    The Info page reminds people that the file is final.

14. Click the **Insert** tab.

    An orange bar appears, notifying you that the document has been marked as final.

15. Click the **Insert** tab again.

    The tab's groups and buttons are displayed, but all of the buttons are inactive.

    Tip If you really want to make changes to the document, you can click a tab to display the orange bar and then click the Edit Anyway button to unmark the file.

 CLEAN UP Save the InfoSheetC document, and then close it.

Tip If you need to distribute a document electronically but you don't want to share the actual file, you can "print" the document to a new file in XML Paper Specification (XPS) format. For information, see "Saving Files in Different Formats" in Chapter 11, "Create Documents for Use Outside of Word."

Key Points

- You should always preview a document before printing it.
- You can use page and section breaks and page break options to ensure that pages break in logical places.
- All the printing options are now gathered together on the Print page of the Backstage view.
- Before distributing a document, you can use the Document Inspector to remove private or inappropriate information.

Part 2

Document Enhancements

Chapter at a Glance

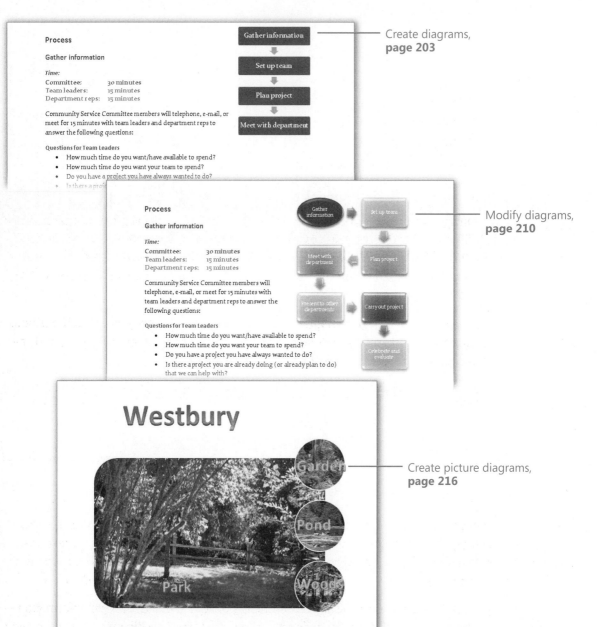

Create diagrams,
page 203

Modify diagrams,
page 210

Create picture diagrams,
page 216

7 Insert and Modify Diagrams

In this chapter, you will learn how to

✔ Create diagrams.

✔ Modify diagrams.

✔ Create picture diagrams.

Diagrams are graphics that convey information. Business documents often include diagrams to clarify concepts, describe processes, and show hierarchical relationships. Microsoft Word 2010 comes with a powerful diagramming tool called *SmartArt* that you can use to create diagrams directly in your documents. By using ready-made diagram templates, you can produce sophisticated results tailored to your needs.

In this chapter, you'll insert a diagram into a document and specify its size and position. Then you'll change the diagram's layout, visual style, and color theme. Finally, you'll see how to use a diagram to arrange pictures in a document.

> **Practice Files** Before you can complete the exercises in this chapter, you need to copy the book's practice files to your computer. The practice files you'll use to complete the exercises in this chapter are in the Chapter07 practice file folder. A complete list of practice files is provided in "Using the Practice Files" at the beginning of this book.

Creating Diagrams

When you need your document to clearly illustrate a concept such as a process, cycle, hierarchy, or relationship, the powerful SmartArt Graphics tool is available to help you create a dynamic, visually appealing diagram. By using predefined sets of sophisticated formatting, you can almost effortlessly put together any of the following diagrams:

● **List** These diagrams visually represent lists of related or independent information— for example, a list of items needed to complete a task, including pictures of the items.

- **Process** These diagrams visually describe the ordered set of steps required to complete a task—for example, the steps for getting a project approved.

- **Cycle** These diagrams represent a circular sequence of steps, tasks, or events, or the relationship of a set of steps, tasks, or events to a central, core element—for example, the looping process for continually improving a product based on customer feedback.

- **Hierarchy** These diagrams illustrate the structure of an organization or entity—for example, the top-level management structure of a company.

- **Relationship** These diagrams show convergent, divergent, overlapping, merging, or containment elements—for example, how using similar methods to organize your e-mail, calendar, and contacts can improve your productivity.

- **Matrix** These diagrams show the relationship of components to a whole—for example, the product teams in a department.

- **Pyramid** These diagrams illustrate proportional or interconnected relationships— for example, the amount of time that should ideally be spent on different phases of a project.

- **Picture** These diagrams rely on pictures instead of text to create one of the other types of diagrams—for example, a process picture diagram with photographs showing the recession of glaciers in Glacier National Park.

You select the type of diagram you want to create from the Choose A SmartArt Graphic dialog box. The categories are not mutually exclusive, meaning that some diagrams appear in more than one category.

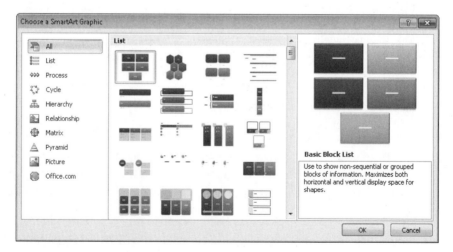

The Choose A SmartArt Graphic dialog box.

After creating the diagram, you insert text by typing either directly in its shapes or in the associated Text pane. Depending on the diagram type, the text appears in or adjacent to its shapes.

In this exercise, you'll create a diagram, add text, adjust its size, and specify its position in relation to the document text and page margins.

SET UP You need the ServiceA_start document located in the Chapter07 practice file folder to complete this exercise. Open the ServiceA_start document, and save it as *ServiceA*. Then follow the steps.

1. Click to the left of the **Gather information** heading, and then on the **Insert** tab, in the **Illustrations** group, click the **SmartArt** button.

   Keyboard Shortcut Press and release Alt, N, and then M to open the Choose A SmartArt Graphic dialog box.

   See Also For more information about keyboard shortcuts, see "Keyboard Shortcuts" at the end of this book.

   The Choose A SmartArt Graphic dialog box opens, displaying all the available graphics.

2. In the left pane, click each diagram category in turn to display only the available layouts of that type in the center pane.

3. In the left pane, click **Process**. Then in the center pane, click each process diagram layout in turn to view an example, along with a description of what the diagram best conveys, in the right pane.

   Tip While you are exploring, keep in mind how much data your own diagrams might contain, and analyze which diagrams will ensure that the data will all fit on one page.

4. When you finish exploring, click the third thumbnail in the sixth row (**Vertical Process**), and then click **OK**.

   The process diagram is inserted at the cursor, and the Design and Format contextual tabs are displayed on the ribbon.

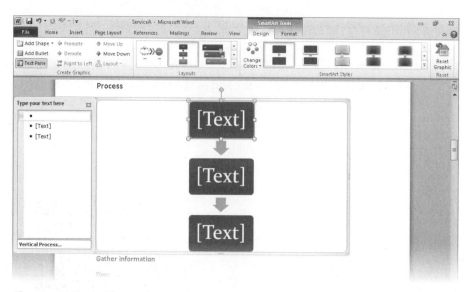

Three text placeholders appear in the diagram shapes and in the adjacent Text pane, where the text placeholders are formatted as a bulleted list.

Troubleshooting The appearance of buttons and groups on the ribbon changes depending on the width of the program window. For information about changing the appearance of the ribbon to match our screen images, see "Modifying the Display of the Ribbon" at the beginning of this book.

Depending on your screen resolution, you might see a description of the Vertical Process diagram at the bottom of the Text pane. If your Text pane looks like the one in our graphic, you can click Vertical Process to display the description.

Troubleshooting If the Text pane is not open, click the tab displaying left and right (open and close) arrows on the left side of the diagram frame. You can also display the Text pane by clicking the Text Pane button in the Create Graphic group on the Design contextual tab.

5. With the first bullet selected in the **Text** pane, type **Gather information**, and then press the Down Arrow key to move the cursor to the next placeholder.

Troubleshooting Be sure to press the Down Arrow key. If you press the Enter key, you'll start a new bullet, and if you press the Tab key, you'll turn the current bullet into a level-two bullet below the one above it.

As you type in the Text pane, the words also appear in the corresponding shape in the diagram.

Tip For a cleaner look, don't type any punctuation at the end of the text in diagram shapes.

6. Repeat step 5 for the remaining two placeholders, entering **Set up team** and **Plan project**.

7. With the cursor at the end of the third bulleted item in the **Text** pane, press Enter to extend the bulleted list and add a new shape to the diagram. Then type **Meet with department**.

   The widths of the shapes in the diagram adjust to accommodate the length of the bullet point you just typed.

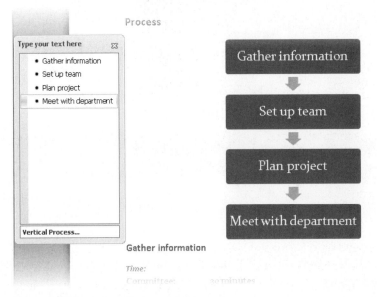

You can add as many shapes as you need.

8. In the **Text** pane, click the **Close** button.

9. On the left side of the diagram frame, point to the sizing handle (the four dots), and when the pointer changes to a double-headed arrow, drag to the right past the diagram and into the white space, until the frame is approximately as wide as the shapes within the diagram.

   Troubleshooting Ensure that the pointer is a double-headed arrow before dragging. Point to the four dots, not to a blank part of the frame or to the Text pane tab on the left side of the frame.

10. If you can't see the diagram after you release the mouse button, scroll up in the document.

The diagram now sits at the left margin of the document, with the *Gather information* heading to its right.

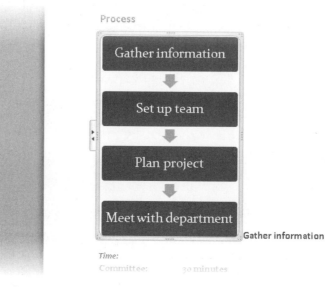

The diagram is anchored to the Gather information *heading and moves with it.*

11. On the **Format** contextual tab, in the **Arrange** group, click the **Wrap Text** button, and then in the gallery, click **Square**.

Troubleshooting Depending on your window size and screen resolution, you might need to click the Arrange button to display the Arrange group.

See Also For information about text wrapping, see "Arranging Objects on the Page" in Chapter 10, "Organize and Arrange Content."

12. In the **Arrange** group, click the **Position** button, and then at the bottom of the gallery, click **More Layout Options**.

The Layout dialog box opens with the Position page displayed. On this page are options for controlling where the diagram appears relative to other elements of the document.

The Position page of the Layout dialog box.

13. In the **Horizontal** area, click **Alignment**. Then click the **Alignment** arrow, and in the list, click **Right**.

14. In the **Vertical** area, click **Alignment**. Leave the **Alignment** setting as **Top**, and then change the **relative to** setting to **Line**.

15. Click **OK**.

    Instead of sitting at the left margin with text before and after it, the diagram now sits to the right of the text, without interrupting its flow.

16. In the lower-left corner of the diagram frame, point to the sizing handle. When the pointer changes to a diagonal double-headed arrow, drag up and to the right until the bottom of the diagram frame sits level with the last line of text in the **Community Service Committee** paragraph.

    Tip You can precisely size the diagram by adjusting the Height or Width setting in the Size group on the Format contextual tab.

17. Click a blank area of the document.

    The diagram now sits neatly to the right of the introductory text.

You can align and size the diagram to fit your text.

CLEAN UP Save the ServiceA document, and then close it.

Modifying Diagrams

After you create a diagram, you can add and remove shapes and edit the text of the diagram by making changes in the Text pane. You can also customize the diagram by using the options on the SmartArt Tools contextual tabs.

You can make changes such as the following by using the commands on the Design contextual tab:

- Switch to a different layout of the same type or of a different type.

   Tip If you have entered more text than will fit in the new layout, the text is not shown, but SmartArt retains it so that you don't have to retype it if you switch the layout again.

- Add shading and three-dimensional effects to all the shapes in a diagram.

- Change the color scheme.

- Add shapes and change their hierarchy.

   Tip You can remove a shape and its text by selecting it and then pressing the Delete key. You can also rearrange shapes by dragging them.

You can customize individual shapes in the following ways by using the commands on the Format contextual tab:

- Change an individual shape—for example, you can change a square into a star.

- Apply a built-in shape style.

- Change the color, outline, or effect of a shape.
- Change the style of the shape's text.

You can use Live Preview to display the effects of these changes before you apply them. If you apply a change and then decide you preferred the original version, you can click the Reset Graphic button in the Reset group on the Design contextual tab.

Reset Graphic

In this exercise, you'll change a diagram's layout, style, and colors. Then you'll change the shape and color of one of its elements, and customize copies of the diagram.

SET UP You need the ServiceB_start document located in the Chapter07 practice file folder to complete this exercise. Open the ServiceB_start document, and save it as *ServiceB*. Then follow the steps.

1. If necessary, adjust your view of the document so that the entire diagram sits in the bottom half of your screen.

2. Click a blank area inside the diagram frame to activate the diagram as a whole.

   Troubleshooting Be sure to click a blank area away from any shapes. If a shape in the diagram is surrounded by handles, that shape is selected, either for editing or for manipulation, instead of the diagram as a whole.

3. On the **Design** contextual tab, in the **Layouts** group, click the **More** button.

   The Layouts gallery appears, showing the other available Process diagram layouts.

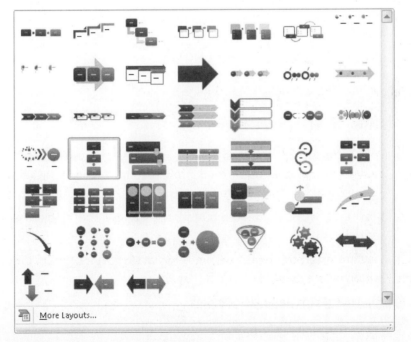

You can switch to any of these layouts.

Tip If a gallery has a sizing handle (three dots) in its lower-right corner, as this one does, you can drag the handle upward to reduce the height of the gallery. You can then see more of the document and the gallery at the same time.

4. In the **Layouts** gallery, point to each thumbnail to preview the diagram with that layout.

   Because changing the layout does not change the width of the diagram frame, some of the horizontal layouts create a very small diagram.

5. In the **Layouts** gallery, click the last thumbnail in the fourth row (**Basic Bending Process**).

   The diagram changes to two columns with arrows indicating the process flow.

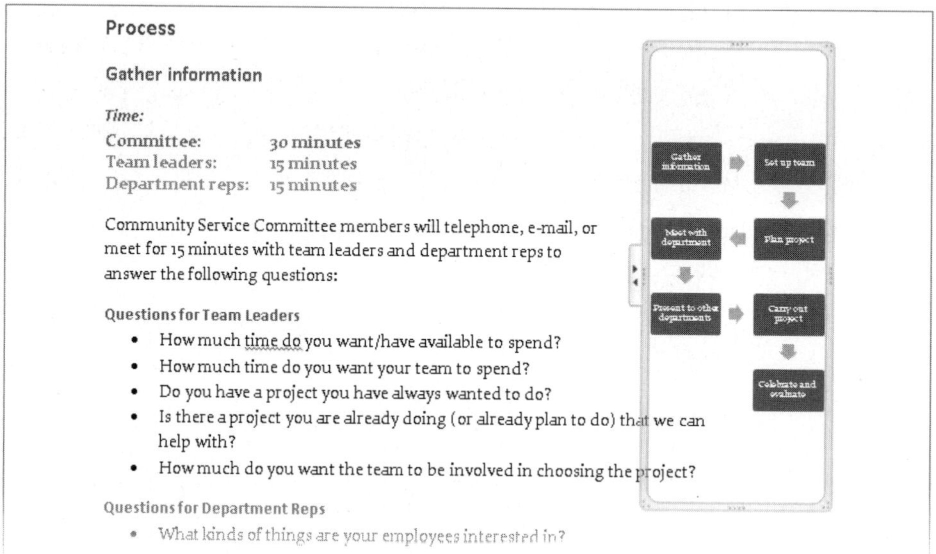

The Basic Bending Process diagram.

6. Point to the sizing handle on the left side of the diagram's frame, and when the pointer changes to a two-headed arrow, drag the frame to the left until the diagram occupies a bit less than half the page width.

   When you release the mouse button, the shapes in the diagram expand to fill the resized frame.

7. On the **Design** contextual tab, in the **SmartArt Styles** group, click the **More** button.

   The SmartArt Styles gallery appears.

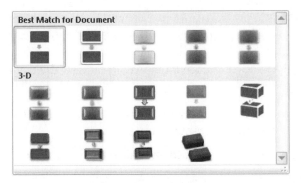

You can apply two-dimensional or three-dimensional styles.

8. In the gallery, point to each style, noticing the changes to your diagram. Then under **3-D**, click the first thumbnail in the first row (**Polished**).

9. In the **SmartArt Styles** group, click the **Change Colors** button.

   The Colors gallery appears, offering sets of different colors or of different shades of the same color.

10. Preview a few color combinations, and then under **Colorful**, click the first thumbnail (**Colorful – Accent Colors**).

   In the document, you can see that the new diagram colors coordinate with the text colors.

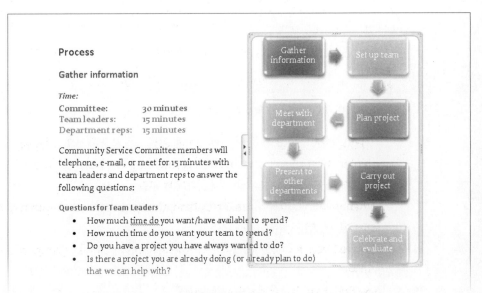

The diagram shapes have a new style and new colors.

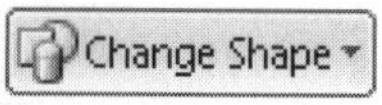

11. In the upper-left corner of the diagram, click the **Gather information** shape (not its text), and then on the **Format** contextual tab, in the **Shapes** group, click the **Change Shape** button.

Change Shape ▾

The Shapes gallery appears, showing all the available built-in shapes.

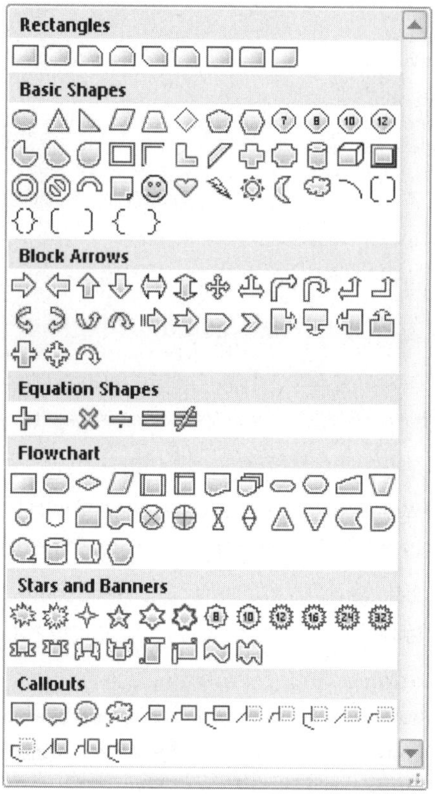

You can use any of these shapes in a diagram.

12. Under **Basic Shapes**, click the first shape in the first row (**Oval**).

The selected shape changes from a rectangle to an oval.

Shape Fill ▾

13. Without changing the selection, in the **Shape Styles** group, click the **Shape Fill** button. Then under **Standard Colors** in the palette, click the first box (**Dark Red**).

14. Click away from the diagram.

You can now see the results.

Process

Gather information

Time:

Committee:	30 minutes
Team leaders:	15 minutes
Department reps:	15 minutes

Community Service Committee members will telephone, e-mail, or meet for 15 minutes with team leaders and department reps to answer the following questions:

Questions for Team Leaders

- How much time do you want/have available to spend?
- How much time do you want your team to spend?
- Do you have a project you have always wanted to do?
- Is there a project you are already doing (or already plan to do) that we can help with?

The shape that corresponds with the heading to the left of the diagram is now accentuated with a different shape and color.

15. Click a blank area within the diagram to select it. Then on the **Home** tab, in the **Clipboard** group, click the **Copy** button.

16. Scroll down the document, click to the left of the **Set up team** heading, and in the **Clipboard** group, click the **Paste** button to paste in a copy of the diagram.

17. On the **Format** tab, in the **Arrange** group, click the **Position** button, and then click **More Layout Options** to display the **Layout** dialog box. Ensure that the **Horizontal** setting is **Alignment**, **Right relative to Column** and the **Vertical** setting is **Alignment**, **Top relative to Line**. Then click **OK**.

18. Click the **Gather information** shape (not its text). In the **Shapes** group, click the **Change Shape** button, and under **Rectangles**, click the second shape (**Rounded Rectangle**). Then in the **Shape Styles** group, click the **Shape Fill** button, and under **Theme Colors** in the palette, click the third box (**Light Turquoise, Background 2**).

    The shape corresponding to the previous heading is now muted to show that it has already been discussed.

19. Click the **Set up team** shape (not its text), and change its shape to **Oval**. Then change its fill color to **Dark Red**.

    The diagram now corresponds with the adjacent topic.

The red oval shape reflects the heading to the left, and the previous topic is a muted color.

20. If you want, repeat steps 15 through 19 to insert a customized copy of the diagram adjacent to each of the remaining headings in the Process section.

> **Tip** Sometimes headings appear too close together, or a heading might appear too close to the bottom of the page, to accommodate a series of diagrams neatly. In that case, insert a page break (press Ctrl+Enter) to push each heading to a new page before inserting the diagram.

CLEAN UP Save the ServiceB document, and then close it.

Creating Picture Diagrams

The SmartArt Graphics tool that comes with Word 2010 includes a sophisticated new category of diagrams that are designed to hold pictures. You can use these diagrams for business uses such as creating organization charts with pictures as well as names and titles or for personal uses such as creating a page of family photographs.

In this exercise, you'll create a page of photographs. You'll size and position the photographs and then enter and format accompanying captions.

SET UP You need the Garden, Park, Pond, and Woods pictures located in the Chapter07 practice file folder to complete this exercise. Create a blank document, and save it as *Westbury* in the folder where you usually save your practice files. Then follow the steps.

1. On the **Page Layout** tab, in the **Page Setup** group, set the orientation to **Landscape**, and set the margins to **Narrow**. Then if necessary, set the zoom percentage so that you can see the entire page on your screen.

2. At the top of the document, type **Westbury**, and press Enter. Select the text, and then on the **Home** tab, in the **Font** group, click the **Text Effects** button. Then in the gallery, click the second thumbnail in the last row (**Gradient Fill - Orange, Accent 6, Inner Shadow**). Finally, set the size to **72**.

3. Press the Down Arrow key, and on the **Insert** tab, in the **Illustrations** group, click the **SmartArt** button. In the left pane of the **Choose a SmartArt Graphic** dialog box, click **Picture**. Then in the middle pane, double-click the first thumbnail in the first row (**Accented Picture**).

The template for the selected diagram is inserted at the cursor.

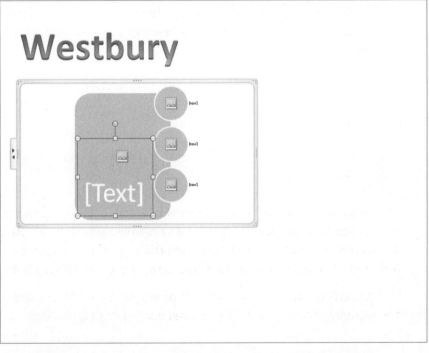

The Accented Picture diagram, ready for you to enter pictures and captions.

4. Click a blank area inside the diagram frame, and then on the **Format** contextual tab, in the **Size** group, change the **Height** setting to **5.75** and the **Width** setting to **9**.

   Tip You don't have to type the inch marks; Word will add them for you. After you enter a Size setting, pressing Enter implements your changes.

5. Click a blank area of the biggest shape, and then in the **Size** group, change the **Height** setting to **5** and the **Width** setting to **8**. Then drag the shape down and to the left until it sits in the lower-left corner of the diagram frame.

6. Click a blank area of the top circle, and then in the **Size** group, use the up arrows in the **Height** and **Width** settings to increase the size to **1.7"**. Repeat this step for the other two circles.

   Troubleshooting Don't type the sizes; use the arrows. Sometimes the shapes don't hold precise measurements when you type them.

7. Drag the top circle to the upper-right corner of the diagram frame, drag the middle circle to the right to align with the frame, and drag the bottom circle to the lower-right corner of the frame.

   The diagram now occupies most of the page.

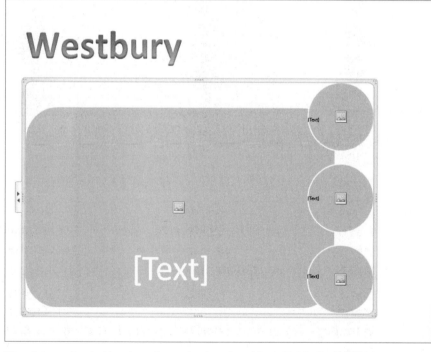

The picture placeholders have been sized and positioned to fit the available space.

8. In the biggest shape, click the **Insert Picture** icon.

   The Insert Picture dialog box opens.

9. Navigate to your **Chapter07** practice file folder, and then double-click **Park**.

10. Repeat step 9 to insert the **Garden** picture in the top circle, the **Pond** picture in the middle circle, and the **Woods** picture in the bottom circle.

11. Open the **Text** pane, and replace the placeholder bullet points with **Park**, **Garden**, **Pond**, and **Woods**.

    The captions appear on the diagram in the position and format specified by the diagram template.

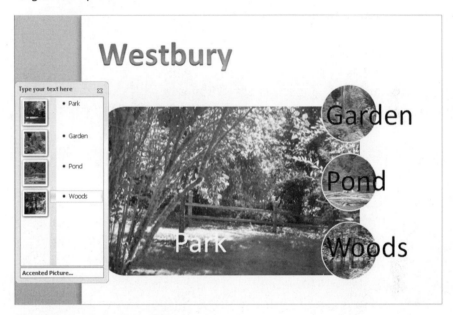

The pictures now have captions.

12. In the **Text** pane, double-click the **Park** bullet point, and then on the **Home** tab, in the **Font** group, apply the **Gradient Fill – Orange, Accent 6, Inner Shadow** text effect and set the size to **40**. Repeat this step for the **Garden**, **Pond**, and **Woods** bullet points. Then close the **Text** pane.

13. To balance the slide, on the **Page Layout** tab, in the **Page Setup** group, click the **Margins** button, and at the bottom of the gallery, click **Custom Margins**. Then in the **Page Setup** dialog box, increase the **Left** margin to **1.25**, and click **OK**.

    Troubleshooting If Word displays a message that one of the margins is outside the printable area of the page, in this case you can click Ignore. If you were going to print this page, you would want to fix the problem.

14. Make any additional adjustment to achieve a balanced slide.

    We indented the title by 1 inch and removed the space after it.

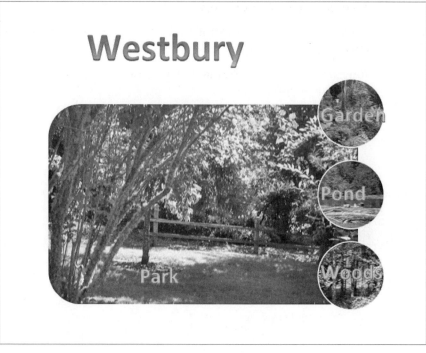

The final picture diagram.

✖ **CLEAN UP** Save the Westbury document, and then close it.

Key Points

- You can easily create a sophisticated diagram to convey a process or the relationship between hierarchical elements.

- Diagrams are dynamic illustrations that you can customize to produce precisely the effect you are looking for.

- You can use a picture diagram to neatly lay out pictures on a page.

Chapter at a Glance

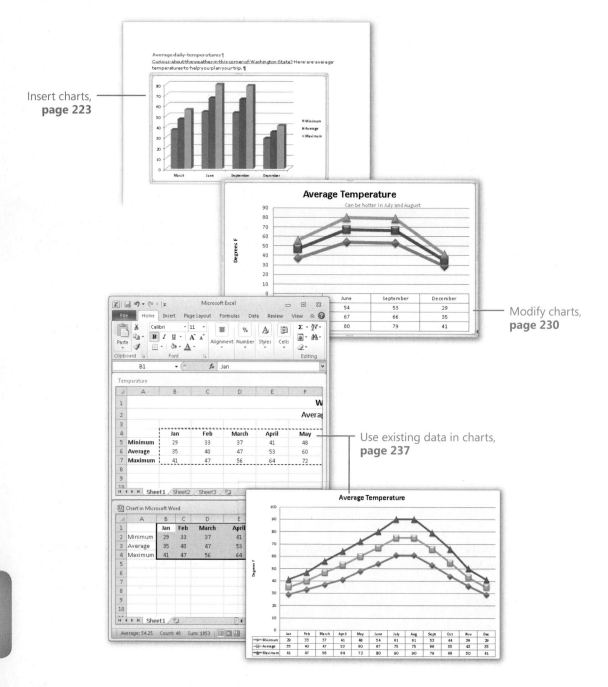

8 Insert and Modify Charts

In this chapter, you will learn how to

✔ Insert charts.

✔ Modify charts.

✔ Use existing data in charts.

You'll often find it helpful to reinforce the argument you are making in a document with facts and figures. When it's more important for your audience to understand trends than identify precise values, you can use a chart to present numerical information in visual ways.

In this chapter, you'll add a chart to a document and modify its appearance by changing its chart type, style, and layout, as well as the color of some elements. Then you'll recreate the chart by plotting data stored in an existing Microsoft Excel worksheet.

Important The exercises in this chapter assume that you have Microsoft Excel 2010 installed on your computer. If you do not have this version of Excel, the steps in the exercises won't work as described.

> **Practice Files** Before you can complete the exercises in this chapter, you need to copy the book's practice files to your computer. The practice files you'll use to complete the exercises in this chapter are in the Chapter08 practice file folder. A complete list of practice files is provided in "Using the Practice Files" at the beginning of this book.

Inserting Charts

When you insert a chart into a document created in Microsoft Word 2010, a sample chart is embedded in the document. The data used to plot the sample chart is stored in an Excel worksheet that is associated with the Word file. (You don't have to maintain a separate Excel file.)

Tip Don't worry: you don't have to know how to use Excel to be able to create the chart.

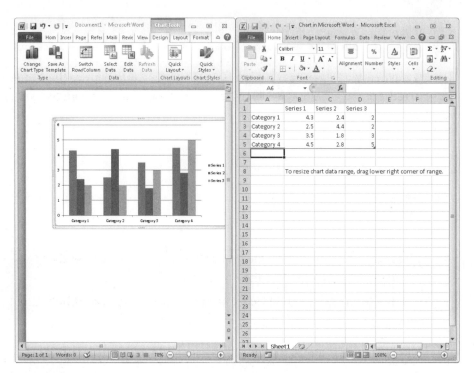

A sample chart plotted from the data in its associated Excel worksheet.

Troubleshooting The appearance of buttons and groups on the ribbon changes depending on the width of the program window. For information about changing the appearance of the ribbon to match our screen images, see "Modifying the Display of the Ribbon" at the beginning of this book.

The Excel worksheet is composed of rows and columns of cells that contain values, which in charting terminology are called *data points*. Collectively a set of data points is called a *data series*. As with Word tables, each worksheet cell is identified by an address consisting of its column letter and row number—for example, A2. A range of cells is identified by the address of the cell in the upper-left corner and the address of the cell in the lower-right corner, separated by a colon—for example, A2:D5.

To customize the sample chart, you replace the sample data in the Excel worksheet with your own data. Because the Excel worksheet is linked to the chart, when you change the values in the worksheet, the chart changes as well. To enter a value in a cell, you click the cell to select it, and start typing. You can select an entire column by clicking the column header—the shaded box containing a letter at the top of each column—and an entire row by clicking the row header—the shaded box containing a number to the left of each row. You can select the entire worksheet by clicking the Select All button— the box at the junction of the column and row headers.

Tip If you create a chart and later want to edit its data, you can open the associated worksheet by clicking the chart and then clicking the Edit Data button in the Data group on the Design contextual tab.

In this exercise, you'll insert a chart into a document and then replace the sample data in the associated worksheet with seasonal minimum, average, and maximum temperature data.

Tip If you open a document created in Word 2003 in Word 2010 and then insert a chart into it, Word uses Microsoft Graph to create the chart. This Word 2003 charting technology has been retained to maintain compatibility with earlier versions of the program. The steps in this exercise will work only with a document created in Word 2010 or Word 2007.

SET UP You need the CottageA_start document located in your Chapter08 practice file folder to complete this exercise. Open the CottageA_start document, and save it as *CottageA*. Then follow the steps.

1. Press Ctrl+End to move to the end of the document. Then set the zoom percentage so that you can see almost the entire page.

2. On the **Insert** tab, in the **Illustrations** group, click the **Chart** button.

   The Insert Chart dialog box opens.

In the Insert Chart dialog box, you can select from a variety of chart types and their variations.

3. In the gallery in the right pane, under **Column**, click the fourth thumbnail in the first row (**3-D Clustered Column**). Then click **OK**.

The document window is resized to fill the left half of the screen, and a sample chart of the type you selected is inserted at the cursor. An Excel worksheet containing the data plotted in the sample chart opens on the right.

4. Click the **Select All** button in the upper-left corner of the Excel worksheet, and then press the Delete key.

   The sample data in the worksheet is deleted, and the worksheet is now blank. The columns in the sample chart in the document disappear, leaving a blank chart area.

5. Click the second cell in row **1** (cell **B1**), type **March**, and then press the Tab key.

   Excel enters the heading and activates the next cell in the same row.

6. In cells **C1** through **E1**, type **June**, **September**, and **December**, pressing Tab after each entry to move to the next cell.

   Tip If you were entering a sequential list of months, you could type *January* and then drag the fill handle in the lower-right corner of the cell to the right to fill subsequent cells in the same row with the names of the months.

7. Click cell **A2**, type **Minimum**, and then press the Enter key.

   Excel enters the heading and activates the next cell in the same column.

   Keyboard Shortcut Press Enter to move down in the same column or Shift+Enter to move up. Press Tab to move to the right in the same row or Shift+Tab to move to the left. Or press the Arrow keys to move up, down, left, or right one cell at a time.

   See Also For more information about keyboard shortcuts, see "Keyboard Shortcuts" at the end of this book.

8. In cells **A3** and **A4**, type **Average** and **Maximum**, pressing Enter after each entry.

   You have now entered the row and column headings for the data you want to plot.

	A	B	C	D	E	F	G
1		March	June	September	December		
2	Minimum						
3	Average						
4	Maximum						
5							
6							
7							
8							

The row and column headings for your data.

9. Point to the border between the headers of columns **A** and **B**, and when the pointer changes to a double-headed arrow, double-click.

Excel adjusts the width of the column to the left of the border to fit the entries in the column.

10. Select columns **B** through **E** by dragging through their headers. Then point to the border between any two selected columns, and double-click.

Excel adjusts the width of all the selected columns to fit their cell entries.

11. In cell **B2**, type **37**, and press Tab. Then in cells **C2** through **E2**, type **54**, **53**, and **29**, pressing Tab to move from cell to cell.

12. Type the following data into the cells of the Excel worksheet:

	B	C	D	E
3	47	67	66	35
4	56	80	70	41

As you enter data, the chart changes to reflect what you type.

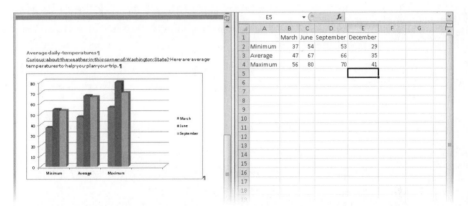

The data series in the columns (the months) are plotted by the categories in the rows (Minimum, Average, and Maximum).

Something is wrong. You entered data for March, June, September, and December, but December is not shown in the chart. This is because the original sample chart plotted only the cells in the range A1:D5, and you have entered data in A1:E4. You need to specify the new range.

13. In the Word document, click a blank area inside the chart frame to activate the chart. Then on the **Design** contextual tab, in the **Data** group, click the **Select Data** button.

Select Data

In the Excel worksheet, the plotted data range is surrounded by a blinking dotted border, and the Select Data Source dialog box opens so that you can make any necessary adjustments.

The Select Data Source dialog box.

14. At the right end of the **Chart data range** box, click the **Collapse Dialog** button to shrink the **Select Data Source** dialog box. Then if you can't see the worksheet data, point to the title bar of the collapsed dialog box, and drag it downward.

15. In the Excel worksheet, point to cell **A1**, and drag down and to the right to cell **E4**. Then in the **Select Data Source** dialog box, click the **Expand Dialog** button.

    In the Select Data Source dialog box, the Chart Data Range box now contains the new range, and the Legend Entries (Series) list now includes December.

16. Click **Switch Row/Column**.

    In the dialog box, Excel switches the entries in the Legend Entries (Series) and Horizontal (Category) Axis Labels boxes.

The data series in the rows will be plotted by the categories in the columns.

17. Click **OK** to close the dialog box. Then in the upper-right corner of the Excel window, click the **Close** button to close the worksheet.

    The Word window expands to fill the screen. The data for December now appears in the chart, which is plotted by month.

    Suppose you realize that you made an error when typing the data for September.

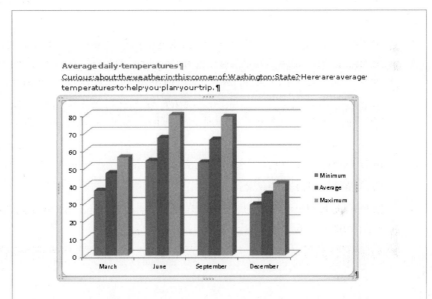

18. Click a blank area inside the chart frame. Then on the **Design** tab, in the **Data** group, click the **Edit Data** button to open the Excel worksheet.

19. In the Excel worksheet, click cell **D4**, type **79** to replace the existing data, and press Enter. Then close the Excel window.

    In the chart, the maximum temperature column for September becomes taller to represent the new value.

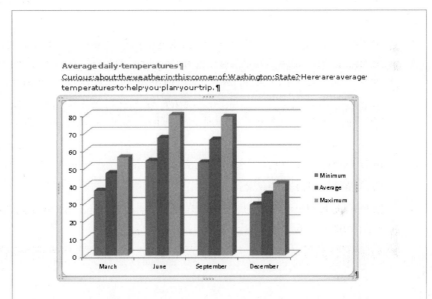

A simple three-dimensional column chart showing seasonal temperatures.

✖ **CLEAN UP** Save the CottageA document, and then close it.

Modifying Charts

If you decide that the chart you created doesn't adequately depict the most important characteristics of your data, you can change the chart type at any time. Word provides 11 types of charts, each with two-dimensional and three-dimensional variations. Common chart types include the following:

- **Column** These charts show how values change over time.
- **Bar** These charts show the values of several items at one point in time.
- **Line** These charts show erratic changes in values over time.
- **Pie** These charts show how parts relate to the whole.

Having settled on the most appropriate chart type, you can modify the chart as a whole or any of its elements, such as the following:

- **Chart area** This is the entire area within the chart frame.
- **Plot area** This is the rectangular area bordered by the axes.
- **Axes** These are the lines along which the data is plotted. The x-axis shows the categories, and the y-axis shows the data series, or values. (Three-dimensional charts also have a z-axis.)
- **Labels** These identify the data along each axis.
- **Data markers** These graphically represent each data point in each data series.
- **Legend** This is a key that identifies the data series.

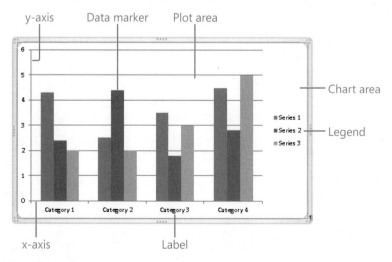

The main elements of a chart.

To modify a specific element, you first select it by clicking it, or by clicking its name in the Chart Elements box in the Current Selection group on the Format tab. You can then modify the element by clicking the buttons on the Design, Layout, and Format contextual tabs.

If you make extensive modifications, you might want to save the customized chart as a template so that you can use it for plotting similar data in the future without having to repeat all the changes.

In this exercise, you'll modify the appearance of a chart by changing its chart type and style. You'll change the color of the plot area and the color of two data series. You'll then hide gridlines and change the layout to display titles and a datasheet. After adding an annotation in a text box, you'll save the chart as a template.

 **SET UP** You need the CottageB_start document located in your Chapter08 practice file folder to complete this exercise. Open the CottageB_start document, and save it as *CottageB*. Then follow the steps.

1. Scroll through the document to display the chart, and click a blank area inside the chart frame to activate it.

   Troubleshooting Be sure to click a blank area inside the chart frame. Clicking any of its elements will activate that element, not the chart as a whole.

   Word displays the Design, Layout, and Format contextual tabs.

2. On the **Design** tab, in the **Type** group, click the **Change Chart Type** button.

   The Change Chart Type dialog box opens. This dialog box is the same as the Insert Chart dialog box shown earlier in the chapter.

3. In the gallery on the right, under **Line**, double-click the fourth thumbnail (**Line with Markers**).

   The column chart changes to a line chart, which depicts data by using colored lines instead of columns.

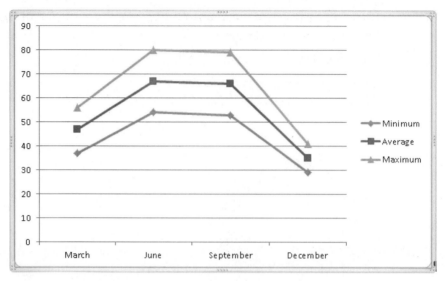

The temperature data plotted as a line chart.

4. In the **Chart Styles** group, click the **More** button.

   The Chart Styles gallery appears.

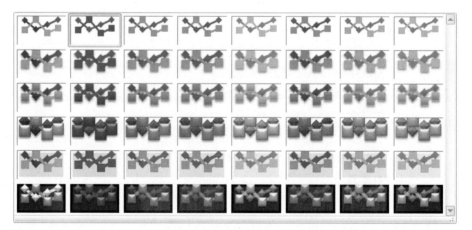

You can quickly switch to a different color scheme or data marker style.

5. In the gallery, click the second thumbnail in the fourth row (**Style 26**).

   The lines are now thicker, and the data markers are three-dimensional.

6. Move the pointer over the chart between the axes that contains the data markers, and when a ScreenTip indicates that you are pointing to the plot area, click to select it.

Shape Fill ▾

7. On the **Format** tab, in the **Shape Styles** group, click the **Shape Fill** button, and then click **More Fill Colors**.

    The Colors dialog box opens.

When none of the theme or standard colors meets your needs, you can pick a color in the Colors dialog box.

8. On the **Standard** page of the **Colors** dialog box, click the pale yellow hexagon below and to the left of the center, and then click **OK**.

    The plot area is now a pale yellow shade to distinguish it from the rest of the chart.

    Tip To change several aspects of the plot area, right-click the area and then click Format Plot Area to open the Format Plot Area dialog box. You can then change the fill, border, shadow, and 3-D format in one location.

9. At the top of the **Current Selection** group, click the **Chart Elements** arrow to display the list of elements, and then click **Series "Average"**.

    An outline appears around the data points of the selected series.

Format Selection

10. In the **Current Selection** group, click the **Format Selection** button.

The Format Data Series dialog box opens.

Format Data Series

Series Options	Series Options
Marker Options	Plot Series On
Marker Fill	● Primary Axis
Line Color	○ Secondary Axis
Line Style	
Marker Line Color	
Marker Line Style	
Shadow	
Glow and Soft Edges	
3-D Format	

Close

You can change several aspects of the selected data series in this dialog box.

11. In the left pane, click **Marker Fill**, and on the **Marker Fill** page, click **Solid Fill**. In the **Fill Color** area, click the **Color** button, and under **Theme Colors**, click the purple box (**Purple, Accent 4**).

12. In the left pane, click **Line Color**. Then on the **Line Color** page, change the color to the same solid purple.

13. Check that the marker line color is also purple, and then click **Close**.

    The Average data series is now represented by the color purple.

Gridlines

14. On the **Layout** tab, in the **Axes** group, click the **Gridlines** button, point to **Primary Horizontal Gridlines**, and then click **None** to remove the horizontal gridlines from the chart.

15. On the **Design** tab, in the **Chart Layouts** group, click the **More** button.

The Chart Layouts gallery appears.

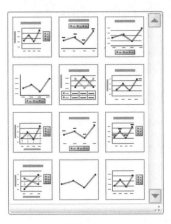

You can quickly change the layout of the chart by selecting one of the predefined options.

16. In the gallery, click the second thumbnail in the second row (**Layout 5**).

    The legend now appears below the chart with the data points in a datasheet. Gridlines have been turned back on, and placeholders for a chart title and axis title have been added to the chart.

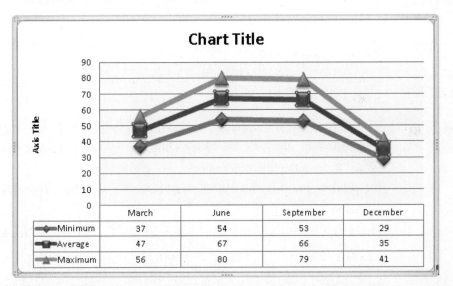

When you don't have a lot of data, displaying a datasheet can clarify without adding clutter.

17. In the chart, drag across the **Chart Title** placeholder at the top, and type **Average Temperature**. Then replace the **Axis Title** placeholder on the left with **Degrees F**.

18. On the **Layout** tab, in the **Insert** group, click the **Draw Text Box** button.

19. Point below the chart title and above the **June** maximum temperature data point, and then drag diagonally down and to the right until the text box stretches as far as the **December** data.

20. Type **Can be hotter in July and August**. Then select the text, and on the **Home** tab, in the **Font** group, change the size to **10** points and the color to **Red**.

21. Click outside the text box (but not outside the chart).

    You can now see the results of your changes.

Average Temperature

Can be hotter in July and August

	March	June	September	December
Minimum	37	54	53	29
Average	47	67	66	35
Maximum	56	80	79	41

The chart with titles and a custom label.

Save As Template

22. On the **Design** tab, in the **Type** group, click the **Save As Template** button.

    The Save Chart Template dialog box opens and displays the contents of your Charts folder, which is a subfolder of your Templates folder.

    Troubleshooting If the Charts folder is not displayed in the Address bar, navigate to the C:\Users\<user name>\AppData\Roaming\Microsoft\Templates\Charts folder.

23. With the **Charts** folder displayed in the **Address** bar, type **My Temperature Chart** in the **File name** box, and then click **Save**.

24. In the **Type** group, click the **Change Chart Type** button, and then in the left pane of the **Change Chart Type** dialog box, click **Templates**. Then, in the right pane, point to the icon under **My Templates**.

    A ScreenTip identifies this template as the one you just created.

Change Chart Type

Templates	**My Templates**
Column	
Line	My Temperature Chart
Pie	
Bar	
Area	
X Y (Scatter)	
Stock	
Surface	
Doughnut	
Bubble	
Radar	

Manage Templates...   Set as Default Chart   OK   Cancel

In the future, you can click the custom template to create a chart with the same layout and formatting.

25. Click **Cancel** to close the dialog box.

 CLEAN UP Save the CottageB document, and then close it.

Using Existing Data in Charts

If the data you want to plot as a chart already exists in a Microsoft Access database, an Excel worksheet, or a Word table, you don't have to retype it in the chart's worksheet. You can copy the data from its source program and paste it into the worksheet.

In this exercise, you'll copy data stored in an Excel worksheet into a chart's worksheet and then expand the plotted data range so that the new data appears in the chart.

SET UP You need the CottageC_start document and the Temperature workbook located in your Chapter08 practice file folder to complete this exercise. Open the CottageC_start document, and save it as *CottageC*. Then follow the steps.

1. Press Ctrl+End to move to the end of the document, and then if necessary, adjust the zoom percentage so that you can see the entire page.

2. Right-click a blank area inside the chart frame, and then click **Edit Data** to open the associated Excel worksheet.

3. In the Excel window, click the **File** tab to display the Backstage view, and in the left pane, click **Open**. In the **Open** dialog box, navigate to your **Chapter08** practice file folder, and double-click the **Temperature** workbook.

Arrange
All

4. On the Excel **View** tab, in the **Window** group, click the **Arrange All** button. Then in the **Arrange Windows** dialog box, click **Horizontal**, and click **OK**.

Excel arranges the Temperature worksheet above the worksheet associated with the chart so that both are visible at the same time.

	A	B	C	D	E	F
1						
2						Aver
3						
4		Jan	Feb	March	April	May
5	Minimum	29	33	37	41	48
6	Average	35	40	47	53	60
7	Maximum	41	47	56	64	72
8						
9						
10						

Chart in Microsoft Word

	A	B	C	D	E	F	G
1		March	June	September	December		
2	Minimum	37	54	53	29		
3	Average	47	67	66	35		
4	Maximum	56	80	79	41		
5							
6							
7							
8							
9							
10							

Displaying two worksheets at the same time makes it easy to copy data between them.

5. In the **Temperature** worksheet, click cell **B4**. Then at the bottom of the **Temperature** pane, to the right of the sheet tabs, drag the horizontal scroll bar until you can see column **M**. Hold down the Shift key, and click cell **M7**.

You have selected the range B4:M7.

6. On the Excel **Home** tab, in the **Clipboard** group, click the **Copy** button.

7. Click the title bar of the **Chart in Microsoft Word** worksheet to activate it, click cell **B1**, and then on the Excel **Home** tab, in the **Clipboard** group, click the **Paste** button.

   The copied data is pasted into the worksheet associated with the chart.

The copied data will be plotted in the chart.

8. Click the **Temperature** title bar to activate that worksheet, and close the **Temperature** workbook. Then maximize the chart worksheet.

   Troubleshooting Be sure to click the Close button at the right end of the Temperature title bar, and not the Close button in the upper-right corner of the Excel program window.

   Now you need to specify that the new data should be included in the chart.

9. In the Word document, click a blank area inside the chart frame, and then on the **Design** contextual tab, in the **Data** group, click the **Select Data** button.

The Select Data Source dialog box opens.

10. In the **Chart data range** box, click to the right of the highlighted cell range, and change the range to read =**Sheet1!$A$1:$M$4**.

You are telling Excel to use the values in A1:M4 on Sheet1 of the associated worksheet. (The $ signs ensure that only that range of cells will be used as the source of the chart's data. Sheet1 is the name defined for the worksheet on the sheet tab at the bottom of the Excel program window.)

11. Click **OK**, and then close the Excel window.

12. In the lower-right corner of the chart frame, drag the sizing handle down and to the right until the chart occupies most of the available space on the page.

Troubleshooting If the chart disappears onto the next page when you release the mouse button, click the Undo button on the Quick Access Toolbar, and then try again.

13. Click **Can be hotter in July and August**, click the border of the text box, and press the Delete key. Then click outside the chart frame.

You can now see twelve months of data.

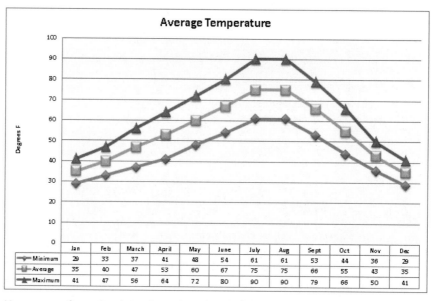

	Jan	Feb	March	April	May	June	July	Aug	Sept	Oct	Nov	Dec
Minimum	29	33	37	41	48	54	61	61	53	44	36	29
Average	35	40	47	53	60	67	75	75	66	55	43	35
Maximum	41	47	56	64	72	80	90	90	79	66	50	41

You can see from the chart that winter is relatively cold, summer is relatively hot, and spring and fall are mild.

CLEAN UP Save the CottageC document, and then close it.

Tip You can also import data into your chart from a text file, Web page, or other external source, such as Microsoft SQL Server. To import data, first display the associated Excel worksheet. Then on the Excel Data tab, in the Get External Data group, click the button for your data source, and navigate to the source. For more information, see Microsoft Excel Help.

Key Points

- A chart is often the most efficient way to present numeric data with at-a-glance clarity.

- You can select the type of chart and change the appearance of its elements until it clearly conveys key information.

- Existing data in a Word table, Excel workbook, Access database, or other structured source can easily be copied and pasted into the associated chart worksheet, eliminating time-consuming typing.

Chapter at a Glance

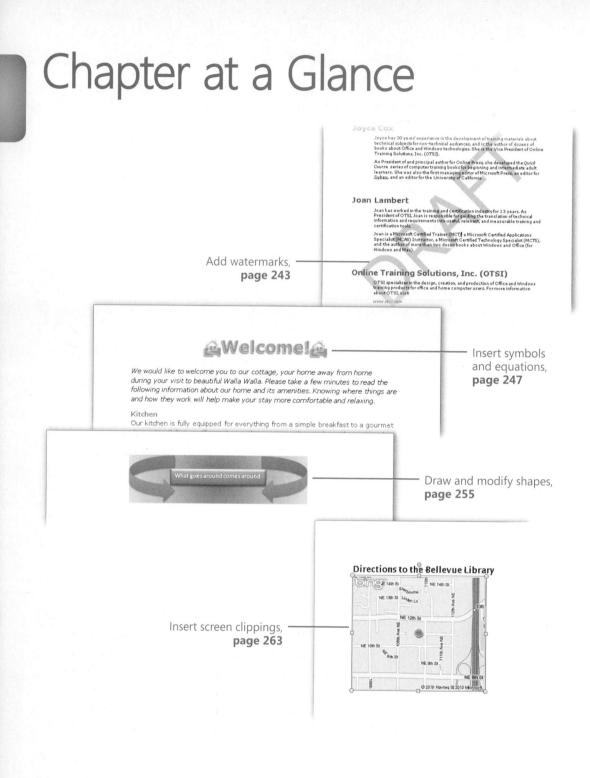

Add watermarks,
page 243

Insert symbols
and equations,
page 247

Draw and modify shapes,
page 255

Insert screen clippings,
page 263

9 Use Other Visual Elements

In this chapter, you will learn how to

✔ Add watermarks.

✔ Insert symbols and equations.

✔ Draw and modify shapes.

✔ Insert screen clippings.

We have looked at some of the more common graphic elements you can add to a document, such as pictures, diagrams, and charts. These elements reinforce concepts or make a document more attention grabbing or visually appealing. But for some documents, you might need other more specialized visual elements.

In this chapter, you'll create text and picture watermarks, insert a symbol, and build a simple equation. You'll also draw shapes to create a simple picture, and insert a screenshot.

> **Practice Files** Before you can complete the exercises in this chapter, you need to copy the book's practice files to your computer. The practice files you'll use to complete the exercises in this chapter are in the Chapter09 practice file folder. A complete list of practice files is provided in "Using the Practice Files" at the beginning of this book.

Adding Watermarks

There might be times when you want words to appear behind the text of a printed or online document. For example, you might want the word *CONFIDENTIAL* to appear faintly behind the text in a contract. When you want to dress up the pages of your document without distracting attention from the main text, you might consider displaying a faint graphic behind the text. These faint background effects are called *watermarks*. Watermarks are visible in a document, but because they are faint, they don't interfere with the readers' ability to view the document's main text.

In this exercise, you'll first add a text watermark to every page of a document, and then you'll add a graphic watermark.

SET UP You need the AuthorsDraft_start document and the OTSI-Logo picture located in your Chapter09 practice file folder to complete this exercise. Open the AuthorsDraft_start document, and save it as *AuthorsDraft*. Turn off formatting marks and the ruler, and set the magnification so that you can see all the text. Then follow the steps.

1. On the **Page Layout** tab, in the **Page Background** group, click the **Watermark** button.

   The Watermark gallery appears.

   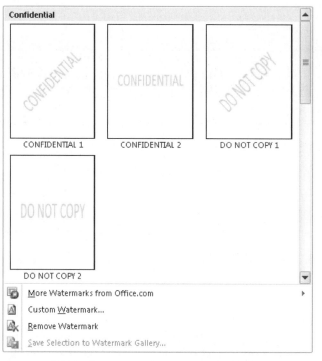

   You can click the thumbnail of a predefined watermark or click Custom Watermark to define your own.

2. Scroll to the bottom of the gallery, noticing the available options.

   Clicking any of these options inserts the specified watermark in pale blue on every page of the current document.

3. At the bottom of the gallery, click **Custom Watermark**.

   The Printed Watermark dialog box opens.

In this dialog box, you can specify a custom picture or text watermark.

4. Click **Text watermark**, display the **Text** list, and then click **DRAFT**.

5. Ensure that **Verdana** appears in the **Font** box.

6. Click the **Color** arrow, and then click the purple box (**Purple, Accent 4**).

7. With the **Semitransparent** check box and **Diagonal** option selected, click **OK**.

   The specified text is inserted diagonally across the page.

Joyce Cox

Joyce has 30 years' experience in the development of training materials about technical subjects for non-technical audiences, and is the author of dozens of books about Office and Windows technologies. She is the Vice President of Online Training Solutions, Inc. (OTSI).

As President of and principal author for Online Press, she developed the *Quick Course* series of computer training books for beginning and intermediate adult learners. She was also the first managing editor of Microsoft Press, an editor for Sybex, and an editor for the University of California.

Joan Lambert

Joan has worked in the training and certification industry for 13 years. As President of OTSI, Joan is responsible for guiding the translation of technical information and requirements into useful, relevant, and measurable training and certification tools.

Joan is a Microsoft Certified Trainer (MCT), a Microsoft Certified Applications Specialist (MCAS) Instructor, a Microsoft Certified Technology Specialist (MCTS), and the author of more than two dozen books about Windows and Office (for Windows and Mac).

Online Training Solutions, Inc. (OTSI)

OTSI specializes in the design, creation, and production of Office and Windows training products for office and home computer users. For more information about OTSI, visit

www.otsi.com

The text watermark is faint enough to read the text but bold enough to be noticed.

8. On the **Page Layout** tab, in the **Page Background** group, click the **Watermark** button, and then click **Custom Watermark**.

9. In the **Printed Watermark** dialog box, click **Picture watermark**, and then click **Select Picture**.

   The Insert Picture dialog box opens.

10. Navigate to your **Chapter09** practice file folder, and double-click the **OTSI-Logo** picture file.

11. In the **Printed Watermark** dialog box, change the **Scale** setting to **200%**, and then click **Apply**.

12. Drag the dialog box by its title bar until you can see the watermark. Then change the **Scale** setting by typing **400%**, and click **Apply**.

13. With the **Washout** check box selected, click **Close**.

   The picture is inserted as a watermark at the size you specified.

Joyce Cox

Joyce has 30 years' experience in the development of training materials about technical subjects for non-technical audiences, and is the author of dozens of books about Office and Windows technologies. She is the Vice President of Online Training Solutions, Inc. (OTSI).

As President of and principal author for Online Press, she developed the *Quick Course* series of computer training books for beginning and intermediate adult learners. She was also the first managing editor of Microsoft Press, an editor for Sybex, and an editor for the University of California.

Joan Lambert

Joan has worked in the training and certification industry for 13 years. As President of OTSI, Joan is responsible for guiding the translation of technical information and requirements into useful, relevant, and measurable training and certification tools.

Joan is a Microsoft Certified Trainer (MCT), a Microsoft Certified Applications Specialist (MCAS) Instructor, a Microsoft Certified Technology Specialist (MCTS), and the author of more than two dozen books about Windows and Office (for Windows and Mac).

Online Training Solutions, Inc. (OTSI)

OTSI specializes in the design, creation, and production of Office and Windows training products for office and home computer users. For more information about OTSI, visit

www.otsi.com

The picture watermark adds visual interest without obscuring the text.

CLEAN UP Save the AuthorsDraft document, and then close it.

Inserting Symbols and Equations

Some documents require characters not found on a standard keyboard. These characters might include the copyright (©) or registered trademark (®) symbols, currency symbols (such as € or £), Greek letters, or letters with accent marks. Or you might want to add arrows (such as ↗ or ↖) or graphic icons (such as ☎ or ✈). Word gives you easy access to a huge array of symbols that you can easily insert into any document.

Like graphics, symbols can add visual information or eye appeal to a document. However, they are different from graphics in that they are characters associated with a particular font.

Keyboard Shortcut You can insert some common symbols by typing a keyboard combination. For example, if you type two consecutive dashes followed by a word and a space, Word changes the two dashes to a professional-looking em-dash—like this one. (This symbol gets its name from the fact that it was originally the width of the character *m*.) To use these keyboard shortcuts, display the Backstage view, click Options, and on the Proofing page of the Word Options dialog box, click AutoCorrect Options. On the AutoCorrect page of the AutoCorrect dialog box, ensure that the Replace Text As You Type check box is selected, and then select or clear check boxes in the Replace Text As You Type area of the AutoFormat As You Type page. You can see many of the available shortcuts on the Special Characters page of the Symbol dialog box.

See Also For more information about keyboard shortcuts, see "Keyboard Shortcuts" at the end of this book.

You can insert mathematical symbols, such as π (pi) or $\sum$ (sigma, or summation), the same way you would insert any other symbol. But you can also create entire mathematical equations in a document. You can insert some predefined equations, including the Quadratic Formula, the Binomial Theorem, and the Pythagorean Theorem, into a document with a few clicks. If you need something other than these standard equations, you can build your own equations by using a library of mathematical symbols.

Equations are different from graphics in that they are accurately rendered mathematical formulas that appear in the document as fields. However, they are similar to graphics in that they can be displayed in line with the surrounding text or in their own space with text above and below them.

The buttons for inserting symbols and equations are in the Symbols group on the Insert tab:

- Clicking the Symbol button displays a Symbol gallery of commonly used symbols.

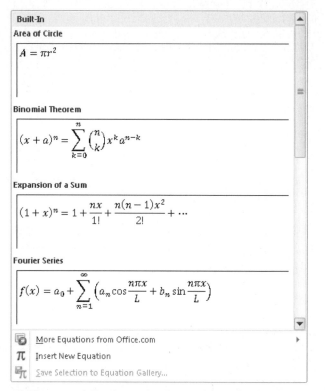

The Symbol gallery is dynamic and changes to reflect recent symbol selections, such as the house symbol in the first row.

From this gallery, you can also open the Symbol dialog box, where you can select from hundreds of symbols and special characters in a variety of fonts.

● Clicking the Equation arrow displays the Equation gallery of commonly used equations.

Built-In

Area of Circle

$$A = \pi r^2$$

Binomial Theorem

$$(x + a)^n = \sum_{k=0}^{n} \binom{n}{k} x^k a^{n-k}$$

Expansion of a Sum

$$(1 + x)^n = 1 + \frac{nx}{1!} + \frac{n(n-1)x^2}{2!} + \cdots$$

Fourier Series

$$f(x) = a_0 + \sum_{n=1}^{\infty} \left(a_n \cos\frac{n\pi x}{L} + b_n \sin\frac{n\pi x}{L} \right)$$

More Equations from Office.com

Insert New Equation

Save Selection to Equation Gallery...

Clicking a predefined equation inserts it into the document at the cursor.

● Clicking the Equation button inserts a box where you can type an equation, and also adds the Design contextual tab to the ribbon. This tab provides access to mathematical symbols, structures such as fractions and radicals, and the Equation Options dialog box. After building your equation, you can add it to the Equation gallery so that it is readily available the next time you need it.

In this exercise, you'll insert a symbol into a document. Then you'll build a simple equation, and you'll add the equation to the Equation gallery.

SET UP You need the Welcome_start document located in your Chapter09 practice file folder to complete this exercise. Open the Welcome_start document, and save it as *Welcome*. Then follow the steps.

1. With the cursor to the left of the document's title, on the **Insert** tab, in the **Symbols** group, click the **Symbol** button, and then click **More Symbols**.

   The Symbol dialog box opens.

The Symbol page of the Symbol dialog box.

Tip The Recently Used Symbols area of the Symbol dialog box is dynamic. If you have already explored this dialog box, you will see the symbols you have inserted into your documents.

2. In the dialog box, display the **Font** list, scroll to the bottom, and then click **Webdings**.

3. In the rows of symbols, click the ninth icon in the third row (the house), click **Insert**, and then click **Close**.

   Word inserts the house symbol at the insertion point.

4. Press the End key, and in the **Symbols** group, click the **Symbol** button.

   The Symbol gallery appears, with the icon you just inserted at the top.

5. Click the house symbol.

The house icon now appears at both ends of the title.

🏠**Welcome!**🏠

We would like to welcome you to our cottage, your home away from home during your visit to beautiful Walla Walla. Please take a few minutes to read the following information about our home and its amenities. Knowing where things are and how they work will help make your stay more comfortable and relaxing.

Kitchen
Our kitchen is fully equipped for everything from a simple breakfast to a gourmet dinner. You'll find a coffee maker on the counter and a grinder in the cupboard

Inserting a picture symbol like the house is easier than inserting a clip art image.

6. Display formatting marks, and then press Ctrl+End to move to the end of the document.

π Equation ▾

7. On the **Insert** tab, in the **Symbols** group, click the **Equation** button.

An equation field is inserted into the document at the cursor so that you can type the equation. The Design contextual tab appears on the ribbon.

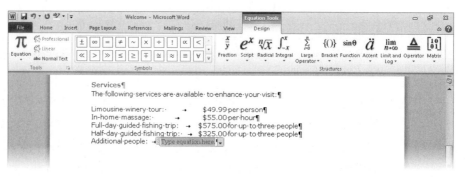

The Design tab includes symbols and structures for building an equation.

Troubleshooting The appearance of buttons and groups on the ribbon changes depending on the width of the program window. For information about changing the appearance of the ribbon to match our screen images, see "Modifying the Display of the Ribbon" at the beginning of this book.

8. In the field, type **(p-3)***.

The asterisk is a multiplication symbol.

9. On the **Design** tab, in the **Structures** group, click the **Fraction** button.

The Fraction gallery appears.

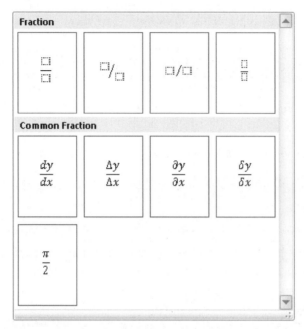

This gallery provides ready-made common fractions as well as the structures for creating your own fractions.

10. In the gallery, click the first thumbnail in the first row (**Stacked Fraction**).

The structure for a simple fraction is inserted in the field at the cursor.

11. Click the top box in the fraction structure, and type **t**. Then click the bottom box, and type **3**.

12. Click the blank area to the right of the equation field. Then press the Spacebar, and type **where p is the number of people and t is the base cost.** (Include the period.)

This equation subtracts 3 from the total number of people and multiplies the result by a per-person amount to calculate the cost of a specific number of additional people. Word has taken care of formatting the equation so that it looks professional.

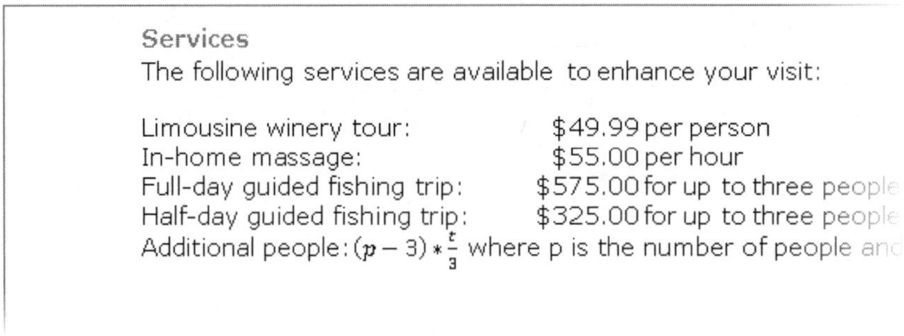

Services
The following services are available to enhance your visit:

Limousine winery tour: $49.99 per person
In-home massage: $55.00 per hour
Full-day guided fishing trip: $575.00 for up to three people
Half-day guided fishing trip: $325.00 for up to three people
Additional people: $(p-3) * \frac{t}{3}$ where p is the number of people and

The p and t variables in the equation are automatically formatted as italic.

13. Click the equation, click the arrow that appears to the right, and then click **Save as New Equation**.

    The Create New Building Block dialog box opens.

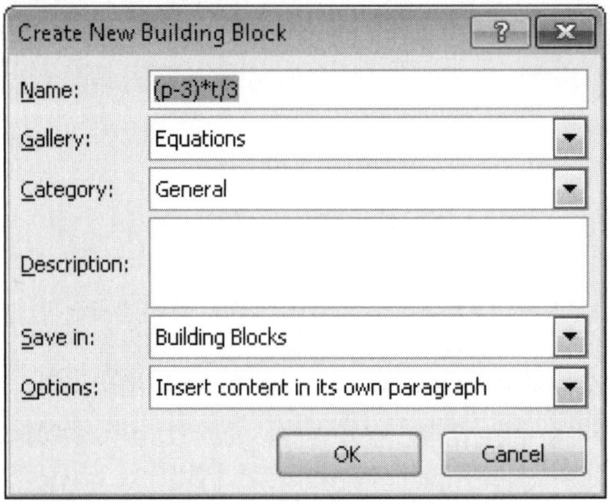

Name:	(p-3)*t/3
Gallery:	Equations
Category:	General
Description:	
Save in:	Building Blocks
Options:	Insert content in its own paragraph

    The equation will be saved as a building block and displayed in the Equation gallery.

    See Also For more information about building blocks, see "Inserting Saved Text" in Chapter 2, "Edit and Proofread Text."

14. In the **Name** box, type **Additional people cost**, and then click **OK**.

15. Press End to release the selection. Then on the **Insert** tab, in the **Symbols** group, click the **Equation** arrow, and scroll to the bottom of the **Equation** gallery.

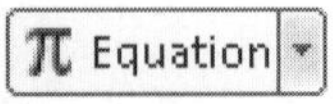

    π Equation

    Your custom equation is now available in the Equation gallery.

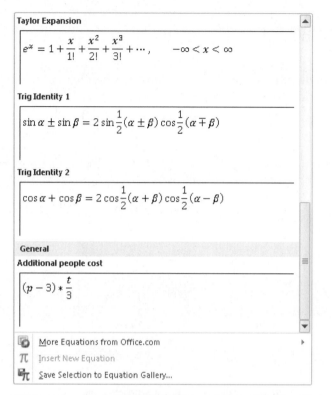

Taylor Expansion

$$e^x = 1 + \frac{x}{1!} + \frac{x^2}{2!} + \frac{x^3}{3!} + \cdots, \qquad -\infty < x < \infty$$

Trig Identity 1

$$\sin \alpha \pm \sin \beta = 2 \sin \frac{1}{2}(\alpha \pm \beta) \cos \frac{1}{2}(\alpha \mp \beta)$$

Trig Identity 2

$$\cos \alpha + \cos \beta = 2 \cos \frac{1}{2}(\alpha + \beta) \cos \frac{1}{2}(\alpha - \beta)$$

General

Additional people cost

$$(p - 3) * \frac{t}{3}$$

More Equations from Office.com   ▸

π Insert New Equation

Save Selection to Equation Gallery...

Custom equations appear in the General area of the Equation gallery.

16. Press the Esc key to close the gallery without making a selection.

17. In the document, click the equation, click its arrow, and then click **Change to Display**.

    Word inserts a line break before and after the equation and positions it in the center of the page.

18. Click the equation's arrow, point to **Justification**, and then click **Left**.

19. Click the equation's arrow, and then click **Change to Inline** to move the equation back in line with the text.

 CLEAN UP Save the Welcome document, and then close it. When you exit Word, remember to click Don't Save when you are asked whether you want to save changes to the Building Block template.

Setting Math AutoCorrect Options

If you frequently create documents that contain mathematical formulas, you don't have to rely on the Design tab to insert mathematical symbols. Instead, you can type a predefined combination of characters and have Word automatically replace it with a corresponding math symbol. For example, if you type \infty, Word replaces the characters with the infinity symbol.

This replacement is made possible by the Math AutoCorrect feature. You can view all the predefined combinations by displaying the Backstage view, clicking Proofing, and then clicking AutoCorrect Options. Then in the AutoCorrect dialog box, click the Math AutoCorrect tab.

The Math AutoCorrect page of the AutoCorrect dialog box.

Tip You can create custom Math AutoCorrect entries in the same way you create text AutoCorrect entries. For information, see "Correcting Spelling and Grammatical Errors" in Chapter 2, "Edit and Proofread Text."

Clicking Recognized Functions at the bottom of the AutoCorrect dialog box displays the Recognized Math Functions dialog box, which lists the math expressions Word recognizes.

Word recognizes most common math expressions.

If you use a math expression that is not included in the list, you can easily make it available in the future by clicking Add.

Drawing and Modifying Shapes

If you want to add visual interest and impact to a document but you don't need anything as fancy as a picture or a clip art image, you can draw a shape. Shapes can be simple, such as lines, circles, or squares, or more complex, such as stars, hearts, and arrows.

To draw a shape directly on the page (Word's default setting), you click the Shapes button in the Illustrations group on the Insert tab, and click the shape you want in the Shapes gallery.

The Recently Used Shapes area of the Shapes gallery is dynamic and reflects any shapes you have drawn.

After selecting the shape you want, you can do one of the following:

● Click the document where you want a drawing with the default size and shape to be placed.

● Drag the pointer across the page to create a drawing the size and shape you want.

When you finish drawing the shape, it is automatically selected. Later, you can select the shape by clicking it. While the shape is selected, you can move and size it, and you can modify it by using commands on the Format contextual tab to do the following:

- Change the shape.

- Change the style, fill color, outline, and effects assigned to the shape, including the three-dimensional aspect, or perspective, from which you are observing the shape.

  Tip If you change the attributes of a shape—for example, its fill color and border weight—and you want all the shapes you draw from now on in this document to have those attributes, right-click the shape, and then click Set As Default Shape.

- Specify the position of the shape on the page, and the way text wraps around the shape.

  Tip You can also position a shape by dragging it, or you can hold down the Ctrl key and press the Arrow keys on your keyboard to move the shape in small increments.

- Control the order of the shape in a stack of shapes.

- Specify the shape's alignment and angle of rotation.

- Precisely control the size of the shape.

  Tip You can also change the size and shape of an object by dragging its handles.

You can right-click a shape and click Add Text to place a cursor in the center of the shape. After you type the text, you can format it with the commands in the WordArt Styles group and control its direction and alignment with the commands in the Text group.

If you build a picture by drawing individual shapes, you can group them so that they act as one object. If you move or size a grouped object, the shapes retain their positions in relation to each other. To break the bond, you ungroup the object.

If your picture consists of more than a few shapes, you might want to draw the shapes on a drawing canvas instead of directly on the page. The drawing canvas keeps the parts of the picture together, helps you position the picture, and provides a frame-like boundary between your picture and the text on the page. To open a drawing canvas, you click New Drawing Canvas at the bottom of the Shapes gallery. You can then draw shapes on the canvas in the usual ways. At any time, you can size and move the drawing canvas and the shapes on it as one unit.

Tip If you prefer to always use the drawing canvas when creating pictures with shapes, display the Backstage view, click Options, and in the Word Options dialog box, click Advanced. Then under Editing Options, select the Automatically Create Drawing Canvas When Inserting AutoShapes check box, and click OK.

In this exercise, you'll draw two shapes and a text box on a drawing canvas to create a logo. Next, you'll change the style of the shapes and the color of the text box. Then you'll size and position the canvas.

SET UP You don't need any practice files to complete this exercise. Open a blank document, and save it as *CSC-Logo*. Display the rulers, and then follow the steps.

1. On the **Insert** tab, in the **Illustrations** group, click the **Shapes** button, and then at the bottom of the **Shapes** gallery, click **New Drawing Canvas**.

   Word inserts a drawing canvas and displays the Format contextual tab on the ribbon.

2. On the **Format** tab, in the **Insert Shapes** group, click the **More** button to display the **Shapes** gallery, and then under **Block Arrows**, click the first shape in the second row (**Curved Right Arrow**).

3. Point to the upper-left corner of the drawing canvas, and then drag down and to the right to draw an arrow about 1.5 inches tall and 1.5 inches wide.

   Tip To draw a shape with equal height and width, such as a square or circle, hold down the Shift key while you drag, and then release the mouse button before releasing the Shift key.

   When you finish drawing, the arrow is selected, as indicated by the handles around it.

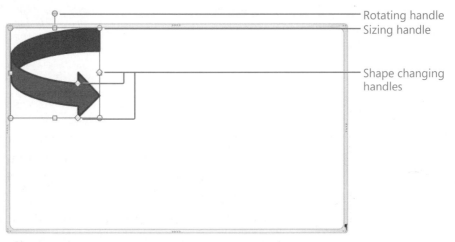

You can drag handles to rotate the arrow, change its size, and change its shape— for example, to make it fatter or make the arrowhead bigger.

4. In the **Size** group, set the **Height** and **Width** to precisely **1.5**.

5. Hold down the Ctrl key, drag a shadow outline of the arrow to the upper-right corner of the drawing canvas, and release first the mouse button and then the Ctrl key.

   Word creates a copy of the arrow in the location where you release the mouse button.

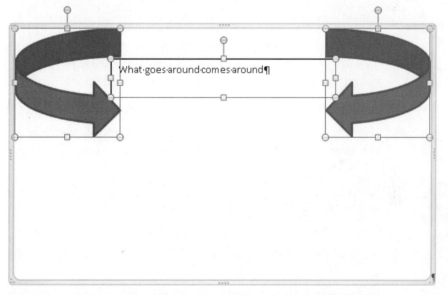

6. In the **Arrange** group, click the **Rotate** button, and then click **Flip Horizontal**.

   The copy of the arrow is now facing to the left.

7. In the **Insert Shapes** group, click the **Draw Text Box** button, and drag a text box between the two arrows. Then type **What goes around comes around**.

8. Select the left arrow, hold down the Shift key, and then select both the text box and the right arrow.

   All three shapes are now selected.

Handles around each shape indicate that they are all selected individually.

9. In the **Arrange** group, click the **Group** button, and then click **Group**.

   The three shapes are grouped as one object.

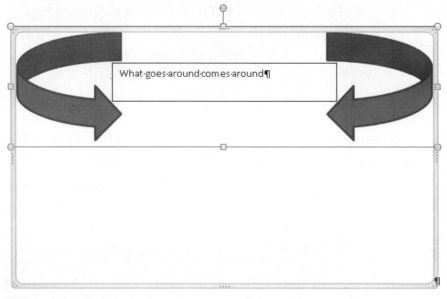

One set of handles appears around a grouped object.

10. In the **Shape Styles** group, click the **More** button, and in the **Shape Styles** gallery, click the fourth thumbnail in the last row (**Intense Effect – Olive Green, Accent 3**).

    The style is applied to all the grouped shapes.

11. Select the text in the text box, and in the **WordArt Styles** group, display the **WordArt Quick Styles** gallery. Then click the third thumbnail in the first row (**Fill – White, Drop Shadow**).

    Tip Depending on your screen resolution, you might need to click the Quick Styles button to display the WordArt Quick Styles gallery.

12. Click a blank area of the drawing canvas to release the selection.

    You can now see the results.

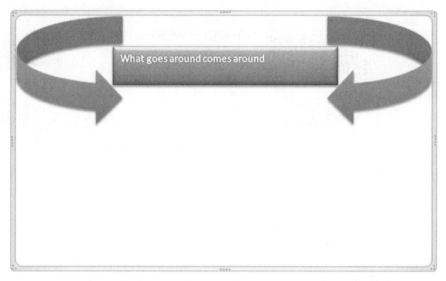

You can format a grouped object as a whole, or format individual shapes within the object.

13. In the **Size** group, click the **Width** down arrow until the drawing canvas is as narrow as it can be without the word *around* disappearing from the text box or wrapping to a second line.

14. Point to the sizing handle (the four dots) in the middle of the bottom border of the drawing canvas frame, and drag upward until the drawing canvas is just tall enough to contain the logo.

15. In the **Arrange** group, click the **Wrap Text** button, and then click **Top and Bottom**.

    You can now move the drawing canvas independently of the text around it.

    See Also For information about text wrapping, see "Arranging Objects on the Page" in Chapter 10, "Organize and Arrange Content."

16. In the **Arrange** group, click the **Position** button, and click **More Layout Options** to display the **Position** page of the **Layout** dialog box.

17. In the **Horizontal** area, set **Alignment** to **Centered, relative to Column**. Then in the **Vertical** area, set **Absolute position** to **0.5"**, **below Top Margin**. Click **OK**.

The logo is now centered at the top of the page.

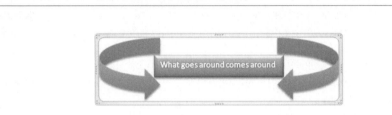

You can position the drawing canvas anywhere on the page.

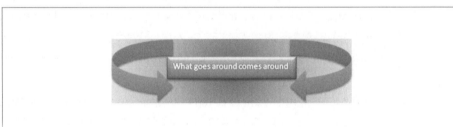

18. In the **Shape Styles** group, click the **Shape Fill** arrow, and then under **Theme Colors**, click the third box (**Tan, Background 2**).

19. Click the **Shape Fill** arrow again, point to **Gradient**, and then under **Variations**, click the second thumbnail in the second row (**From Center**).

20. Click outside of the drawing canvas.

The logo is now ready to use as part of a letterhead.

You can format the drawing canvas or leave it blank.

✖ **CLEAN UP** Save the CSC-Logo document, and then close it.

Inserting Screen Clippings

These days, many people rely on the Web as a source of the information they use in their daily life. Sometimes that information is presented in a graphic that would be useful in a Word document. Included in Word 2010 is a screen clipping tool that you can use to capture an image of anything that is visible on your computer screen.

After you display the content you want to include in a document, you click the Screenshot button in the Illustrations group on the Insert tab. You can then insert a screen clipping in one of two ways:

- Clicking a window thumbnail in the Screenshot gallery inserts a picture of that window into the document at the cursor.

- Clicking Screen Clipping at the bottom of the gallery enables you to drag across the part of the screen you want to capture, so that only that part is inserted as a picture into the document.

In this exercise, you'll insert a screen clipping from a Web site into a document.

SET UP You need the AgendaDraft_start document located in your Chapter09 practice file folder to complete this exercise. Open the AgendaDraft_start document, and save it as *AgendaDraft*. Then follow the steps.

1. Press Ctrl+End to move to the end of the document, and then at the right end of the program window title bar, click the **Minimize** button.

2. Start your Web browser, and display a Web site from which you want to capture a screen clipping.

   For example, we searched for a map showing the location of the Bellevue public library. You might want to display a map of the location of your office or a local landmark.

3. On the Windows Taskbar, click the button for the **AgendaDraft** document. Then on the **Insert** tab, in the **Illustrations** group, click the **Screenshot** button.

   A gallery displays the open windows from which you can capture a screen clipping.

Clicking the thumbnail of a window inserts an image of the window in the document.

4. At the bottom of the gallery, click **Screen Clipping**.

   The Word program window is minimized on the Windows Taskbar, and a translucent white layer covers the entire screen.

   Tip If you change your mind about capturing the screen clipping, press the Esc key to remove the white layer.

5. Drag to select the area of the Web page you want.

   For example, we dragged across the map showing the Bellevue public library location.

As you drag, the white layer is removed from the selected area so that you can see what you are selecting.

When you release the mouse button, Word inserts the screen clipping into the document at the cursor.

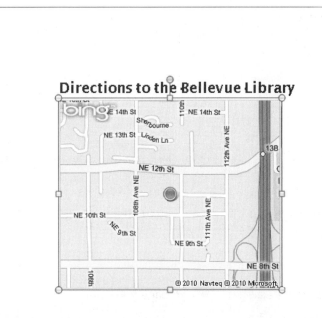

The screen clipping is a picture that can be formatted by using the commands on the Format contextual tab, just like any other picture.

See Also For information about formatting pictures, see "Inserting and Modifying Pictures" in Chapter 5, "Add Simple Graphic Elements."

❌ **CLEAN UP** Save the AgendaDraft document, and then close it.

Key Points

- By using a watermark, you can flag every page of a document with a faint word, such as *Confidential*, or a faint picture. Watermarks appear behind the text of the document, so the text can still be read.

- The Symbols dialog box provides access not only to the symbols you might need in a professional document but also to little icons that add pizzazz.

- You can construct complex math equations in your documents and have Word display them in traditional math formats.

- To dress up a document, you can draw shapes. You can also group shapes on a drawing canvas to create simple pictures.

- You can capture graphical information from other programs by using the Screenshot command.

Chapter at a Glance

Reorganize document outlines,
page 268

Arrange objects
on the page,
page 273

Use tables to control page layout,
page 282

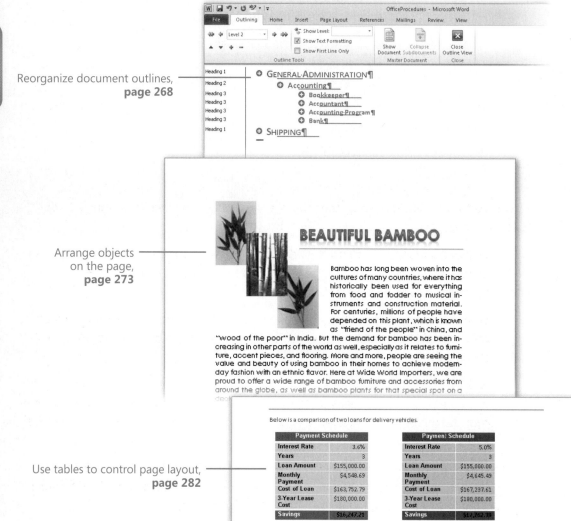

10 Organize and Arrange Content

In this chapter, you will learn how to

✔ Reorganize document outlines.

✔ Arrange objects on the page.

✔ Use tables to control page layout.

Microsoft Word 2010 gives you the following tools for organizing and arranging your document's content:

● **Outlining tools** You can use these tools to control the organization of the content in a styled document. In Outline view, you can reorganize content by moving it or by promoting or demoting it.

● **Object arranging tools** You can use these tools to control the layout of objects on the page. You can precisely position objects and control their alignment and stacking order.

● **Nested tables** You can use a table to control the positions of blocks of information on the page. For example, a table with two columns and two rows can hold a set of four paragraphs, four bulleted lists, or four tables in a format in which they can be easily compared.

In this chapter, you'll first reorganize a document by working with its outline. Then you'll modify the text-wrapping, position, and stacking order of multiple pictures in a document. Finally, you'll create a table to hold nested tables of information.

> **Practice Files** Before you can complete the exercises in this chapter, you need to copy the book's practice files to your computer. The practice files you'll use to complete the exercises in this chapter are in the Chapter10 practice file folder. A complete list of practice files is provided in "Using the Practice Files" at the beginning of this book.

Reorganizing Document Outlines

When you create a document that contains headings, you can format the headings with built-in heading styles that include outline levels. Then it is easy to view and organize the document in Outline view. In this view, you can hide all the body text and display only the headings at and above a particular level. You can also rearrange the sections of a document by moving their headings.

See Also   For information about formatting headings with styles, see "Quickly Formatting Text" in Chapter 3, "Change the Look of Text." For information about styles in general, see "Working with Styles and Templates" in Chapter 16, "Work in Word More Efficiently."

When you view a document in Outline view, the document is displayed with a hierarchical structure, and the Outlining tab appears on the ribbon.

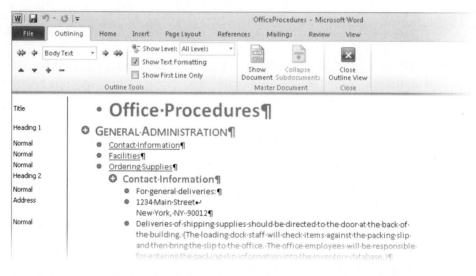

A styled document, displayed in Outline view.

Troubleshooting   The appearance of buttons and groups on the ribbon changes depending on the width of the program window. For information about changing the appearance of the ribbon to match our screen images, see "Modifying the Display of the Ribbon" at the beginning of this book.

The indentations and symbols used in Outline view to indicate the level of a heading or paragraph in the document's structure don't appear in the document in other views or when you print it. To the left of the document, the style area pane shows the style applied to each paragraph. This pane is available only in Draft and Outline views, and it is not visible by default.

Tip By default, the style area pane is 0 inch wide, which effectively closes it. We find it useful to work in Outline view with the style area pane open. If you want your screen to look like the ones shown in our graphics, display the Advanced page of the Word Options dialog box and in the Display area, change the Style Area Pane Width In Draft And Outline Views setting to 1".

You can use commands in the Outline Tools group of the Outlining tab to do the following:

- Display only the headings at a specific level and above.
- Promote or demote headings or body text by changing their level.
- Move headings and their text up or down in the document.

Tip You can click the buttons in the Master Document group to create a master document with subdocuments that you can then display or hide. The topic of master documents and subdocuments is beyond the scope of this book. For information, see Word Help.

In this exercise, you'll switch to Outline view, promote and demote headings, move headings, and expand and collapse the outline.

SET UP You need the OfficeProcedures_start document located in your Chapter10 practice file folder to complete this exercise. Open the OfficeProcedures_start document, and save it as *OfficeProcedures*. Turn on formatting marks, open the style area pane (see the tip at the top of the page), and then follow the steps.

1. In the lower-right corner of the window, on the **View Shortcuts** toolbar, click the **Outline** button.

   The document is displayed in Outline view, and the Outlining tab appears at the left end of the ribbon.

2. On the **Outlining** tab, in the **Outline Tools** group, click the **Show Level** arrow, and in the list, click **Level 1**.

   The document collapses to display only level-1 headings.

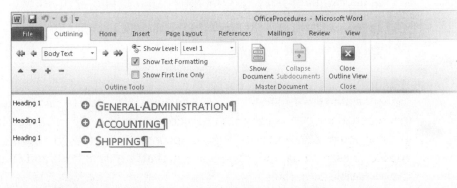

Level-1 headings are those that have the Heading 1 style applied to them.

3. Click anywhere in the **ACCOUNTING** heading.

4. In the **Outline Tools** group, click the **Expand** button.

   Keyboard Shortcut Press Alt+Shift++ to expand a heading.

   See Also For more information about keyboard shortcuts, see "Keyboard Shortcuts" at the end of this book.

   Word expands the ACCOUNTING section to display its level-2 headings.

5. In the **Outline Tools** group, click the **Demote** button.

   Keyboard Shortcut Press Alt+Shift+Right Arrow to demote a heading.

   The ACCOUNTING heading changes to a level-2 heading.

The style of the Accounting heading changes to Heading 2 when it is demoted.

6. On the Quick Access Toolbar, click the **Undo** button.

   The ACCOUNTING heading changes back to a level-1 heading.

7. In the **Outline Tools** group, click the **Collapse** button.

   Keyboard Shortcut Press Alt+Shift+_ to collapse a heading.

8. Click the **Demote** button.

   Again, the ACCOUNTING heading changes to a level-2 heading.

9. Click the **Expand** button.

Because the subheadings were hidden when you demoted the ACCOUNTING heading, all the subheadings are demoted to level 3 to maintain the hierarchy of the section.

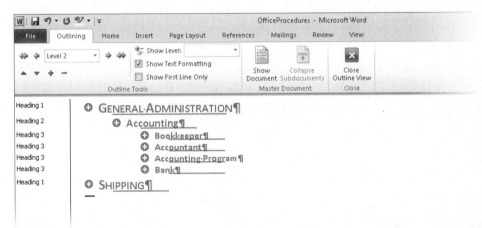

The Accounting heading changes to Heading 2, and all its subheadings change to Heading 3.

10. Click the **Collapse** button, and then in the **Outline Tools** group, click the **Promote** button.

    Keyboard Shortcut Press Alt+Shift+Left Arrow to promote a heading.

    The ACCOUNTING heading is now a level-1 heading again.

11. Press Ctrl+Home to move to the top of the document, and then in the **Outline Tools** group, in the **Show Level** list, click **Level 2**.

    The outline shows all the level-1 and level-2 headings.

12. Click the plus sign to the left of the **SHIPPING** heading, and then in the **Outline Tools** group, click the **Move Up** button five times.

    Keyboard Shortcut Press Alt+Shift+Up Arrow to move a selected heading upward in an outline.

    The SHIPPING heading and all its subheadings move above the ACCOUNTING heading.

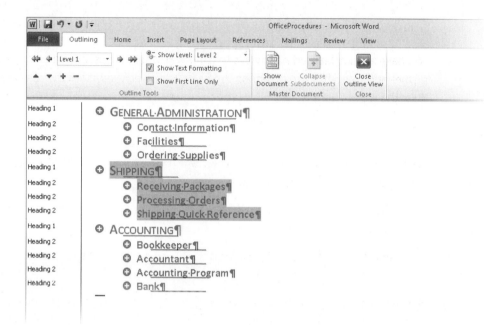

Clicking the plus sign adjacent to a heading selects all the headings and text in that section.

13. Press Ctrl+Home to release the selection, and then in the **Outline Tools** group, in the **Show Level** list, click **All Levels**.

    Keyboard Shortcut Press Alt+Shift+A to display all levels.

    You can now scroll through the document to see the effects of the reorganization.

14. In the **Close** group, click the **Close Outline View** button.

    Word displays the reorganized document in Print Layout view.

✖ **CLEAN UP** Save the OfficeProcedures document, and then close it.

Arranging Objects on the Page

You have already learned basic ways to control how text wraps around an object such as a picture and to position an object on the page. However, sometimes things don't work out quite the way you expect them to, especially when you are dealing with multiple objects.

Tip In the exercise for this chapter, you work with photographs, but the concepts discussed here also apply to other graphic objects, such as clip art images, diagrams, and shapes.

When you choose a text wrapping option other than In Line With Text, you can specify that an object be positioned in one of two ways:

- **Absolutely** This option positions the object at a distance you set from a margin, page, paragraph, or line.

- **Relatively** This type of positioning is determined by the relationship of the object to a margin or page.

However, you can take the guesswork out of setting an object's position by choosing one of nine predefined position options from the Position gallery. These options all implement square text wrapping in a specific location relative to the margins of the page.

If you use one of the position options to locate an object, you can still move it manually by dragging it. Often it is easier to drag objects into position if you display an onscreen grid to align against. You can also use alignment commands to align objects with the margins and with each other.

After you position an object, adding text might upset the arrangement of the page. You can specify whether the object should move with its related text or should remain anchored in its position. You can also specify whether the object should be allowed to overlap other objects.

If you insert several objects and then position them so that they overlap, they are said to be *stacked*. The stacking order (which object appears on top of which) is initially determined by the order in which you inserted the objects, but can also be determined by other factors such as the type of text wrapping assigned to each object. Provided all the objects have the same kind of text wrapping, you can change their order by selecting an object and clicking the Bring Forward or Send Backward button in the Arrange group to move the object to the top or bottom of the stack. If you click either button's arrow and then click Bring Forward or Send Backward, the object moves forward or backward in the stack one position at a time.

After you have arranged objects on the page, you can use the Selection And Visibility task pane to hide and show them so that you can judge each object's contribution to the whole.

In this exercise, you'll modify the text-wrapping, position, and stacking order of pictures that have already been inserted into a document. Then you'll hide one of the pictures.

SET UP You need the BambooInfo_start document located in your Chapter10 practice file folder to complete this exercise. Open the BambooInfo_start document, and save it as *BambooInfo*. Turn off formatting marks and the rulers, and set the zoom percentage so that you can see the entire first page. Then follow the steps.

1. Click the first picture, and on the **Format** tab, in the **Arrange** group, click the **Wrap Text** button.

   The Wrap Text gallery appears.

⊠	In Line with Text
⊠	Square
⊠	Tight
⊠	Through
⊠	Top and Bottom
≋	Behind Text
⊠	In Front of Text
⊠	Edit Wrap Points
⊟	More Layout Options...

   The selected picture is assigned the In Line With Text text-wrapping option.

2. In the **Wrap Text** gallery, click **More Layout Options**. Then in the **Layout** dialog box, click the **Position** tab.

   All the options on the Position page are unavailable. You cannot manually change these settings when text wrapping is set to In Line With Text.

3. Click the **Text Wrapping** tab, and in the **Wrapping style** area, click **Tight**. Then in the **Wrap Text** area, click **Right only**. Finally, in the **Distance from text** area, set both **Left** and **Right** to **0.3"**.

4. Click the **Position** tab.

   The options on the Position page are now available. Notice that the Horizontal and Vertical settings are Absolute and that the Move Object With Text check box is selected.

The selected picture is anchored to its paragraph.

5. Click **OK**.

The text now wraps to the right of the picture.

You have controlled the text wrapping and position of this picture, as well as the distance from the adjacent text.

6. Click anywhere in the first line of text to the right of the picture, and press the Home key to position the cursor at the beginning of the line. Then press Enter.

Word inserts a blank paragraph below the document title.

BEAUTIFUL BAMBOO

 Bamboo has long been woven into the cultures of many countries, where it has historically been used for everything from food and fodder to musical instruments and construction material. For centuries, millions of people have depended on this plant, which is known as "friend of the people" in China, and "wood of the poor" in India. But the demand for bamboo has been increasing in other parts of the world as well, especially as it relates to furniture, accent pieces, and flooring. More and more, people are seeing the value and beauty of using bamboo in their homes to achieve modern-day fashion with an ethnic flavor. Here at Wide World Importers, we are proud to offer a wide range of bamboo furniture and accessories from around the globe, as well as bamboo plants for that special spot on a deck or patio.

The picture moves down with the paragraph to which it is attached.

7. On the Quick Access Toolbar, click the **Undo** button to remove the blank paragraph.

8. Click the picture to select it. Then on the **Format** tab, in the **Arrange** group, click the **Position** button.

The Position gallery appears.

In Line with Text

With Text Wrapping

More Layout Options...

This gallery offers nine With Text Wrapping positions.

9. In the **Position** gallery, point to each thumbnail in turn to see a live preview of its effects. Then under **With Text Wrapping**, click the first thumbnail in the first row (**Position in Top Left with Square Text Wrapping**).

The picture moves to the upper-left corner of the document.

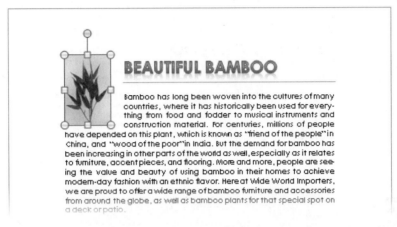

The picture is now aligned with the top and left page margins.

10. Click to the left of **Beautiful** in the title, and press Enter.

Word inserts a blank paragraph above the document title, but the picture does not move down with the title.

11. Click the picture, and then at the bottom of the **Position** gallery, click **More Layout Options** to display the **Position** page of the **Layout** dialog box.

Notice that the Horizontal and Vertical settings have changed to Alignment and that the Move Object With Text check box is no longer selected. The relationship of the picture with the text is broken, and the picture is now sitting in a fixed position relative to the margins of the page.

12. Click **Cancel** to close the dialog box.

13. Click the second bamboo picture, display the **Position** gallery, and under **With Text Wrapping**, click the third thumbnail in the first row (**Position in Top Left with Square Text Wrapping**).

Selecting one of the predefined Position options is a quick way of both setting text wrapping and breaking the relationship of the picture with the text.

14. In the **Arrange** group, click the **Align** button.

The Align gallery appears.

📇	Align <u>L</u>eft
🔱	Align <u>C</u>enter
🗐	Align <u>R</u>ight
🗓	Align <u>T</u>op
◈	Align <u>M</u>iddle
📊	Align <u>B</u>ottom
▫▫▫	Distribute <u>H</u>orizontally
🔱	Distribute <u>V</u>ertically
	Align to <u>P</u>age
✓	Align to Margin
	Align Selected O<u>b</u>jects
	View Gridline<u>s</u>
⊞	<u>G</u>rid Settings...

The Align gallery provides easy access to all the alignment options.

Tip When pictures have a text wrapping setting other than In Line With Text, you can use the options in the Align gallery to align multiple objects horizontally or vertically. You can also distribute selected objects equally between the first and last objects in the selection. Understanding how these options work takes practice. It is a good idea to test various settings with multiple objects to see the results. Remember, the Undo button is your ally!

15. At the bottom of the gallery, click **Grid Settings**.

The Drawing Grid dialog box opens.

The settings in this dialog box control the appearance of an onscreen grid.

16. In the **Grid settings** area, set both **Horizontal spacing** and **Vertical spacing** to **0.25"**. Then in the **Show grid** area, select the **Display gridlines on screen** check box, and click **OK**.

    The text column is filled with a grid of quarter-inch squares.

17. Drag the selected picture down and to the left until it sits three squares from the top margin and three squares from the left margin, overlapping the first picture.

    Notice as you drag that the picture snaps to the grid.

    Tip To move a picture without snapping to the grid, hold down the Ctrl key while pressing an Arrow key. The picture moves in tiny increments in the direction of the key.

18. Click the third picture in the document, set its position to **Position in Bottom Left with Square Text Wrapping**, and then drag it up and to the right until it sits six squares from the top margin and six squares from the left margin, overlapping the second picture.

    The text wraps on both sides of the picture, which is not the effect you want.

    Aligning objects doesn't always produce the results you expect. To behave predictably, the objects need to have the same text-wrapping settings.

19. Click the first picture, display the **Text Wrapping** page of the **Layout** dialog box, and in the **Wrapping style** area, click **Tight**. In the **Wrap Text** area, ensure that the setting is **Right only**. Then in the **Distance from text** area, ensure that both **Left** and **Right** are set to **0.3"**, and click **OK**.

20. Repeat step 19 for the second and third pictures.

21. With the third picture still selected, in the **Arrange** group, click the **Send Backward** button.

    The middle picture now overlaps the first and third pictures.

22. In the **Arrange** group, click the **Align** button, and click **View Gridlines** to turn them off. Then click away from the picture to release the selection.

    The text now wraps to the right of the pictures.

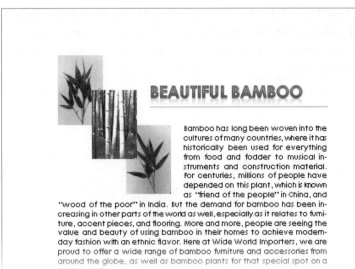

It is easier to judge the balance of your layout if you turn off gridlines.

Selection Pane

23. Click the third picture, and then in the **Arrange** group, click the **Selection Pane** button.

The Selection And Visibility task pane opens, identifying the three objects on this page.

You can click buttons to show, hide, and change the order of objects on a page.

24. At the bottom of the task pane, click the **Hide All** button. Then in turn, click the boxes adjacent to the three pictures.

    When an object is hidden, its box is blank, and when it is visible, its box contains an eye icon.

25. Click the check box for **Picture 3** to hide just that picture. Then close the task pane.

 CLEAN UP Save the BambooInfo document, and then close it.

Using Tables to Control Page Layout

Most people are accustomed to thinking of a table as a means of displaying data in a quick, easy-to-grasp format. But tables can also serve to organize your pages in creative ways. For example, suppose you want to display two tables next to each other. The simplest way to do this is to first create a table with one tall row and two wide columns and no gridlines. You can then insert one table in the first cell and the other table in the second cell. These nested tables then seem to be arranged side by side.

Consultation Fees	
Location	Hourly Rate
In home	$50.00
Phone	$35.00
In store	$40.00

In-Home Trip Charge	
Distance	Fee
0-10 miles	No charge
11-50 miles	$10.00
Over 50 miles	$20.00

These tables are nested within the cells of a one-row, two-column table.

As with regular tables, you can create a nested table in one of three ways:

● From scratch

● By formatting existing information

● By inserting Microsoft Excel data

And just like other tables, you can format a nested table either manually or by using one of the ready-made table styles.

Tip You can use tables to organize a mixture of elements such as text, tables, charts, and diagrams.

When creating a table to contain other elements, you might want to take advantage of the Word table-drawing feature. If you click Draw Table below the grid displayed when you click the Table button on the Insert tab, the pointer changes to a pencil you can use to draw cells on the page. You can set up the container table visually, without having to fuss with dialog boxes and precise dimensions while you are designing the layout. Then after everything is set up the way you want it, you can use the Table Properties dialog box to fine-tune the table specifications.

In this exercise, you'll draw a table to contain two other tables. You'll then insert and format the nested tables.

SET UP You need the Loan workbook, the DeliveryTruckPurchase document, and the LoanComparisons_start document located in your Chapter10 practice file folder to complete this exercise. Open the Loan workbook in Excel, and open the DeliveryTruckPurchase document in Word. Then open the LoanComparisons_start document, and save it as *LoanComparisons*. Turn on formatting marks and the rulers, and then follow the steps.

1. With the **LoanComparisons** document active, on the **Insert** tab, in the **Tables** group, click the **Table** button, and then click **Draw Table**.

    The pointer becomes a pencil.

2. Point below the last paragraph mark in the document, and drag across and down to create a cell about 3 inches wide and 1.5 inches tall.

    Tip The location of the pencil is marked with guides on the horizontal and vertical rulers. You can use these guides to help you draw cells of specific dimensions.

3. Point to the upper-right corner of the cell (you don't have to be precise), and drag to create another cell about the same size as the first.

    When you release the mouse button, Word joins the two cells.

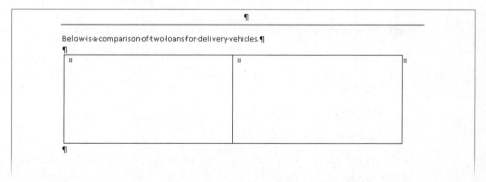

The structure of a table, created with the drawing tool.

Troubleshooting If your table is not placed between the two paragraph marks, as shown in the graphic, click the Undo button and redraw your table, being sure to start below the last paragraph mark. When you finish drawing the first cell, Word positions the table correctly.

Switch Windows ▾

4. On the **View** tab, in the **Window** group, click the **Switch Windows** button, and then click **DeliveryTruckPurchase**.

5. Scroll to the bottom of the page, and click anywhere in the **Payment Schedule** table. Then on the **Layout** contextual tab, in the **Table** group, click **Select**, and click **Select Table**.

6. On the **Home** tab, in the **Clipboard** group, click the **Copy** button.

7. Switch to the **LoanComparisons** document, right-click the first cell in the table, and then under **Paste Options**, click the **Nest Table** button.

Word inserts the table you copied into the cell and adjusts the height of the container table to fit the size of the nested table.

8. On the Windows Taskbar, click the **Microsoft Excel** button to activate **Sheet1** of the **Loan** workbook. Then select cells **A1:B8**, and on the Excel **Home** tab, in the **Clipboard** group, click the **Copy** button.

9. Switch back to the **LoanComparisons** document, click the second cell in the table, and then on the **Home** tab, in the **Clipboard** group, click the **Paste** button.

Word inserts the worksheet data as a nested table in the cell.

Paste ▾

Payment·Schedule¤		¤	Payment·Schedule¤		¤	¤
Interest·Rate¤	3.6%¤	¤	Interest·Rate¤	5.0%¤	¤	
Years¤	3¤	¤	Years¤	3¤	¤	
Loan·Amount¤	$155,000.00·	¤	Loan·Amount¤	$155,000.00·	¤	
Monthly· Payment¤	$4,548.69¤	¤	Monthly· Payment¤	$4,645.49¤	¤	
Cost·of·Loan¤	$163,752.79¤	¤	Cost·of·Loan¤	$167,237.61¤	¤	
3-Year·Lease· Cost¤	$180,000.00¤	¤	3-Year·Lease· Cost¤	$180,000.00¤	¤	
Savings¤	$16,247.21¤	¤	Savings¤	$12,762.39¤	¤	

Below·is·a·comparison·of·two·loans·for·delivery·vehicles.¶

These nested tables come from a Word document and an Excel worksheet.

10. Move the pointer to the selection area adjacent to the container table, and then click to select its two cells.

11. On the **Home** tab, in the **Paragraph** group, click the **Border** arrow, and then in the list, click **No Border**.

Word removes the borders from the container cells.

12. Click anywhere in the left table, and on the **Design** contextual tab, in the **Table Style Options** group, ensure that the **Header Row** check box is selected, select the **Total Row** check box, and clear any other check boxes.

13. In the **Table Styles** group, display the **Table Styles** gallery, and click the thumbnail of the table style you want to apply to the nested table.

    We used Medium Grid 3 – Accent 1.

14. Repeat steps 12 and 13 to format the right table, perhaps using a similar table style with a different color.

    We used Medium Grid 3 – Accent 2.

15. Turn off formatting marks to see the results.

    The nested tables now clearly contrast the two loans.

Below is a comparison of two loans for delivery vehicles.

Payment Schedule	
Interest Rate	3.6%
Years	3
Loan Amount	$155,000.00
Monthly Payment	$4,548.69
Cost of Loan	$163,752.79
3-Year Lease Cost	$180,000.00
Savings	$16,247.21

Payment Schedule	
Interest Rate	5.0%
Years	3
Loan Amount	$155,000.00
Monthly Payment	$4,645.49
Cost of Loan	$167,237.61
3-Year Lease Cost	$180,000.00
Savings	$12,762.39

Although invisible, the container table provides the structure to display these two tables effectively.

✖ CLEAN UP Save the LoanComparisons document, and then close it. Then close the DeliveryTruckPurchase document. Finally, close the Loan workbook without saving any changes.

Key Points

- If you take the time to apply heading styles to a document, you can use the document's outline to rearrange its sections.
- You can position an object in relation to the text that surrounds it and in relation to other objects on the page.
- By using tables in creative ways, you can place information in non-linear arrangements for easy comparison or analysis.

Chapter at a Glance

Save files in different formats, **page 288**

ParkingRules.xps - XPS Viewer

File ▾ Permissions ▾ Signatures ▾   Find

6.   Parking and Vehicles

6.1   The Association shall not be responsible for any vehicles parked in the Common Areas the complex.

6.2   Owners shall park their vehicles only in their assigned areas or stalls in the common ga except under the circumstances specified in rule 6.4.

6.3   Five parking spaces are reserved for guest parking for the entire complex. Commercial vehicles may park in these spaces only as long as necessary to perform services.

6.4   No Owner shall park his or her vehicle in the guest parking spaces except on a tempora short-term basis.

• Temporary is defined as not routine and not recurring.

Create and modify Web documents, **page 293**

Room Planner - Windows Internet Explorer

C:\Users\Sidney Higa\Desktop\Word2010SBS\Chapter11\My Web Page.htm   Bing

Favorites   Suggested Sites ▾   Web Slice Gallery ▾

Room Planner   Page ▾ Safety ▾ Tools ▾   100%

Wide World Importers

INFORMATION SHEET

Simple Room Design

With the Room Planner, you'll never make another design mistake. Created by acclaimed interior designers to simplify the redecorating process, this award-winning planning tool incorporates elements of color, dimension, and style to guide your project. It includes a furniture location guide; room grid; drawing tools; and miniature furniture, rugs, accessories, and color swatches that match our large in-store selection. Here's how to use the planner to create the room of your dreams!

Take a look at how your home is decorated and notice the things you like and dislike. Pay special attention to the color scheme and to how you react to each room. Is it inviting? Does it feel comfortable? Does it relax you or does it invigorate you?

Focus on the room(s) you would most like to change. Brainstorm all the things you would change in that room if you could. Don't think about what it would cost; just let your imagination go wild! It might be helpful to write down all the negatives and positives. You don't need to come up with solutions all at once. Just be clear about what you like and what you hate about that room.

> Go with what you love, and the rest will fall into place.

Visit our showroom and purchase a Room Planner. While you're there, take a look around and see what really appeals to you. Sometimes entire room...

Blog

Add | Summary

March 02
Walla Walla Music

If you are a music lover, you'll want to explore the Walla Walla music scene. This little town offers music for everyone: ethereal choral, funky blues, downhome country, refined chamber, rock, and pop. But the jewel of them all is the Walla Walla Symphony Orchestra, the oldest continuously operating symphony west of the Mississippi.

From humble beginnings, this outstanding orchestra has matured into one of the best we have heard in recent years. Maestro Yaacov Bergman, in his 20th season, continues to deliver inspired programs that challenge his musicians and his audiences. In April, we look forward to a night of *Flora and Fauna* at the orchestra's 416th concert since its inception in 1907. As usual, the performance will be held in beautiful Cordiner Hall on the Whitman College campus. Be sure to check out this and their other offerings at www.wwsymphony.org.

1:17 PM | Add a comment | Permalink | Blog it

Create and publish blog posts, **page 299**

11 Create Documents for Use Outside of Word

In this chapter, you will learn how to

✔ Save files in different formats.

✔ Create and modify Web documents.

✔ Create and publish blog posts.

Sometimes you'll create a document in Microsoft Word 2010 and then want to send it to someone who doesn't have Word 2010 installed on his or her computer. Word comes with several conversion utilities that you can use to save documents in other file formats so that you can distribute documents that your colleagues can read and use in almost any program.

If you need to distribute a document electronically but you don't want to share the actual file, you can "print" the document to a new file in Portable Document Format (PDF) or XML Paper Specification (XPS) format. When people view the PDF or XPS file, they see it just as it would look if you printed it. If they print the file, no matter what computer or what printer they use, the pages look just as they do when printed from your computer on your printer.

One way of distributing the information in your documents is by converting them to Web pages so that people can read them on the Web. The Web has become a major part of our everyday lives. We use it to research topics, shop, check the news, and find out how our favorite sports team is doing. It's also a great publishing tool if you are trying to reach a broad audience. For example, your organization might want to publish a Web newsletter to provide information while advertising its goods or services. Or you might want to use built-in Word tools to create and post articles to a blog (short for *Web log*) about a particular topic.

In this chapter, you'll first save a document in a different file format. Then you'll preview a document in Web Layout view, save the document as a Web page, and make any adjustments necessary for optimum presentation in a Web browser. Finally, you'll create a blog post, register an existing blog account, and then publish the blog post.

> **Practice Files** Before you can complete the exercises in this chapter, you need to copy the book's practice files to your computer. The practice files you'll use to complete the exercises in this chapter are in the Chapter11 practice file folder. A complete list of practice files is provided in "Using the Practice Files" at the beginning of this book.

Saving Files in Different Formats

When you save a Word document, the default file format is the Word 2010 .docx format. To save a document in a different file format, you display the Backstage view, click Save As to open the Save As dialog box, and then change the Save As Type setting to the format you want to use.

Viewing the .docx Format

The .docx format actually consists of a set of files in various folders. The entire set is compressed so that the "file" has the smallest possible footprint. If you are interested in taking a look at a "file," you can change the .docx file name extension to .zip and then view the files in Windows Explorer.

To view the components of a .docx file:

1. Display Windows Explorer, click Organize, and then click Folder And Search Options to display the Folder Options dialog box.

2. Click the View tab, and in the Advanced Settings list, clear the Hide Extensions For Known File Types check box. Then click OK.

3. Navigate to the folder containing the file you want to view, and change the file name extension from .docx to .zip. Click Yes to acknowledge the warning message.

4. Double click the .zip file, and then double-click any folders you want to view.

   You can see the component files in the expanded folder.

5. When you have finished exploring, change the file name extension back to .docx, and in the Folder Options dialog box, hide the display of file name extensions.

If you want to save the file so that it can be used with an earlier version of Word, you need to save it in the .doc format. You do this by changing the Save As Type setting to Word 97-2003 Document.

You can save Word documents in many different formats.

If you want to save a Word document in a format that can be opened by the widest variety of programs, use one of the following formats:

- **Rich Text Format (*.rtf)** This format preserves the document's formatting.

- **Plain Text (*.txt)** This format preserves only the document's text.

If you want people to be able to view a document but not change it, you can save the document in one of two formats:

- **PDF (.pdf)** This format is preferred by commercial printing facilities. You should also use this format if you know that recipients have a PDF reader, such as Adobe Acrobat Reader, installed on their computer.

- **XPS (.xps)** This format precisely renders all fonts, images, and colors on recipients' computers.

Both the PDF and XPS formats are designed to deliver documents as electronic representations of the way they look when printed. The text and graphics in .pdf and .xps files are essentially static and content cannot be easily edited, so these formats are ideal for legal documents. Both types of files can easily be sent by e-mail to many recipients and can be made available on a Web page for downloading by anyone who wants them. However, the files are no longer Word documents, and they cannot be opened, viewed, or edited in Word.

When you indicate that you want to save a Word document in PDF or XPS format, the Save As dialog box expands so that you can optimize the file size of the document for your intended distribution method. You can also click Options to display a dialog box where you can do the following:

- Specify the pages to include in the .pdf or .xps version of the document.
- Include or exclude comments and tracked changes.
- Include or exclude items such as bookmarks and properties.
- Set specific PDF options.

Tip Another way to create an .xps file or a .pdf file is to display the Backstage view, and in the left pane, click Save & Send. Then in the File Types area of the center pane, click Create PDF/XPS Document to display information about this task in the right pane. Clicking the Create PDF/XPS button displays the Publish As PDF Or XPS dialog box, in which you can save (publish) the file in the usual way.

You can also click Change File Type in the center pane of the Save & Send page to display information about common file formats. Selecting a format and then clicking the Save As button in the right pane opens the Save As dialog box with that file type already selected.

In this exercise, you'll save one page of a multipage document in XPS format for publication online. Then you'll view the XPS page.

SET UP You need the ParkingRules_start document located in your Chapter11 practice file folder to complete this exercise. Open the ParkingRules_start document, and then follow the steps.

1. Scroll down to page **3** of the document.

   You want to save only this page in XPS format.

2. Display the Backstage view, and then in the left pane, click **Save As**.

3. In the **File name** box of the **Save As** dialog box, change the name to **ParkingRules**.

4. Display the **Save as type** list, and click **XPS Document**.

   The Save As dialog box expands so that you can select options for the file.

The expanded Save As dialog box for the XPS format.

5. In the **Optimize for** area, click **Minimum size (publishing online)**. Then click **Options**.

    The Options dialog box opens.

You can choose from these options to tailor the .xps file to your needs.

6. In the **Page range** area, click **Current page**.

7. In the **Include non-printing information** area, clear the **Document properties** check box, and then click **OK**.

8. Back in the **Save As** dialog box, select the **Open file after publishing** check box, and then click **Save**.

    The document is saved in XPS format. Because you indicated that you wanted to open the file after saving it, the XPS Viewer starts and displays the file.

Only page 3 of the Word document appears in the .xps file.

✖ CLEAN UP Close the XPS Viewer, and then close the ParkingRules_start document.

Creating and Modifying Web Documents

You don't need to be a Web designer to create a Web page. From within Word 2010, you can view a document in Web Layout view, make any necessary adjustments in Word, and then save the document as a Web page, as easily as you would save it in any other format. During the process of saving the Web page, you can assign a page title that will appear in the title bar of the viewer's Web browser.

When you save a document as a Web page, Word converts the styles and formatting in the document to Hypertext Markup Language (HTML) codes, which are called *tags*. These tags tell a Web browser how to display the document. During the conversion, some of the document's formatting might be changed or ignored because it is not supported by all Web browsers. If that is the case, Word alerts you and gives you the option of stopping the conversion process so that you can make adjustments to the formatting to make it more compatible.

Tip In the Web Options dialog box, you can specify which browsers you anticipate will be used to view your Web pages. You can also have Word disable any features that are incompatible with the specified browsers.

You can save a document as a Web page in any of three formats:

- **Web Page** This format saves the Web page as a .htm file with a folder of supporting files that ensure the page is rendered exactly as you want it.

- **Single File Web Page** This format embeds all the information necessary to render the Web page in one MIME-encapsulated aggregate HTML (.mhtml) file that can be distributed via e-mail.

- **Web Page, Filtered** This format removes any Office-specific tags from the file and significantly reduces the size of the Web document and its accompanying folder of supporting files. However, it can also radically change the look of the document. For example, it might change a shaded background to a solid color, making the resulting page difficult to read.

After you save a document as a Web page, it is no longer a Word document. However, you can still open, view, and edit the Web page in Word, just as you would a normal document. (You can also open and edit HTML-format Web pages created in other programs.) Making changes can be as basic as replacing text and adjusting alignment, or as advanced as moving and inserting graphics. When you finish modifying the Web page, you can resave it as a Web page, or save it as a regular Word document.

In this exercise, you'll check that your computer is optimized for displaying documents as Web pages in Windows Internet Explorer 6, Internet Explorer 7, or Internet Explorer 8. You'll preview a document in Web Layout view and make adjustments necessary for online presentation. Finally, you'll save the document as a Web page, provide a title for the Web page, open the Web page in Word to make some modifications, and then save and view your changes.

SET UP You need the RoomPlannerWeb_start document located in your Chapter11 practice file folder to complete this exercise. You also need a Web browser. Internet Explorer 8 is recommended; the steps might be different for other browsers and versions. Open the RoomPlannerWeb_start document, and save it as *RoomPlannerWeb*. Hide formatting marks, display the rulers, and be sure the zoom percentage is set to 100%. Then follow the steps.

1. Display the Backstage view, and in the left pane, click **Options**.

   The Word Options dialog box opens.

2. In the left pane, click **Advanced**. Then at the bottom of the **Advanced** page, in the **General** area, click **Web Options**.

   The Web Options dialog box opens.

The Browsers page of the Web Options dialog box.

3. On the **Browsers** page, verify that the **People who view this Web page will be using** option is set to **Microsoft Internet Explorer 6 or later** and that under **Options**, all five check boxes are selected.

4. If you want, view the other pages of the **Web Options** dialog box to familiarize yourself with the kinds of settings available for your Web pages. Then click **OK**.

5. Click **OK** to close the **Word Options** dialog box.

6. On the **View Shortcuts** toolbar in the lower-right corner of the screen, click the **Web Layout** button.

   Word displays the page as it will appear in your Web browser.

In Web Layout view, the document expands to fill the screen.

Troubleshooting The appearance of buttons and groups on the ribbon changes depending on the width of the program window. For information about changing the appearance of the ribbon to match our screen images, see "Modifying the Display of the Ribbon" at the beginning of this book.

As you can see, the page margins are ignored. The page will be easier to read if the text lines are shorter, which you can accomplish by indenting the paragraphs. You also need to adjust the size of the quote box for a more dramatic visual effect.

7. On the **Home** tab, in the **Editing** group, click the **Select** button, and then click **Select All**.

   Keyboard Shortcut Press Ctrl+A to select an entire document.

   See Also For more information about keyboard shortcuts, see "Keyboard Shortcuts" at the end of this book.

8. With the document selected, click the **Paragraph** dialog box launcher.

9. On the **Indents and Spacing** page of the **Paragraph** dialog box, in the **Indentation** area, change the **Left** and **Right** settings to **1.25"**, and then click **OK**.

   The text is now indented from the left and right edges of the window.

10. Click the frame of the quote box to select it, and then on the **Format** contextual tab, in the **Size** group, change the **Width** setting to **2.5"**. Press Enter to implement the change, and then click away from the quote box to release the selection.

Troubleshooting If the quote box jumps to the middle of the window when you change its size, select it and then in the Arrange group, click the Wrap Text button, and click Square to reapply that text wrapping option.

The Web document is now more readable. (Depending on your screen configuration, your line breaks might be different than those shown here.)

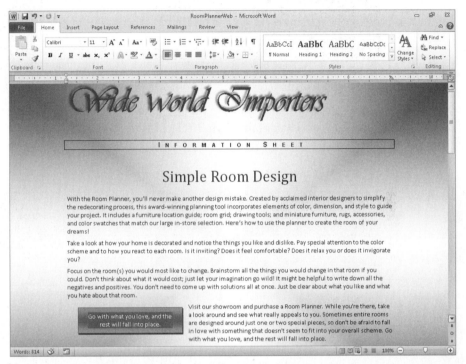

The "margins" are wider and the quote box is half its original width, making the quote wrap to two lines.

11. Display the Backstage view, and in the left pane, click **Save As**.

12. With the contents of the **Chapter11** practice file folder displayed in the **Save As** dialog box, type **My Web Page** in the **File name** box.

13. Display the **Save as type** list, and click **Web Page**. Then when the **Save As** dialog box expands, click **Change Title**.

    The Enter Text dialog box opens.

14. In the **Page title** box, type **Room Planner**, and click **OK**.

    This title will appear in the title bar of the Web browser window when the Web page is displayed.

15. In the **Save As** dialog box, click **Save**.

The Microsoft Word Compatibility Checker tells you that the Small Caps effect used for the *Information Sheet* subtitle is not supported by the specified Web browsers and will be changed to all capital letters.

16. In the **Compatibility Checker**, click **Continue**.

    Word saves the document as an HTML file called *My Web Page*.

17. Press Ctrl+End to move to the end of the document, and then type **Looking for free advice? Check our schedule of decorating seminars.** (Include the period.)

18. If you want, format the text to make it stand out. Then save the Web page.

19. Open Windows Explorer, and navigate to the **Chapter11** practice file folder.

    The Chapter11 folder contains the My Web Page file and a folder named My Web Page_files, which contains supporting files for the Web page.

20. Double-click **My Web Page**.

    Your Web browser starts, and the Web page opens.

The Web document looks the same in a Web browser as it did in Web Layout view.

You can scroll to the bottom of the page to see the changes you made to the HTML file in Word.

 CLEAN UP Close your Web browser and Windows Explorer. Then close the My Web Page HTML file.

Creating and Publishing Blog Posts

Blogs used to be personal Web sites—online spaces where individuals expressed their opinions about anything and everything. With the evolution of social sites such as Facebook and MySpace, blogs are now less likely to be personal online diaries intended for a limited audience, such as the author's family or circle of friends, and are more likely to serve a promotional purpose. For example, they might provide news and information about an industry. Or they might offer commentary on a specific subject, such as a genre of music, a political point of view, a medical condition, or local news.

A blog consists of posts that can include text, images, and links to related blogs, Web pages, and other media. Word 2010 makes it easy to create posts that you can upload to your blog. If you have already set up a blog account with a blog service provider, you can register your account with Word the first time you create a blog post. If you haven't yet set up the blog account, you'll need to register with a service provider before you can publish your first post. Thereafter, Word uses your registered account information when you create or publish a blog post.

To create a blog post, you can use a template designed specifically for that purpose. You then publish a draft of the post to your blog space, where you can review and make any necessary changes before actually publishing the final version.

If you create a regular document and then want to publish it as a blog post, display the Backstage view, and in the left pane, click Save & Send. Then in the Save & Send area of the center pane, click Publish As Blog Post to display information about blogging in the right pane. Clicking the Publish As Blog Post button converts the active document to a new blog post containing the content of the document. You can then save and publish the blog post the same way you would a regular blog post.

In this exercise, you'll register your existing blog account in Word, create a blog post, publish it to your blog, and then view the published blog post.

SET UP You need the BlogPost document located in your Chapter11 practice file folder to complete this exercise. You need to have an existing blog account with Windows Live Spaces or another blog service provider, with e-mail publishing or the equivalent turned on. Then follow the steps.

1. Display the Backstage view, and in the left pane, click **New**.

2. In the center pane of the **New** page, under **Available Templates**, click **Blog post**. Then in the right pane, click **Create**.

   Word creates a document and the Register A Blog Account dialog box opens. If you already have a blog account, you can click Register Now, and follow the instructions to register your existing account. If you don't have a blog account, you can click the Office.com link for information about getting an account.

Setting Up a Blog Account

Before setting up a blog account, you must decide which blog service provider you want to use. Many service providers, such as Windows Live Spaces (*spaces.live.com*) and Blogger (*www.blogger.com*), offer blog spaces free of charge. If your organization is running Microsoft SharePoint 2007 or SharePoint 2010, the site manager might be able to set up a blog space for you.

Tip The following instructions were current at the time of writing, but because the Windows Live site is constantly being updated, the steps might have changed.

To open a Windows Live Spaces account and create a blog space:

1. Start your Web browser, and then in the Address bar, type *spaces.live.com*, and press Enter. Then if necessary, enter your credentials to sign into your account.

2. On the Spaces - Windows Live home page, click Create Your Space.

3. On the [Your Name] Space page, under Welcome To Your Space, click Choose A Web Address.

4. In the box between *http://* and *.spaces.live.com* on the Web Address page, enter the address you want to use. Then click Check Availability.

5. If Windows Live Spaces reports that the Web address is available, click Save; if the address is not available, repeat step 4 with another name.

You can then enter information about yourself (your profile), give access to friends, and add content directly on your blog's home page.

If you want to publish to your blog from Word, you need to activate the blog and turn on e-mail publishing.

To activate the blog:

1. Under Welcome To Your Space, click Add Blog Entry.

   A Blog button is added to the toolbar of your blog page header, and a window opens so that you can enter a blog post.

2. Click Cancel, and then in the Exit Without Saving Changes message box, click OK.

To turn on e-mail publishing:

1. At the right end of the toolbar of your blog page header, click Options, and then click E-mail Publishing.

   On this page, you specify the locations from which you will post blog materials.

The Windows Live Spaces E-mail Publishing page.

2. On the E-mail Publishing page, do the following:

   a. Select the Turn On E-mail Publishing check box.

   b. Type up to three e-mail addresses from which you'll publish blog posts.

   c. Type a secret word (the password you'll use to register your blog account in Word).

   d. Select photo albums to share (optional).

   e. Choose whether to publish e-mail submissions immediately or review them online before publishing.

3. Record the e-mail addresses given at the bottom of the page, and then click Save.

This dialog box appears the first time you create a blog post.

Tip If you don't already have a blog account, you can click Register Later and skip to step 8. Word will prompt you again to register your account the first time you publish a blog post or the next time you create a blog post.

The following steps are for registering a blog account created on Windows Live Spaces.

3. Click **Register Now**.

   The New Blog Account dialog box opens.

Remember, you are not creating a new account but registering one you have already created.

4. In the **Blog** list, click **Windows Live Spaces**, and then click **Next**.

   The New Windows Live Spaces Account dialog box opens.

You need the space name and secret word assigned to your blog account to complete the registration process.

5. Enter your space name and secret word, and then click **OK**.

    Tip With Windows Live Spaces, your space name is part of your space address. For example, if your space address is http://lucernepublishing.spaces.live.com/, the space name is *lucernepublishing*.

    The Picture Options dialog box opens.

6. In the **Picture Options** dialog box, verify that **None – Don't upload pictures** is selected in the **Picture provider** box, and then click **OK**.

    Tip If you want to be able to upload pictures, you can get information about setting up a provider by clicking the links in the Picture Options dialog box.

    A message box appears when your account has been successfully registered.

You can now publish blog posts from Word to your blog account.

7. In the **Microsoft Word** message box, click **OK**.

    Word displays a blank blog post with a title placeholder at the top.

For a blog post, the ribbon displays only the File, Blog Post, and Insert tabs.

8. Click the title placeholder, and type **Walla Walla Music**.

9. Display the Backstage view, and in the left pane, click **Open**. Then in the **Open** dialog box, navigate to your **Chapter11** practice file folder, and double-click the **BlogPost** document.

10. Select and copy the two paragraphs, and then close the **BlogPost** document.

11. In the blog post, click below the line, and then paste the two paragraphs from the Microsoft Office Clipboard.

12. If you want, use the commands in the **Basic Text** group on the **Blog Post** tab to format the title and text.

We left the default formatting.

The entry is ready to be posted to your blog.

Tip Before you publish this blog post, you can turn wwsymphony.org in the last line of the second paragraph into a Web link by clicking the Hyperlink button in the Links group on the Insert tab. For information about inserting Web links, see "Adding Hyperlinks" in Chapter 12, "Explore More Text Techniques." You can also insert tables and illustrations by clicking their buttons and using the techniques you would use in a regular Word document.

13. On the Quick Access Toolbar, click the **Save** button.

14. With the contents of your **Chapter11** practice file folder displayed in the **Save As** dialog box, type **My Blog Post** in the **File name** box, and then click **Save**.

15. On the **Blog Post** tab, in the **Blog** group, click the **Publish** arrow, and then click **Publish as Draft**.

The Connect To <Blog Title> dialog box opens.

You can specify the blog account for each blog post.

Troubleshooting If you have only one blog account, you might not see this dialog box.

16. Enter your space name and secret word, and then click **OK**.

A message appears when the blog post has been published to your blog.

> This post was published to Margie's Blog at 1:10:29 PM 3/2/2010
>
> ## Walla Walla Music
>
> If you are a music lover, you'll want to explore the Walla Walla music scene. This
> country, refined chamber, rock, and pop. But the jewel of them all is the Walla W
> the Mississippi.
>
> From humble beginnings, this outstanding orchestra has matured into one of the
> season, continues to deliver inspired programs that challenge his musicians and
> orchestra's 416th concert since its inception in 1907. As usual, the performance w
> check out this and their other offerings at www.wwsymphony.org.

This message confirms that the draft blog post was successfully published.

17. In the **Blog** group, click the **Home Page** button.

    Your default Web browser opens, displaying the home page of your registered blog space.

18. Under **Blog**, click **Summary**. On the Web page that opens, click the **Walla Walla Music** link.

    Word displays the draft of the Word blog post in the Windows Live Spaces blog window.

You can edit and format the blog post here, just as you would edit it in Word.

19. After making any necessary changes, click **Publish Entry**.

    Word publishes the post to your blog.

Blog   ⚙

Add | Summary

March 02
Walla Walla Music

If you are a music lover, you'll want to explore the Walla Walla music scene. This little town offers music for everyone: ethereal choral, funky blues, downhome country, refined chamber, rock, and pop. But the jewel of them all is the Walla Walla Symphony Orchestra, the oldest continuously operating symphony west of the Mississippi.

From humble beginnings, this outstanding orchestra has matured into one of the best we have heard in recent years. Maestro Yaacov Bergman, in his 20th season, continues to deliver inspired programs that challenge his musicians and his audiences. In April, we look forward to a night of *Flora and Fauna* at the orchestra's 416th concert since its inception in 1907. As usual, the performance will be held in beautiful Cordiner Hall on the Whitman College campus. Be sure to check out this and their other offerings at www.wwsymphony.org.

1:17 PM | Add a comment | Permalink | Blog it

The blog post, after it has been published to the blog.

 CLEAN UP Close Internet Explorer, and then save and close the My Blog Post document.

Key Points

- You can save a document in a file format that allows it to be opened in other programs.

- To distribute information in a format that cannot be easily changed, you can save the document as an XPS file so that it looks on the screen the way it will when it is printed.

- A Word document can easily be converted to a Web page. You can see how it will look in a Web browser, and you can adjust the layout from within Word.

- If you have a blog space, you can easily create and publish blog posts in Word.

Part 3

Additional Techniques

Chapter at a Glance

If you are a music lover, you'll want to explore the Walla Walla music scene. This little town offers music for everyone: ethereal choral, funky blues, downhome country, refined chamber, rock, and pop. But the jewel of them all is the Walla Walla Symphony Orchestra, the oldest continuously operating symphony west of the Mississippi. ¶

From humble beginnings, this exceptional orchestra has matured into one of the best we have heard in recent years. The latest in a series of outstanding conductors, Maestro Yaacov Bergman continues to deliver inspired programs that challenge his musicians and his audiences. In April, we look forward to a night of *Flora and Fauna* at the orchestra's 416th concert since it Send e-mail message to Margie's Travel performance will be held in beautiful Cordiner Hall on the Whit **Ctrl+Click to follow link** ck out this and their other offerings at www.wwsymphony.org, or e-mail us for more information. ¶

Add hyperlinks, **page 310**

The office employees will be responsible for entering the packing slip information into the inventory database.) ¶

Phone numbers: ¶

Telephone: (972)-555-0123 ↵
Fax: (972)-555-0124 ¶

E-mail: ¶

CustomerService@consolidatedmessenger.com ¶

Web-site: ¶

www.consolidatedmessenger.com ¶

. Facilities ¶

Office ¶

Warehouse ¶

Phone System ¶

Insert fields, **page 316**

First Page Footer

3/9/2010·11:54·AM → Office·Procedures → File·name: proceduresinfo ¶

4. Storage

4.1 No bicycles, tricycles, scooters, roller skates, skateboards, wagons, toys, or other personal belongings shall be stored or left in any Common Area.

4.2 No trailers, boats, vans, campers, house trailers, buses, or trucks shall be stored in any parking space in any Common Area. See also 6. Parking

Add bookmarks and cross-references, **page 322**

4.3 No Owner shall use his or her garage to store personal belongings in such a way that there is not enough space for his or her vehicles.

4.4 No Owner shall use his or her parking spaces in the common garage to store personal belongings, except that with prior written permission of the Board, bicycles may be stored in the front end of the assigned parking stall or in the Owner's unused assigned stall. Bicycles must be standing upright, by using the bicycle's own stand or in an approved type of bicycle stand. Storage of anything other than automobiles, motorcycles, and bicycles in the common garage may be a violation of fire code and subject to citation and fines by the Bellevue Fire Department.

5. Garbage

5.1 Owners shall keep their garbage and recycling bins in the designated garbage area. Nothing else shall be stored in this area.

5.2 Garbage and recycling bins may be put out at the road the day before pickup day, which is currently Friday. Bins must be placed approximately 2 feet apart to allow for mechanical pickup. (The garbage company will complain and can refuse to pick up if the bins are so close together that they have to be handled manually.)

5.3 Garbage and recycling bins shall be retrieved from the road the same day as pickup. (One truck usually comes early in the morning and the other early in the afternoon.) If an Owner will be away, arrangements must be made for a neighbor to retrieve the bins and, if necessary, place them in an unobtrusive place until the Owner returns.

6. Parking

12 Explore More Text Techniques

In this chapter, you will learn how to

✔ Add hyperlinks.

✔ Insert fields.

✔ Add bookmarks and cross-references.

Microsoft Word 2010 has several tools that make creating professional documents easy and efficient:

● **Hyperlinks** To help a reader move to a location in the same file, in another file, or on a Web page, you can add links from text or graphics to the target location.

● **Fields** Instead of typing information that is associated with a document, you can have Word insert it for you in a field. Then if the information changes, you can simply update the field to ensure that the information is current.

● **Bookmarks** You can quickly return to a specific location in a document by inserting a bookmark. You can jump to a bookmarked location by selecting it from a list, and you can help a reader find information by inserting hyperlinks or cross-references to bookmarks.

● **Cross-references** To help a reader move to a related location in a document, you can insert a cross-reference. Then if the text at the location changes, you can tell Word to update the cross-reference to reflect the change.

In this chapter, you'll insert two different kinds of hyperlinks and three different types of fields. Then you'll create and modify bookmarks and cross-references.

> **Practice Files** Before you can complete the exercises in this chapter, you need to copy the book's practice files to your computer. The practice files you'll use to complete the exercises in this chapter are in the Chapter12 practice file folder. A complete list of practice files is provided in "Using the Practice Files" at the beginning of this book.

Adding Hyperlinks

Like Web pages, Word documents can include hyperlinks that provide a quick way to perform tasks such as the following:

- Open another document.
- Link to a Web site.
- Download a file.
- Send an e-mail message.

You insert hyperlinks into a Word document by displaying the Insert Hyperlink dialog box, specifying the type of link you want to create, and then entering an appropriate destination for that type of link.

While creating a hyperlink to a document or a Web page, called the *target*, you can specify whether the target information should appear in the same window or frame as the active document or in a new one. You can also make a particular setting the default for all hyperlinks.

Within a document, hyperlinks appear underlined and in the color specified for hyperlinks by the document's theme. You can jump to the target of the hyperlink by holding down the Ctrl key and clicking the link. After you click the hyperlink, its color changes to the color specified for followed hyperlinks.

To edit or remove a hyperlink, you can select it and click Hyperlink in the Links group on the Insert tab or you can right-click the selection and then click the appropriate command.

In this exercise, you'll insert and test a hyperlink to a different document. Then you'll insert, modify, and test a hyperlink that opens an e-mail message window.

SET UP You need the VisitorGuide_start and Conductors documents located in your Chapter12 practice file folder to complete this exercise. Open the VisitorGuide_start document, and save it as *VisitorGuide*. Then follow the steps.

1. In the second sentence of the second paragraph, select **series of outstanding conductors**. Then on the **Insert** tab, in the **Links** group, click the **Hyperlink** button.

   Keyboard Shortcut Press Ctrl+K to open the Insert Hyperlink dialog box.

   See Also For more information about keyboard shortcuts, see "Keyboard Shortcuts" at the end of this book.

The Insert Hyperlink dialog box opens. On the Link To bar, Existing File Or Web Page is selected, and the dialog box shows the contents of your Chapter12 practice file folder.

You can select the target type in the Link To bar.

Troubleshooting If you don't see the contents of the Chapter12 folder, ensure that Existing File Or Web Page is selected on the Link To bar, and then click the Look In arrow, and navigate to your Chapter12 practice file folder.

2. In the list of file names, click (don't double-click) the **Conductors** document, and then click **Target Frame**.

The Set Target Frame dialog box opens with Page Default (None) selected as the frame in which the document will open.

In the Set Target Frame dialog box, you can change the way the target of the hyperlink will be displayed.

3. Display the **Select the frame** list, and click **New window**. Then click **OK**.

4. Click **OK** to close the **Insert Hyperlink** dialog box.

   Word inserts a hyperlink from the selected text in the VisitorGuide document to the Conductors document. The hyperlink is indicated by an underline and the color assigned to hyperlinks by the document's theme.

5. Point to the hyperlink.

   Word displays a ScreenTip.

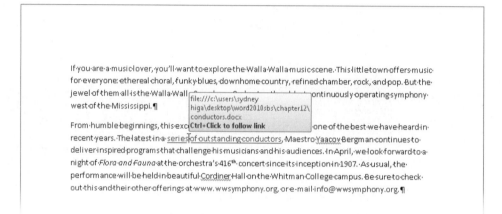

The ScreenTip shows the path to the Conductors document and instructions for following the link.

6. Hold down the Ctrl key, and then click the hyperlink.

   Word opens the Conductors document in a new window.

7. On the **View** tab, in the **Window** group, click the **Switch Windows** button, and then click **VisitorGuide**.

   In the VisitorGuide document, the color of the hyperlink has changed to indicate that you have followed this link to its target.

8. In the last line of the document, select **e-mail us**, and then on the **Insert** tab, in the **Links** group, click the **Hyperlink** button.

9. At the bottom of the **Link to** bar of the **Insert Hyperlink** dialog box, click **E-mail Address**.

The dialog box changes so that you can enter the information appropriate for an e-mail hyperlink.

If you have already inserted a hyperlink to an e-mail address, it will appear in the Recently Used list, and you can click it to use it again.

10. In the **E-mail address** box, type **margie@margiestravel.com**.

   Tip When you begin typing in the E-Mail Address box, Word inserts *mailto:* in the box, in front of the address you type.

   When a person clicks the link, Word will start his or her default e-mail program and open a new e-mail message window.

11. In the **Subject** box, type **Flora and Fauna inquiry**.

   This text will be automatically entered in the Subject box of the new e-mail message window.

12. Click **OK**.

   The hyperlinked text is indicated by an underline and its assigned theme color. Pointing to it displays a ScreenTip with the hyperlink's target.

13. Right-click the **e-mail us** hyperlink, and then click **Edit Hyperlink**.

    The Edit Hyperlink dialog box opens with the current destination for this link in the E-Mail Address box.

14. In the upper-right corner of the dialog box, click **ScreenTip**.

    The Set Hyperlink ScreenTip dialog box opens.

You can specify the text you want for the ScreenTip that appears when someone points to the hyperlink.

15. In the **ScreenTip text** box, type **Send e-mail message to Margie's Travel**, and then click **OK**.

16. In the **Edit Hyperlink** dialog box, click **OK**.

17. Point to the hyperlink.

    Word displays your custom ScreenTip.

The custom ScreenTip.

18. Hold down Ctrl, and click the hyperlink.

    Your e-mail program starts, and a message window opens. (This is the message window displayed by Microsoft Outlook 2010.)

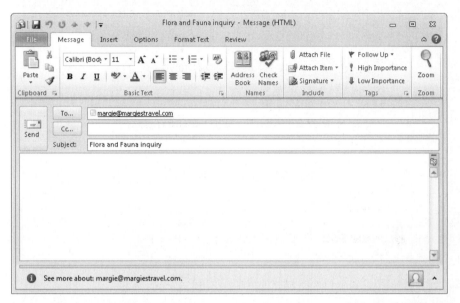

The specified e-mail address has been inserted in the To box, and the specified description appears in the Subject box.

See Also For information about the many features of Outlook 2010, see *Microsoft Outlook 2010 Step by Step* by Joan Lambert and Joyce Cox (Microsoft Press, 2010).

19. Close the message window, clicking **No** when asked whether you want to save the changes.

    The hyperlinked text is now displayed in the color assigned to followed hyperlinks by the document's theme.

 CLEAN UP Save and close the VisitorGuide document, and then close the Conductors document.

Inserting Fields

When you insert a hyperlink into a document, you are actually inserting a HYPERLINK field. A field is a placeholder that tells Word to supply the specified information or perform the specified action in the specified way.

Word inserts fields to control certain processes, such as the creation of a table of contents or the merging of a form letter with a data source. You can use fields to insert information that can be updated with the click of a button if the information changes. You can't type a field in your document; instead, you must tell Word to insert the field you want. You do this by clicking the Quick Parts button in the Text group on the Insert tab and then clicking Field to display the Field dialog box.

The Field dialog box provides a comprehensive list of all the available fields. In this dialog box, you can also set options that refine the field.

Each field consists of a set of curly braces containing the field name and any required or optional instructions or settings. These settings, called *switches*, refine the results of the field—for example, by formatting it in a particular way. When you insert a field from the Field dialog box, you can click Field Codes in the lower-left corner of the dialog box to display the field's syntax. Clicking Options in the lower-left corner displays the Field Options dialog box, in which you can add general and specific optional settings to the field code.

Descriptions in the Field and Field Options dialog boxes guide you in defining the field.

Tip After Word inserts the field, you see the field results; for example if you insert a FILESIZE field, you see the size of the file. To see the field code that tells Word to insert the file size, either click the field to select it and press Alt+F9, or right-click the field and click Toggle Field Codes.

Inserting some types of fields requires advanced knowledge of the fields and how to control them. However, some fields are very easy. For example, to insert today's date or the current time in a document, you simply click the Date & Time button in the Text group on the Insert tab to display the Date And Time dialog box and select the format you want. to use. To insert the information as regular text, you click OK. If you want to be able to update the date or time, you insert the information as a field by selecting the Update Automatically check box. Word then inserts a Date or Time field matching the format you selected and retrieves the date or time from your computer's internal calendar or clock.

Tip You can insert other types of date and time fields, such as a PrintDate field or an EditTime field. Insert a date or time field in the usual way, right-click the field, and then click Edit Field to display the Field dialog box. Then change the Categories setting to Date And Time, and in the Field Names list, click the field you want. (Clicking a field in the list displays a brief description, so it is easy to choose the one you want.) When you click OK, the information corresponding to the field type you specified is shown in the document.

By default, date and time fields are updated every time you open the document. You can prevent this updating by selecting the field and pressing Ctrl+F11 to lock the field; press Ctrl+Shift+F11 to unlock it again. If a field is not locked, you can click it and then click the Update button that appears above it or press the F9 key to update it with the most current information.

Another type of field you might want to insert in a document—for example, in its header or footer—is one that contains a document property, such as the author, title, or last modification date. This type of information is easily inserted by clicking the Quick Parts button, pointing to Document Property, and then clicking the property you want. If you insert the field and then you edit the contents of the field in the document, the change is carried over to the list of properties displayed on the Info page in Backstage view.

See Also For information about document properties, see "Preparing Documents for Electronic Distribution" in Chapter 6, "Preview, Print, and Distribute Documents."

In this exercise, you'll insert a field that displays the current date and time in the footer of a document, and you'll update the field. Then you'll insert a field that displays the Title property, and you'll change the property by changing the field. You'll also add the file name. Finally, you'll convert the current date and time to the date and time when the document was last saved.

SET UP You need the ProceduresFields_start document located in your Chapter12 practice file folder to complete this exercise. Open the ProceduresFields_start document, and save it as *ProceduresFields*. Display formatting marks, and then follow the steps.

📄 Footer ▾

1. On the **Insert** tab, in the **Header & Footer** group, click the **Footer** button, and then click **Edit Footer**.

   Word dims the text and displays the footer area at the bottom of the first page of the document.

2. With the cursor in the blank paragraph of the footer, on the **Design** contextual tab, in the **Insert** group, click the **Date & Time** button.

   The Date And Time dialog box opens.

You can specify the date and/or time format you want.

3. In the **Available formats** list, click the first format that combines the date and time.

4. Ensure that the **Update automatically** check box is selected, and then click **OK**.

5. Press the Tab key. Then in the **Insert** group, click the **Quick Parts** button, point to **Document Property**, and then click **Title**.

   Word inserts a field for the Title property in the document.

The Title property of this document is currently blank.

6. With the **Title** property active, type **Office Procedures**. Then press the Right Arrow key to release the selection.

7. Display the Backstage view, and if the **Info** page is not displayed, click **Info**.

   Notice that under Properties in the right pane, the Title property is *Office Procedures*.

Properties ▾	
Size	47.6KB
Pages	9
Words	1898
Total Editing Time	0 Minutes
Title	Office Procedures
Tags	Add a tag
Comments	Add comments

Related Dates

The Title property on the Info page reflects the change you made in the document.

8. Click the **Design** contextual tab to redisplay the document footer.

9. Press the Tab key, type **File name:** (including the colon), and press the Spacebar. Then in the **Insert** group, click the **Quick Parts** button, and click **Field**.

10. In the **Field names** list in the **Field** dialog box, click **FileName**. Then in the **Format** list, click **Lowercase**, and click **OK**.

11. Save the document.

    At the left end of the footer, the date and time still reflect the moment when you inserted that field.

12. Click the field, and then click the **Update** button that appears.

    The time is updated to reflect the current time. You want this field to reflect the date and time when the document was last saved.

13. Right-click the field, and click **Edit Field**.

14. In the **Field** dialog box, display the **Categories** list, and then click **Date and Time**.

   The list is filtered to display only the fields that relate to dates and times.

Word has four date fields and two time fields.

15. In the **Field names** list, click **SaveDate**, and in the **Date formats** list, click the first format that combines the date and time.

16. Select the **Preserve formatting during updates** check box, and click **OK**.

17. Save the document. Then right-click the field, and click **Update Field**.

   The time is updated to reflect the most recent save.

The information in this footer is supplied by three fields.

✖ **CLEAN UP** Save the ProceduresFields document, and then close it.

Adding Bookmarks and Cross-References

Word provides two tools that you can use to jump easily to designated places within the same document:

- **Bookmarks** Whether the document you are reading was created by you or by someone else, you can insert bookmarks to flag information to which you might want to return later. Like a physical bookmark, a Word bookmark marks a specific named place in a document. After inserting a bookmark, you can quickly jump to it by displaying the Bookmark dialog box, clicking the bookmark you want to locate, and then clicking Go To.

  Tip Alternatively, you can display the Go To page of the Find And Replace dialog box, click Bookmark in the Go To What list, and then select the bookmark you want from the Enter Bookmark Name list.

- **Cross-references** You use cross-references to quickly move readers to associated information elsewhere in the document. You can create cross-references to headings, figures, and tables, for which Word automatically creates pointers. You can also create cross-references to manually inserted bookmarks. If you delete an item you have designated as the target of a cross-reference, you must update the cross-reference.

See Also For information about using hyperlinks to jump to other locations, see "Adding Hyperlinks" earlier in this chapter. For information about using the Navigation task pane to jump to any paragraph styled as a heading, see "Viewing Documents in Different Ways" in Chapter 1, "Explore Word 2010."

In this exercise, you'll insert a bookmark and then jump to it. You'll also create a cross-reference, edit the referenced item, and then update the cross-reference.

 SET UP You need the RulesBookmarks_start document located in your Chapter12 practice file folder to complete this exercise. Open the RulesBookmarks_start document, and save it as *RulesBookmarks*. Then follow the steps.

1. On the **Home** tab, in the **Editing** group, click the **Find** arrow, and in the list, click **Go To**.

   Keyboard Shortcut Press Ctrl+G to display the Go To tab of the Find And Replace dialog box.

   The Find And Replace dialog box opens, with the Go To page active.

You can select the type of element and the specific element to which you want to jump.

2. With **Page** selected in the **Go to what** list, in the **Enter page number** box, type **5**. Then click **Go To**, and click **Close**.

3. On page **5**, click to the left of the **10. Building Maintenance** heading. Then on the **Insert** tab, in the **Links** group, click the **Bookmark** button.

   The Bookmark dialog box opens.

You create and manage your bookmarks in this dialog box.

4. In the **Bookmark name** box, type **Maintenance**, and then click **Add**.

   The Bookmark dialog box closes, and although you can't see it, a bookmark named *Maintenance* is inserted into the document.

5. Below the **10.3** paragraph, select the six bulleted items. Then display the **Bookmark** dialog box, type **LimitedCommon** in the **Bookmark name** box, and click **Add**.

   Troubleshooting Bookmark names cannot contain spaces. If you enter a space and then type a character, the Add button becomes inactive. To name bookmarks with multiple words, either run the words together and capitalize each word, or replace the spaces with underscores for readability.

6. Press the Home key to release the selection. Then display the **Advanced** page of the **Word Options** dialog box, and under **Show Document Content**, select the **Show Bookmarks** check box. Click **OK**.

   The location of the bookmark you inserted without selecting text is identified by a large, gray I-beam. The location of the one you inserted after selecting the bulleted items is identified by large, gray square brackets around the selection.

The identifiers for the two types of bookmarks.

7. Press Ctrl+Home to move to the beginning of the document. Then display the **Go To** page of the **Find and Replace** dialog box.

8. In the **Go to what** list, click **Bookmark**.

   The dialog box changes so that you can specify the bookmark you want to jump to.

Find and Replace	?	X

   Find   Replace   Go To

   Go to what:

   Page
   Section
   Line
   Bookmark
   Comment
   Footnote

   Enter bookmark name:

   LimitedCommon

   Previous   Go To   Close

   The bookmarks you created are accessible on the Go To page.

9. Display the **Enter bookmark name** list, click **Maintenance**, and then click **Go To**.

   The cursor moves to the location of the bookmark. The dialog box remains open in case you want to move somewhere else.

10. Close the **Find and Replace** dialog box.

    Tip You can also jump to a bookmark by displaying the Bookmark dialog box, clicking the bookmark you want, and then clicking Go To. In the Bookmark dialog box, you can sort the bookmarks alphabetically or in the order in which they are located. To delete a bookmark, click its name, and then click Delete.

11. Scroll upward to page **2**, and click at the end of the **4.2** paragraph. Press the Spacebar, type **See also**, and then press the Spacebar again.

12. On the **Insert** tab, in the **Links** group, click the **Cross-reference** button.

    Cross-reference

    The Cross-Reference dialog box opens. You can specify the type of item you want to reference and what you want the cross-reference inserted in the document to say.

13. Display the **Reference type** list, and click **Heading**.

    The list box in the Cross-Reference dialog box now displays all the headings in this document.

Word can identify the headings in a document only if you have applied heading styles.

14. With **Heading text** selected in the **Insert reference to** box, click **6. Parking and Vehicles** in the **For which heading** list. Then click **Insert**, and click **Close**.

    The text *6. Parking and Vehicles* appears in the document at the cursor. Although it's not obvious, the text is inserted as a field.

15. Hold down the Ctrl key, and then click the cross-reference to move to the **6. Parking and Vehicles** heading.

16. In the heading, delete **and Vehicles**.

17. Move back to page **2**, and at the end of the **4.2** paragraph, click **6. Parking and Vehicles** to select the cross-reference field.

    Troubleshooting Click the field; don't try to select the text.

18. Right-click the selected cross-reference, and then click **Update Field**.

    Word deletes the words *and Vehicles* at the end of the cross-reference.

The cross-reference reflects the change you made to the target heading.

19. Hold down Ctrl, and click the cross-reference to jump to the associated heading.

 CLEAN UP Turn off the display of bookmark identifiers by displaying the Advanced page of the Word Options dialog box and clearing the Show Bookmarks check box in the Show Document Content area. Then save and close the RulesBookmarks document.

Key Points

- Documents can contain hyperlinks to Web pages, files, or e-mail addresses.
- You can use fields to tell Word to supply the specified information or perform the specified action in the specified way.
- Flagging information with a bookmark makes it easy to look up the information later.
- Using Word to insert cross-references makes them easier to maintain.

Chapter at a Glance

Office·Procedures¶

······················Page Break··················¶

Create and modify tables of contents, **page 332**

Create and modify indexes, **page 340**

Index

Add sources and compile bibliographies, **page 347**

Bibliography

American Bamboo Society. 2006. www.americanbamboo.org/BooksOnBamboo.html.
Freitas, Victor, and Sean Stewart. *Bamboo Garden.* Lucerne Publishing, 2009.
Goldberg, Jossef. *Black Bamboo.* Litware, 2008.

13 Use Reference Tools for Longer Documents

In this chapter, you will learn how to

✔ Create and modify tables of contents.

✔ Create and modify indexes.

✔ Add sources and compile bibliographies.

If you create long documents and are concerned about helping your readers find the information they're looking for, you can rely on the following Microsoft Word 2010 tools to do the job:

● **Table of contents** You can provide an overview of the information contained in a document and help readers locate topics by compiling a table of contents from the document headings. Depending on the intended delivery format (printed or electronic), you can choose to include page numbers or hyperlinks to each heading.

● **Index** You can help readers locate specific information by inserting index entry fields within a document and compiling an index of keywords and concepts that directs the reader to the corresponding page numbers.

● **Information sources and a bibliography** You can appropriately attribute information to its source by inserting citations into a document. Word will then compile a professional bibliography from the citations.

In this chapter, you'll create and update a table of contents. Then you'll mark index entries in a document and compile an index. Finally, you'll use the Source Manager to enter source information, insert a few citations, and compile a bibliography.

Practice Files Before you can complete the exercises in this chapter, you need to copy the book's practice files to your computer. The practice files you'll use to complete the exercises in this chapter are in the Chapter13 practice file folder. A complete list of practice files is provided in "Using the Practice Files" at the beginning of this book.

Adding Footnotes and Endnotes

When you want to make a comment about a statement in a document—for example, to explain an assumption or cite the source for a different opinion—you can enter the comment as a footnote or an endnote. Doing so inserts a number or symbol called a *reference mark*, and your associated comment appears with the same number or symbol, either as a footnote at the bottom of the page or as an endnote at the end of the document or document section. In most views, footnotes or endnotes are divided from the main text by a note separator line.

To create a footnote or endnote:

1. With the cursor where you want the reference mark to appear, on the References tab, in the Footnotes group, click either the Insert Footnote or the Insert Endnote button.

    Keyboard Shortcut Press Alt+Ctrl+F to insert a footnote or Alt+Ctrl+D to insert an endnote.

    See Also For more information about keyboard shortcuts, see "Keyboard Shortcuts" at the end of this book.

    Word inserts the reference mark in the document and creates a linked area at the bottom of the page or end of the section.

2. Type the note text.

Word applies default styles to the reference marks for footnotes and endnotes. By default, footnote reference marks use the 1, 2, 3 format, and endnote reference marks use i, ii, iii.

To change the number format of footnotes or endnotes:

1. On the References tab, click the Footnotes dialog box launcher.

    The Footnote And Endnote dialog box opens.

You can change the format before or after you enter footnotes or endnotes.

2. In the Location area, click Footnotes or Endnotes.

3. In the Format area, display the Number Format list, and click the number format you want.

4. With Whole Document shown in the Apply Changes To box, click Apply.

   All footnotes or endnotes change to the new number format.

To change the formatting applied to existing footnote or endnote reference marks:

1. In the document text, select the reference mark for any footnote or endnote.

2. On the Home tab, in the Editing group, click the Select button, and then click Select Text With Similar Formatting.

   All the footnote or endnote reference marks are selected.

3. On the Home tab, apply the character formatting you want the reference marks to have.

   All the reference marks in the body of the document now appear with the character formatting you applied.

Creating and Modifying Tables of Contents

If you create a long document with headings and subheadings, such as an annual report or a catalog that has several sections, you might want to add a table of contents to the beginning of the document to give your readers an overview of the document's contents and help them navigate to specific sections. In a document that will be printed, you can indicate with a page number the page where each heading is located. If the document will be distributed electronically, you can link each entry in the table of contents to the corresponding heading in the document so that readers can jump directly to the heading with a click of the mouse.

By default, Word expects to create a table of contents based on paragraphs within the document that you have formatted with the standard heading styles: Heading 1, Heading 2, and so on. (Word can also create a table of contents based on outline levels or on fields that you have inserted in the document.) When you tell Word to create the table, Word identifies the table of contents entries and inserts the table at the cursor as a single field. You can modify the elements on which Word bases the table at any time.

Office Procedures

Contents

General Administration 1

    Contact Information 2

    Facilities 3

      Office 3

      Warehouse 3

      Phone System 3

    Ordering Supplies 5

      Business Stationery, Letterheads, Invoices, Packing Slips, Receipts 5

      Supplies 5

Shipping 7

    Receiving Packages 8

The table of contents is a field that can be updated.

See Also For information about applying styles, see "Quickly Formatting Text" in Chapter 3, "Change the Look of Text."

The Table Of Contents gallery offers three standard table options:

- **Automatic Table 1** This option inserts a table of contents with the heading Contents.

- **Automatic Table 2** This option inserts a table of contents with the heading Table of Contents.

- **Manual Table** This option inserts a table of contents with placeholders that you replace manually.

The formatting of the entries in a table of contents is controlled by nine levels of built-in TOC styles (TOC 1, TOC 2, and so on). By default, Word uses the styles that are assigned in the template attached to the document. If you want to use a different style, instead of clicking one of the three options in the Table Of Contents gallery, you can click Insert Table Of Contents below the gallery to display the Table Of Contents dialog box, where you can choose from several variations, such as Classic, Fancy, and Simple.

After you create a table of contents, you can format it manually by selecting text and then applying character or paragraph formatting or styles.

If you change a heading in the document or if edits to the text change the page breaks, the easiest way to update the table of contents is to click the Update Table button and have Word do the work for you. You have the option of updating only the page numbers, or if you have changed, added, or deleted headings, you can update (re-create) the entire table.

In this exercise, you'll create a table of contents for a document based on heading styles. You'll alter the document by deleting page breaks, and then you'll update the table of contents to reflect your changes.

 SET UP You need the ProceduresContents_start document located in your Chapter13 practice file folder to complete this exercise. Open the ProceduresContents_start document, and save it as *ProceduresContents*. Display formatting marks, and then follow the steps.

1. Click to the left of **GENERAL ADMINISTRATION**, and then on the **References** tab, in the **Table of Contents** group, click the **Table of Contents** button.

   The Table Of Contents gallery appears.

Built-In

Automatic Table 1

Contents

Heading 1 .... *1*

    Heading 2 1

        Heading 3 1

Automatic Table 2

Table of Contents

Heading 1 .... *1*

    Heading 2 1

        Heading 3 1

Manual Table

Table of Contents

Type chapter title (level 1) *1*

    Type chapter title (level 2) 2

        Type chapter title (level 3) 3

    <u>M</u>ore Table of Contents from Office.com   ▶

    <u>I</u>nsert Table of Contents...

    <u>R</u>emove Table of Contents

    <u>S</u>ave Selection to Table of Contents Gallery...

You can choose from three built-in styles or insert a custom table of contents.

2. In the **Table of Contents** gallery, click **Automatic Table 1**.

3. Press Ctrl+Home to return to the beginning of the document.

   Word has inserted a table of contents at the cursor.

Office·Procedures¶

˙Contents¶

General·Administration ....➔................................. *1¶*

    Contact·Information ....➔................................. 2¶

    Facilities ....➔................................. 3¶

        Office ....➔................................. 3¶

        Warehouse ....➔................................. 3¶

        Phone·System ....➔................................. 3¶

    Ordering·Supplies ....➔................................. 5¶

        Business·Stationery,·Letterheads,·Invoices,·Packing·Slips,·Receipts ....➔............... 5¶

        Supplies ....➔................................. 5¶

Each heading level is assigned its own TOC style.

4. In the **Table of Contents** group, click the **Table of Contents** button, and then below the gallery, click **Remove Table of Contents**.

5. Click at the right end of the **Office Procedures** title, and press Enter. Then type **Table of Contents**, and make this heading bold.

6. Click at the left end of **GENERAL ADMINISTRATION**, and on the **Insert** tab, in the **Pages** group, click the **Page Break** button. Then press the Up Arrow key to position the cursor at the left end of the empty page-break paragraph.

7. On the **References** tab, in the **Table of Contents** group, click the **Table of Contents** button, and then below the gallery, click **Insert Table of Contents**.

    The Table Of Contents dialog box opens.

You can specify the format for both print and the Web.

8. In the **General** area of the **Table of Contents** page, display the **Formats** list, and click **Classic**.

    Examples of entries with the Classic table of contents styles applied appear in the Print Preview and Web Preview boxes.

Tip If you create a table of contents based on the document's template, you can customize the TOC styles during the creation process. With Formats set to From Template in the General area of the Table Of Contents dialog box, click Modify. The Style dialog box opens, displaying the nine TOC styles. You can modify the font, paragraph, tabs, border, and other formatting of these styles the same way you would modify any other style. For information about creating styles, see "Working with Styles and Templates" in Chapter 16, "Work in Word More Efficiently."

9. Display the **Tab leader** list, click the dotted leader option, and then click **OK** to insert the table of contents.

10. Press Ctrl+Home to move to the beginning of the document, and then point to any entry in the table of contents.

   A ScreenTip tells you that you can hold down the Ctrl key and click any entry in the table of contents to jump to that heading in the document.

11. Click anywhere in the table.

   The table of contents is contained in one large field, and clicking anywhere in the field selects the entire field.

   See Also For information about fields, see "Inserting Fields" in Chapter 12, "Explore More Text Techniques."

12. Scroll down to page **2**, click in the selection area to the left of the page break, and then press the Delete key to delete the page break.

   The *Contact Information* heading is now on page 2.

13. Scroll down to the next page break, and delete it.

   The *Facilities* heading is now also on page 2.

14. On the **References** tab, in the **Table of Contents** group, click the **Update Table** button.

   The Update Table Of Contents dialog box opens.

If you make a change to a document that affects the headings or page breaks, you can easily update the table of contents.

15. Click **Update entire table**, and click **OK**. Then press Ctrl+Home.

    Word has updated the table of contents to reflect the new page numbers.

16. Drag in the selection area to select all the lines of the table of contents.

    Troubleshooting You need to drag to select the actual text of the table of contents, not just click to select the field.

17. On the **Home** tab, in the **Paragraph** group, click the **Line and Paragraph Spacing** button, and then click **Remove Space Before Paragraph**.

18. Press Ctrl+Home to release the selection and move to the top of the document.

    Word has removed the extra space between the lines in the table of contents.

You can format the text of a table of contents just like any other text.

✖ **CLEAN UP** Save the ProceduresContents document, and then close it.

Tables of Figures

If a document includes figures or tables that have captions, you can tell Word to create a table of figures.

To insert a caption:

1. Position the cursor where you want the caption to appear (usually in an empty paragraph immediately after the figure), and then on the References tab, in the Captions group, click the Insert Caption button.

   The Caption dialog box opens.

2. If you want to change the label shown in the Caption box (the default is *Figure*), in the Label list, click Table or Equation; or click New Label, type the label you want, and then click OK.

   Tip The number 1 in the Caption box is a field that reflects the graphic's position in the figure sequence. If you add or delete graphics, this number is automatically updated.

3. In the Caption box, click to the right of the label and number, press the Spacebar, type the caption, and then click OK.

   Word adds the caption to the document.

To create a table of figures:

1. Position the cursor where you want to insert the table of figures, and then on the References tab, in the Captions group, click Insert Table Of Figures.

   The Table Of Figures dialog box opens. This dialog box looks similar to the Table Of Contents dialog box.

2. If you want to change the default caption label, in the General area, display the Caption Label list, and click the label you want.

3. If you want to change the default format, display the Formats list, and click the format you want.

4. Select any additional options you want, and then click OK.

   Word inserts the table of figures in the specified format above the cursor.

Tables of Authorities

If a legal document contains items such as regulations, cases, and statutes that are identified as legal citations, you can tell Word to create a table of authorities. Word uses the citations to create this type of table the same way it uses headings to create a table of contents.

To insert a legal citation:

1. Select the first legal reference that you want to mark with a citation.
2. On the References tab, in the Table Of Authorities group, click the Mark Citation button.

   Keyboard Shortcut Press Alt+Shift+D to open the Mark Citation dialog box.

   The Mark Citation dialog box opens.

   Tip You can leave the Mark Citation dialog box open to facilitate the marking of citations.

3. In the Short Citation box, edit the citation to reflect the way you want it to appear in the table.
4. If you want to change the category, display the Category list, and click the category that applies to the citation.
5. To mark one citation, click Mark. To mark all citations that match the selected citation, click Mark All.

To create a table of authorities:

1. Position the cursor where you want the table of authorities to appear, and then on the References tab, in the Table Of Authorities group, click the Insert Table Of Authorities button.

   The Table Of Authorities dialog box opens.

2. In the Category list, click the category of citations that you want to appear in the table, or click All to include all categories.
3. Select formatting options for the table, and then click OK.

   Word inserts the table in the specified format above the cursor.

Creating and Modifying Indexes

To help readers find specific concepts and terms that might not be readily located by looking at a table of contents, you can include an index at the end of a document. Word creates an index by compiling an alphabetical listing with page numbers based on index entry fields that you mark in the document. As with a table of contents, an index is inserted at the cursor as one field.

Tip You don't need to create indexes for documents that will be distributed electronically because readers can use the Navigation task pane to search for the information they need. For information about searching for information in a document, see "Finding and Replacing Text" in Chapter 2, "Edit and Proofread Text."

In the index, an index entry might apply to a word or phrase that appears on one page or is discussed on several pages. The entry might have related subentries. For example, in the index to this book, the main index entry *text effects* might have below it the subentries *applying* and *live preview of.* An index might also include cross-reference entries that direct readers to related entries. For example, the main index entry *text wrapping breaks* might be cross-referenced to *line breaks.*

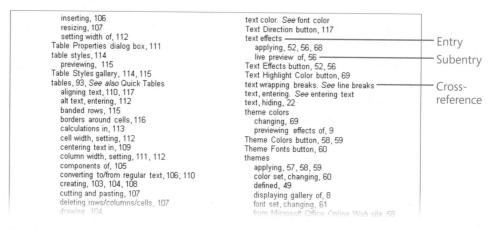

The three types of index entries, as they appear in an index.

To insert an index entry field into the document, you select the text you want to mark, and click the Mark Entry button in the Index group on the References tab to open the Mark Index Entry dialog box, where you can do the following:

- Use the selected text as is, modify the entry, or add a subentry.

- Format the entry—for example, to make it appear bold or italic in the index—by right-clicking it, clicking Font, and selecting the options you want; or by using keyboard shortcuts.

- Designate the entry as a cross-reference, one-page entry, or a page-range entry.

    Tip Cross-references appear in the index in the following format:

    garages. *See* parking

    In this manner, you can direct readers to index terms they might not think of when looking for specific information.

- Specify the formatting of this entry's page number.

Keyboard Shortcut Press Alt+Shift+X to open the Mark Index Entry dialog box.

After you have set the options in the dialog box the way you want them, you can insert an index entry field adjacent to the selected text by clicking Mark, or adjacent to every occurrence of the selected text in the document by clicking Mark All. The Mark Index Entry dialog box remains open to simplify the process of inserting multiple index entry fields, so you don't have to click the Mark Entry button for each new entry. You can move the dialog box off to the side so that it doesn't block the text you're working with.

Tip When building an index, you should choose the text you mark carefully, bearing in mind what terms readers are likely to look up. One reader might expect to find information about *cell phones* by looking under *cell*, whereas another might look under *mobile*, another under *phones*, and another under *telephones*. A good index will include all four entries.

Index entry fields are formatted as hidden; you cannot see them unless you click the Show/Hide ¶ button in the Paragraph group on the Home tab to turn on formatting marks and hidden characters. When the index entry field is visible, it appears in the document enclosed in quotation marks within a set of braces, with the designator *XE* and a dotted underline.

Hidden index entry
field with main entry
and subentry

In·addition·to·applying·styles·to·quickly·change·the·look·of·
paragraphs·and·characters,·you·can·add·more·zing·by·applying·
predefined·text·effects{·XE·"text·effects:applying"·}·to·a·
selection.·Clicking·the·Text·Effects·button·in·the·Font·group·on·the·
Home·tab·displays·a·gallery·of·effects·to·choose·from.¶

These·effects·are·dramatic,·so·you'll·probably·want·to·restrict·
their·use·to·document·titles·and·similar·elements·to·which·you·want·
to·draw·particular·attention.¶

An index entry as it appears when formatting marks and hidden characters are turned on.

Tip You can hide any text in a document by selecting it, clicking the Font dialog box launcher on the Home tab, selecting the Hidden check box, and clicking OK. When you print the document, Word will not include the hidden text unless you select the Print Hidden Text check box in the Printing Options area of the Display page in the Word Options dialog box.

To create an index based on the index entries in a document, you position the cursor where you want the index to appear and then click the Insert Index button in the Index group on the References tab. The Index dialog box opens, and you can then specify the following:

● Whether the index formatting should use styles from the current template or be based on one of four predefined formats that you can preview in the Print Preview box.

● Whether page numbers should be right-aligned, and if so whether they should have dotted, dashed, or solid tab leaders.

● Whether the index should be indented, with each subentry on a separate line below the main entries, or run-in, with subentries on the same line as the main entries.

● The number of columns you want.

When you click OK in the Index dialog box, Word calculates the page numbers of all the entries and subentries, consolidates them, and inserts the index as one field in the specified format at the specified location in the document.

Tip If you make changes to the document that affect its index entries or page numbering, you can update the index by clicking it and then clicking the Update Index button in the Index group on the References tab. You can also right-click the index and then click Update Field.

You can edit the text of the index generated from the entries, but the changes you make are not permanent; regenerating the index restores the original entries. It is more efficient to edit the text within the quotation marks in the index entry fields. To delete an index entry, you select the entire hidden field and then press the Delete key. You can move and copy index entries by using the techniques you would use for regular text.

Tip Dragging through any part of an index entry field that includes one of the enclosing braces selects the entire field.

In this exercise, you'll first mark a few index entries and a cross-reference entry. Then you'll create and format an index, delete an index entry from the document, and update the index.

SET UP You need the RulesIndex_start document located in your Chapter13 practice file folder to complete this exercise. Open the RulesIndex_start document, and save it as *RulesIndex*. Then display formatting marks, and follow the steps.

Mark Entry

1. In the first item in the first bulleted list, select the word **Declaration**. Then on the **References** tab, in the **Index** group, click the **Mark Entry** button.

The Mark Index Entry dialog box opens.

The selected text appears in the Main Entry box. You can edit it, format it, add a subentry, and otherwise adjust the index entry in this dialog box.

2. Drag the dialog box by its title bar to the upper-right corner of the screen. Then click **Mark All**.

   Word inserts hidden index entry fields adjacent to every occurrence of the word *Declaration* in the document.

   Tip If this document contained instances of the word *declaration*, those would not be marked because their capitalization does not match the selected word.

3. In the same paragraph, select the word **Bylaws**, and click the title bar of the **Mark Index Entry** dialog box to activate it and enter the selected text. Then click **Mark All**.

4. In section **2.1**, select the word **professional**, and click the dialog box title bar. Then click at the right end of the entry in the **Main entry** box, press the Spacebar, and type **businesses**. Click **Mark**. Then select and mark **administrative businesses**.

5. In the **Main entry** box, delete the word **administrative**, and then click **Mark**.

6. In section **2.4**, select the words **hobby shop**, click the dialog box title bar, and in the **Main entry** box, add an **s** to **shop** to make it *shops*. Then click **Mark**. Repeat this step to mark **carpenter shop**, and then create an entry for **shops**.

   Tip Index entries will appear in the index exactly as they appear in the Mark Index Entry dialog box. For consistency, make all nouns lowercase and plural except proper nouns and those where only one exists.

7. In section **4.3**, select the word **garage**, change the entry in the **Mark Index Entry** dialog box to **garages**, and click **Mark All**.

8. In the **Mark Index Entry** dialog box, in the **Options** area, click **Cross-reference**.

   The cursor moves to the space after the word *See* in the adjacent box.

9. Without moving the cursor, type **also parking**. Select the word **also**, press Ctrl+I to make it italic, and then click **Mark**.

   A cross-reference to the *garages* index entry appears adjacent to the word *garage*.

The cross-reference in the document reflects your specifications in the Mark Index Entry dialog box.

10. In section **7.2**, select the words **Common Area**, and click the dialog box title bar. Then type **landscaping** in the **Subentry** box, and click **Mark**.

    Word inserts an index entry with the entry and subentry separated by a colon.

11. In section **8.2**, mark the words **Common Area** with a subentry of **alterations**.

12. Close the **Mark Index Entry** dialog box.

13. Press Ctrl+End to move to the end of the document, press Enter, and then press Ctrl+Enter to insert a page break.

    The cursor moves to the top of the new page.

14. Type **Index**, and press Enter. Apply the **Heading 1** style to the new heading, and press Ctrl+End to move to the empty paragraph.

15. On the **Home** tab, in the **Paragraph** group, click the **Show/Hide ¶** button to hide formatting marks and hidden characters.

> **Troubleshooting** When hidden text is visible, the document might not be paginated correctly. Always turn off the display of formatting marks and hidden characters before creating an index.

16. On the **References** tab, in the **Index** group, click the **Insert Index** button.

The Index dialog box opens.

You can use the settings in this dialog box to tailor the look of the index.

17. In the **Columns** box, change the setting to **1**.

18. Display the **Formats** list, and click **Fancy**. Then click **OK**.

Word compiles a short index based on the index entries you just marked.

Index

A

administrative businesses, 1

B

businesses, 1
Bylaws, 1, 7

C

carpenter shops, 1
Common Area
   alterations, 4
   landscaping, 3

D

Declaration, 1, 7

G

garages, 2, 3, 4, 5, *See also* parking

H

hobby shops, 1

P

This index is formatted in one column with the page numbers adjacent to their index entries.

19. Display hidden characters so that you can see the index entry fields in the document, and scroll up to section **4.3**.

20. Select the entire cross-reference entry following **garage**, and press the Delete key.

   Troubleshooting If you find it hard to select just this entry, try pointing to the right of the closing brace (}) and dragging slightly to the left.

   The cross-reference entry is deleted from the document.

21. Press Ctrl+End to move to the end of the document, and click anywhere in the index to select its field.

22. Hide the formatting marks and hidden characters. Then on the **References** tab, in the **Index** group, click the **Update Index** button.

 Update Index

   The index is updated to reflect that you have deleted the cross-reference.

✖ **CLEAN UP** Save the RulesIndex document, and then close it.

Adding Sources and Compiling Bibliographies

In Word 2010, you can use the Source Manager to help you keep track of sources you use while researching a document and to ensure that you reference them in the proper format. Whether your sources are books, periodicals, Web pages, or interviews, you can record details about them and then select a common style guide, such as the *Chicago Manual of Style*, to have Word automatically list your sources in that style guide's standard format.

There are two ways to enter a new source:

- You can enter all the sources in the Source Manager dialog box and then insert the sources from the Source Manager into the document.

- You can enter the information for one specific source in the Create Source dialog box and click OK to insert the citation at the cursor.

No matter which method you use to enter the source information, Word stores the sources in a separate file on your computer's hard disk so that you can cite them in any document you create. You can view this Master List and select which sources will be available to the current document from the Source Manager dialog box.

After you enter citations in a document, you can easily compile their sources into one of two types of lists by clicking the Bibliography button in the Citations & Bibliography group on the References tab:

- **Bibliography** This option inserts the source list with a Bibliography heading.

- **Works Cited** This option inserts the source list with a Works Cited heading.

You can also click Insert Bibliography at the bottom of the gallery to insert the source list without a heading. The type of bibliography you use is usually specified by the organization or person for whom you are preparing the document, such as your company, your instructor, or the publication in which you intend to publish the document.

When you compile a bibliography, Word inserts it at the cursor as one field. You can edit the text of a bibliography, but if the source information changes, it is more efficient to edit the source in the Source Manager and then update the bibliography the same way you would update a table of contents or index.

Tip You can update a bibliography by clicking the bibliography and then clicking the Update Citations And Bibliography button that appears above the field. If you used the Insert Bibliography command to compile the source list, the Update Citations And Bibliography button does not appear when you click the field. In that case, you can update the bibliography by right-clicking anywhere in the field and then clicking Update Field.

In this exercise, you'll enter information for a couple of sources, insert citations for existing sources, add a new source, compile a bibliography, and then change its format.

SET UP You need the AllAboutBamboo_start and BambooBibliography_start documents located in your Chapter13 practice file folder to complete this exercise. Open the AllAboutBamboo_start document, and save it as *AllAboutBamboo*. Then follow the steps.

1. On the **References** tab, in the **Citations & Bibliography** group, display the **Style** list, and then click **Chicago Fifteenth Edition**.

   Any sources you create and citations you insert will be formatted according to the *Chicago Manual of Style* rules.

2. In the **Citations & Bibliography** group, click the **Manage Sources** button.

   The Source Manager dialog box opens.

![Source Manager dialog box with Search field, Sort by Author dropdown, Master List and Current List panes, and Browse, Copy, Delete, Edit, New buttons. A legend shows "✓ cited source" and "? placeholder source". A Preview (Chicago Fifteenth Edition) pane is at the bottom with a Close button.]

   The Source Manager accumulates sources from all documents on your hard disk, so if other documents contain citations, their source information might appear in here.

3. In the **Source Manager** dialog box, click **New**.

   The Create Source dialog box opens.

The sources you enter in this dialog box will become part of the Source Manager's Master List.

4. Ensure that **Book** is selected in the **Type of Source** list. Then in the **Bibliography Fields for Chicago Fifteenth Edition** area, type Goldberg, Jossef in the **Author** box, Black Bamboo in the **Title** box, 2008 in the **Year** box, and Litware in the **Publisher** box. Then click **OK**.

The new source is added to the Source Manager and appears not only in the Master List but also in the Current List, which is the list of sources that can be used in this document.

5. In the **Source Manager** dialog box, click **New**, and then in the **Create Source** dialog box, click **Edit**.

The Edit Name dialog box opens.

If a source has more than one author, you enter their names in the Edit Name dialog box.

6. Under **Add name**, type **Freitas** in the **Last** box, type **Victor** in the **First** box, and then click **Add**.

   Freitas, Victor appears in the Names box.

7. To enter a second author for the same book, type **Stewart** in the **Last** box, type **Sean** in the **First** box, click **Add**, and then click **OK**.

8. In the **Create Source** dialog box, type **Bamboo Garden** in the **Title** box, **2009** in the **Year** box, and **Lucerne Publishing** in the **Publisher** box. Then click **OK**.

   The new source is added to the Master List and the Current List.

9. Close the **Source Manager** dialog box.

10. Open the **BambooBibliography_start** document, and save it as **BambooBibliography**. Then open the **Source Manager** dialog box.

    The two sources you just entered appear in the Master List but not in the Current List, meaning they are not available for use in this document.

Source Manager		? ✕
Search:		Sort by Author ▾

Sources available in:
Master List

Freitas, Victor, Stewart, Sean; Bamboo Garden (2009)
Goldberg, Jossef; Black Bamboo (2008)

Browse...
Copy ->
Delete
Edit...
New...

Current List

✓ cited source
? placeholder source

Preview (Chicago Fifteenth Edition):

Citation: (Freitas and Stewart 2009)

Bibliography Entry:
Freitas, Victor, and Sean Stewart. *Bamboo Garden*. Lucerne Publishing, 2009.

Close

You can select the sources in the Master List that you want to be available for a particular document.

11. With the **Freitas** source selected in the **Master List** box, click **Copy** to make that source available in this document. Then copy the **Goldberg** source to the **Current List** box, and click **Close**.

12. In the document, position the cursor to the right of **Black Bamboo** on the last line of the first paragraph. Then in the **Citations & Bibliography** group, click the **Insert Citation** button, and in the list of citations, click **Goldberg, Jossef**.

Word inserts the source in parentheses.

BEAUTIFUL BAMBOO

Bamboo has long been woven into the cultures of many countries, where it has historically been used for everything from food and fodder to musical instruments and construction material. For centuries, millions of people have depended on this plant, which is known as "friend of the people" in China, and "wood of the poor" in India. But the demand for bamboo has been increasing in other parts of the world as well, especially as it relates to furniture, accent pieces, and flooring. More and more, people are seeing the value and beauty of using bamboo in their homes to achieve modern-day fashion with an ethnic flavor. Entire books have been written on the subject, including *Black Bamboo* (Goldberg 2008) and *Bamboo Garden*.

There are many different sizes and varieties of bamboo. It is both tropical and subtropical, growing in climates as diverse as jungles and mountain-

Citation

Information stored in the Source Manager is used to create the citation in the specified format (in this case, the Chicago Manual of Style, Fifteenth Edition *format).*

13. Insert a **Freitas, Victor, Stewart, Sean** citation to the right of **Bamboo Garden** (but before the period) at the end of the same paragraph.

14. Click to the right of **Entire books** (one line up in the same paragraph). Then in the **Citations & Bibliography** group, click the **Insert Citation** button, and in the list, click **Add New Source**.

15. In the **Create Source** dialog box, display the **Type of Source** list, and click **Web site**.

16. In the **Name of Web Page** box, type **American Bamboo Society**, and in the **Year** box, type **2006**. Then type **www.americanbamboo.org/BooksOnBamboo.html** in the **URL** box, and click **OK**.

Word inserts the source in parentheses at the insertion point.

17. In the **Citations & Bibliography** group, click the **Manage Sources** button.

In the Source Manager dialog box, the new citation appears in both the Master List and the Current List.

Because the sources in the Current List are actually cited in the document, they have a check mark beside them.

18. Close the **Source Manager** dialog box, and then press Ctrl+End to move to the end of the document.

19. In the **Citations & Bibliography** group, click **Bibliography**.

The Bibliography gallery appears.

You can choose from two built-in styles or insert a bibliography with no heading.

20. In the gallery, click **Bibliography**.

Word inserts a bibliography of all the citations in the document in alphabetical order.

Bibliography

American Bamboo Society. 2006. www.americanbamboo.org/BooksOnBamboo.html.
Freitas, Victor, and Sean Stewart. *Bamboo Garden.* Lucerne Publishing, 2009.
Goldberg, Jossef. *Black Bamboo.* Litware, 2008.

A bibliography formatted in the specified format (in this case, the Chicago Manual of Style Fifteenth Edition).

21. In the **Citations & Bibliography** group, display the **Style** list, and click **APA Fifth Edition**.

Tip You don't have to select the bibliography to apply this change; you can do it from anywhere in the document.

The format of the bibliography and of the citations changes to bring it in line with the style specified by the *Publication Manual of the American Psychological Association*.

 CLEAN UP Save and close the BambooBibliography and AllAboutBamboo documents.

Key Points

- A table of contents provides an overview of the topics covered in a document and lets readers navigate quickly to a topic.

- After marking index entries for key concepts, words, and phrases, you can use the Insert Index command to tell Word to compile an index.

- Word can keep track of sources and compile a bibliography of cited sources based on the style of your choosing.

Chapter at a Glance

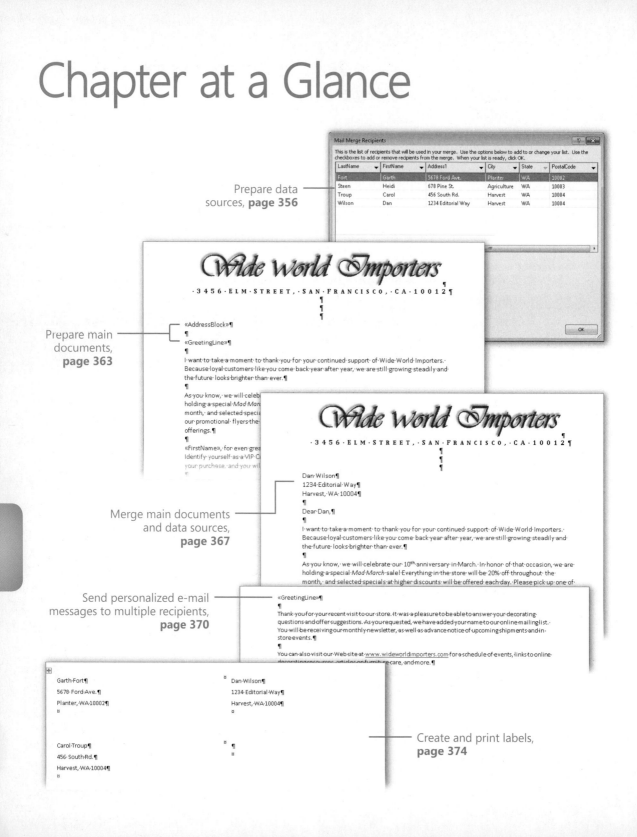

Prepare data sources, **page 356**

Prepare main documents, **page 363**

Merge main documents and data sources, **page 367**

Send personalized e-mail messages to multiple recipients, **page 370**

Create and print labels, **page 374**

14 Work with Mail Merge

In this chapter, you will learn how to

- ✔ Understand mail merge.
- ✔ Prepare data sources.
- ✔ Prepare main documents.
- ✔ Merge main documents and data sources.
- ✔ Send personalized e-mail messages to multiple recipients.
- ✔ Create and print labels.

Many business and other organizations communicate with their customers or members by means of letters, newsletters, and promotional pieces that are sent to everyone on a mailing list. The easiest way to generate a set of documents that are identical except for certain information—such as the name, address, and greeting of a letter—is to use a process called *mail merge*. If you have a list of potential recipients stored in a consistent format, you can use the mail merge process to easily produce a set of personalized documents and mailing labels.

In this chapter, you'll use the Mail Merge wizard in Microsoft Word 2010 to guide you through the process of creating a form letter. You'll select a data source, add a record to it, sort it, and filter it. You'll then add merge fields for an address and greeting line to an existing form letter, preview the merged data, exclude recipients from the merge, merge the letters into a new document, and save the merged file. You'll also set up and send a merged e-mail message. Finally, you'll create and print mailing labels.

> **Practice Files** Before you can complete the exercises in this chapter, you need to copy the book's practice files to your computer. The practice files you'll use to complete the exercises in this chapter are in the Chapter14 practice file folder. A complete list of practice files is provided in "Using the Practice Files" at the beginning of this book.

Understanding Mail Merge

The mail merge process combines the static information stored in one document with variable information stored in another document, as follows:

- **Main document** This document contains the static text that will appear in all the merged documents. It also contains placeholders—called *merge fields*—that tell Word where to insert the variable information.

- **Data source** This is a structured document, such as a Word table, Microsoft Excel worksheet, Microsoft Access database table, or Microsoft Outlook contacts list, that contains sets of information—called *records*—in a predictable format. You can use an existing data source, or you can create a new one as part of the mail merge process.

You can use the Mail Merge wizard to merge a main document with a data source in easy steps. The first step is to select the document type, which can be a letter, an e-mail message, envelopes, labels, or a directory. The type you select determines the subsequent steps. When you have some experience with mail merge, you can use the buttons on the Mailings tab to create and merge documents, instead of the Mail Merge wizard. Regardless of the method, the end result is one copy of the merged document for every record in the data source.

You can merge the main document and data source into a new document, with each merged document separated from the next by a page break. You can then personalize the merged documents before printing them, and you can save the document for later use. If you don't need to edit or save the merged documents, you can merge the main document and data source directly to the printer or to an e-mail message.

Preparing Data Sources

The first step in the mail merge process is to either specify an existing data source or create one. The data source consists of a matrix of rows and columns. Each row contains one record, such as the complete name and address of a customer, and each column contains a particular type of information—called a *field*—such as the first name of all the customers. In the first row of the data source, each field is identified by its column heading—called a *field name*.

◢	A	B	C	D	E	F	G
1	FirstName	LastName	Address1	City	State	PostalCode	
2	Isabel	Martins	7899 38th St.	Tucker	NJ	90025	
3	Garth	Fort	5678 Ford Ave.	Planter	WA	10002	
4	Dan	Wilson	1234 Editorial Way	Harvest	WA	10004	
5	Carol	Troup	456 South Rd.	Harvest	WA	10004	
6	John	Rodman	987 Hard Rock Way	Potential	DE	97540	
7							

Field name — points to row 1

Record — points to row 4

Field — points to column C

The data source stores information in a structured way so that individual items can easily be identified and retrieved.

Tip Because the field names are also used as the merge fields in the main document, they cannot contain spaces. To make the field names readable with no spaces, capitalize each word, as in *PostalCode*, or replace the spaces with underscores, as in *Last_Name*.

If the data source contains many records and it changes frequently, you might want to create it in a program designed for working with large amounts of data, such as Excel or Access. You can also use the contacts list from Outlook. If the data source contains only a few records and it won't be updated often, you can create it in Word, either as a table or as a list with each field separated by a tab. Or you can create it as part of the mail merge process.

What if you want to create merge documents for only a subset of the data in the data source? For example, you might have mail-order customers from all over the United States but want to send an announcement about a store sale only to customers with addresses in your state. After you specify the data source, you can do the following:

- Filter the data source to create merged documents for only some of its data.
- Create a query (a set of selection criteria) to extract only the information you're interested in—for example, all the postal codes for your state.
- Sort the data source—for example, in postal code order for a bulk mailing.

When you use a filter or a query, all the data remains in the data source, but only the data that meets your specifications is used for the mail merge.

In this exercise, you'll open a document that you want to send to multiple people (the main document) and use the Mail Merge wizard to select the list of recipients (the data source). After you add information for a new recipient (a record) to the data source, you'll sort and filter it.

Important The mail merge process is discussed in this topic and the two following topics, each with its own exercise. You need to complete the exercises in sequence. Be sure to read the SET UP paragraphs of each exercise closely to ensure that you can successfully complete the exercises.

SET UP You need the AnniversaryLetter_start document and CustomerList_start workbook located in your Chapter14 practice file folder to complete this exercise. In Windows Explorer, navigate to your Chapter14 folder, double-click the CustomerList_start workbook to open it in Excel, save it as *CustomerListLetter*, and then close it. (To save the file, click the File tab to display the Backstage view, and click Save As in the usual way.) Open the AnniversaryLetter_start document, save it as *AnniversaryLetter*, and leave it open. Then display formatting marks, and follow the steps.

1. On the **Mailings** tab, in the **Start Mail Merge** group, click the **Start Mail Merge** button, and then click **Step by Step Mail Merge Wizard**.

   The Mail Merge task pane opens.

   The first of the wizard's six mail merge steps.

2. With **Letters** selected as the document type, at the bottom of the **Mail Merge** task pane, click **Next: Starting document**.

3. With **Use the current document** selected in the step 2 task pane, click **Next: Select recipients**.

4. With **Use an existing list** selected in the step 3 task pane, click **Browse**.

   The Select Data Source dialog box opens so that you can select the file in which your recipient information is stored.

5. Navigate to your **Chapter14** practice file folder, and double-click the **CustomerListLetter** workbook.

The Select Table dialog box opens.

This workbook contains three sheets, so you need to specify which sheet contains the data.

6. With **Customers$** selected in the **Select Table** dialog box, click **OK**.

The Mail Merge Recipients dialog box opens.

The dialog box shows the records contained in the data source.

7. In the box in the **Data Source** area, click **CustomerListLetter.xlsx**, and then click **Edit**.

The Edit Data Source dialog box opens.

	FirstName ▼	LastName ▼	Address1 ▼	City ▼	State ▼
▷	Isabel	Martins	7899 38th St.	Tucker	NJ
	Garth	Fort	5678 Ford Ave.	Planter	WA
	Dan	Wilson	1234 Editorial ...	Harvest	WA
	Carol	Troup	456 South Rd.	Harvest	WA
	John	Rodman	987 Hard Rock ...	Potential	DE

You can make changes to the data source in this dialog box.

8. Click **New Entry**, and then in the cell below **John**, type the following, pressing Tab to move from field to field:

FirstName	Heidi
LastName	Steen
Address1	678 Pine St.
City	Agriculture
State	WA
PostalCode	10003

Tip You can add multiple records by clicking New Entry after you enter each record.

9. Click **OK**, and then click **Yes** to update the recipient list.

The new record appears at the bottom of the list of recipients in the Mail Merge Recipients dialog box.

10. In the **Refine recipient list** area, click **Sort**.

The Filter And Sort dialog box opens, with the Sort Records page displayed.

You can sort the records on up to three fields, each in ascending or descending order.

11. Display the **Sort by** list, and click **PostalCode**. Then with **Ascending** selected, click **OK**.

   Tip You can also sort data in the Mail Merge Recipients dialog box by clicking the arrow to the right of the field you want to sort on and then clicking Sort Ascending or Sort Descending.

12. Drag the horizontal scroll box to the right, and verify that the records are sorted in ascending order by the **PostalCode** field. Then in the **Refine recipient list** area, click **Filter**.

   The Filter And Sort dialog box opens, with the Filter Records page displayed.

You can specify that only the records that match certain criteria should be included in the merge.

   Tip You can also open the Filter And Sort dialog box by clicking the arrow to the right of any field name and then clicking Advanced.

13. Display the **Field** list, and click **State**.

    The Comparison box displays the default Equal To criterion.

14. In the **Compare to** box, type **WA**, and then click **OK**.

    The Mail Merge Recipients dialog box is updated to show only Washington State residents in ascending PostalCode order.

LastName ▼	FirstName ▼	Address1 ▼	City ▼	State ▼	PostalCode ▼
Fort	Garth	5678 Ford Ave.	Planter	WA	10002
Steen	Heidi	678 Pine St.	Agriculture	WA	10003
Troup	Carol	456 South Rd.	Harvest	WA	10004
Wilson	Dan	1234 Editorial Way	Harvest	WA	10004

Mail Merge Recipients

This is the list of recipients that will be used in your merge. Use the options below to add to or change your list. Use the checkboxes to add or remove recipients from the merge. When your list is ready, click OK.

Data Source

CustomerListLetter.xlsx

Refine recipient list

- ↓ Sort...
- Filter...
- Find duplicates...
- Find recipient...
- Validate addresses...

Edit...   Refresh

OK

The records for customers who do not live in Washington State are hidden and will be excluded from the merge process.

15. Click **OK** to close the **Mail Merge Recipients** dialog box.

 CLEAN UP Save the AnniversaryLetter document, and leave it open for the next exercise.

Using an Outlook Contacts List as a Data Source

Using information from an Outlook contacts list as the data source for the merge process requires a few extra steps in the Mail Merge wizard.

To use Outlook information as the data source for a form letter:

1. In the Mail Merge task pane, display the step 3 task pane.

2. Under Select Recipients, click Select From Outlook Contacts, and then click Choose Contacts Folder.

3. If you are prompted to select your Outlook profile, select the one you want to use, and then click OK.

   The Select Contacts dialog box opens.

4. In the Select A Contact Folder To Import list, click the folder you want to use, and then click OK.

   The Mail Merge Recipients dialog box opens, displaying your Outlook contacts.

5. In the contacts table, clear the check boxes of any contacts you want to exclude from the merge process, or sort and filter the list to display the contacts you want to include in the desired order.

6. Click OK.

You can then continue with the next steps in the merge process, as explained in later topics in this chapter.

Preparing Main Documents

One common type of main document used in the mail merge process is a form letter. This type of document typically contains merge fields for the name and address of each recipient along with text that is the same in all the letters. In the form letter, each merge field is enclosed in « and » characters, which are called *chevrons*—for example, «AddressBlock».

If you have already written the letter, you can insert the merge fields during the merge process; if you haven't written the letter, you can write it as part of the process. Either way, you first enter the text that will be common to all the letters and then insert the merge fields that will be replaced by the variable information from the data source.

Tip If you need to stop before you finish the merge process, you can save the form letter to retain the work you have done so far. You can then open the form letter and resume from where you left off. Because you have specified a data source for the form letter, you will be asked to confirm that you want to run a command to reattach the same data source.

You can insert merge fields in two ways:

● From the Mail Merge task pane in step 4 of the Mail Merge wizard

● By clicking buttons in the Write & Insert Fields group on the Mailings tab

Either way, clicking Address Block or Greeting Line opens a dialog box in which you can refine the fields' settings, whereas clicking individual fields inserts them with their default settings.

month, and selected specials at higher discounts will be offered each day
our promotional flyers the next time you visit the store for a complete sc
offerings.¶

¶ —————————————————————————————— Merge field
«FirstName», for even greater savings, be sure to bring this letter with yo
Identify yourself as a VIP Customer by presenting the letter to your sales
your purchase, and you will receive an additional 5% off your total bill.¶
¶

You can insert a merge field anywhere in the main document.

Tip To save the form letter without any mail merge information, click Start Mail Merge in the Start Mail Merge group on the Mailings tab, and then click Normal Word Document.

In this exercise, you'll modify an existing form letter by adding merge fields for a standard address, an informal greeting line, and the recipient's first name.

SET UP This exercise uses the AnniversaryLetter document to which you attached the CustomerListLetter workbook as the data source in the previous exercise. If you didn't complete that exercise, you should do so now. If you closed the AnniversaryLetter document at the end of the previous exercise, open it, and when a message asks whether you want to run the command that will attach the data source to the document, click Yes. Then open the Mail Merge task pane by clicking the Start Mail Merge button in the Start Mail Merge group on the Mailings tab and clicking Step by Step Mail Merge Wizard. The Mail Merge task pane opens to the step 3 task pane. Then display formatting marks, and follow the steps.

1. At the bottom of the **Mail Merge** task pane, click **Next: Write your letter**.

2. In the document, position the cursor in the first empty left-aligned paragraph, and then in the **Mail Merge** task pane, click **Address block**.

   The Insert Address Block dialog box opens.

In this dialog box, you can refine the format of the fields that make up the Address Block merge field.

3. Click **OK** to accept the default settings.

   Word inserts the «AddressBlock» merge field into the document. When you merge the form letter with the data source, Word will substitute the component name and address information for this merge field.

4. Press the Enter key twice, and then in the **Mail Merge** task pane, click **Greeting line**.

   The Insert Greeting Line dialog box opens.

In this dialog box, you can specify how the greeting line should appear in the merged letters.

5. Under **Greeting line format**, display the list for the second box, and then click **Joshua**.

6. In the **Preview** area, click the **Next** button three times to view the greeting line for each of the recipients in the linked data source. Then click **OK** to close the **Insert Greeting Line** dialog box.

   Word inserts the «GreetingLine» merge field into the document. When you merge the form letter with the data source, Word will replace this merge field with the word *Dear* and a space, followed by the information in the FirstName field, followed by a comma.

7. Click to the left of the **For even greater savings** paragraph, and in the **Mail Merge** task pane, click **More items**.

   The Insert Merge Field dialog box opens.

   You can insert individual fields from the data source.

8. With **Database Fields** selected and **FirstName** highlighted in the **Fields** box, click **Insert**, and then click **Close**.

   The «FirstName» merge field appears at the beginning of the third paragraph.

9. Without moving the cursor, type a comma and press the Spacebar. Then change **For** to **for**.

   The form letter is now ready for merging.

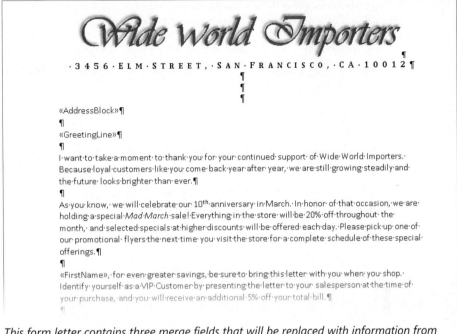

This form letter contains three merge fields that will be replaced with information from the data source.

✖ **CLEAN UP** Save the AnniversaryLetter document, and leave it open for the next exercise.

Merging Main Documents and Data Sources

After you specify the data source you want to use and enter merge fields in the main document, you can preview the merged documents before performing the actual merge. You can exclude recipients during this preview. When you are ready, you can either send the merged documents directly to the printer or you can merge them one after the other into a new document, separated by page breaks. If you merge to a new document, you have another chance to review and, if necessary, edit the merged documents before sending them to the printer.

In this exercise, you'll preview merged letters, exclude recipients from the merge, merge the letters into a new document, and then save the merged file.

SET UP This exercise uses the AnniversaryLetter document to which you attached the CustomerListLetter workbook as the data source and in which you inserted merge fields in the previous two exercises. If you didn't complete those exercises, you should do so now. If you closed the AnniversaryLetter document at the end of the last exercise, open it, and when a message asks whether you want to run the command that will attach the data source to the document, click Yes. Then open the Mail Merge task pane by clicking the Start Mail Merge button in the Start Mail Merge group on the Mailings tab and clicking Step by Step Mail Merge Wizard. The Mail Merge task pane opens to the step 3 task pane. Then display formatting marks, and follow the steps.

1. At the bottom of the **Mail Merge** task pane, click **Next** until the step 5 task pane is displayed.

2. If necessary, scroll down the letter until you can see the address block, the greeting line, and the third paragraph at the same time.

Word displays a preview of how the personalized letter will look when merged with the data source.

You can preview how the personalized letters will look before you proceed with the merge.

3. Under **Preview your letters** in the **Mail Merge** task pane, click the **Previous Record** button three times to preview all the letters.

Tip You can also preview the next or previous documents by clicking the Next Record or Previous Record button in the Preview Results group on the Mailings tab. You can jump to the first merged document by clicking the First Record button or the last merged document by clicking the Last Record button.

4. To exclude the displayed recipient (*Garth Fort*) from the merge, under **Make changes** in the **Mail Merge** task pane, click **Exclude this recipient**.

5. Preview the letters again. Then at the bottom of the **Mail Merge** task pane, click **Next: Complete the merge**.

6. In the **Mail Merge** task pane, click **Edit individual letters**.

   The Merge To New Document dialog box opens.

If you want to merge only some of the records, you can specify which ones in this dialog box.

7. With the **All** option selected, click **OK**.

   Word creates a document called *Letters1* that contains a personalized copy of the form letter for each of the selected records.

8. On the Quick Access Toolbar, click the **Save** button.

   Keyboard Shortcut Press Ctrl+S to save files.

   See Also For more information about keyboard shortcuts, see "Keyboard Shortcuts" at the end of this book.

   The Save As dialog box opens so that you can save the new document with a more specific name.

9. Navigate to your **Chapter14** practice file folder, type **My Merged Letters** in the **File name** box, and then click **Save**.

   Word saves the new document in the specified folder with the name *My Merged Letters*.

CLEAN UP Close the My Merged Letters document. Then save and close the AnniversaryLetter document.

Printing Envelopes

You can print an envelope based on an address in a document. To do this:

1. In the document, select the lines of the address. (Do not select any blank lines above or below the address.)

2. On the Mailings tab, in the Create group, click the Envelopes button.

   The Envelopes And Labels dialog box opens. You can edit the address in the Delivery Address box and enter a return address in the Return Address box.

   Tip You can have Word supply the return address. Display the Advanced page of the Word Options dialog box. Toward the bottom of the page, under General, enter the return address in the Mailing Address box, and click OK. The address then appears by default as the Return Address in the Envelopes And Labels dialog box. If you want to use envelopes with a preprinted return address, you must select the Omit check box to avoid duplication.

3. Size 10 is the default envelope size. If you want to select a different envelope size, click Options, make your selection, and then click OK.

   In the Envelope Options dialog box, you can also specify the feed method (horizontally or vertically and face up or face down), and the font and font size of both the address and the return address.

   If you have electronic postage software installed on your computer, you can include electronic postage.

4. Insert an envelope in the printer, and then click Print.

Alternatively, you can click Add To Document to have Word insert the address in the format required for an envelope on a separate page at the beginning of the current document.

Sending Personalized E-Mail Messages to Multiple Recipients

When you want to send the same information to all the people on a list—for example, all your customers, or all the members of a club or your family—you don't have to print letters and physically mail them. Instead, you can use mail merge to create a personalized e-mail message for each person in a data source. As with a form letter that will be printed, you can either use the Mail Merge wizard or use the buttons on the Mailings tab to insert merge fields into the form message. These merge fields will be replaced with information from the specified data source.

If you are using the wizard, be sure to click E-Mail Messages in step 1. If you are not using the wizard, you can specify the list of e-mail addresses you want to send the message to by clicking the Select Recipients button in the Start Mail Merge group on the Mailings tab. In either case, you have three options:

- Type an entirely new list of recipients.
- Use an existing list of recipients.
- Select recipients from an Outlook contacts list.

You can quickly add merge fields to a form message by using the buttons in the Write & Insert Fields group. Many e-mail messages need only a greeting line. Because e-mail messages tend to be less formal than printed letters, you might want to start the messages with something other than the predefined greeting options (*Dear* and *To:*) by typing a custom greeting.

In this exercise, you'll open an existing form message, use the buttons on the Mailings tab to create a short mailing list, add a custom greeting line merge field, and then complete the merge.

SET UP You need the ThankYouEmail_start document located in your Chapter14 practice file folder to complete this exercise. Open the ThankYouEmail_start document, and save it as *ThankYouEmail*. Display formatting marks, and then follow the steps.

Select
Recipients ▾

1. On the **Mailings** tab, in the **Start Mail Merge** group, click the **Select Recipients** button, and then in the list, click **Type New List**.

   The New Address List dialog box opens.

Title ▾	First Name ▾	Last Name ▾	Company Name ▾	Address Line 1 ▾

New Address List

Type recipient information in the table. To add more entries, click New Entry.

New Entry   Find...
Delete Entry   Customize Columns...   OK   Cancel

If you don't have an existing data source, you can create one as part of the mail merge process.

2. Skipping over the Title field, type **Andrea** in the **First Name** field, type **Dunker** in the **Last Name** field, press the Tab key until you reach the **E-mail Address** field (the last field in the table), and then type **andrea@consolidatedmessenger.com**.

3. Click **New Entry**, and then add **Judy Lew**, whose e-mail address is **judy@lucernepublishing.com**.

    Tip If you have several e-mail addresses to add to the list, you can press Tab in the last field of the last entry, instead of clicking New Entry each time.

4. Repeat step 3 to add **Ben Miller**, whose e-mail address is **ben@wingtiptoys.com**, and then click **OK**.

    The Save Address List dialog box opens, with the contents of your My Data Sources folder displayed. This dialog box is very similar to the Save As dialog box.

    Troubleshooting If the dialog box doesn't appear, it might be hidden behind the program window, which will start flashing to indicate that you need to attend to the dialog box before you can proceed. Click the program window title bar to make the dialog box appear, or click the Word button on the Windows Taskbar and then click the dialog box thumbnail.

5. Navigate to your **Chapter14** practice file folder, type **My E-Mail Data Source** in the **File name** box, and then click **Save**.

    Word saves the data source in the specified location as a database.

6. With the cursor at the beginning of the form message, press Enter twice, and then press the Up Arrow key twice.

7. On the **Mailings** tab, in the **Write & Insert Fields** group, click the **Greeting Line** button.

    The Insert Greeting Line dialog box opens.

8. In the first box under **Greeting line format**, replace **Dear** with **Hello** followed by a comma and a space. Display the list of options for the second box, and click **Joshua**. Then display the list of options for the third box, and click **:** (the colon).

9. In the **Preview** area, click the **Next** button twice to preview the greetings as they will appear in the e-mail messages.

10. Click the **First** button to return to the first record, and then click **OK**.

    Word inserts the «GreetingLine» merge field at the top of the form message.

Greeting
Line

«GreetingLine»¶

¶

Thank·you·for·your·recent·visit·to·our·store.·It·was·a·pleasure·to·be·able·to·answer·your·decorating·
questions·and·offer·suggestions.·As·you·requested,·we·have·added·your·name·to·our·online·mailing·list.·
You·will·be·receiving·our·monthly·newsletter,·as·well·as·advance·notice·of·upcoming·shipments·and·in-
store·events.¶

¶

You·can·also·visit·our·Web·site·at·<u>www.wideworldimporters.com</u>·for·a·schedule·of·events,·links·to·online·
decorating·resources,·articles·on·furniture·care,·and·more.¶

¶

*If you want to edit the custom greeting, you can right-click its merge field and then click
Edit Greeting Line.*

11. On the **Mailings** tab, in the **Preview Results** group, click the **Preview Results**
button.

Word shows a preview of the first message. You can click the Next Record button in
the Preview Results group to preview the messages for other recipients. Clicking the
Preview Results button again turns off the preview.

12. In the **Write & Insert Fields** group, click the **Highlight Merge Fields** button.

Word indicates the merge field with a gray highlight.

13. In the **Finish** group, click the **Finish & Merge** button, and then in the list, click
Send E-mail Messages.

The Merge To E-Mail dialog box opens.

You set up the e-mail message header information and format in this dialog box.

14. In the **Message options** area, verify that **Email_Address** is selected in the **To** box, type **Welcome to Wide World Importers!** in the **Subject line** box, and verify that **HTML** is selected in the **Mail format** box.

15. In this case, click **Cancel**.

If you click OK, Word converts the form message to an e-mail message and transmits it to your default e-mail program, which then sends the message to each of the selected addresses in the data source.

Tip Your e-mail program might require that you log in or manually send the messages (they will be held in the outbox until sent). If you are using Outlook, a copy of each sent message appears in your Outlook Sent Items folder. If you plan to send a large number of messages, you might want to turn off the saving of sent messages.

❌ **CLEAN UP** Save the ThankYouEmail document, and then close it.

Creating and Printing Labels

Most organizations keep information about their customers or clients in a worksheet or database that can be used for several purposes. For example, the address information might be used to send billing statements, form letters, and brochures. It might also be used to print sheets of mailing labels that can be attached to items such as packages and catalogs.

To create sheets of mailing labels, you first prepare the data source and then prepare the main document by selecting the brand and style of labels you plan to use. Word creates a table with cells the size of the labels on a page the size of the label sheet, so that each record will print on one label on the sheet. You insert merge fields into the first cell as a template for all the other cells. When you merge the main document and the data source, you can print the labels or create a new label document that you can use whenever you want to send something to the same set of recipients.

In this exercise, you'll use the Mail Merge wizard to create mailing labels. You'll then print the labels on standard paper to proofread them.

➡ **SET UP** You need the CustomerList_start workbook located in your Chapter14 practice file folder to complete this exercise. Open the CustomerList_start workbook, save it as *CustomerListLabels*, and then close it. Display formatting marks, and be sure to turn on your printer. (If you don't want to print the labels, you can proof them on-screen.) Then with the Word program window active, follow the steps.

1. Display the Backstage view, click **New**, and then double-click **Blank document**.

A new blank document opens.

Start Mail
Merge ▾

2. On the **Mailings** tab, in the **Start Mail Merge** group, click the **Start Mail Merge** button, and then click **Step by Step Mail Merge Wizard**.

3. In the **Mail Merge** task pane, click **Labels**, and then click **Next: Starting document**.

4. With **Change document layout** selected in the step 2 task pane, click **Label options**.

The Label Options dialog box opens.

Label Options   ? ✕

Printer information
  ○ C̲ontinuous-feed printers
  ● P̲age printers   T̲ray: Default tray (Automatically Select) ▾

Label information
  Label v̲endors: Avery US Letter ▾

Find updates on Office.com

Product n̲umber: Label information

5143 Print or Write Name Badge Labels	Type: Mailing Labels
5144 Print or Write Name Badge Labels	Height: 1.5"
5146 Print or Write Name Badge Labels	Width: 4"
5147 Print or Write Name Badge Labels	Page size: 8.5" × 11"
5155 Easy Peel Return Address Labels	
5159 Mailing Labels	

  [D̲etails...] [New Label...] [Delete]   [OK] [Cancel]

Every label is different. You need to specify the print method, the manufacturer and/or type, and the product number so that Word can set up the labels correctly.

5. In the **Label information** area, ensure that the **Label vendors** setting is **Avery US Letter**.

6. In the **Product number** box, ensure that the setting is **5159 Mailing Labels**, and then click **OK**.

Word inserts a table that fills the first page of the main document.

7. At the bottom of the **Mail Merge** task pane, click **Next: Select recipients**.

8. With **Use an existing list** selected, click **Browse**, navigate to your **Chapter14** practice file folder, double-click the **CustomerListLabels** workbook, and then in the **Select Table** dialog box, click **OK**.

9. In the **Mail Merge Recipients** dialog box, clear the check boxes of the two recipients whose addresses are not in Washington State (WA), and then click **OK**.

Word inserts a «Next Record» merge field in all the cells in the main document except the first.

10. At the bottom of the **Mail Merge** task pane, click **Next: Arrange your labels**, and then ensure that you can see the left edge of the main document.

11. With the cursor positioned in the first cell, in the **Mail Merge** task pane, click **Address block**.

12. In the **Insert Address Block** dialog box, click **OK** to accept the default settings.

    Word inserts an «AddressBlock» merge field into the first cell.

    ┌──┐
    │ ⊞   │
    │   «AddressBlock»¶   ¤   «Next·Record»¶   │
    │   ¤   ¤   │
    │   │
    │   │
    │   │
    │   «Next·Record»¶   ¤   «Next·Record»¶   │
    │   ¤   ¤   │
    └──┘

    The merge fields in the first cell in the table will be used as a template for all the other cells.

13. In the **Mail Merge** task pane, click **Update all labels**.

    The «AddressBlock» merge field is copied to the other cells, after the «Next Record» merge field.

14. At the bottom of the **Mail Merge** task pane, click **Next: Preview your labels**. Then in the **Preview Results** group, click the **First Record** button.

    The merge fields are replaced by the specified information from the data source.

    ┌──┐
    │ ⊞   │
    │   Garth·Fort¶   ¤   Dan·Wilson¶   │
    │   5678·Ford·Ave.¶   1234·Editorial·Way¶   │
    │   Planter,·WA·10002¶   Harvest,·WA·10004¶   │
    │   ¤   ¤   │
    │   │
    │   │
    │   Carol·Troup¶   ¤   ¶   │
    │   456·South·Rd.¶   ¤   │
    │   Harvest,·WA·10004¶   │
    │   ¤   │
    └──┘

    Labels for the three recipients who live in Washington State, as they will appear after the merge.

15. At the bottom of the **Mail Merge** task pane, click **Next: Complete the merge**. Then in the **Mail Merge** task pane, click **Print**.

The Merge To Printer dialog box opens.

Merge to Printer

Print records

○ A̲ll

○ Curre̲nt record

○ F̲rom: [   ]   T̲o: [   ]

[OK]   [Cancel]

You have the opportunity to exclude records from the merge before printing the labels.

16. With the **All** option selected, click **OK**.

17. In the **Print** dialog box, verify that the name of the printer you want to use to print the labels appears in the **Name** box, and then click **OK** to print the labels.

    The labels are printed on regular paper on the printer you selected. If you want to print on label sheets, insert the sheets in the printer's paper tray before clicking OK in the Print dialog box.

✖ **CLEAN UP** Save the label document as *My Merged Labels*, and then close it.

Key Points

- The mail merge process works by combining static information in a main document with variable information in a data source.

- The main document can be any type of document, such as a letter, e-mail message, envelope or label template, or a directory or catalog.

- The data source is organized into sets of information, called *records*, with each record containing the same items, called *fields*.

- You insert placeholders called *merge fields* into the main document to tell Word where to merge items from the data source.

- You don't have to use all the records in a data source for a mail merge. You can filter the data and exclude specific records.

- You can send the mail merged results directly to your printer or to a new document that you can edit and save.

Chapter at a Glance

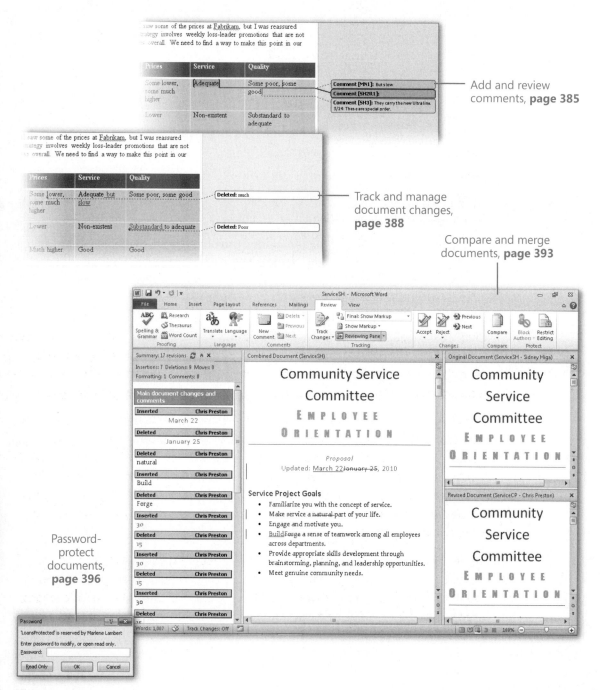

Add and review comments, **page 385**

Track and manage document changes, **page 388**

Compare and merge documents, **page 393**

Password-protect documents, **page 396**

15 Collaborate on Documents

In today's workplace, many documents are developed collaboratively by a team of people. You might be the lead author of some documents that are reviewed by your colleagues and managers, and you might be a reviewer of other documents. With Microsoft Word 2010, you can collaborate on the development of documents in new and exciting ways. You can also easily attach a document to an e-mail message and send it to colleagues for review.

These days, most documents are reviewed on the screen rather than on paper printouts. With Word, it's easy to edit documents on-screen without losing track of the original text, and it's easy to accept or reject changes. You can also make comments, ask questions, and respond to comments made by others. If you send a document out for review and then receive several copies with changes and suggestions back from different people, you can merge the different versions into one file to simplify the process of reviewing and accepting or rejecting changes.

Sometimes you'll want other people to review a document but not change it. You can prevent other people from making changes to a document by assigning a password to it. You can also specify that only certain people are allowed to make changes, and what types of formatting and content changes are allowed.

In this chapter, we'll first discuss the new Word coauthoring capabilities., and then you'll send a document directly from Word. You'll track changes that you make to a document, and then accept and reject changes. You'll review, add, delete, and hide comments, and merge three versions of the same document. Finally, you'll set and remove a password and set up editing and formatting restrictions.

> **Practice Files** Before you can complete the exercises in this chapter, you need to copy the book's practice files to your computer. The practice files you'll use to complete the exercises in this chapter are in the Chapter15 practice file folder. A complete list of practice files is provided in "Using the Practice Files" at the beginning of this book.

Coauthoring Documents

Whether you work for a large organization or a small business, you might need to collaborate with other people on the development of a document. Or perhaps you are working with a team of students or volunteers on a document that requires input from everyone. No matter what the circumstances, it can be difficult to keep track of different versions of a document produced by different people. With Word 2010, however, it is now possible to store one version of the document that can be worked on by multiple people simultaneously.

To develop a document with other users, you need to save it to a Microsoft SharePoint 2010 site. Display the Save & Send page of the Backstage view, click Save To SharePoint, and then use the settings in the Save As dialog box to save the document to the site. You then continue to work on it from the site. When another contributor begins making changes to the file stored on the site, Word alerts you to that person's presence. You can display a list of the other people who are actively working on the document and their availability.

As the people working on the document make changes, Word keeps track of them. When you finish working with the document, you save and close it as usual. The next time you open it, you'll see the changes made by anyone else who has worked on the document. In this way, people can work efficiently on a document whether they are in the same office building, on the other side of town, or in a different time zone.

If your organization has implemented the Word 2010 Web App on a server, team members who travel frequently can review documents while on the road. With the Web App, you can review and edit a document stored on your organization's server on any computer running Windows Internet Explorer 7 or Internet Explorer 8, FireFox 3.5, or Safari 4 on the Mac.

You can also save a document to a Windows Live SkyDrive space and share it with other people from there. SkyDrive is part of Windows Live Online Services, a suite of useful programs that are available over the Internet from your computer or from mobile devices, such as portable computers or smartphones. You can visit www.windowslive.com/Online/ to learn about these services. All you need to start using them is a Windows Live ID.

You save a document to SkyDrive by displaying the Save & Send page of the Backstage view, clicking Save To Web, and then specifying the location where you want to save the file. You can make the document publicly available by saving it in the Public folder, or you can save it in your My Documents folder and then assign access permissions to specific people. You and colleagues who can access the file can then work on it by using the Word Web App from the site. (At the time of writing, editing capabilities were not yet available.)

If you have a smartphone, you might be able to use the Word 2010 Mobile App to view and edit documents.

More in-depth discussion of the Web App and the Mobile App, which allow you to continue collaborating with your team no matter where you are, is beyond the scope of this book, but if you are a "road warrior," you will certainly want to research them further.

Sending Documents Directly from Word

After you create a document, you can quickly send it via e-mail from the Save & Send page of the Backstage view, without starting your e-mail program.

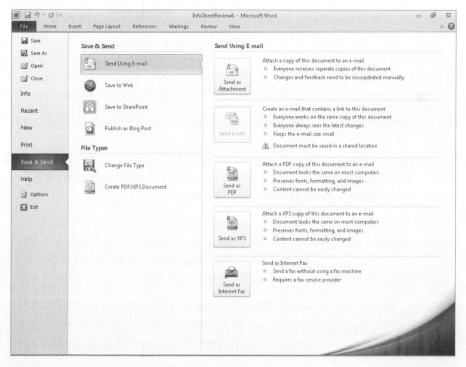

You can send a file in .docx, .pdf, or .xps format.

Clicking Send As Attachment opens a message window with the current document already attached as a .docx file. All you have to do is enter the e-mail addresses of anyone you want to receive the message and its attachment. If you want, you can modify the subject line, which contains the name of the document you're sending.

Similarly, you can click Send As PDF or Send As XPS to attach a version of the document saved in the corresponding file format.

In addition to sending a document as an e-mail attachment from within Word, if you have signed up with an Internet fax service provider, you can send the document as a fax. Although the exact terms vary from one provider to another, these services let you send and receive faxes from your computer without needing a fax machine or dedicated fax line. After establishing an Internet fax service account, you can send the current document as a fax by clicking Send As Internet Fax on the Save & Send page. You then follow the procedure specified by your fax service provider.

Tip If you do not sign up with an Internet fax service provider before clicking Send As Internet Fax, a message box appears. Clicking OK opens a Web page where you can choose a fax service provider.

In this exercise, you'll attach three documents to an e-mail message so that you can simulate sending them for review.

SET UP You need the InfoSheetReviewA_start, InfoSheetReviewB_start, and InfoSheetReviewC_start documents located in your Chapter15 practice file folder to complete this exercise. Open each document and save it without _start as part of the file name. Be sure to have an e-mail program installed on your computer and an e-mail account set up before beginning this exercise. Microsoft Outlook 2010 is recommended. You can use another e-mail program, but the steps for attaching and sending a message might vary from those given in this exercise. Then with only the InfoSheetReviewA document open, follow the steps.

1. Display the Backstage view, and click **Save & Send**.

2. With **Send Using E-mail** selected in the center pane of the **Save & Send** page, click **Send as Attachment**.

   A message window opens.

Word enters the name of the document in the Subject line and attaches the document to the message.

3. In the **To** box, type your own e-mail address.

4. In the message content pane, type **Please review the attached documents and let me know which title you prefer.**

   You can format the text of the message in the same way you would the text of a document.

5. On the **Message** tab, in the **Include** group, click the **Attach File** button.

   The Insert File dialog box opens.

6. Navigate to your **Chapter15** practice file folder.

7. Click **InfoSheetReviewB**, hold down the Ctrl key, click **InfoSheetReviewC**, and then click **Insert**.

   In the message window, the Attached box shows that three files are attached to the message.

8. On the **Message** tab, in the **Tags** group, click the **High Importance** button.

   If the message recipient is using Outlook, the message header will display a red exclamation mark to indicate that it is important.

Send

9. In the message header, click the **Send** button.

   Outlook sends the e-mail message with the attached documents. You'll receive the message the next time Outlook connects to your mail server.

✖ **CLEAN UP** Close the InfoSheetReviewA document.

Adding Digital Signatures

When you create a document that will be circulated to other people via e-mail or the Web, you might want to attach a digital signature, which is an electronic stamp of authentication. The digital signature confirms the origin of the document and indicates that no one has tampered with the document since it was signed.

To add a digital signature to a Word document:

1. Display the Backstage view, and click Info.

2. On the Info page, click the Protect Document button, and then click Add A Digital Signature.

   If you do not already have a digital signature stored on this computer, a dialog box opens.

3. If you want to obtain a signature from a third-party company such as ARX CoSign or IntelliSafe, click Signature Services From The Office Marketplace to display a Web site with instructions.

4. If you want to create your own signature, click OK. Then in the Get A Digital ID dialog box, click Create Your Own Digital ID, and click OK. Then in the Create A Digital ID dialog box, enter the information you want included in the boxes provided, and click Create.

5. In the Sign dialog box, enter the purpose for signing the document, if you want, and click Sign. Then click OK in the message that the signature has been saved with the document.

   The Info page now indicates that the document is signed and final. When you click any of the other ribbon tabs, an info bar at the top of the document discourages editing by announcing that the document is final, and the ribbon commands are hidden.

Adding and Reviewing Comments

When reviewing a document, you can insert notes, called *comments*, to ask questions, make suggestions, or explain edits. To insert a comment, you select the text to which the comment refers, click the New Comment button in the Comments group on the Review tab, and type what you want to say in the balloon that appears. In Print Layout view, Word highlights the associated text in the document in the same color as the balloon and adds your initials and a sequential number to the balloon itself.

You can work with comments in the following ways:

- To display the reviewer's name and the date and time the comment was inserted, point to either the commented text or the balloon.

- To review comments, scroll through the document, or in the case of long documents, click the Next or Previous button in the Comments group to jump from balloon to balloon.

- To edit a comment, click the balloon and use normal editing techniques.

- To delete a comment, click its balloon and then click the Delete button in the Comments group; or right-click the balloon and then click Delete Comment.

- To respond to a comment, simply add text to its existing balloon. You can also click the existing balloon and then click the New Comment button to attach a new balloon to the same text in the document.

- If the complete text of a comment isn't visible in its balloon, view it in its entirety by clicking the Reviewing Pane button to display the Reviewing pane. To change the size of the pane, point to its border, and when the pointer changes to a double-headed arrow, drag the border. To close the Reviewing pane, click its Close button, or click the Reviewing Pane button again.

  Tip In addition to displaying comments, the Reviewing pane displays all the editing and formatting changes made to a document in Track Changes, with the number of each type of change summarized at the top of the pane. For information about Track Changes, see the next topic in this chapter.

- Turn off the display of comment balloons by clicking the Show Markup button in the Tracking group and then clicking Comments.

- If multiple people have reviewed a document and you want to see only the comments of a specific person, click the Show Markup button, click Reviewers, and then click the name of any reviewer whose comments you don't want to see.

In this exercise, you'll show and review comments in a document, add and respond to comments, delete one that is no longer needed, and then hide the remaining comments.

 SET UP You need the CompetitiveAnalysisA_start document located in your Chapter15 practice file folder to complete this exercise. Open the CompetitiveAnalysisA_start document, and save it as *CompetitiveAnalysisA*. Then follow the steps.

1. If comments are not visible in the document, click the **Review** tab, and in the **Tracking** group, ensure that the **Display for Review** box displays **Final: Show Markup**. If comments are still not visible, in the **Tracking** group, click the **Show Markup** button, and if **Comments** does not have a check mark to its left in the list, click it.

2. On the **Review** tab, in the **Comments** group, click the **Next** button.

In the document, Word highlights the first instance of commented text.

Word positions the cursor in the highlighted comment balloon, in case you want to edit the comment.

Tip If a document contains both comments and tracked changes, clicking the Next or Previous button in the Changes group on the Review tab moves sequentially among both elements, whereas clicking the Next or Previous button in the Comments group moves only among comments.

3. In the **Comments** group, click the **Next** button.

Word moves to the next comment.

4. In the table, point to **Adequate**.

A ScreenTip displays information about who inserted the comment and when.

5. In the fifth column of the same row, select the words **some good**, and then in the **Comments** group, click the **New Comment** button.

Word highlights the selection and displays a new balloon in the right margin.

6. In the comment balloon, type **They carry the new Ultra line.**

Delete

7. Click the comment balloon associated with the word **competitors**, and in the **Comments** group, click the **Delete** button.

   Word deletes the comment and its balloon.

Reviewing Pane

8. In the **Tracking** group, click the **Reviewing Pane** button.

   The Reviewing pane opens at the left side of the program window.

The Reviewing pane shows the two remaining comments.

Tip You can click the Reviewing Pane arrow and then click Reviewing Pane Horizontal to display the pane across the bottom of the page.

9. In the **Reviewing** pane, click at the right end of the second comment, press Enter, type the date and a colon (:), press the Spacebar, and then type **These are special order.**

   The new text is added to the same comment in the Reviewing pane.

10. In the **Tracking** group, click the **Reviewing Pane** button to close the pane, and then scroll through the document so that you can see its text.

11. Click anywhere in the comment balloon associated with **Adequate**, and then in the **Comments** group, click the **New Comment** button.

    Word attaches a response comment to the same text in the document.

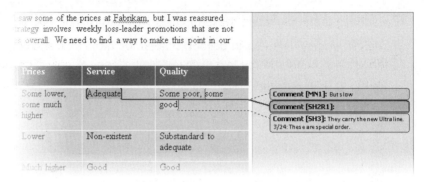

The response comment is labeled with your initials, the sequential comment number 2, and R1, which indicates that this is a response to comment 1.

12. In the response comment balloon, type **If you had been a real customer, would you have left?**

13. In the **Tracking** group, click the **Show Markup** button, and then click **Comments** to hide them.

✖ **CLEAN UP** Save the CompetitiveAnalysisA document, and then close it.

Tracking and Managing Document Changes

When two or more people collaborate on a document, one person usually creates and "owns" the document and the others review it, adding or revising content to make it more accurate, logical, or readable. In Word, reviewers can turn on the Track Changes feature so that the revisions they make to the document are recorded without the original text being lost. (Note that turning on Track Changes affects only the active document, not any other documents that might also be open.)

To turn on Track Changes, you click the Track Changes button in the Tracking group on the Review tab. You then edit the text as usual.

Tip If you want to know whether Track Changes is turned on when the Review tab is not displayed, right-click the status bar and then click Track Changes on the Customize Status Bar menu. Word then adds a Track Changes button to the status bar that you can click to turn the feature on and off.

By default, your revisions appear in a different color from the original text, as follows:

● Insertions and deletions are inserted in the text in your assigned color and are underlined.

● Formatting changes appear in balloons in the right margin.

- All changes are marked in the left margin by a vertical line.

- You can display deletions in balloons instead of in the text, and you can display formatting changes in the text instead of in balloons. Simply click the Show Markup button in the Tracking group on the Review tab, click Balloons, and then click the options you want.

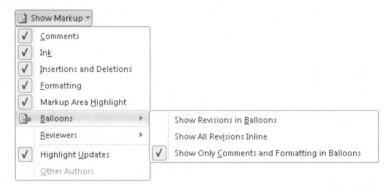

You can specify whether you want revisions to be displayed in the text or in balloons.

Tip The colors used for revisions are controlled by the settings in the Track Changes Options dialog box, which you can display by clicking the Track Changes arrow and then clicking Change Tracking Options.

You can display a ScreenTip identifying the name of the reviewer who made a specific change and when the change was made, by pointing to a revision or balloon. The reviewer name is taken from the user information stored with the user account. You can change the user information by clicking the Track Changes arrow, clicking Change User Name, typing the name and initials you want in the Word Options dialog box, and then clicking OK.

By using the commands available on the Review tab, you can work with revisions in the following ways:

- To track changes without showing them on the screen, hide the revisions by clicking the Display For Review arrow in the Tracking group and clicking Final in the list. To display the revisions again, click Final: Show Markup in the Display For Review list. You can also display the original version, with or without revisions.

- When revisions are visible in the document, select which types of revisions you want to display from the Show Markup list in the Tracking group—for example, you can display only comments or only insertions and deletions. You can also display or hide the revisions of specific reviewers from this list.

- Move forward or backward from one revision or comment to another by clicking the Next or Previous button in the Changes group.

- Incorporate a selected change into the document and move to the next change by clicking the Accept button in the Changes group. Click the Reject button to remove the selected change, restore the original text, and move to the next change.

  Tip You can also right-click the change and then click Accept Change or Reject Change.

- Accept or reject all the changes in a block of text, such as a paragraph, by selecting the block and clicking the Accept or Reject button.

- Accept all the changes in the document by clicking the Accept arrow and then clicking Accept All Changes In Document. Reject all the changes at once by clicking the Reject arrow and then clicking Reject All Changes In Document.

- Accept or reject only certain types of changes or changes from a specific reviewer by displaying only the changes you want to accept or reject, clicking the Accept or Reject arrow, and then clicking Accept All Changes Shown or Reject All Changes Shown in the list.

In this exercise, you'll turn on Track Changes, edit the document, and accept and reject changes.

SET UP You need the CompetitiveAnalysisB_start document located in your Chapter15 practice file folder to complete this exercise. Open the CompetitiveAnalysisB_start document, and save it as *CompetitiveAnalysisB*. Then follow the steps.

Track Changes ▾

1. On the **Review** tab, in the **Tracking** group, click the **Track Changes** button.

   The active (orange) button indicates that Track Changes is turned on. Any changes that you make now will be indicated in the document as revisions.

Show Markup ▾

2. To display changes the same way we do in our graphics, in the **Tracking** group, click the **Show Markup** button, point to **Balloons**, and then click **Show All Revisions Inline**.

3. In the table at the end of the document, in **Some much lower** in the third column, double-click **much**, and then press the Delete key.

   Word changes the font color of the word *much* and indicates with strikethrough formatting that you deleted it.

4. In the fourth column of the same row, position the insertion point at the right end of **Adequate**, press the Spacebar, and then type **but slow**.

   Word inserts the new text in the same color as the deletion.

first, I was alarmed when I saw some of the prices at Fabrikam, but I was reassured when I realized that their strategy involves weekly loss-leader promotions that are not representative of their prices overall. We need to find a way to make this point in our marketing materials.

Store	Type	Prices	Service	Quality
Fabrikam	Traditional	Some ~~much~~ lower, some much higher	Adequate but slow	Some poor, some good
Northwind Traders	Warehouse	Lower	Non-existent	Poor to adequate
Contoso	Traditional	Much higher	Good	Good

A vertical line in the left margin draws your attention to revisions.

5. In the fifth column of the **Northwind Traders** row, select the word **Poor**, and then type **Substandard**.

   Word interprets this one change as both a deletion and an insertion.

6. Point to **Substandard**.

   A ScreenTip appears.

Fabrikam, but I was reassured
ss-leader promotions that are not
a way to make this point in our

	Quality
ate but	Some poor, some good
istent	~~Poor~~ Substandard to adequate
	Good

Sidney Higa, 3/21/2010 5:59:00 PM
inserted:
Substandard

Revision ScreenTips display your user name, the date and time you made the change, the type of change, and the affected text.

7. In the **Tracking** group, click **Show Markup**, point to **Balloons**, and then click **Show Revisions in Balloons**.

Word removes the deletions from the text and displays them in balloons in the right margin.

Prices	Service	Quality	
Some lower, some much higher	Adequate but slow	Some poor, some good	Deleted: much
Lower	Non-existent	Substandard to adequate	Deleted: Poor
Much higher	Good	Good	

The text is less cluttered if you display deletions in balloons.

8. In the **Tracking** group, display the **Display for Review** list, and then click **Final**.

Word hides the revisions, displaying the document as it would appear if all the changes are accepted.

9. Display the **Display for Review** list, and click **Final: Show Markup** to make the revisions visible again.

10. Press Ctrl+Home to move to the beginning of the document.

11. In the **Changes** group, click the **Next** button.

Word selects the first change in the document—the deleted word *much*.

12. In the **Changes** group, click the **Accept** button.

Word accepts the change, removes the revision and associated balloon, and moves to the next change (*but slow*).

13. In the **Changes** group, click the **Reject** button.

Word removes the inserted text, and because there are no more changes in this row of the table, it also removes the adjacent vertical bar from the left margin. It then moves to the next change (*Substandard*).

14. In the **Changes** group, click the **Accept** button to implement the deletion, and then click the same button again to implement the insertion.

A message box tells you that there are no more changes in the document.

15. Click **OK** to close the message box.

16. In the **Tracking** group, click the **Track Changes** button to stop tracking changes made to the active document.

 CLEAN UP Change the balloons setting to the one you want. Then save and close the CompetitiveAnalysisB document.

Comparing and Merging Documents

Sometimes you might want to compare several versions of the same document. For example, if you have sent a document out for review by colleagues, you might want to compare their edited versions with the original document.

Instead of comparing multiple open documents visually, you can tell Word to compare the documents and merge the changes into one document. Even if the changes were not made with Track Changes turned on, they are recorded in the merged document as revisions. From within that one document, you can view all the changes from all the reviewers or view only those from a specific reviewer.

In this exercise, you'll merge three versions of the same document: your version, a version edited by Chris Preston, and a version edited by Terry Adams. You'll then evaluate and resolve the differences between the versions.

SET UP You need the ServiceSH_start, ServiceCP_start, and ServiceTA_start documents located in your Chapter15 practice file folder to complete this exercise. Open each document and save it without _start as part of the file name. Then with only the ServiceSH document open, follow the steps.

1. On the **Review** tab, in the **Compare** group, click the **Compare** button, and then click **Combine**.

   Tip Click the Compare option to compare two documents and display the differences between them in a third document. The documents being compared are not changed.

   The Combine Documents dialog box opens.

Combine Documents

Original document
Label unmarked changes with:

Revised document
Label unmarked changes with:

More >>   OK   Cancel

You select the two documents you want to combine in this dialog box.

2. Display the **Original document** list, and click **ServiceSH**. Then ensure that **Sidney Higa** appears in the **Label unmarked changes with** box.

   Troubleshooting If ServiceSH doesn't appear in the list, browse to your Chapter15 practice file folder, and then double-click the file.

3. Display the **Revised document** list, and click **ServiceCP**. Then ensure that **Chris Preston** appears in the **Label unmarked changes with** box.

4. In the lower-left corner of the dialog box, click **More**, and then in the **Comparison settings** area, verify that all the check boxes are selected.

5. In the **Show changes** area, under **Show changes in**, click **Original document**, and then click **OK**.

   Troubleshooting If the documents contain conflicting formatting, you'll see a message box asking you to confirm which document's formatting should be used.

Word compares the two documents and marks the differences in the ServiceSH document, which is displayed in the center pane. To the left, it displays the Reviewing pane, and to the right, it displays the two documents being compared.

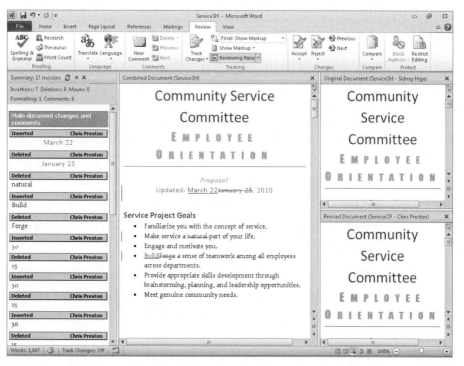

The document in the center pane combines the changes from the two documents on the right.

Troubleshooting The appearance of buttons and groups on the ribbon changes depending on the width of the program window. For information about changing the appearance of the ribbon to match our screen images, see "Modifying the Display of the Ribbon" at the beginning of this book.

Troubleshooting If the Reviewing pane is not open, click the Reviewing Pane button in the Tracking group on the Review tab. If the source documents are not displayed, click the Compare button, point to Show Source Documents, and then click Show Both.

6. On the **Review** tab, in the **Compare** group, click the **Compare** button, and then click **Combine** to display the **Combine Documents** dialog box.

7. Display the **Original document** list, and click **ServiceSH**. Then display the **Revised document** list, and click **ServiceTA**. Ensure that the changes are assigned to **Sidney Higa** and **Terry Adams**, respectively. Then with **Original document** selected, click **OK**.

   The changes from the ServiceTA version of the document are added to those of the other two versions.

8. In the center pane, scroll through the document to see all the revisions, and then in the **Reviewing** pane, scroll through the individual revisions.

9. In the **Tracking** group, click the **Show Markup** button, point to **Reviewers**, and then click **Sidney Higa**.

   The revisions made by Sidney Higa are hidden.

10. Display the **Reviewers** list again, and then click **All Reviewers** to redisplay all the revisions.

11. Press Ctrl+Home to ensure that the cursor is at the top of the document. Then in the **Changes** group, click the **Accept** arrow, and in the list, click **Accept All Changes in Document**.

    All the changes are accepted.

12. Close the **Reviewing** pane, and then close the two windows on the right side of the screen.

    Tip The next time you combine documents, the Reviewing pane and the source windows will be closed. You can open the Reviewing pane by clicking the Reviewing Pane button in the Tracking group on the Review tab, and you can open the source windows by clicking Show Source Documents in the Compare list and then clicking the option you want.

CLEAN UP Save the ServiceSH document, and then close it.

Password-Protecting Documents

Sometimes, you might want only certain people to be able to open and change a document. The easiest way to exercise this control is to assign a password to protect the document. Word then requires that the password be entered correctly before it will allow the document to be opened and changed.

Word offers two levels of password protection:

- **Unencrypted** The document is saved in such a way that only people who know the password can open it, make changes, and save the file. People who don't know the password can open a read-only version. If they make changes and want to save them, they have to save the document with a different name or in a different location, preserving the original.

- **Encrypted** The document is saved in such as way that people who do not know the password cannot open it at all.

In this exercise, you'll set an unencrypted password for a document and then test the document's security by entering an incorrect password. You'll open a read-only version of the document and then reopen it with the correct password. You'll remove the unencrypted password-protection from the document and then set an encrypted password.

SET UP You need the LoansProtected_start document located in your Chapter15 practice file folder to complete this exercise. Open the LoansProtected_start document, and then follow the steps.

1. Display the Backstage view, and click **Save As**.

2. With your **Chapter15** practice file folder displayed in the **Save As** dialog box, change the name in the **File name** box to **LoansProtected**.

3. At the bottom of the dialog box, click **Tools**, and then in the list, click **General Options**.

   The General Options dialog box opens.

Assigning a password to open a document encrypts the document; assigning a password to modify the document does not encrypt it.

Tip If you want people to be able to read the document's contents but you don't expect them to change the document, you can select the Read-Only Recommended check box to tell Word to display a message suggesting that the document be opened as read-only. Then click OK to close the General Options dialog box without assigning a password.

4. In the **Password to modify** box, type **P@ssword**.

   As you type the password, dots appear instead of the characters to keep the password confidential.

   Important Don't use common words or phrases as passwords, and don't use the same password for multiple documents. After assigning a password, make a note of it in a safe place. If you forget it, you won't be able to open the password-protected document.

5. Click **OK**.

   The Confirm Password dialog box opens.

6. In the **Reenter password to modify** box, type **P@ssword**, and then click **OK** to set the password.

7. In the **Save As** dialog box, click **Save**.

   Word protects the document by assigning the selected password, and then saves it in the Chapter15 folder.

8. Display the Backstage view, and click **Close** to close the **LoansProtected** document.

9. Display the Backstage view, and on the **Recent** page, click the **LoansProtected** document.

   Because this document is protected by the password you just set, the Password dialog box opens.

You must enter the password or open the document as read-only.

10. In the **Password** box, type **password**, and click **OK**.

    A message tells you that you typed an incorrect password.

11. In the message box, click **OK**.

12. In the **Password** dialog box, click **Read Only**.

    The LoansProtected document opens as a read-only document, as indicated by *(Read-Only)* in its title bar.

13. Close the document from the Backstage view, and then reopen it.

    Word asks whether you want to open a read-only version of the document again.

Word displays this dialog box because you opened the document as read-only last time.

14. Click **No**. Then when the **Password** dialog box opens, type **P@ssword**, and click **OK**.

    Because you typed the correct password, the document opens.

15. Display the Backstage view, and click **Save As**. Then click **Tools**, and click **General Options**.

16. In the **General Options** dialog box, select the contents of the **Password to modify** box, press Delete, and click **OK** to close the dialog box.

17. In the **Save As** dialog box, click **Save**. Then click **Yes** to confirm that you want to replace the existing file.

    The document is no longer protected by a password.

18. Display the Backstage view, and in the **Permissions** area of the **Info** page, click **Protect Document**. Then click **Encrypt with Password**.

    The Encrypt Document dialog box opens.

![Encrypt Document dialog box. Title "Encrypt Document". Section labeled "Encrypt the contents of this file" with a "Password:" field. Caution text reads: "If you lose or forget the password, it cannot be recovered. It is advisable to keep a list of passwords and their corresponding document names in a safe place. (Remember that passwords are case-sensitive.)" with OK and Cancel buttons.]

After the password is assigned, you will no longer be able to open the document without it.

19. In the **Password** box, type **P@ssword**, and click **OK**. Then type the password again in the **Confirm Password** dialog box, and click **OK**.

    The Info page now reports that a password is required to open the LoansProtected document.

20. In the Backstage view, click **Save**. Then redisplay the Backstage view, and close the document.

21. Test the document's security by trying to open it with an incorrect password.

 CLEAN UP If you want, remove the encrypted password by opening the LoansProtected document with the P@ssword password, reversing steps 18 and 19, and then saving and closing the document.

Restricting Who Can Do What to Documents

If rights management software is installed on your computer, you can control who can see and work with your documents. The minimum required software is Windows Rights Management Services (RMS) Client Service Pack 1 (SP1). If your computer is running Windows 7 or Windows Vista, the software is already installed. (Rights management is usually configured by an administrator for an entire company.)

If you have this capability, you will see a Restrict Permission By People option in the list displayed when you click the Protect Document button in the Permissions area of the Info page. Pointing to the Restrict Permission By People command and then clicking Restricted Access displays the Permission dialog box. In this dialog box, you can click Restrict Permission To This Document and then allow specific people to perform specific tasks, such as opening, printing, saving, or copying the document. When this protection is in place, other people cannot perform these tasks. The assigned permissions are stored with the document and apply no matter where the file is stored.

Before you can work on a document to which access has been restricted, you must verify your credentials with a licensing server. You can then download a use license that defines the tasks you are authorized to perform with the document. You need to repeat this process with each restricted document.

See Also For more information about rights management, search for Information Rights Management in Word Help.

Controlling Changes

Sometimes you'll want people to be able to open and view a document but not make changes to it. Sometimes you'll want to allow changes, but only of certain types. For example, you can specify that other people can insert comments in the document but not make changes, or you can require that people track their changes.

To prevent anyone from introducing inconsistent formatting into a document, you can limit the styles that can be applied. You can select the styles individually, or you can implement the recommended minimum set, which consists of all the styles needed by Word for features such as tables of contents. (The recommended minimum set doesn't necessarily include all the styles used in the document.)

To protect a document from unauthorized changes, you display the Restrict Formatting And Editing task pane.

Restrict Formatting and Editing ▼ ✕

1. Formatting restrictions

☐ Limit formatting to a selection of styles

Settings…

2. Editing restrictions

☐ Allow only this type of editing in the document:

No changes (Read only) ▼

3. Start enforcement

Are you ready to apply these settings? (You can turn them off later)

Yes, Start Enforcing Protection

You specify the changes that are allowed in the document in this task pane.

In this exercise, you'll set editing and formatting restrictions to selectively allow modifications to a document.

SET UP You need the ProceduresRestricted_start document located in your Chapter15 practice file folder to complete this exercise. Open the ProceduresRestricted_start document, and save it as *ProceduresRestricted*. Then follow the steps.

1. On the **Review** tab, in the **Protect** group, click the **Restrict Editing** button.

   The Restrict Formatting And Editing task pane opens.

2. Under **Formatting restrictions** in the task pane, select the **Limit formatting to a selection of styles** check box, and then click **Settings**.

   The Formatting Restrictions dialog box opens.

All the available styles are currently allowed.

3. Scroll through the **Checked styles are currently allowed** list.

   The styles reflect those in the template attached to the open document, including styles that are available but not currently in use.

4. Click **Recommended Minimum**, and then scroll through the list again.

   All the selected styles are designated by the word *recommended*. The recommended set does not include some of the styles used in the document, so you need to add them.

5. Toward the top of the list, select the **Address** check box. Then scroll through the list, and select the **BulletList1** and **BulletList2** check boxes.

6. In the **Formatting** area, select the **Block Theme or Scheme switching** and the **Block Quick Style Set switching** check boxes.

7. Click **OK** to implement the restricted set of styles.

   Word displays a message stating that the document might contain formatting that is not allowed, and asking if you want the formatting to be removed.

8. In the message box, click **Yes**.

9. Under **Editing restrictions** in the task pane, select the **Allow only this type of editing in the document** check box. Then click the arrow to the right of the box below, and in the list, click **Tracked changes**.

10. Under **Start enforcement** in the task pane, click **Yes, Start Enforcing Protection**.

    The Start Enforcing Protection dialog box opens.

Start Enforcing Protection	?	✕

    Protection method

    ◉ Password
    (The document is not encrypted. Malicious users can edit the file and remove the password.)

    Enter new password (optional): [   ]

    Reenter password to confirm: [   ]

    ○ User authentication
    (Authenticated owners can remove document protection. The document is encrypted and Restricted Access is enabled.)

    [OK]   [Cancel]

    People who don't know the password can't turn off the restrictions.

11. Without entering a password, click **OK**.

    The Restrict Formatting And Editing task pane indicates that formatting and editing in this document is now restricted.

12. Close the task pane, and then display the **Home** tab.

    Many of the buttons in the Font and Paragraph groups are now unavailable.

13. Display the **Review** tab, and notice that you cannot turn off **Track Changes**.

14. In the document title, double-click the word **Office**, and type **Operations**.

    Your change is marked as a revision. Any edits you make will be recorded, and because the Track Changes button is unavailable, you cannot turn it off.

✖ **CLEAN UP** Save the ProceduresRestricted document, and then close it.

Key Points

- You can send a document for review via e-mail. When you receive the reviewed versions, you can merge them so that all the changes are recorded in one document.

- You can insert comments in a document to ask questions or explain suggested edits.

- When you collaborate on a document, you can record the revisions you make to the document without losing the original text.

- If only specific people should work on a document, you can protect it with a password. You can also restrict what people can do to it.

Chapter at a Glance

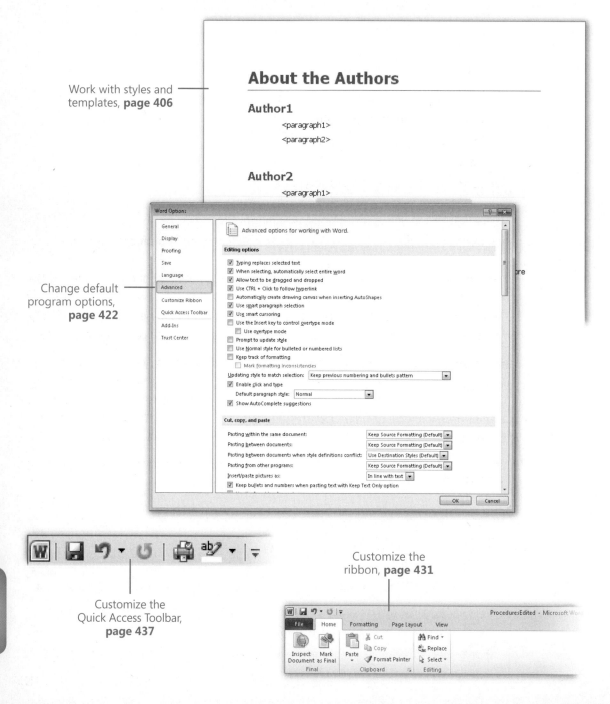

Work with styles and templates, **page 406**

Change default program options, **page 422**

Customize the Quick Access Toolbar, **page 437**

Customize the ribbon, **page 431**

16 Work in Word More Efficiently

In this chapter, you will learn how to

- ✔ Work with styles and templates.
- ✔ Change default program options.
- ✔ Customize the ribbon.
- ✔ Customize the Quick Access Toolbar.

If you use Microsoft Word 2010 only occasionally, you might be perfectly happy creating new documents with the wide range of tools we have already discussed in this book. And you might be comfortable with the default working environment options and behind-the-scenes settings. However, if you create a lot of documents of various types, you might find yourself wishing that you could streamline the document development process or change aspects of the program to make it more suitable for the kinds of documents you create.

In this chapter, you'll explore styles and templates, which can greatly enhance document development efficiency. You'll also take a tour of the pages of the Word Options dialog box to understand the ways in which you can customize the program. Then you'll manipulate the ribbon and the Quick Access Toolbar to put the tools you need for your daily work at your fingertips.

> **Practice Files** Before you can complete the exercises in this chapter, you need to copy the book's practice files to your computer. The practice files you'll use to complete the exercises in this chapter are in the Chapter16 practice file folder. A complete list of practice files is provided in "Using the Practice Files" at the beginning of this book.

Working with Styles and Templates

When you want to quickly create an effective, visually attractive document, you can take advantage of your previous work or even the work of other people by saving an existing document with a new name and then customizing it to suit the current purpose. However, if you frequently create the same type of document, such as a monthly or quarterly report, one of the most efficient ways to generate the document is to base it on a template that already contains the text, character and paragraph styles, page formatting, and graphic elements that you generally use in that type of document.

When it comes to making your work in Word more efficient, styles and templates are among the most powerful tools available to you. Entire books have been written about them; this discussion can only scratch the surface. We'll talk about templates first; then we'll discuss styles.

Templates

Although you might not have realized it, all documents are based on a template. New blank documents are based on the built-in Normal template, which defines paragraph styles for regular text paragraphs, a title, and different levels of headings. It also defines a few character styles that you can use to change the look of selected text. These styles appear in the Quick Styles gallery on the Home tab, and you can apply these Quick Styles to format the text in the document.

See Also For information about applying Quick Styles, see "Quickly Formatting Text" in Chapter 3, "Change the Look of Text."

In addition to the Normal template, Word 2010 comes with a variety of templates for a variety of types of documents. To create a document based on one of these templates, you start by displaying the New page in the Backstage view. At the top of the New page are icons for templates or categories of templates that were installed with Word on your computer. The Office.com Templates area lists categories of templates that are available for downloading from the Office.com Web site.

Tip If the designation *(Compatibility Mode)* appears in the title bar when you create a document based on a template, it indicates that the template was created in an earlier version of Word. Usually this will have no effect on your use of the template, but bear in mind that sometimes compatibility can have an impact on functionality.

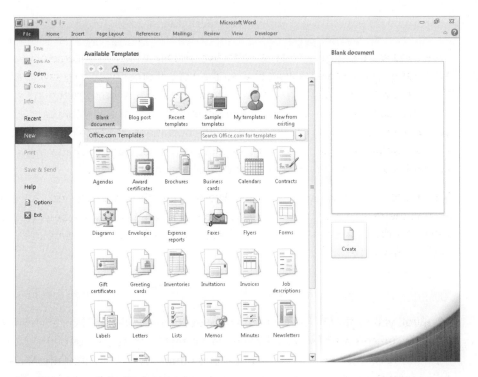

The New page of the Backstage view.

In general, templates can contain the following:

● **Formatting** Most templates contain formatting information, which in addition to styles can include page layout settings, backgrounds, themes, and other types of formatting. A template that contains only formatting defines the look of the document, and you add your own content.

● **Text** Templates can also contain text that you customize for your own purposes. For example, if you base a new document on an agenda template from Office.com, the text of the agenda is already in place, and all you have to do is customize it. Sometimes, a document based on a template displays formatted text placeholders surrounded by square brackets—for example, *[Company Name]*—instead of actual text. You replace a placeholder with your own text by clicking it and then typing the replacement. If you don't need a placeholder, you simply delete it.

● **Graphics, tables, charts, and diagrams** Templates can contain ready-made graphic elements, either for use as is or as placeholders for elements tailored to the specific document.

- **Building blocks** Some templates make custom building blocks, such as headers and footers or a cover page, available for use with a particular type of document. They might also include AutoText, such as contact information or standard copyright or privacy paragraphs.

    See Also For information about creating building blocks, see "Inserting Building Blocks" in Chapter 5, "Add Simple Graphic Elements."

- **Macros** Sophisticated templates contain macros that allow users to perform processes with the click of a button. The topic of macros is beyond the scope of this book; for information, search for *macros* in Word Help.

Tip Word 2010 template files have one of two file name extensions, depending on their content. Those that contain macros have the *.dotm* file name extension; those that don't contain macros have the .dotx extension.

When you base a new document on a template, that template is said to be *attached* to the document. The styles defined in the attached template appear in the Quick Styles gallery so that you can easily apply them to any content you add to the document.

In addition to attaching a document template, you can load global templates to make their contents available to a document. Two global templates are automatically loaded by Word—the Normal template and the Building Blocks template—but you can load others. For example, your organization might have a Custom Building Blocks template containing items that it wants you to use in all documents.

See Also For information about attaching a different template to an existing document and about loading global templates, see the sidebar "Switching to a Different Template" later in this chapter.

If none of the templates that come with Word or that you download from Office.com meets your needs, you can create your own template. If you routinely create the same type of document, such as a monthly financial report, you can create the appropriate styles, format the document, and then save it as a template on which to base future versions of that type of document. You can save your new template with text in it, which is handy if you create many documents with only slight variations. Or you can delete the text so that a new document based on the template will open as a blank document with the set of predefined styles available to apply to whatever content you enter.

You can save a custom template anywhere and then browse to and double-click the file name to open a new document based on the template. However, if you save the template in your default Templates folder, it will be available when you click My Templates on the New page of the Backstage view.

Tip On a Windows 7 computer, the default Templates folder location is C:\Users\<user name>\AppData\Roaming\Microsoft\Templates. By default, this folder is hidden.

Styles

Even if you don't want to create your own templates, it's useful to know how to create and modify styles. When you apply direct character formatting or paragraph formatting, you affect only the selected characters or paragraphs. If you change your mind about the formatting, you have to change the formatting manually everywhere it is applied. When you apply a style to characters or paragraphs, you can change the way those characters or paragraphs look simply by changing the style definition. With one change in one place, you can completely change the look of the document.

You already know that when you create a blank document, it is based on the Normal template. Initially, the Normal template displays only a limited number of styles in the Quick Styles gallery, but in fact it contains styles for just about every element you can think of. Although they are available, these styles aren't actually used unless you apply the style or add the corresponding element to the document. For example, nine paragraph styles are available for an index, but none of them is used until you create and insert an index in the document. You can access the unused styles and manually apply them to characters and paragraphs in two ways:

● Clicking the Styles dialog box launcher displays the Styles task pane. By default, the task pane shows only the styles in use in the document. Clicking Options at the bottom of the task pane opens the Style Pane Options dialog box.

You can specify which styles should be shown and how.

By selecting All Styles in the Select Styles To Show list and Alphabetical in the Select How List Is Sorted list, you can display all the available styles in alphabetical order. You can then apply a style from the Styles task pane by clicking it.

Styles	▾ ×
Clear All	
Balloon Text	¶a
Bibliography	¶
Block Text	¶
Body Text	¶a
Body Text 2	¶a
Body Text 3	¶a
Body Text First Indent	¶a
Body Text First Indent 2	¶a
Body Text Indent	¶a
Body Text Indent 2	¶a
Body Text Indent 3	¶a
Book Title	a
Caption	¶
Closing	¶a
Comment Reference	a
Comment Subject	¶a
Comment Text	¶a
Date	¶a
Default Paragraph Font	a
Document Map	¶a
E-mail Signature	¶a
Emphasis	a
Endnote Reference	a

☐ Show Preview
☐ Disable Linked Styles

Options...

The Styles task pane, as it looks when all the available styles are shown.

Tip Selecting the Show Preview check box below the style list displays the style names in the formatting assigned to the style. Pointing to a style displays a ScreenTip with its formatting specifications.

● Clicking Apply Styles at the bottom of the Quick Styles gallery opens the Apply Styles dialog box. The Style Name box displays the name of the style applied to the active paragraph or selected text.

Clicking Reapply reapplies the formatting defined in the style, stripping away any direct formatting.

Selecting a different style from the Style Name list applies it to the active paragraph or selected text. The Style Name list reflects the display in the Styles task pane; that is, if the task pane shows only the styles in use, so does the Style Name list in the Apply Styles dialog box.

There are three major types of styles, identified in the Styles task pane by icons:

- **Paragraph** These styles can include any formatting that can be applied to a paragraph. They can also include character formatting. Paragraph styles are applied to the entire paragraph containing the cursor. In the Styles task pane, they are identified by a paragraph mark to the right of their names.

- **Character** These styles can include any formatting that can be applied to selected text. They are applied on top of the character formatting defined for the paragraph style. Like direct character formatting, character styles are applied to selected text; to apply them to an entire paragraph, you must select it.

- **Linked** These styles are hybrids. If you click in a paragraph and then apply the style, the style is applied to the entire paragraph like a paragraph style. If you select text and then apply the style, the style is applied to the selection only.

  Tip Two additional style types, Table and List, are reserved for styles for those document elements.

The simplest way to customize the look of a document is to modify an existing style in one of the following ways:

- Apply the style to a paragraph or selected text, and adjust the formatting so that the paragraph or selection looks the way you want it. Then update the style definition with the new formatting by right-clicking the style in the Quick Styles gallery, or by clicking the arrow to the right of the style in the Styles task pane, and then clicking Update <style> To Match Selection.

● Right-click the style in the Quick Styles gallery, and click Modify; or click the arrow to the right of the style in the Styles task pane; or display the style name in the Apply Styles dialog box and click Modify. Then in the Modify Style dialog box, change the settings in the Formatting area to achieve the look you want.

You can adjust the formatting definition of any style by changing the settings in this dialog box.

If you modify the existing styles, you can save the new style definitions as a style set. (Each new style must have the same name as its corresponding existing style.) Clicking the Change Styles button in the Styles group on the Home tab, pointing to Style Set, and then clicking Save As Quick Style Set opens the Save Quick Style Set dialog box, where you name the set. Without changing the storage location, click Save to save the style set in the QuickStyles folder. You can then make the style set accessible to any document by selecting it from the Style Set list.

See Also For information about switching style sets, see "Quickly Formatting Text" in Chapter 3, "Change the Look of Text."

If you want to create a style rather than redefine an existing one, you apply the formatting you want for the style to a paragraph or selection and then click Save Selection As A New Quick Style at the bottom of the Quick Styles gallery to open the Create New Style From Formatting dialog box.

You can see the formatting applied to the selected text in the Paragraph Style Preview box.

If you want to refine the definition of the new style, clicking Modify expands the dialog box so that it resembles the Modify Style dialog box. (You can go directly to the expanded dialog box by clicking the New Style button at the bottom of the Styles task pane.) There you can specify the style name and type and all formatting for the style. If you are building on an existing style, you can select that style in the Style Based On list and then specify the formatting differences rather than defining the style from scratch. If you are creating the style as part of a new template, you can make the style part of the template instead of only part of the current document.

After you have created the styles you want, you might want to remove any you don't want from the Quick Styles gallery. Right-click the style in the gallery and click Remove From Quick Style Gallery. The styles will still be available in the Styles task pane, and you can add them back to the Quick Styles gallery at any time by clicking the arrow to the right of the style in the task pane and then clicking Add To Quick Style Gallery. To remove a style from the Styles task pane, click the arrow to the right of the style, click Delete or Revert, and then click Yes to confirm the deletion.

Tip You cannot delete a built-in style, but if you have modified it, you can revert it back to its original formatting.

In this exercise, you'll create a template based on a predefined Word template, and then you'll create a document based on the custom template. You'll also create a template based on a document, modify the template's styles, and create a style. Finally, you'll create a document based on that template.

 SET UP You need the AuthorsTemplate_start document located in your Chapter16 practice file folder to complete this exercise, but don't open it yet. Just follow the steps.

1. Display the **New** page in the Backstage view, and then under **Available Templates**, click **Sample templates**.

   The center pane displays thumbnails of the installed templates.

2. Scroll down the **Available Templates** list, and double-click the **Oriel Fax** template.

   Word opens a new fax cover page document based on the selected template.

[Pick the date]

TO: [TYPE THE RECIPIENT NAME]

FAX: [Type the recipient fax number]

PHONE: [Type the recipient phone number]

FROM: Sidney Higa

FAX: [Type the sender fax number]

PHONE: [Type the sender phone number]

PAGES: [Type the number of pages]

RE: [Type text]

CC: [Type text]

COMMENTS:
[Type comments]

FAX [Type the sender company name] [Type the company address]

The fax cover page has placeholders for the text you need to supply.

3. On the right side of the page, click the **[Type the sender company name]** place-holder, and type **Lucerne Publishing** or your company name. Then if you want, replace the other placeholders in the banner on the right side of the page. Also replace the placeholders in the **FROM** area of the cover page.

4. On the right side of the page, click **Lucerne Publishing** or your company name, and drag across it to select it. Then display the **Quick Styles** gallery, and click the **Strong** thumbnail.

5. Open the **Save As** dialog box, and in the **File name** box, type **My Fax Template**.

6. Display the **Save as type** list, and click **Word Template**.

   Tip If you want users who have older versions of Word to be able to use the template, click Word 97-2003 Template instead.

7. At the top of the **Navigation** pane, click **Templates**.

   Word displays your default Templates folder.

   See Also For information about changing default file locations, see "Changing Default Program Options" later in this chapter.

8. Click **Save**, and then close the template.

9. Display the **New** page in the Backstage view, and under **Available Templates**, click **My templates**.

   The New dialog box opens.

The customized template is available in the Personal Templates list.

Tip If you frequently create your own templates, you might want to organize them by storing them in subfolders of the default Templates folder. With the contents of the Templates folder displayed in the Save As dialog box, click the New Folder button, and name the folder in the usual way. When you click My Templates on the New page to create a document based on one of your custom templates, the subfolders of the Templates folder will appear as tabs in the New dialog box.

10. With **My Fax Template** highlighted and **Document** selected in the **Create New** area, click **OK**.

    Word opens a new document based on your custom fax cover page template.

The customized template produces fax cover pages with all the information that doesn't change already filled in.

11. Make any changes you want to the fax cover page document, save it in your **Chapter16** practice file folder with the name **My Fax**, and then close the document.

12. Open the **AuthorsTemplate_start** document from the **Chapter16** folder, and save it as a template named **AuthorsTemplate** in your default **Templates** folder.

13. Select all the text in the document, and change the font to **Tahoma**. Change the color of **About the Authors** and **Author1** to **Purple, Accent 4**. Then change the size of the first paragraph under the **Author1** heading to **12** points.

14. Click anywhere in the **About the Authors** heading, and then in the **Quick Styles** gallery, right-click the **Title** style, and click **Update Title to Match Selection**.

15. Repeat step 14 to update the styles assigned to **Author1** (**h1**) and the first **<paragraph1>** (**Normal**).

   All the paragraphs to which the h1 and Normal styles are applied are updated to reflect your formatting changes.

About the Authors

Author1

   <paragraph1>
   <paragraph2>

Author2

   <paragraph1>
   <paragraph2>

Online Training Solutions, Inc. (OTSI)

   OTSI specializes in the design, creation, and production of Office and Windows training products for office and home computer users. For more information about OTSI, visit

   www.otsi.com

   Copyright © 2010 by Online Training Solutions, Inc.

Updating a style changes the formatting of any paragraphs to which the style is applied.

16. Select the last paragraph in the document. Then change the size to **9** pts, and make the selection bold, underlined, and purple.

17. Display the **Quick Styles** gallery, and below the thumbnails, click **Save Selection as a New Quick Style**.

   The Create New Style From Formatting dialog box opens.

18. In the **Name** box, replace **Style1** with **Copyright**, and then click **Modify**.

   The dialog box expands to display options for modifying the new style.

Because the Style Type setting is Linked, you will be able to apply this style to entire paragraphs or selected text.

19. At the bottom of the expanded dialog box, click **New documents based on this template**, and then click **OK**.

    The new style will be available to other documents.

20. Display the **Quick Styles** gallery.

    The new style appears as a thumbnail.

The new style in the Quick Styles gallery.

21. Save and close the template.

22. Display the **New** page in the Backstage view, click **My templates** in the center pane, and from the **New** dialog box, create a document based on the **AuthorsTemplate** template.

    Word opens a new document with the template's title and headline already in place.

23. Replace **Author1** with **Joyce Cox** and **Author2** with **Joan Lambert**.

✖ **CLEAN UP** Save the document as *AuthorsDocument*, and then close it.

Tip If you want to change an existing template, you need to open the template file, not a document based on the template. Display the Backstage view, and click Open. Then in the Open dialog box, set the file type to Word Templates, navigate to your Templates folder, and then double-click the template.

Switching to a Different Template

Although style sets provide a quick and easy way to change the look of an existing document, there might be times when you want to attach a different template to a document. The simplest way to attach a new template is from the Developer ribbon tab, which by default is hidden. To display the Developer tab:

1. Display the Word Options dialog box, and in the left pane, click Customize Ribbon.

2. Under Main Tabs in the list on the right, select the Developer check box, and click OK.

To attach a new template to an open document:

1. On the Developer tab, in the Templates group, click Document Template.

   The Templates And Add-ins dialog box opens.

The Template page of the Templates And Add-ins dialog box.

2. In the Document Template area, click Attach.

   The Attach Template dialog box opens.

3. Navigate to the template you want to attach, and double-click its file name.

4. In the Templates And Add-ins dialog box, select the Automatically Update Document Styles check box, and then click OK to attach the new template.

5. In the Styles group, click the Change Styles button, point to Style Set, and then at the bottom of the style set list, click Reset To Quick Styles From *<template name>* Template.

   The document changes to reflect the style definitions in the new template.

To load a global template and make it available for use:

1. Display the Templates And Add-ins dialog box, and in the Global Templates And Add-ins area, click Add.

2. In the Add Template dialog box, navigate to the global template you want to load, and double-click its file name.

3. With the check box adjacent to the template's name selected, click OK.

   You can deactivate the global template by clearing its check box, and you can unload it by selecting it in the list and clicking Remove.

To replace all instances of one style with another style (if style names don't match):

1. Open the Word Options dialog box, and on the Advanced page, under Editing Options, select the Keep Track Of Formatting check box. Then click OK.

2. Display the Styles task pane, point to a style you want to replace, and click the arrow that appears to its right.

   A list of actions you can perform with the style appears.

Heading 1,h1 ▼
Update Heading 1 to Match Selection
✍ Modify...
Select All 3 Instance(s)
Clear Formatting of 3 Instance(s)
Delete Heading 1...
Remove from Quick Style Gallery

You can select or clear all instances of a particular style.

3. Click Select All <n> Instance(s). Then in the Styles list, click the new style you want to apply.

4. Repeat steps 3 and 4 for each style that needs to be replaced.

To avoid the style-checking overhead, when you have finished replacing styles, you might want to repeat step 1 to clear the Keep Track Of Formatting check box.

Changing Default Program Options

In earlier chapters, we mentioned that you can change settings in the Word Options dialog box to customize the Word environment in various ways. For example, we told you how to create AutoCorrect entries, how to adjust the save period for AutoRecover information, and how to recheck the spelling and grammar of a document. After you work with Word for a while, you might want to refine more settings to tailor the program to the way you work. Knowing which settings are where in the Word Options dialog box makes the customizing process more efficient.

In this exercise, you'll open the Word Options dialog box and explore several of the available pages.

SET UP You don't need any practice files to complete this exercise. With a blank document open and active, follow the steps.

1. On the **Home** tab, in the **Font** group, point to the **Bold** button.

   Word displays a ScreenTip that includes the button name, its keyboard shortcut, and a description of its purpose.

   See Also For information about keyboard shortcuts, see "Keyboard Shortcuts" at the end of this book.

2. Display the Backstage view, and click **Options**.

   The Word Options dialog box opens, displaying the General page.

   The General page of the Word Options dialog box.

If having the Mini Toolbar appear when you select text is more of a hindrance than a help, you can disable that feature by clearing the Show Mini Toolbar On Selection check box. Similarly, you can disable the live preview of styles and formatting by clearing the Enable Live Preview check box.

3. Under **User Interface options**, display the **Color scheme** list, and click **Black**.

4. Display the **ScreenTip style** list, and click **Don't show feature descriptions in ScreenTips**.

5. Under **Personalize your copy of Microsoft Office**, verify that the **User name** and **Initials** are correct, or change them to the way you want them to appear.

6. Click **OK** to close the **Word Options** dialog box.

   The program window elements are now black and shades of gray.

7. In the **Font** group, point to the **Bold** button.

   The ScreenTip now includes only the button name and its keyboard shortcut.

8. Open the **Word Options** dialog box, and in the left pane, click **Display**.

   On this page, you can adjust how documents look on the screen and when printed.

The Display page of the Word Options dialog box.

9. In the left pane, click **Proofing**.

   This page provides options for adjusting the AutoCorrect settings and for refining the spell-checking and grammar-checking processes.

   See Also For information about AutoCorrect and checking spelling, see "Correcting Spelling and Grammatical Errors" in Chapter 2, "Edit and Proofread Text."

The Proofing page of the Word Options dialog box.

10. Display the **Save** page.

    On this page, you can change the default document format; the AutoRecover file save rate and location; the default location to which Word saves files you create; and the default location for files you check out from document management servers (such as Microsoft SharePoint) and drafts of those files saved while you are working offline.

    Tip Although we mention SharePoint in "Co-Authoring Documents" in Chapter 15, "Collaborate on Documents," a discussion of SharePoint is beyond the scope of this book.

The Save page of the Word Options dialog box.

The Save page also has options for specifying whether you want the fonts used within the current document to be embedded in the document, in the event that someone who opens the document doesn't have those fonts on his or her computer.

11. Under **Save documents**, display the **Save files in this format** list.

Notice the many formats in which you can save files. One of these is the Word 97-2003 Document format that creates .doc files compatible with earlier versions of Word. If you have upgraded to Word 2010 but your colleagues are still working in an earlier version of the program, you might want to select this option so that they will be able to view and work with any document you create.

Tip If you want to save just one document in a format that is compatible with earlier versions of the program, you can click Word 97-2003 in the Save As Type list of the Save As dialog box.

12. Click away from the list to close it, and then display the **Language** page.

     If you create documents for international audiences, you can make additional editing languages available on this page. You can also specify the Display, Help, and ScreenTip languages.

The Language page of the Word Options dialog box.

13. Display the **Advanced** page.

     This page includes options related to editing document content; displaying documents on-screen; printing, saving, and sharing documents; and a variety of other options. Although these options are labeled *Advanced*, they are the ones you're most likely to want to adjust to suit the way you work.

The Advanced page of the Word Options dialog box.

14. Take a few minutes to explore all the options on this page.

In the General area at the bottom of the page are two buttons:

○ **File Locations** You click this button to change the default locations of various types of files associated with Word and its documents.

○ **Web Options** You click this button to adjust settings for converting a document to a Web page.

See Also For information about converting a Word document to a Web page, see "Creating and Modifying Web Documents" in Chapter 11, "Create Documents for Use Outside of Word."

15. Skipping over **Customize Ribbon** and **Quick Access Toolbar**, which we discuss in later topics in this chapter, click **Add-Ins**.

   This page displays all the active and inactive add-ins and enables you to add and remove them.

The Add-Ins page of the Word Options dialog box.

   See Also For information about add-ins, see the sidebar "Using Add-ins" at the end of this topic.

16. Display the **Trust Center** page.

   This page provides links to information about privacy and security. It also provides access to the Trust Center settings that control the actions Word takes in response to documents that are provided by certain people or companies, that are saved in certain locations, or that contain ActiveX controls or macros.

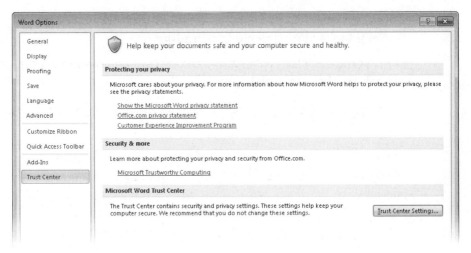

The Trust Center page of the Word Options dialog box.

17. Under **Microsoft Word Trust Center**, click **Trust Center Settings**, and then in the left pane of the **Trust Center** dialog box, click **Trusted Locations**.

    On this page, you can specify the locations from which Word will not block content.

The Trusted Locations page of the Trust Center dialog box.

18. Explore the other pages of the **Trust Center** dialog box, and then click **Cancel** to return to the **Word Options** dialog box.

✖ CLEAN UP Reverse any changes you don't want to keep before moving on. Then close the Word Options dialog box.

Using Add-ins

Add-ins are utilities that add specialized functionality to a program (but aren't full-fledged programs themselves). Word includes two primary types of add-ins: COM add-ins and Word add-ins. The first type uses the Component Object Model to create utilities that extend the functionality of Office programs. The second type includes templates that incorporate sophisticated functionality such as macros.

There are several sources of add-ins:

● You can purchase add-ins from third-party vendors—for example, you can purchase an add-in that augments the ability to work with numbers in tables.

● You can download free add-ins from the Microsoft Web site or other Web sites.

● When installing a third-party program, you might install an add-in to allow it to interface with Microsoft Office 2010 programs. For example, you can install an add-in to capture screens from within an Office document.

Important Be careful when downloading add-ins from Web sites other than those you trust. Add-ins are executable files that can easily be used to spread viruses and otherwise wreak havoc on your computer. For this reason, default settings in the Trust Center intervene when you attempt to download or run add-ins.

To use some add-ins, you must first install them on your computer and then load them into your computer's memory, as follows:

1. At the bottom of the Add-Ins page of the Word Options dialog box, display the Manage list, click either COM Add-ins or Word Add-ins, and then click Go.

    A dialog box corresponding to the type of add-in you selected opens. For example, if you select COM Add-ins in the Manage list, the COM Add-ins dialog box opens.

2. In the dialog box, click Add.

3. In the Add-In dialog box, navigate to the folder where the add-in you want to install is stored, and double-click its name.

   The new add-in appears in the list of those that are available for use.

4. In the list, select the check box of the new add-in, and then click OK.

   The add-in is now loaded and available for use in Word.

To unload an add-in, open the Add-Ins dialog box and clear the add-in's check box to remove the add-in from memory but keep its name in the list. To remove the add-in from the list entirely, click the add-in name, and then click Remove.

Tip The Templates And Add-Ins dialog box that is displayed when you select Word Add-Ins and click Go includes pages that allow you to add XML schemas, expansion packs, and cascading style sheets. These topics are beyond the scope of this book. For information, search on *XML* or the particular type of Word add-in in Word Help.

Customizing the Ribbon

Even if Word 2010 is the first version of the program you have ever worked with, you will by now be accustomed to working with commands represented as buttons on the ribbon. The ribbon was designed to make all the commonly used commands visible, so that people could more easily discover the full potential of the program. But many people use Word to perform the same set of tasks all the time, and for them, the visibility of buttons (or even entire groups of buttons) that they never use is just another form of clutter.

See Also For information about minimizing and expanding the ribbon, see "Customizing the Quick Access Toolbar" later in this chapter.

Would you prefer to see fewer commands, not more? Or would you prefer to see more specialized groups of commands? Well, you can. Clicking Customize Ribbon in the left pane of the Word Options dialog box displays the Customize Ribbon page, which is new in Word 2010.

The Customize Ribbon page of the Word Options dialog box.

On this page, you can customize the ribbon in the following ways:

- If you rarely use a tab, you can turn it off.

- If you use the commands in only a few groups on each tab, you can remove the groups you don't use. (The group is not removed from the program, just from its tab.)

- You can move a predefined group by removing it from one tab and then adding it to another.

- You can duplicate a predefined group by adding it to another tab.

- You can create a custom group on any tab and then add commands to it. (You cannot add commands to a predefined group.)

- For the ultimate in customization, you can create a custom tab. For example, you might want to do this if you use only a few commands from each tab and you find it inefficient to flip between them.

Don't be afraid to experiment with the ribbon to come up with the configuration that best suits the way you work. If at any point you find that your new ribbon is harder to work with rather than easier, you can always reset everything back to the default configuration.

Tip If you have upgraded from Word 2003 or an earlier version, you might have identified a few commands that no longer seem to be available. A few old features have been abandoned, but others that people used only rarely have simply been pushed off to one side. If you sorely miss one of these sidelined features, you can make it a part of your Word environment by adding it to the ribbon. You can find a list of all the commands that do not appear on the ribbon but are still available in Word by displaying the Customize Ribbon page of the Word Options dialog box and then clicking Commands Not In The Ribbon in the Choose Commands From list.

In this exercise, you'll turn off tabs, remove groups, create a custom group, and add a command to the new group. Then you'll create a tab and move predefined groups of buttons to it. Finally, you'll reset the ribbon to its default state.

SET UP You need the ProceduresEdited_start document located in your Chapter16 practice file folder to complete this exercise. Open the ProceduresEdited_start document, and save it as *ProceduresEdited*. Then follow the steps.

1. Open the **Word Options** dialog box, and then click **Customize Ribbon**.

   The Customize Ribbon page is displayed.

2. In the list on the right, clear the check boxes of the **Insert**, **Page Layout**, **References**, **Mailings**, and **Review** tabs. Then click **OK**.

   The ribbon now displays only the File, Home, and View tabs.

You cannot turn off the File tab.

3. Redisplay the **Customize Ribbon** page of the **Word Options** dialog box, and in the right pane, select the **Page Layout** check box. Then click the plus sign to display the groups on this tab.

4. Above the left pane, display the **Choose commands from** list, and click **Main Tabs**. Then in the list below, click the plus sign adjacent to **Page Layout** to display the groups that are predefined for this tab.

5. In the right list, click the **Paragraph** group, and then click **Remove**.

   The group is removed from the Page Layout tab on the ribbon (the list on the right), but is still available in the list on the left. You can add it back to the Page Layout tab, or add it to a different tab, at any time.

6. In the right pane, click the plus sign adjacent to **Home** to display its groups, and then click the word **Home**.

7. Below the right pane, click **New Group**. When the **New Group (Custom)** group is added to the bottom of the **Home** group list, click **Rename**, type **Final** in the **Display name** box, and click **OK**. Then click the **Move Up** button until the **Final** group is at the top of the list.

   Because of its location in the list, the new group will appear at the left end of the Home tab.

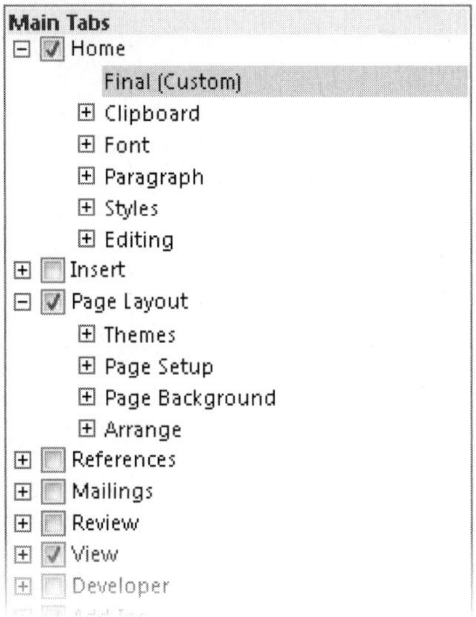

You have created a custom group on the Home tab.

8. Above the list on the left, display the **Choose commands from** list, and click **File Tab**.

   The available commands list changes to include only the commands that are available in the Backstage view, which you display by clicking the File tab.

9. In the available commands list, click **Inspect Document**, and click **Add**. Then repeat this step to add **Mark as Final**.

The two commands are added to the custom group.

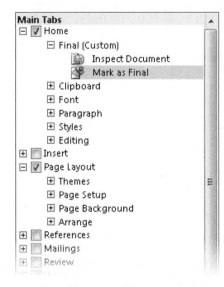

You can add commands to a custom group, but not to a predefined group.

10. In the list on the right, remove the **Font**, **Paragraph**, and **Styles** groups from the **Home** tab, and remove the **Page Background** group from the **Page Layout** tab.

11. Click the word **Home**, and then below the list, click **New Tab**.

    A new tab is added to the right pane and is selected for display on the ribbon. It has automatically been given one custom group.

12. Click **Remove** to remove the custom group.

13. Click **New Tab (Custom)**, then click **Rename**. In the **Rename** dialog box, type **Formatting** in the **Display name** box, and click **OK**.

14. Display **Main Tabs** in the list on the left, and then expand the **Home** and **Page Layout** tabs.

15. With the **Formatting (Custom)** tab selected in the right pane, add the **Font**, **Paragraph**, and **Styles** groups from **Home** in the left pane, and then add **Page Background** from **Page Layout**.

    The right pane shows the new configuration of the Home, Formatting, and Page Layout tabs.

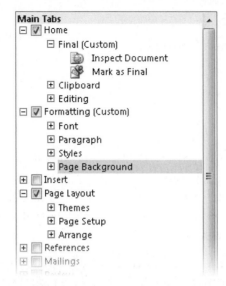

You have moved groups from the Home and Page Layout tabs to a new Formatting tab.

16. In the **Word Options** dialog box, click **OK**.

    The Home tab displays the new Final group.

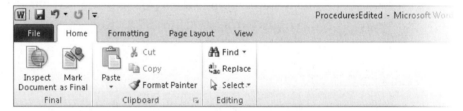

The custom Home tab.

17. Click the **Formatting** tab.

    The formatting commands are now collected on the Formatting tab.

The custom Formatting tab.

18. Display the **Customize Ribbon** page of the **Word Options** dialog box. In the lower-right corner, click **Reset**, and then click **Reset all customizations**. Then in the message box asking you to confirm that you want to delete all ribbon and Quick Access Toolbar customizations, click **Yes**.

19. Click **OK** to close the **Word Options** dialog box.

    The default ribbon configuration is restored.

✖ **CLEAN UP** Close the ProceduresEdited document.

Customizing the Quick Access Toolbar

By default, the Save, Undo, and Redo buttons appear on the Quick Access Toolbar. If you regularly use a few buttons that are scattered on various tabs of the ribbon and you don't want to switch between tabs to access the buttons or crowd your ribbon with a custom tab, you might want to add these frequently used buttons to the Quick Access Toolbar. They are then always visible in the upper-left corner of the program window.

Clicking Quick Access Toolbar in the left pane of the Word Options dialog box displays the page where you specify which commands you want to appear on the toolbar.

The Quick Access Toolbar page of the Word Options dialog box.

On this page, you can customize the Quick Access Toolbar in the following ways:

● You can define a custom Quick Access Toolbar for all documents, or you can define a custom Quick Access Toolbar for a specific document.

● You can add any command from any group of any tab, including contextual tabs, to the toolbar.

● You can display a separator between different types of buttons.

● You can move buttons around on the toolbar until they are in the order you want.

● You can reset everything back to the default Quick Access Toolbar configuration.

If you never use more than a few buttons, you can add those buttons to the Quick Access Toolbar and then hide the ribbon by double-clicking the active tab or by clicking the Minimize The Ribbon button. Only the Quick Access Toolbar and tab names remain visible. You can temporarily redisplay the ribbon by clicking the tab you want to view. You can permanently redisplay the ribbon by double-clicking any tab or by clicking the Expand The Ribbon button.

As you add buttons to the Quick Access Toolbar, it expands to accommodate them. If you add many buttons, it might become difficult to view the text in the title bar, or all the buttons on the Quick Access Toolbar might not be visible, defeating the purpose of adding them. To resolve this problem, you can move the Quick Access Toolbar below the ribbon by clicking the Customize Quick Access Toolbar button and then clicking Show Below The Ribbon.

In this exercise, you'll add a couple of buttons to the Quick Access Toolbar for all documents, and then you'll test the buttons.

SET UP You need the AgendaSH_start document located in your Chapter16 practice file folder to complete this exercise. Open the AgendaSH_start document, and save it as *AgendaSH*. Then follow the steps.

1. Open the **Word Options** dialog box, and then click **Quick Access Toolbar**.

   A list of available commands appears on the left, and a list of the commands currently displayed on the Quick Access Toolbar appears on the right.

   Tip If you want to create a Quick Access Toolbar that is specific to the active document, on the right side of the Word Options dialog box, click the arrow at the right end of the box below Customize Quick Access Toolbar, and then click For <name of document>. Then any command you select will be added to that specific toolbar instead of the toolbar for all documents.

2. At the top of the available commands list on the left, double-click **Separator**.

3. Scroll down the available commands list, click the **Quick Print** command, and then click **Add**.

4. Repeat step 3 to add the **Text Highlight Color** command.

   The list of commands that will appear on the Quick Access Toolbar now includes the items you have added.

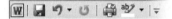

   The arrow to the right of the Text Highlight Color command indicates that clicking this button on the Quick Access Toolbar will display a menu of options.

5. Click **OK** to close the **Word Options** dialog box.

   The Quick Access Toolbar now includes the default Save, Undo, and Repeat buttons and the custom Quick Print and Text Highlight Color buttons, separated by a line.

   You have added two buttons to the Quick Access Toolbar.

   To print a document with the default settings, you no longer have to click the File tab to display the Backstage view, click Print in the left pane, and then click the Print button.

6. If you want to test printing from the Quick Access Toolbar, ensure that your printer is turned on, and then on the Quick Access Toolbar, click the **Quick Print** button.

   Now let's see how easy it is to highlight or remove highlighting from text when you are working primarily with the commands on a tab other than the Home tab.

7. Click the **Review** tab. Then select the first highlighted paragraph, **Proof of notice of meeting**.

8. On the Quick Access Toolbar, click the **Text Highlight Color** arrow, and then click **No Color**.

   The yellow highlight is removed from the selection. The No Color option becomes the default for the Text Highlight Color button.

9. Select the next highlighted paragraph, and on the Quick Access Toolbar, click the **Text Highlight Color** button.

   The yellow highlight is removed from the selection.

10. Display the **Quick Access Toolbar** page of the **Word Options** dialog box, click **Reset**, and then click **Reset only Quick Access Toolbar**.

11. In the **Reset Customizations** message box, click **Yes** to return the Quick Access Toolbar to its default contents. Then click **OK** to close the **Word Options** dialog box.

✖ CLEAN UP Save the AgendaSH document, and then close it.

Key Points

- The Word environment is flexible and can be customized to meet your needs.
- You can create styles and templates to speed up the work of formatting a document. Styles and templates ensure that formatting is consistent within a document and between documents.
- Most of the settings that control the working environment are gathered on the pages of the Word Options dialog box.
- You can customize the ribbon to put precisely the document development tools you need at your fingertips.
- You can provide one-click access to any Word 2010 command by adding a button for it to the Quick Access Toolbar, either for all documents or for one document.

Glossary

aspect ratio The ratio of the width of an image to its height.

attribute Individual items of character formatting, such as size or color, which determine how text looks.

balloon In Print Layout view or Web Layout view, a box that shows comments and tracked changes in the margins of a document, making it easy to see and respond to them.

bar chart A chart with bars that compares the quantities of two or more items.

blog A frequently updated online journal or column. Blogs are often used to publish personal or company information in an informal way. Short for *web log*.

building block Frequently used text saved in a gallery, from which it can be inserted quickly into a document.

caption Descriptive text associated with a figure, photo, illustration, or screen shot.

cell A box formed by the intersection of a row and column in a worksheet or a table, in which you enter information.

cell address The location of a cell, expressed as its column letter and row number, as in A1.

character formatting Formatting you can apply to selected text characters.

character spacing The distance between characters in a line of text. Can be adjusted by pushing characters apart (expanding) or squeezing them together (condensing).

character style A combination of any of the character formatting options identified by a style name.

chart area A region in a chart object that is used to position chart elements, render axes, and plot data.

chevron A small control or button that indicates that there are more items than can be displayed in the allotted space. You click the chevron to see the additional items. Also the « and » characters that surround each merge field in a main document; also known as *guillemet characters*.

Click and Type A feature that allows you to double-click a blank area of a document to position the cursor in that location, with the appropriate paragraph alignment already in place.

Clipboard A storage area shared by all Office programs where cut or copied items are stored.

column Either the vertical arrangement of text into one or more side-by-side sections or the vertical arrangement of cells in a table.

column break A break inserted in the text of a column to force the text below it to move to the next column.

column chart A chart that displays data in vertical bars to facilitate data comparison.

column header In an Excel worksheet, a shaded rectangular area at the top of each column containing a letter. You can click a column header to select an entire column. See also *row header*.

comment A note or annotation that an author or reviewer adds to a document. Word displays the comment in a balloon in the margin of the document or in the Reviewing pane.

cross-reference entry An entry in an index that refers readers to a related entry.

cursor A representation on the screen of the mouse pointer location.

cycle diagram A diagram that shows a continuous process.

data marker A customizable symbol or shape that identifies a data point on a chart. A data marker can be formatted with various sizes and colors.

data point An individual value plotted in a chart and represented together with other data points by bars, columns, lines, pie or doughnut slices, dots, and various other shapes referred to as *data markers*.

data series Related data points that are plotted in a chart. One or more data series in a chart can be plotted. A pie chart has just one data series.

data source A file containing variable information, such as names and addresses, that is merged with a main document containing static information.

demoting In an outline, changing a heading to body text or to a lower heading level; for example, changing from Heading 5 to Heading 6. See also *promoting*.

desktop publishing A process that creates pages by combining text and objects, such as tables and graphics, in a visually appealing way.

destination file The file that a linked or embedded object is inserted into. The source file contains the information that is used to create the object. When you change information in a destination file, the information is not updated in the source file.

diagram A graphic in which shapes, text, and pictures are used to illustrate a process, cycle, or relationship.

dialog box launcher On the ribbon, a button at the bottom of some groups that opens a dialog box with features related to the group.

digital signature Data that binds a sender's identity to the information being sent. A digital signature may be bundled with any message, file, or other digitally encoded information, or transmitted separately. Digital signatures are used in public key environments and provide authentication and integrity services.

Draft view A document view that displays the content of a document with a simplified layout.

drag-and-drop editing A way of moving or copying selected text by dragging it with the mouse pointer.

dragging A way of moving objects by pointing to them, holding down the mouse button, moving the mouse pointer to the desired location, and releasing the button.

drawing object Any graphic you draw or insert, which can be changed and enhanced. Drawing objects include AutoShapes, curves, lines, and WordArt.

drop cap An enlarged, decorative capital letter that appears at the beginning of a paragraph.

embedded object An object created with one program and embedded into a document created by another program. Embedding the object, rather than simply inserting or pasting it, ensures that the object retains its original format. If you double-click the embedded object, you can edit it with the toolbars and menus from the program used to create it.

endnote A note that appears at the end of a section or document and that is referenced by text in the main body of the document. An endnote consists of two linked parts, a reference mark within the main body of text and the corresponding text of the note. See also *footnote*.

Extensible Markup Language (XML) A format for delivering rich, structured data in a standard, consistent way. XML tags describe the content of a document, whereas HTML tags describe how the document looks. XML is extensible because it allows designers to create their own customized tags.

field A placeholder that tells Word to supply the specified information in the specified way. Also, the set of information of a specific type in a data source, such as all the last names in a contacts list.

field name A first-row cell in a data source that identifies data in the column below.

file format The structure or organization of data in a file. The file format of a document is usually indicated by the file name extension.

filtering Displaying files or records in a data source that meet certain criteria; for example, filtering a data source so that you see only the records for people who live in a particular state. Filtering does not delete files, it simply changes the view so that you see only the files that meet your criteria.

font A graphic design applied to a collection of numbers, symbols, and characters. A font describes a certain typeface, along with other qualities such as size, spacing, and pitch.

font effect An attribute, such as superscript, small capital letters, or shadow, that can be applied to a font.

font size The height (in points) of a collection of characters, where one point is equal to approximately 1/72 of an inch.

font style The emphasis placed on a font by using formatting such as bold, italic, underline, or color.

footer One or more lines of text in the bottom margin area of a page in a document, typically containing elements such as the page number and the name of the file. See also *header*.

footnote A note that appears at the end of a page, section, chapter, or publication that explains, comments on, or provides references for text in the main body of a document. A footnote consists of two linked parts, a reference mark within the main body of the document and the corresponding text of the note. See also *endnote*.

formatting See *character formatting* and *paragraph formatting*.

formula A sequence of values, cell references, names, functions, or operators in a cell of a table or worksheet that together produce a new value. A formula always begins with an equal sign (=).

Full Screen Reading view A document view that displays a document as it would appear on a printed page. The view is optimized for reading documents on a computer screen and was previously referred to as *Reading Layout view*.

gallery A grouping of thumbnails that display options visually.

graphic Any piece of art used to illustrate or convey information or to add visual interest to a document.

grayscale The spectrum (range) of shades of black in an image.

gridlines In a table, thin lines that indicate the cell boundaries in a table. Table gridlines do not print when you print a document. In a chart, lines that visually carry the values on the y-axis across the plot area.

group On a ribbon tab, an area containing buttons related to a specific document element or function.

grouping Assembling several objects, such as shapes, into a single unit so that they act as one object. Grouped objects can easily be moved, sized, and formatted.

header A line, or lines, of content in the top margin area of a page in a document, typically containing elements such as the title, page number, or name of the author.

hierarchy diagram A diagram that illustrates the structure of an organization or entity.

Hypertext Markup Language (HTML) An application of the Standard Generalized Markup Language (SGML) that uses tags to mark elements in a document to indicate how Web browsers should display these elements to the user and should respond to user actions.

hyphenating Splitting a word that would otherwise extend beyond the right margin of the page.

indent marker A marker on the horizontal ruler that controls the indentation of text from the left or right margin of a document.

index A list of the words and phrases that are discussed in a printed document, along with the page numbers they appear on.

index entry A field code that marks specific text for inclusion in an index. When you mark text as an index entry, Word inserts an XE (Index Entry) field formatted as hidden text.

index entry field The XE field, including the braces ({ }), that defines an index entry.

justifying Making all lines of text in a paragraph or column fit the width of the document or column, with even margins on each side.

keyboard shortcut Any combination of keystrokes that can be used to perform a task that would otherwise require a mouse or other pointing device.

landscape The orientation of a picture or page where the width is greater than the height.

legend A key in a chart that identifies the colors and names of the data series or categories that are used in the chart.

line break A manual break that forces the text that follows it to the next line. Also called a *text wrapping break*.

line graph or line chart A type of chart in which data points in a series are connected by a line.

linked object An object that is inserted into a document but still exists in the source file. When information is linked, the document is updated automatically if the information in the original document changes.

list diagram A diagram in which lists of related or independent information are visually represented.

Live Preview A feature that temporarily displays the effect of applying a specific format to the selected document element.

mail merge The process of merging information into a main document from a data source, such as an address book or database, to create customized documents, such as form letters or mailing labels.

main document In a mail merge operation in Word, the document that contains the text and graphics that are the same for each version of the merged document.

manual page break A page break inserted to force subsequent information to appear on the next page.

margin The blank space outside the printing area on a page.

matrix diagram A diagram that shows the relationship of components to a whole.

merge field A placeholder inserted in the main document that is replaced with variable information from a data source during the merge process.

Microsoft Office Clipboard See *Clipboard*.

Navigation task pane A task pane that displays an outline of a document's headings, or thumbnails of a document's pages, and allows you to jump to a heading or page in the document by clicking it. Also provides content search capabilities.

nested table A table inserted into a cell of a table that is being used to arrange information on a page.

note separator A set of characters that separates document text from footnotes or endnotes. The default separator is a horizontal line.

object An item, such as a graphic, video clip, sound file, or worksheet, that can be inserted into a document and then selected and modified.

orientation The direction—horizontal or vertical—in which a page is laid out.

orphan The first line of a paragraph printed by itself at the bottom of a page.

Outline view A view that shows the headings of a document indented to represent their level in the document's structure. You can also use outline view to work with master documents.

paragraph In word processing, a block of text of any length that ends when you press the Enter key.

paragraph formatting Formatting that controls the appearance of a paragraph. Examples include indentation, alignment, line spacing, and pagination.

paragraph style A combination of character formatting and paragraph formatting that is named and stored as a set. Applying the style to a paragraph applies all the formatting characteristics at one time.

path A sequence of folders (directories) that leads to a specific file or folder. A backslash is used to separate each folder in the path. For example, the path to a file called *invoice.txt* might be C:\Documents\July\invoice.txt.

picture A photograph, clip art image, illustration or another type of image created with a program other than Word.

picture diagram A diagram that uses pictures to convey information, rather than or in addition to text.

pie chart A round chart that shows the size of items in a single data series, proportional to the sum of the items.

plot area In a two-dimensional chart, the area bounded by the axes, including all data series. In a three-dimensional chart, the area bounded by the axes, including the data series, category names, tick-mark labels, and axis titles.

point The unit of measure for expressing the size of characters in a font, where 72 points equals 1 inch.

pointing to Pausing a pointing device over an area of the display.

portrait The orientation of a picture or page where the page is taller than it is wide.

post A message published on a blog, message board, or help board.

Print Layout view A view of a document as it will appear when printed; for example, items such as headers, footnotes, columns, and text boxes appear in their actual positions.

process diagram A diagram that visually represents the ordered set of steps required to complete a task.

promoting In an outline, to change body text to a heading, or to change a heading to a higher-level heading.

pull quote Text taken from the body of a document and showcased in a text box to create visual interest.

pyramid diagram A diagram that shows foundation-based relationships.

query Selection criteria for extracting information from a data source for use in the mail merge process.

Quick Access Toolbar A small, customizable toolbar that displays frequently used commands.

Quick Style A collection of character and paragraph formatting that makes formatting documents and objects easier. Quick Styles appear in the Quick Styles gallery and are organized into ready-made Quick Style sets that are designed to work together to create an attractive and professional-looking document.

Quick Table A table with sample data that you can customize.

read-only A setting that allows a file to be read or copied, but not changed or saved. If you change a read-only file, you can save your changes only if you give the document a new name.

record A collection of data about a person, a place, an event, or some other item. Records are the logical equivalents of rows in a table.

reference mark The number or symbol displayed in the body of document when you insert a footnote or endnote.

relationship diagram A diagram that shows convergent, divergent, overlapping, merging, or containment elements.

revision A change in a document.

ribbon A user interface design that organizes commands into logical groups, which appear on separate tabs.

row header In an Excel worksheet, a shaded rectangular area to the left of each row containing a number. You can click a row header to select an entire row. See also *column header*.

saturation In color management, the purity of a color's hue, moving from gray to the pure color.

ScreenTip A note that appears on the screen to provide information about a button, tracked change, or comment, or to display a footnote or endnote. ScreenTips also display the text that will appear if you choose to insert a date or AutoText entry.

section break A mark you insert to show the end of a section. A section break stores the section formatting elements, such as the margins, page orientation, headers and footers, and sequence of page numbers.

selecting Highlighting text or activating an object so that you can manipulate or edit it in some way.

selection area An area in a document's left margin in which you can click and drag to select blocks of text.

sizing handle A small circle, square, or set of dots that appears at the corner or on the side of a selected object. You drag these handles to change the size of the object horizontally, vertically, or proportionally.

SmartArt graphic A predefined set of shapes and text used as a basis for creating a diagram.

soft page break A page break that Word inserts when the text reaches the bottom margin of a page.

source file A file containing an object that is inserted in a destination file.

stack A set of graphics that overlap each other.

status bar A row of information related to the current program. The status bar is usually located at the bottom of a window. Not all windows have a status bar.

subentry An index entry that falls under a more general heading; for example, "Mars" and "Venus" might be subentries of the index entry "planets."

switch In fields, a setting that refines the results of the field; for example, by formatting it in a particular way.

tab A tabbed page on the ribbon that contains buttons organized in groups.

tab leader A repeating character (usually a dot or dash) that separates text before the tab from text or a number after it.

tab stop A location on the horizontal ruler that indicates how far to indent text or where to begin a column of text.

tabbed list A list that arranges text in simple columns separated by left, right, centered, or decimal tab stops.

table of authorities A list of the references in a legal document, such as references to cases, statutes, and rules, along with the numbers of the pages the references appear on.

table of contents A list of the headings in a document, along with the numbers of the pages the headings appear on.

table of figures A list of the captions for pictures, charts, graphs, slides, or other illustrations in a document, along with the numbers of the pages the captions appear on.

table style A set of formatting options, such as font, border style, and row banding, that are applied to a table. The regions of a table, such as the header row, header column, and data area, can be variously formatted.

tag A text string used in HTML and XML to identify a page element's type, format, or appearance. Many elements have start and end tags that define where the element starts and stops.

target A path that identifies a linked object, such as a location in a document or a Web page.

template A file that can contain predefined formatting, layout, text, or graphics, and that serves as the basis for new documents with a similar design or purpose.

text box A movable, resizable container used to give text a different orientation from other text in the document.

text wrapping The way text wraps around an object on the page.

text wrapping break A manual break that forces the text that follows it to the next line. Also known as a *line break*.

theme A set of unified design elements that combine color, fonts, and graphics to provide a professional look for a document.

thumbnail A small representation of an item, such as an image, a page of content, or a set of formatting, obtained by scaling a snapshot of it. Thumbnails are typically used to provide visual identifiers for related items.

tick-mark A small line of measurement, similar to a division line on a ruler, that intersects an axis in a chart.

View Shortcuts toolbar A toolbar located at the right end of the status bar that contains tools for switching between views of document content and changes the display magnification.

Web Layout view A view of a document as it will appear in a Web browser. In this view, a document appears as one long page (without page breaks), and text and tables wrap to fit the window.

Web page A World Wide Web document. A Web page typically consists of a Hypertext Markup Language (HTML) file, with associated files for graphics and scripts, in a particular folder on a particular computer. It is identified by a Uniform Resource Locator (URL).

widow The last line of a paragraph printed by itself at the top of a page.

wildcard character A keyboard character that can be used to represent one or many characters when conducting a search. The question mark (?) represents a single character, and the asterisk (*) represents one or more characters.

Word Help button The button located at the right end of the ribbon and labeled with a question mark (?), that provides access to the Word Help system.

word processing The writing, editing, and formatting of documents in a program designed for working primarily with text.

word wrap The process of breaking lines of text automatically to stay within the page margins of a document or window boundaries.

WordArt object A text object you create with ready-made effects to which you can apply additional formatting options.

x-axis Also called a *category axis*, the axis for grouping data in a chart, usually the horizontal axis.

y-axis Also called a *value axis*, the axis for plotting values in a chart, usually the vertical axis.

z-axis Also called a *series axis*, the optical axis that is perpendicular to the x-axis and y-axis, usually the "floor."

Keyboard Shortcuts

This section presents a comprehensive list of all the keyboard shortcuts built into Microsoft Word 2010. The list has been excerpted from Word Help and formatted in tables for convenient lookup. Some of these shortcuts might not be available for your edition of Word 2010 or for your keyboard layout.

Creating Custom Keyboard Shortcuts

If a command you use frequently doesn't have a built-in keyboard shortcut, you can create one from the Customize Ribbon page of the Word Options dialog box. To create a keyboard shortcut:

1. Click the File tab to display the Backstage view, and then in the left pane, click Options.

2. In the left pane of the Word Options dialog box, click Customize Ribbon.

3. To the right of Keyboard Shortcuts at the bottom of the dialog box, click Customize.

   The Customize Keyboard dialog box opens.

The ribbon tabs are listed in the Categories box on the left, and the commands in the selected category are listed in the Commands box on the right.

4. In the Categories list, click Home Tab, and then in the Commands list, click Bold.

   In the Current Keys box, Word displays the keyboard shortcuts already assigned to the Bold command.

5. Scroll down the Commands list, and click DecreaseIndent.

   This command has no built-in keyboard shortcut.

6. Click in the Press New Shortcut Key box, and then press Ctrl+D.

   Under the Current Keys box, Word tells you that this keyboard shortcut is already assigned to the FormatFont command.

7. Press the Backspace key (not Delete) to clear the Press New Shortcut Key box, and then press Alt+D.

   Under the Current Keys box, Word tells you that this keyboard shortcut is currently unassigned (unless you have already assigned it to a different command).

8. If you want to assign this keyboard shortcut to the current document, not all documents based on the current template, display the Save Changes In list, and click the document name.

9. Click Assign.

10. Assign the keyboard combination Alt+I to the IncreaseIndent command.

11. Close the Customize Keyboard dialog box, and click OK in the Word Options dialog box.

> **Tip** To delete an existing keyboard shortcut to make it available for reassignment, select it in the Current Keys box, and then at the bottom of the dialog box, click Remove.

Keyboard Shortcut Lists from Word Help

In the following lists, keys you press at the same time are separated by a plus sign (+), and keys you press sequentially are separated by a comma (,).

Microsoft Office General Tasks

Display and Use Windows

Action	Keyboard shortcut
Switch to the next window.	Alt+Tab
Switch to the previous window.	Alt+Shift+Tab
Close the active window.	Ctrl+W or Ctrl+F4
Restore the size of the active window after you maximize it.	Alt+F5
Move to a task pane from another pane in the program window (clockwise direction). (You might need to press F6 more than once.)	F6
Move to a task pane from another pane in the program window (counterclockwise direction).	Shift+F6
When more than one window is open, switch to the next window.	Ctrl+F6
Switch to the previous window.	Ctrl+Shift+F6
Maximize or restore a selected window.	Ctrl+F10
Copy a picture of the screen to the Microsoft Office Clipboard.	Print Screen
Copy a picture of the selected window to the Clipboard.	Alt+Print Screen

Use Dialog Boxes

Action	Keyboard shortcut
Move to the next option or option group.	Tab
Move to the previous option or option group.	Shift+Tab
Switch to the next tab in a dialog box.	Ctrl+Tab
Switch to the previous tab in a dialog box.	Ctrl+Shift+Tab

(continued)

Action	Keyboard shortcut
Move between options in an open drop-down list, or between options in a group of options.	Arrow keys
Perform the action assigned to the selected button; select or clear the selected check box.	Spacebar
Select an option; select or clear a check box.	Alt+ the letter underlined in an option
Open a selected drop-down list.	Alt+Down Arrow
Select an option from a drop-down list.	First letter of an option in a drop-down list
Close a selected drop-down list; cancel a command and close a dialog box.	Esc
Run the selected command.	Enter

Use Edit Boxes Within Dialog Boxes

Action	Keyboard shortcut
Move to the beginning of the entry.	Home
Move to the end of the entry.	End
Move one character to the left or right.	Left Arrow or Right Arrow
Move one word to the left.	Ctrl+Left Arrow
Move one word to the right.	Ctrl+Right Arrow
Select or unselect one character to the left.	Shift+Left Arrow
Select or unselect one character to the right.	Shift+Right Arrow
Select or unselect one word to the left.	Ctrl+Shift+Left Arrow
Select or unselect one word to the right.	Ctrl+Shift+Right Arrow
Select from the insertion point to the beginning of the entry.	Shift+Home
Select from the insertion point to the end of the entry.	Shift+End

Use the Open and Save As Dialog Boxes

Action	Keyboard shortcut
Display the Open dialog box.	Ctrl+F12 or Ctrl+O
Display the Save As dialog box.	F12
Open the selected folder or file.	Enter
Open the folder one level above the selected folder.	Backspace

Action	Keyboard shortcut
Delete the selected folder or file.	Delete
Display a shortcut menu for a selected item such as a folder or file.	Shift+F10
Move forward through options.	Tab
Move back through options.	Shift+Tab
Open the Look In list.	F4 or Alt+I

Undo and Redo Actions

Action	Keyboard shortcut
Cancel an action.	Esc
Undo an action.	Ctrl+Z
Redo or repeat an action.	Ctrl+Y

Access and Use Task Panes and Galleries

Action	Keyboard shortcut
Move to a task pane from another pane in the program window. (You might need to press F6 more than once.)	F6
When a menu is active, move to a task pane. (You might need to press Ctrl+Tab more than once.)	Ctrl+Tab
When a task pane is active, select the next or previous option in the task pane.	Tab or Shift+Tab
Display the full set of commands on the task pane menu.	Ctrl+Spacebar
Perform the action assigned to the selected button.	Spacebar or Enter
Open a drop-down menu for the selected gallery item.	Shift+F10
Select the first or last item in a gallery.	Home or End
Scroll up or down in the selected gallery list.	Page Up or Page Down

Close a Task Pane

1. Press F6 to move to the task pane, if necessary.

2. Press Ctrl+Spacebar.

3. Use the Arrow keys to select Close, and then press Enter.

Move a Task Pane

1. Press F6 to move to the task pane, if necessary.

2. Press Ctrl+Spacebar.

3. Use the Arrow keys to select Move, and then press Enter.

4. Use the Arrow keys to move the task pane, and then press Enter.

Resize a Task Pane

1. Press F6 to move to the task pane, if necessary.

2. Press Ctrl+Spacebar.

3. Use the Arrow keys to select Size, and then press Enter.

4. Use the Arrow keys to resize the task pane, and then press Enter.

Access and Use Available Actions

Action	Keyboard shortcut
Display the shortcut menu for the selected item.	Shift+F10
Display the menu or message for an available action or for the AutoCorrect Options button or the Paste options button. If more than one action is present, switch to the next action and display its menu or message.	Alt+Shift+F10
Move between options in a menu of available actions.	Arrow keys
Perform the action for the selected item on a menu of available actions.	Enter
Close the available actions menu or message.	Esc

Ribbon Tasks

Access Any Command with a Few Keystrokes

1. Press Alt.

   The KeyTips are displayed over each feature that is available in the current view.

2. Press the letter shown in the KeyTip over the feature that you want to use.

3. Depending on which letter you press, you may be shown additional KeyTips. For example, if the Home tab is active and you press N, the Insert tab is displayed, along with the KeyTips for the groups on that tab.

4. Continue pressing letters until you press the letter of the command or control that you want to use. In some cases, you must first press the letter of the group that contains the command.

Tip To cancel the action and hide the KeyTips, press Alt.

Change the Keyboard Focus Without Using the Mouse

Action	Keyboard shortcut
Select the active tab of the ribbon and activate the access keys.	Alt or F10. Press either of these keys again to move back to the document and cancel the access keys.
Move to another tab of the ribbon.	F10 to select the active tab, and then Left Arrow or Right Arrow
Expand or collapse the ribbon.	Ctrl+F1
Display the shortcut menu for the selected item.	Shift+F10
Move the focus to select each of the following areas of the window: • Active tab of the ribbon • Any open task panes • Status bar at the bottom of the window • Your document	F6
Move the focus to each command on the ribbon, forward or backward, respectively.	Tab or Shift+Tab
Move down, up, left, or right, respectively, among the items on the ribbon.	Down Arrow, Up Arrow, Left Arrow, or Right Arrow
Activate the selected command or control on the ribbon.	Spacebar or Enter
Open the selected menu or gallery on the ribbon.	Spacebar or Enter
Activate a command or control on the ribbon so that you can modify a value.	Enter
Finish modifying a value in a control on the ribbon, and move focus back to the document.	Enter
Get help on the selected command or control on the ribbon. (If no Help topic is associated with the selected command, a general Help topic about the program is shown instead.)	F1

Microsoft Word Tasks

Common Tasks

Action	Keyboard shortcut
Create a nonbreaking space.	Ctrl+Shift+Spacebar
Create a nonbreaking hyphen.	Ctrl+Shift+Hyphen
Make letters bold.	Ctrl+B
Make letters italic.	Ctrl+I
Make letters underlined.	Ctrl+U
Decrease font size one value.	Ctrl+Shift+<
Increase font size one value.	Ctrl+Shift+>
Decrease font size 1 point.	Ctrl+[
Increase font size 1 point.	Ctrl+]
Remove paragraph or character formatting.	Ctrl+Spacebar
Copy the selected text or object.	Ctrl+C
Cut the selected text or object.	Ctrl+X
Paste text or an object.	Ctrl+V
Refine paste action (Paste Special).	Ctrl+Alt+V
Paste formatting only.	Ctrl+Shift+V
Undo the last action.	Ctrl+Z
Redo the last action.	Ctrl+Y
Open the Word Count dialog box.	Ctrl+Shift+G

Work with Documents and Web Pages

Create, View, and Save Documents

Action	Keyboard shortcut
Create a new document.	Ctrl+N
Open a document.	Ctrl+O
Close a document.	Ctrl+W
Split the document window.	Alt+Ctrl+S
Remove the document window split.	Alt+Shift+C or Alt+Ctrl+S
Save a document.	Ctrl+S

Find, Replace, and Browse Through Text

Action	Keyboard shortcut
Open the Navigation task pane (to search the document).	Ctrl+F
Repeat a Find action (after closing the Find And Replace dialog box).	Alt+Ctrl+Y
Replace text, specific formatting, and special items.	Ctrl+H
Go to a page, bookmark, footnote, table, comment, graphic, or other location.	Ctrl+G
Switch between the last four places that you have edited.	Alt+Ctrl+Z
Open a list of browse options. Press the Arrow keys to select an option, and then press Enter to browse through a document by using the selected option.	Alt+Ctrl+Home
Move to the previous browse object (set in browse options).	Ctrl+Page Up
Move to the next browse object (set in browse options).	Ctrl+Page Down

Switch to Another View

Action	Keyboard shortcut
Switch to Print Layout view.	Alt+Ctrl+P
Switch to Outline view.	Alt+Ctrl+O
Switch to Draft view.	Alt+Ctrl+N

Work in Outline View

Action	Keyboard shortcut
Promote a paragraph.	Alt+Shift+Left Arrow
Demote a paragraph.	Alt+Shift+Right Arrow
Demote to body text.	Ctrl+Shift+N
Move selected paragraphs up.	Alt+Shift+Up Arrow
Move selected paragraphs down.	Alt+Shift+Down Arrow
Expand text under a heading.	Alt+Shift+Plus sign
Collapse text under a heading.	Alt+Shift+Minus sign
Expand or collapse all text or headings.	Alt+Shift+A
Hide or display character formatting.	The slash (/) key on the numeric keypad
Show the first line of body text or all body text.	Alt+Shift+L
Show all headings with the Heading 1 style.	Alt+Shift+1
Show all headings up to the Heading 9 style.	Alt+Shift+9
Insert a tab character.	Ctrl+Tab

Print and Preview Documents

Action	Keyboard shortcut
Print a document.	Ctrl+P
Display the Print page of the Backstage view.	Alt+Ctrl+I
Move around the preview page when zoomed in.	Arrow keys
Move by one preview page when zoomed out.	Page Up or Page Down
Move to the first preview page when zoomed out.	Ctrl+Home
Move to the last preview page when zoomed out.	Ctrl+End

Review Documents

Action	Keyboard shortcut
Insert a comment.	Alt+Ctrl+M
Turn change tracking on or off.	Ctrl+Shift+E
Close the Reviewing pane if it is open.	Alt+Shift+C

Work in Full Screen Reading View

Action	Keyboard shortcut
Go to the beginning of the document.	Home
Go to the end of the document.	End
Go to page <n>.	<n>, Enter
Exit reading layout view.	Esc

Work with References, Footnotes, and Endnotes

Action	Keyboard shortcut
Mark a table of contents entry.	Alt+Shift+O
Mark a table of authorities entry (citation).	Alt+Shift+I
Mark an index entry.	Alt+Shift+X
Insert a footnote.	Alt+Ctrl+F
Insert an endnote.	Alt+Ctrl+D

Work with Web Pages

Action	Keyboard shortcut
Insert a hyperlink.	Ctrl+K
Go back one page.	Alt+Left Arrow
Go forward one page.	Alt+Right Arrow
Refresh.	F9

Edit and Move Text and Graphics

Delete Text and Graphics

Action	Keyboard shortcut
Delete one character to the left.	Backspace
Delete one word to the left.	Ctrl+Backspace
Delete one character to the right.	Delete
Delete one word to the right.	Ctrl+Delete
Cut selected text to the Clipboard.	Ctrl+X
Undo the last action.	Ctrl+Z

Copy and Move Text and Graphics

Action	Keyboard shortcut
Open the Clipboard.	Press Alt+H to move to the Home tab, and then press F,O.
Copy selected text or graphics to the Clipboard.	Ctrl+C
Cut selected text or graphics to the Clipboard.	Ctrl+X
Paste the most recent addition or pasted item from the Clipboard.	Ctrl+V
Move text or graphics once.	F2 (then move the cursor and press Enter)
Copy text or graphics once.	Shift+F2 (then move the cursor and press Enter)
When text or an object is selected, open the Create New Building Block dialog box.	Alt+F3
When a building block—for example, a SmartArt graphic—is selected, display the shortcut menu that is associated with it.	Shift+F10
Copy the header or footer used in the previous section of the document.	Alt+Shift+R

Insert Special Characters

Action	Keyboard shortcut
A field	Ctrl+F9
A line break	Shift+Enter
A page break	Ctrl+Enter
A column break	Ctrl+Shift+Enter
An em dash	Alt+Ctrl+Minus sign
An en dash	Ctrl+Minus sign
An optional hyphen	Ctrl+Hyphen
A nonbreaking hyphen	Ctrl+Shift+Hyphen
A nonbreaking space	Ctrl+Shift+Spacebar
The copyright symbol	Alt+Ctrl+C
The registered trademark symbol	Alt+Ctrl+R
The trademark symbol	Alt+Ctrl+T
An ellipsis	Alt+Ctrl+Period
A single opening quotation mark	Ctrl+` (single quotation mark), ` (single quotation mark)
A single closing quotation mark	Ctrl+' (single quotation mark), ' (single quotation mark)
Double opening quotation marks	Ctrl+` (single quotation mark), Shift+' (single quotation mark)
Double closing quotation marks	Ctrl+' (single quotation mark), Shift+' (single quotation mark)
An AutoText entry	Enter (after you type the first few characters of the AutoText entry name and when the ScreenTip appears)

Insert Characters by Using Character Codes

Action	Keyboard shortcut
Insert the Unicode character for the specified Unicode (hexadecimal) character code. For example, to insert the euro currency symbol (€), type 20AC, and then hold down Alt and press X.	<Unicode>, Alt+X
Find out the Unicode character code for the selected character.	Alt+X
Insert the ANSI character for the specified ANSI (decimal) character code. For example, to insert the euro currency symbol, hold down Alt and press 0128 on the numeric keypad.	Alt+ <ANSI code> (on the numeric keypad)

Select Text and Graphics

Action	Keyboard shortcut
Select text and graphics.	Hold down Shift and use the Arrow keys to move the cursor

Extend a Selection

Action	Keyboard shortcut
Turn extend mode on.	F8
Select the nearest character.	F8, and then press Left Arrow or Right Arrow
Increase the size of a selection.	F8 (press once to select a word, twice to select a sentence, and so on)
Reduce the size of a selection.	Shift+F8
Turn extend mode off.	Esc
Extend a selection one character to the right.	Shift+Right Arrow
Extend a selection one character to the left.	Shift+Left Arrow
Extend a selection to the end of a word.	Ctrl+Shift+Right Arrow
Extend a selection to the beginning of a word.	Ctrl+Shift+Left Arrow
Extend a selection to the end of a line.	Shift+End
Extend a selection to the beginning of a line.	Shift+Home
Extend a selection one line down.	Shift+Down Arrow
Extend a selection one line up.	Shift+Up Arrow
Extend a selection to the end of a paragraph.	Ctrl+Shift+Down Arrow
Extend a selection to the beginning of a paragraph.	Ctrl+Shift+Up Arrow
Extend a selection one screen down.	Shift+Page Down
Extend a selection one screen up.	Shift+Page Up
Extend a selection to the beginning of a document.	Ctrl+Shift+Home
Extend a selection to the end of a document.	Ctrl+Shift+End
Extend a selection to the end of a window.	Alt+Ctrl+Shift+Page Down
Extend a selection to include the entire document.	Ctrl+A
Select a vertical block of text.	Ctrl+Shift+F8, and then use the Arrow keys; press Esc to cancel selection mode
Extend a selection to a specific location in a document.	F8+Arrow keys; press Esc to cancel selection mode

Select Text and Graphics in a Table

Action	Keyboard shortcut
Select the preceding cell's contents.	Shift+Tab
Extend a selection to adjacent cells.	Hold down Shift and press an Arrow key repeatedly
Select a column.	Use the Arrow keys to move to the column's top or bottom cell, and then do one of the following: ● Press Shift+Alt+Page Down to select the column from top to bottom. ● Press Shift+Alt+Page Up to select the column from bottom to top.
Extend a selection (or block).	Ctrl+Shift+F8, and then use the Arrow keys; press Esc to cancel selection mode
Select an entire table.	Alt+5 on the numeric keypad (with Num Lock off)
Select the next cell's contents.	Tab

Move Through Documents

Action	Keyboard shortcut
One character to the left	Left Arrow
One character to the right	Right Arrow
One word to the left	Ctrl+Left Arrow
One word to the right	Ctrl+Right Arrow
One paragraph up	Ctrl+Up Arrow
One paragraph down	Ctrl+Down Arrow
One cell to the left (in a table)	Shift+Tab
One cell to the right (in a table)	Tab
Up one line	Up Arrow
Down one line	Down Arrow
To the end of a line	End
To the beginning of a line	Home
To the top of the window	Alt+Ctrl+Page Up
To the end of the window	Alt+Ctrl+Page Down
Up one screen (scrolling)	Page Up
Down one screen (scrolling)	Page Down
To the top of the next page	Ctrl+Page Down
To the top of the previous page	Ctrl+Page Up

Action	Keyboard shortcut
To the end of a document	Ctrl+End
To the beginning of a document	Ctrl+Home
To a previous revision	Shift+F5
After opening a document, to the location you were working in when the document was last closed	Shift+F5

Move Around in Tables

Action	Keyboard shortcut
To the next cell in a row	Tab
To the previous cell in a row	Shift+Tab
To the first cell in a row	Alt+Home
To the last cell in a row	Alt+End
To the first cell in a column	Alt+Page Up
To the last cell in a column	Alt+Page Down
To the previous row	Up Arrow
To the next row	Down Arrow
Row up	Alt+Shift+Up Arrow
Row down	Alt+Shift+Down Arrow

Insert Paragraphs and Tab Characters in Tables

Action	Keyboard shortcut
New paragraphs in a cell	Enter
Tab characters in a cell	Ctrl+Tab

Use Overtype Mode

To change the overtype settings so that you can access overtype mode by pressing Insert, do the following:

1. Press Alt+F, T to open the Word Options dialog box.

2. Press A to display the Advanced page, and then press Tab.

3. Press Alt+O to move to the Use The Insert Key To Control Overtype Mode check box.

4. Press the Spacebar to select the check box, and then press Enter.

To turn Overtype mode on or off, press Insert.

Character and Paragraph Formatting

Copy Formatting

Action	Keyboard shortcut
Copy formatting from text.	Ctrl+Shift+C
Apply copied formatting to text.	Ctrl+Shift+V

Change or Resize the Font

Action	Keyboard shortcut
Open the Font dialog box to change the font.	Ctrl+Shift+F
Increase the font size.	Ctrl+Shift+>
Decrease the font size.	Ctrl+Shift+<
Increase the font size by 1 point.	Ctrl+]
Decrease the font size by 1 point.	Ctrl+[

Apply Character Formats

Action	Keyboard shortcut
Open the Font dialog box to change the formatting of characters.	Ctrl+D
Change the case of letters.	Shift+F3
Format all letters as capitals.	Ctrl+Shift+A
Apply bold formatting.	Ctrl+B
Apply an underline.	Ctrl+U
Underline words but not spaces.	Ctrl+Shift+W
Double-underline text.	Ctrl+Shift+D
Apply hidden text formatting.	Ctrl+Shift+H
Apply italic formatting.	Ctrl+I
Format letters as small capitals.	Ctrl+Shift+K
Apply subscript formatting (automatic spacing).	Ctrl+Equal sign
Apply superscript formatting (automatic spacing).	Ctrl+Shift+Plus sign
Remove manual character formatting.	Ctrl+Spacebar
Change the selection to the Symbol font.	Ctrl+Shift+Q

View and Copy Text Formats

Action	Keyboard shortcut
Display nonprinting characters.	Ctrl+Shift+* (asterisk on numeric keypad does not work)
Review text formatting.	Shift+F1 (then click the text with the formatting you want to review)
Copy formats.	Ctrl+Shift+C
Paste formats.	Ctrl+Shift+V

Set the Line Spacing

Action	Keyboard shortcut
Single-space lines.	Ctrl+1
Double-space lines.	Ctrl+2
Set 1.5-line spacing.	Ctrl+5
Add or remove one line space preceding a paragraph.	Ctrl+0 (zero)

Align Paragraphs

Action	Keyboard shortcut
Switch a paragraph between centered and left-aligned.	Ctrl+E
Switch a paragraph between justified and left-aligned.	Ctrl+J
Switch a paragraph between right-aligned and left-aligned.	Ctrl+R
Left align a paragraph.	Ctrl+L
Indent a paragraph from the left.	Ctrl+M
Remove a paragraph indent from the left.	Ctrl+Shift+M
Create a hanging indent.	Ctrl+T
Reduce a hanging indent.	Ctrl+Shift+T
Remove paragraph formatting.	Ctrl+Q

Apply Paragraph Styles

Action	Keyboard shortcut
Open the Apply Styles task pane.	Ctrl+Shift+S
Open the Styles task pane.	Alt+Ctrl+Shift+S
Start AutoFormat.	Alt+Ctrl+K
Apply the Normal style.	Ctrl+Shift+N
Apply the Heading 1 style.	Alt+Ctrl+1
Apply the Heading 2 style.	Alt+Ctrl+2
Apply the Heading 3 style.	Alt+Ctrl+3

Close the Styles Task Pane

1. If the Styles task pane is not selected, press F6 to select it.
2. Press Ctrl+Spacebar.
3. Use the Arrow keys to select Close, and then press Enter.

Insert and Edit Objects

Insert Objects

1. Press Alt, N, J, and then J to open the Object dialog box.
2. Do one of the following.
    - ○ Press Down Arrow to select an object type, and then press Enter to create an object.
    - ○ Press Ctrl+Tab to switch to the Create From File page, press Tab, and then type the file name of the object that you want to insert or browse to the file.

Edit Objects

1. With the cursor positioned to the left of the object in your document, select the object by pressing Shift+Right Arrow.
2. Press Shift+F10.
3. Press the Tab key to get to the command you want, and then press Enter.

Insert SmartArt Graphics

1. Press and release Alt, N, and then M to select SmartArt.
2. Press the Arrow keys to select the type of graphic that you want.
3. Press Tab, and then press the Arrow keys to select the graphic that you want to insert.
4. Press Enter.

Insert WordArt

1. Press and release Alt, N, and then W to select WordArt.

2. Press the Arrow keys to select the WordArt style that you want, and then press Enter.

3. Type the text that you want.

4. Press Esc to select the WordArt object, and then use the Arrow keys to move the object.

5. Press Esc again to return to the document.

Mail Merge and Fields

Perform Mail Merges

Important The Mailings tab must be displayed when you use these keyboard shortcuts.

Action	Keyboard shortcut
Preview a mail merge.	Alt+Shift+K
Merge a document.	Alt+Shift+N
Print the merged document.	Alt+Shift+M
Edit a mail-merge data document.	Alt+Shift+E
Insert a merge field.	Alt+Shift+F

Work with Fields

Action	Keyboard shortcut
Insert a DATE field.	Alt+Shift+D
Insert a LISTNUM field.	Alt+Ctrl+L
Insert a PAGE field.	Alt+Shift+P
Insert a TIME field.	Alt+Shift+T
Insert an empty field.	Ctrl+F9
Update linked information in a Microsoft Word source document.	Ctrl+Shift+F7
Update selected fields.	F9
Unlink a field.	Ctrl+Shift+F9
Switch between a selected field code and its result.	Shift+F9
Switch between all field codes and their results.	Alt+F9
Run GOTOBUTTON or MACROBUTTON from the field that displays the field results.	Alt+Shift+F9

(continued)

Action	Keyboard shortcut
Go to the next field.	F11
Go to the previous field.	Shift+F11
Lock a field.	Ctrl+F11
Unlock a field.	Ctrl+Shift+F11

Language Bar

Handwriting Recognition

Action	Keyboard shortcut
Switch between languages or keyboard layouts.	Left Alt+Shift
Display a list of correction alternatives.	Windows logo key+C
Turn handwriting on or off.	Windows logo key +H
Turn Japanese Input Method Editor (IME) on 101 keyboard on or off.	Alt+~
Turn Korean IME on 101 keyboard on or off.	Right Alt
Turn Chinese IME on 101 keyboard on or off.	Ctrl+Spacebar

Function Key Tasks

Function Keys

Action	Keyboard shortcut
Get Help or visit Microsoft Office.com.	F1
Move text or graphics.	F2
Repeat the last action.	F4
Choose the Go To command (Home tab).	F5
Go to the next pane or frame.	F6
Choose the Spelling command (Review tab).	F7
Extend a selection.	F8
Update the selected fields.	F9
Show KeyTips.	F10
Go to the next field.	F11
Choose the Save As command.	F12

Shift+Function Key

Action	Keyboard shortcut
Start context-sensitive Help or reveal formatting.	Shift+F1
Copy text.	Shift+F2
Change the case of letters.	Shift+F3
Repeat a Find or Go To action.	Shift+F4
Move to the last change.	Shift+F5
Go to the previous pane or frame (after pressing F6).	Shift+F6
Choose the Thesaurus command (Review tab, Proofing group).	Shift+F7
Reduce the size of a selection.	Shift+F8
Switch between a field code and its result.	Shift+F9
Display a shortcut menu.	Shift+F10
Go to the previous field.	Shift+F11
Choose the Save command.	Shift+F12

Ctrl+Function Key

Action	Keyboard shortcut
Expand or collapse the ribbon.	Ctrl+F1
Choose the Print Preview command.	Ctrl+F2
Close the window.	Ctrl+F4
Go to the next window.	Ctrl+F6
Insert an empty field.	Ctrl+F9
Maximize the document window.	Ctrl+F10
Lock a field.	Ctrl+F11
Choose the Open command.	Ctrl+F12

Ctrl+Shift+Function Key

Action	Keyboard shortcut
Edit a bookmark.	Ctrl+Shift+F5
Go to the previous window.	Ctrl+Shift+F6
Update linked information in a Word 2010 source document.	Ctrl+Shift+F7
Extend a selection or block.	Ctrl+Shift+F8, and then press an Arrow key

(continued)

Action	Keyboard shortcut
Unlink a field.	Ctrl+Shift+F9
Unlock a field.	Ctrl+Shift+F11
Choose the Print command.	Ctrl+Shift+F12

Alt+Function Key

Action	Keyboard shortcut
Go to the next field.	Alt+F1
Create a new building block.	Alt+F3
Exit Word 2010.	Alt+F4
Restore the program window size.	Alt+F5
Move from an open dialog box back to the document, for dialog boxes that support this behavior.	Alt+F6
Find the next misspelling or grammatical error.	Alt+F7
Run a macro.	Alt+F8
Switch between all field codes and their results.	Alt+F9
Display the Selection And Visibility task pane.	Alt+F10
Display Microsoft Visual Basic code.	Alt+F11

Alt+Shift+Function Key

Action	Keyboard shortcut
Go to the previous field.	Alt+Shift+F1
Choose the Save command.	Alt+Shift+F2
Display the Research task pane.	Alt+Shift+F7
Run GOTOBUTTON or MACROBUTTON from the field that displays the field results.	Alt+Shift+F9
Display a menu or message for an available action.	Alt+Shift+F10
Choose the Table Of Contents button when the Table Of Contents is active.	Alt+Shift+F12

Ctrl+Alt+Function Key

Action	Keyboard shortcut
Display Microsoft System Information.	Ctrl+Alt+F1
Choose the Open command.	Ctrl+Alt+F2

Index

L

M

T

About the Authors

Joyce Cox

Joyce has 30 years' experience in the development of training materials about technical subjects for non-technical audiences, and is the author of dozens of books about Office and Windows technologies. She is the Vice President of Online Training Solutions, Inc. (OTSI).

As President of and principal author for Online Press, she developed the *Quick Course* series of computer training books for beginning and intermediate adult learners. She was also the first managing editor of Microsoft Press, an editor for Sybex, and an editor for the University of California.

Joan Preppernau

Joan has worked in the training and certification industry for 13 years. As President of OTSI, Joan is responsible for guiding the translation of technical information and requirements into useful, relevant, and measurable training and certification tools.

Joan is a Microsoft Office Master (MOM), a Microsoft Certified Application Specialist (MCAS), a Microsoft Certified Technology Specialist (MCTS), a Microsoft Certified Trainer (MCT), and the author of more than two dozen books about Windows and Office (for Windows and Mac).

The Team

This book would not exist without the support of these hard-working members of the OTSI publishing team:

- Kathleen Atkins
- Jan Bednarczuk
- Jenny Moss Benson
- Rob Carr
- Susie Carr
- Jeanne Craver
- Patty Gardner
- Elizabeth Hansford
- Kathy Krause
- Marlene Lambert
- Patty Masserman
- Brianna Morgan
- Jaime Odell
- Jean Trenary
- Liv Trenary
- Elisabeth Van Every

We are especially thankful to the support staff at home who make it possible for our team members to devote their time and attention to these projects.

Devon Musgrave provided invaluable support on behalf of Microsoft Learning.

Online Training Solutions, Inc. (OTSI)

OTSI specializes in the design, creation, and production of Office and Windows training products for information workers and home computer users. For more information about OTSI, visit:

www.otsi.com

How To Download Your eBook

Thank you for purchasing this Microsoft Press® title. Your companion PDF eBook is ready to download from O'Reilly Media, official distributor of Microsoft Press titles.

To download your eBook, go to
http://go.microsoft.com/FWLink/?Linkid=224345
and follow the instructions.

Please note: You will be asked to create a free online account and enter the access code below.

Your access code:

RVZJZXW

Microsoft® Word 2010 Step by Step

Your PDF eBook allows you to:

- Search the full text
- Print
- Copy and paste

Best yet, you will be notified about free updates to your eBook.

If you ever lose your eBook file, you can download it again just by logging in to your account.

Need help? Please contact:
mspbooksupport@oreilly.com
or call 800-889-8969.

What do you think of this book?

We want to hear from you!

To participate in a brief online survey, please visit:

microsoft.com/learning/booksurvey

Tell us how well this book meets your needs—what works effectively, and what we can do better. Your feedback will help us continually improve our books and learning resources for you.

Thank you in advance for your input!

Stay in touch!

To subscribe to the *Microsoft Press® Book Connection Newsletter*—for news on upcoming books, events, and special offers—please visit:

microsoft.com/learning/books/newsletter